AF552535

CREATIVITY IN ADOLESCENTS

CREATIVITY IN ADOLESCENTS

By

Dr. Y. Sudhakara Reddy
M.A., M.Ed., Ph.D.
Directorate of Distance Associate Professor Education
Sri Venkateswara University
Tirupati–517 502 (A. P.)

Editor

Dr. Digumarti Bhaskara Rao
M.Sc., M.A., M.A., M.Ed., Ph.D.
R.V.R. College of Education
D—43, Srinivasa Nagar
Guntur—522 006
A.P., India

DISCOVERY PUBLISHING HOUSE
NEW DELHI-110002

First Published – 2003

Reprinted – 2017

ISBN: 978-81-7141-659-2

Creativity in Adolescents

Published by:

DISCOVERY PUBLISHING HOUSE PVT. LTD.

4383/4B, Ansari Road Darya Ganj
New Delhi - 110 002 (India)
Phone: +91-11-23279245, 43596064-65
Fax: +91-11-23253475
E-mail: discoverypublishinghouse@gmail.com
sales@discoverypublishinggroup.com
web: www.discoverypublishinggroup.com

Printed at:
Infinity Imaging Systems
Delhi

Preface

Creative individuals are assets to any society and hence the individuals with creative talents be identified early and their abilities be nourished and channelised to help the progress of the people. Identifying the importance of the creativity, a study has been undertaken to study the creativity and some of its correlates.

The present study was aimed at analysing the creativity of adolescents in relation to variables like sex, locality, length of schooling, personality traits, mental ability and socio-economic status. The sample, selected by multi-stage stratified random sampling procedure for the study, consisted of 900 adolescent students. The tools, namely Reddy's Creative Test Battery, Cattell's High School Personality Questionnaire, Raven's Progressive Matrices, and Reddy's Socio-Economic Status Scale were used to measure creativity, personality, mental ability and socio-economic status of adolescents. The data was analysed employing analysis of variance, chi-square test, multiple regression analysis, etc.

Sex and locality of the students did not have any significant influence on creativity, but class has its influence on creativity. High and low creatives differed significantly on the personality factors. High creatives were more intelligent then low creatives. High creatives belonged to higher socio-economic strata when compared to low creatives.

High creatives were characterised by the habit of frequent reading. High creatives liked to do things in a new way rather than in a conventional way.

Creativity is the urgent need of the individuals as it helps to adopt quickly to the changing environment and as it promotes the progress of the mankind.

Bhaskara Rao Digumarti

Contents

1

Introduction

Creativity is man's greatest asset. It is the most highly valued qualities of human beings. There is no gainsaying that man over a few thousand years ago, was barbaric and brutal. He was nude, lived in caves eating raw flesh of animals. He was probably no more than the many animals among which he lived. When the first ray of creativity flashed into his mind, no one knows. His innerself would have started thundering due to his innate creative potentialities, like an ocean surging with its roaring waves, ever since he started thinking, to adjust himself to the environment.

Man's creative potentialities are indeed unfathomable. The deeper we plunge into the ocean of creativity, the more we unearth and the richer we become in terms of the progress of civilisation and the comforts of life. There was an era of the bullock cart and no more than that was known, when the pedastrian probably envied the comfort the traveller in the bullock cart enjoyed! Then came the era of the steam engine, which is also gradually receding into the oblivion. Then we entered the age of the aeroplane. Today we are in the age of jets and rockets which are capable of generating a few thousand times more speed than that of the first steam engine that George Stevenson developed.

The world is changing rapidly. The change is bewilderingly fast. It may not be an exaggeration to say that the discoveries of the next twenty years may make the last 100 years seem to have progressed at snail's space. We may not be able to foresee today what type of knowledge one needs five or ten years hence, to meet his life's needs. We will, indeed, need a different kind of thinking process, for different from the conventional thinking that we are accustomed to, to be able to live in a world which is changing so fast.

When conformity and stereotype guarantees a comfortable position in a culture bound community, why hanker after creativity? Why should man sail off into probable doom, in order to look for the unknown land or other civilisations? Is it for acquisition of riches? or power? Nay, it is because of the natural inquisitiveness and desire to explore the unknown that is inherent in man. To discover is the basic urge for all kinds of intellectual behaviour.

According to Rogers (1969) "at a time when knowledge, constructive or destructive, is advancing by the most incredible leaps and bounds into a fantastic atomic age, genuinely creative adoptation seems to represent the only possibility that man can keep abreast of the kaleideoscopic change in his world. Unless man can make original adoptations to his environment as rapidly as his own science can change it (the environment), our culture will perish".

Who is responsible for this incredibly great progress in science, technology, medicine, surgery, agriculture and industry? An equally incredibly small proportion of the world's population! It is these few men of eminence that could devise new methods, reorganise existing ideas and offer ingeneous solutions to problems. The achievement of creative persons can not be easily evaluated. One can not evaluate Einstein by saying that his work is equivalent to the combined production of some 50 average physicists. These rare creative persons are invaluable to the society. They produce something no other collection of persons can.

Where are these rare pillars of civilisation, who will solve the problems of today and tomorrow? They are no where else than in our classrooms. It is our duty to identify them and help them realise their potentialities. Anything that is done to help these young people to realise their creative energies will be a forward step in the direction of building a better world.

It may not be unreasonable to assume that the progress of a nation depends not so much on its physical resources, as on its human resources, upon the persons of high calibre, on whose shoulders ultimately lies the task of exploitation of the natural resources.

Though the concept of creativity is as old as the Hindu Vedic literature, it has entered into the researchers' parlance only recently. Even Guilford in his presidential address to the American Psychological Association in 1950, which became the spark that kindled scientific research on creativity, "addressed himself to the topic with certain amount of diffidence, beginning with these words: 'I discuss the subject of creativity with considerable hesitation, for it represents an area in which psychologists whether they be angles or not, have feared to tread" (Barron, 1969). Guilford's statement only summarises the elusiveness of creativity for systematic research.

The personal quality of the creative vision has put creativity outside the domain of scientific study and left it as a matter to be shared with congenial souls. The various schools of psychology have used insufficient methods of investigation to study creativity or have considered it as sublimation, a pathological symptom of neurosis.

It looks strange that only within the past three or four decades that creativity has become central concern for educational research, inspite of the fact that creative thinking has been considered as the highest of mental functions. As mentioned earlier this growing concern for research in creativity has been necessitated by the fast changing world, which is itself a consequence of man's creative geneous. This increasing concern of the psychologist for research in creativity is reflected in the successive editions of the Encyclopaedia of Educational Research. In the 1941 edition of the Encyclopaedia, no mention was made of the concept! In 1950 creativity was added to the catalogue of higher mental processes. By 1969 the subject has gained the status of an independent article. Guilford observed in his presidential address that between 1930 and 1950 only 186 books or articles appeared on creativity. But by 1965, the psychological abstracts have listed as many as 132 items on creativity for only one year.

It was indeed, Guilford's presidential address that gave good impetus to recent research in the area of creativity. Endless questions are asked and reasked about different aspects of creativity beginning with the very nature of creativity. But it must be agreed that not much is known about the various ramifications of creativity.

Till recently only the child whose IQ was high was considered as gifted. But a distinction is made now between such aspects of giftedness as intelligence, musical ability, artistic ability, creative writing, leadership, etc. (Burt, 1962; De Haan, 1961; Witty, 1962). Today it is proved beyond doubt that if we were to identify the children as gifted on the basis of intelligence, or scholastic aptitude we would eliminate from consideration approximately 70 per cent of the most creative.

Systematic educational research in creativity is as new as it is a fruitful field of endeavour. The problems are as complex, the concepts are as uncertain, and the results often as conflicting as the subject is enticing and vital. Whether it is about the relation between creativity and intelligence, about that between divergent thinking and creative achievement, about the threshold hypothesis, or about the possibility of facilitating creativity in the classroom, there seems to be almost as many points of view as there are studies. Among the many difficulties is the shifting nature of the criterion. Although IQ tests possess reasonable generality, measures of creativity as yet do not. All instruments labelled as measures of creativity are not interchangeable, and cut off points even with single instruments are frequently referable only to the particular sample under study. Work on the facilitation of creativity through education is just now getting under way, and the criterion is often no more than pre and post performance on divergent thinking tests. With rare exceptions replications are non-existent.

Inevitably one discovers inadequacy of the methodology of human research and the shortcomings, especially in the techniques for studying creativity.

It is needless to mention that schools put more emphasis on cognitive achievement more often than not, than on creativity. Some school practices, such as rigid scheduling may even hamper creativity. The bulk of research on creativity has left little doubt as to which of the two personal orientations—convergent or divergent—receives greater attention in most of our educational institutions. Perceiving this bias Guilford stated,

"(Education) has emphasised abilities in the area of convergent thinking and evaluation, often at the expense of development in the area of divergent thinking. We have attempted to teach students how to arrive at correct answers that our civilisation has taught us are correct. This is convergent thinking ... outside the arts we have generally discouraged the development of divergent thinking abilities, unintentionally but effectively" (Guilford, 1957).

In the same vein Bloom (1958) opined that there is some reasons to believe that the educational system can reduce originality and creativity. This negative effect on creativity is most marked when examinations, instructional materials and processes all emphasise learning by rote and the goal is centred on getting through examinations.

Torrance (1965) obtained teachers' concept of the ideal pupil. Among the 62 characteristics, teachers voted independence in thinking second, independence in judgement nineteenth and courage twenty ninth! The child who answered questions correctly, produced what he was told, knew what the text books contained, was considered superior by the teachers. Needless to mention, the creative child does not fit this model.

A Review Committee was appointed by the Government of India in 1977 to review the whole curriculum and make suitable suggestions for necessary modifications. In its concluding remark the Review Committee emphasized the need for creative education. Without any mincing of words, it maintained:

"If the purpose of education is to nurture the child's capabilities to the full and to give our people not only a useful occupation but a full and abundant life, then the creative urge in the children must in every possible way be actively stimulated and cultivated in as many directions as possible".

One of the objectives of primary education, the NCERT has suggested is that "the child should be able to express itself freely in creative activities and should acquire habits of self learning" (NCERT, 1975).

What is necessary today is to bring about the optimum development of the whole individual. To realise this aim, "We will have to teach the child to think creatively about the yet-to-be discovered" (Crutchfield, 1967). The greatest joy of the teacher and the greatest hope for better world lies in the cultivation of creative power. "To teach toward creativity is to teach toward the future of society" (Lowenfield and Britain, 1966).

According to Arasteh and Arasteh (1976) research studies of creativity and the development of talent have proceeded from both childhood and adulthood with an obvious gap in the adolescent period. The recent concern with increasing scientific personnel has highlighted the need for fostering creative endeavour at the high school level, particularly in the sciences. Of interest, here are the 1960 statistics of the National Science Foundation which indicate that out of the top 10 per cent of American youth, only half ultimately complete college, and the figures are about 15 per cent lower for girls than for boys.

Not only is there a wastage of talent in adolescence, but not much is known of the process of creativity during these years. In this review of creativity, Torrance has commented: "Of the different educational levels, the high school years have been the most neglected in creativity research. Information has accumulated concerning the preschool and elementary school years because of interest in 'creative imagination'. Apparently educators have not had much interest in the 'creative imagination' of high school students. Information has accumulated concerning creativity during the college years, because many outstanding creative students, writers and performers of many kinds began their productivity during these years and because it has deemed appropriate for colleges to produce professionally trained people who make creative contributions. No such expectations exist for high schools" (Torrance, 1964).

Moreover whatever research has been done on creativity is negligible in comparison to the hundred years of experimental psychological research on the mechanistic dimensions of man (such as stimulus—response studies) which has utilised untold amounts of time, personnel and equipment, including laboratory animals, but still has not moved any closer to the core of what is 'human' and what is 'humane'.

While research on creativity is of recent origin even in the advanced countries, it is needless to point out that not many studies have been carried out in this area in the Indian context. There are several aspects of creativity on which clear cut answers are yet to be found out by sustained empirical research. For example, what is the effect of differences in urban—rural environment on creativity of the individual? Do boys and girls differ in the various components of creativity—like fluency, flexibility and originality? What is the effect of personality on creativity? How does creativity develop during the adolescent period? What is the relative effect of each of many independent variables like socioeconomic status, intelligence, personality factors, length of schooling, etc., on creativity? The present investigation is designed to find answers to questions such as the above.

Review of Literature

I. CREATIVITY AND SEX

Who are more creative boys or girls? Results of research are not unequivocal on this aspect. Three contradictory trends of results are observable on this issue: *(i)* Males are superior to females in creative thinking, *(ii)* Females are superior to males in creative thinking, *(iii)* There are no sex differences in creative ability.

There are several researches reporting male superiority in creative thinking. Kelly (1965) for example, observed that males scored higher than females on nonverbal creativity measures in his study on high school students. Middents (1968) obtained similar results on colleges students. Mar'I also found male superiority in creativity over females in a study of Arab and American eighth graders. In this study boys were better on nine out of 13 scores derived on Torrance Tests of Creative Thinking (Mar'I, 1971). Similar results were obtained by Hutchinson (1967). Straus and Straus (1968) reported that boys performed better than girls on measures of creativity in both Indian and American culture, while sex differences were more prominent in India. This finding was also supported by other Indian studies (Raina, 1968; 1969; Prakash, 1966; Gagneja, 1972; Sharma, 1979; Dharmangadan, 1981; Venkata Rami Reddy and Balakrishna Reddy, 1984).

Awasthy (1979) found that male students were significantly higher than female students in fluency and originality areas of creativity. Boys scored significantly higher than girls in verbal originality and verbal total creativity (Badrinath and Satyanarayanan, 1979). Raina (1970) also observed that males were significantly superior to females in originality. Jayaswal (1977) found that male teacher trainees were significantly higher than the female trainees on the originality factor of creativity.

From a series of studies, mostly cross-sectional, Torrance (1961) found that sex and age trends of creativity were evident even in the early grades. The product improvement task, administered to 259 first, second and third graders, revealed that sex differences became more pronounced with age, and by grade 3 boys scored higher than girls on all the three tasks. Torrance (1963) believes that from an early point in time girls are trained to accept things as they are.

On his tests of creative thinking, Torrance (1963a) found little difference in the ability of boys and girls until five years, from then on boys begin to acquire superior ability in manipulating and experimenting, whereas girls excel only in fluency of responses. Cultural sanctions apparently discourage girls from becoming interested in boy's activities. However, junior high school girls, who were given special training in science concepts subsequently demonstrated an increased ability to explain science principles.

If non-conformity is considered a component of creativity, then there is evidence from Starkweather and Cowling's (1964) experiment that pre-school girls tend to conform to adult behaviour, whereas boys of that age may be either conformists or non-comformists. In these experiments, two tasks designed to measure social conformity (to parents and peers) and impersonal conformity (to a form board) were presented to the child in such a way that he was free to copy the model or freely make his own choice (Arasteh and Arasteh, 1976).

Hussain (1976) compared the creativity of 2 groups of children 10–14 years old: 100 girls from an urban high school, from families of middle or upper socio-economic class, most of the parents being well educated, and boys from a rural high school from lower middle class families most of the parents being illiterate. Four tests of creativity, scored for fluency, flexibility and originality were administered. Girls scored significantly higher than boys on the 'unusual uses' test, on the other three tests also the trend was in favour of girls but was not statistically significant. The results contradict the common belief that boys are more creative than girls, but also fail to support the hypothesis that girls would be more creative than boys. The higher creativity scores of the girls may be due to the fact that they came from a higher socio-economic class and thus were less restricted in expressing their ideas.

Orcutt (1968) gave a series of creativity, conformity and originality tests to 197 children, who were participating in an experimental programme of educational stimulation. When the responses were analysed by sex, the result showed that girls were significantly more conforming than boys.

In a study on 300 students of classes VIII and X of Agra city, Rawat and Agarwal (1977) found that boys significantly outperformed girls in creativity.

Dave (1980) and Shukla (1982) also found that boys were more creative than girls.

Mulk Raj Tuli (1982) designed a study to explore the relation between sex and mathematical creativity. The study was conducted on a sample of 172 boys and 132 girls of IX grade. He found that boys were significantly more creative than girls.

Similarly in a study on a simple of 1014 boys and girls of X classes, boys were found to be more creative than girls (Chandrakant, 1987).

Syama Thrimurthy (1987) also found that boys were significantly more creative than girls on a sample of 200 Gujarati speaking children (70 boys and 130 girls) randomly selected from four different schools. The interaction effect among the three independent variables sex, IQ and study habits was highly significantly. It revealed that boys with high IQ and low study habits were more creative than girls with low IQ and high study habits.

The second trend of observation that girls are better in creative thinking than boys is also supported by findings of quite a good number of investigations where children from first through sixth grades were involved (Yamamoto, 1960; Mac Gregor and Smith, 1965; Solomon, 1968; Walker, 1969; Cacha, 1971; Burgess, 1971). Yamamoto (1960) quoting Torrance, reports, "there was a consistent tendency among the groups, for girls to excel boys on creativity scores through grades IV to VI even when the mean IQs were almost equal". Torrance and his associates found that in USA after about the age of 10, girls consistently perform better than boys on almost every verbal test of creative thinking (Torrance, 1967b).

In one cross-cultural study, Ogletree studied 1165 students of third to sixth grades in England, Scotland and Germany and found that girls excelled boys on all creativity measures except in Scotland where boys obtained higher figural creativity scores than girls, but there again the difference was not significant (Ogletree, 1968). Similar findings were obtained in a study on high school children also (Fletcher, 1963).

Razik (1964) observed on a sample of students from colleges of Agriculture, Education, Engineering and Applied Arts that females outranked males in their creative ability on four out of six tests.

After reviewing a large number of studies, Maccoby and Jacklin (1974) concluded that from about the age of seven, girls show an advantage in a majority of studies. They further commented, "In general, then, it may be said that tests of creativity reflect the already documented difference between the sexes in verbal skills. Clearly girls and women are at least as able as boys and men, to generate a variety of hypotheses and produces unusual ideas..." This observation was substantiated by Olton, *et al.,* (1969) and Goyal (1972) also.

Chada and Ghose (1985) found a statistically significant difference between males and females on all the components of creativity. The result is in line with those of Getzels and Jackson (1962), Passi (1972), Hussain (1974), Singh (1975), Pandit (1976), Brodley (1976), Rawat and Garg (1977), Jarial (1981) and Chadha (1981) who found that females scored higher than males on all the four components of creativity.

Raina (1970) observed that females scored higher than males on all the dimensions of creativity except originality, but these differences were not significant.

Bedi (1974) found a significant difference between the performance of males and females in favour of females in measure of nonverbal creativity. Jayaswal (1977) found that females teacher trainees were significantly superior to male trainees on fluency and flexibility scores. Bharadwaj (1985) also found that verbal fluency was greater among females than males. Similarity, Pandey (1984) studied the relationship between creativity and sex among high school students and reported that females scored significantly higher than males on elaboration.

Singh (1978) suggested that girls scored higher than boys mainly in semantic content. On the figural elaboration the two groups performed upto the same level. The girl's group was also able to demonstrate higher level of autonomy in thinking, non-conformity to conventions and mores and less rigidity in belief system than boys. These personality dimensions associated with the divergent thinking abilities would provide girls better chances to grow as creative persons but only in respect of semantic content. This was probably due to the fact that girls tended to keep themselves free from all sense of responsibility likely to occur in different occupations and jobs (Getzels and Jackson, 1962).

Some investigations, involving samples ranging from elementary school children through high school to college students, however, indicated no sex differences in creativity (Phatak, 1962; Pogue, 1964; Jackson, 1968; Simpkins and Eisenman, 1968; Burns, 1969, Kaltsounis, 1971; Philips and Torrance, 1971; Kloss, 1972; Gakhar, 1974; Thammaprateep, 1976; Dutt, Bountra and Sabhrawal, 1977; Rasool, 1977; Cheek, 1979; Gupta, 1979; Saxena, 1981; Sharma, 1981; Jarial, 1981; Agarwal and Gupta, 1982; Pandey and Pandey, 1984; Flang Dexie, 1985).

Rastogi and Nathawat's (1982) study on a sample of 50 boys and 50 girls from IX, X and XI standards of the central schools revealed no significant sex differences in creativity.

Harnek, Gurusagar and Manjit (1988) conducted a study to find out the relationship of sex and creativity on a sample of 200 IXth class students (100 boys and 100 girls) from 5 rural government schools of Ludhiana and found no significant difference between the creative potential of boys and girls.

Research on creativity amongst teacher trainees lends further support to this generalisation (Lal, 1977; Singh, 1978; Arora, 1978; Maish, 1979; Pandey, 1980). Raina (1971) found that though female teachers scored higher than males, the differences were not significant except on originality factor.

Similarly, Jayaswal (1977) found no sex differences in the creativity scores of male and female teacher trainees belonging to the science group.

Bajpai and Ahmed (1986) also reported no significant difference between the composite creativity of male and female teacher trainees.

Markey (1935) used a modified dairy technique to collect information on the imaginative play activities of 54 pre-school children, supplementary data were obtained in two structural situations: one involving blocks, the other a 'house keeping game'. No consistent sex differences were noted.

Olshin (1965) tried to determine what factors affected creativity and found no sex differences in creativity. Vohra (1975) also found no significant relation between nonverbal creativity and sex. Thorat (1977) conducted a study to compare the creativity of male and female student players and found no sex differences in their creativity scores.

From the findings on sex differences in creativity cited above one naturally gets the impression that the results are controversial, inconsistent and inconclusive. While concluding this section of review of literature we may cite one such controversial finding by two leading researchers in the field, (viz.), Torrance and Harlow. Harlow (1967) reported that seventh and ninth grade boys obtained higher scores on flexibility whereas girls obtained higher scores on originality. On the other hand, Torrance in several investigations found that boys were more original than girls even though the girls scored higher than boys on most of the verbal measures of creativity and on measures of ability to elaborate ideas (Torrance, 1962, 1965).

II. CREATIVITY AND AGE

Markey noted age changes in terms of frequency and complexity of imaginative responses as early as in 1935. He found that a child exhibited more imaginative play if he associated himself with older children than with those of his own age (Markey, 1935).

The most impressive information about the peak period of productiveness has been provided by Lehman through his studies of biographies of eminent people (Lehman and Heidler, 1949; Lehman, 1953). Lehman found that highest quality production comes most often in early thirties. The optimal years for chemists seem to be 26–30 years, for Mathematicians 30–40 years, for Musicians 30–40 years and for philosophers between 35 and 39 years of age. For writers, specialised in specific field of literature, this peak period ranged between 27 and 45 years (Lehman and Heidler, 1949). Lehman has given some examples of exceptionally creative like, Aristotle, Francis Bacon, William Crook, Leonhard Euler, etc., whose contribution was outstanding even as teenagers.

Papanek (1964) reported an interesting research effort. Years ago some psychologists at a university in U.S.A. were discussing creativity and age. They agreed that by age 45 one is over the hill and creativity is pretty much gone. They decided to establish this fact experimentally and tested a universe of 45 year olds. To no one's surprise only 2 per cent of the tested were highly creative. They wanted to find the age when creativity seemed to 'wearout' and tested universes of 44 years old, 43 years old and so on. This proved to be a monotonous task, because the 2 per cent highly creative remained the same until the weary psychologists reached the universe of seven years old. At this stage the percentage of highly creative jumped to 10. For five years old the figure was 90 per cent creative!

In one of the earliest studies McCloy (1939) showed that imaginative behaviour correlated more highly with mental age than with chronological age. Lehman's investigations (1953) showed that adult creativity matures early, reaches its highest point in the thirties and then gradually declines. These conclusions are, however, disputed (Dennis, 1956). Since no systematic criteria of creative output can be established for children, Torrance (1962a) examined changes in performance on divergent thinking tests and found the following generalised pattern: an increase in divergent thinking abilities from ages 3 to 4½, a small drop upon entrance to kindergarten, a sharp decrement at about grade 4, and then, with variations by sex and certain sub-tests, except for a small decrement at grade 7, a steady growth through grade 11.

Noteworthy in this curve is that each decrement seems to occur at a period marking a transition from one to another of Sullivan's stages of interpersonal development (1953).

To examine the possibility that distinctive American pressures may account for his data, Torrance (1962a) studied the developmental curves of children in grades 1–6 in Australia, Germany, India, and Samoa and those of segregated Negro children in the United States. Dissimilarities as well as similarities were found among the different cultures. The German and Australian curves were similar but levelled off earlier than those of the United States. The pattern in India was much the same as the American pattern, although the level was lower. The curve for the American Negro children showed a continuity of development, second only to that of the Samoan children, which had almost no breaks. Torrance suggested that the development of creativity may be related to continuities and discontinuities in the particular culture.

Torrance (1961, 1962, 1964) observed steady growth from grade one through three, a sharp decline at about fourth grade followed by some recovery during fifth and sixth grades, a small decrement at grade seven and then a steady growth till the end of the high school stage. The third grade status was not exceeded till the ninth grade by girls and tenth grade by boys. After tenth grade, the locus of slumps, if any, was not clear.

Simpson (1922) included grades three through eight in his studies of creative imagination. Beginning with a low point at the beginning of the third grade he found a sharp increase by the end of the year followed by a decline at the beginning of the fourth grade. This was followed by an upward trend until a peak was reached in the second half of the sixth grade, after which there was a decline in the seventh and a still further one by the beginning of the eighth.

Mearns (1941) maintained that a decline which set in during sixth grade continued throughout the high school period, unless revived by a special encouragement. He has drawn the above conclusion on the basis of experiences in stimulating creative writing, but apparently without any measurement.

In the Minnesota studies (Yamamoto, 1960; Torrance, *et al.*, 1960) the abilities measured show a decline between sixth and seventh grades, after which there is a fairly steady raise until near the end of the high school period. Most of the growth curves then show, either a levelling off or slight decline.

According to Torrance (1962) some clues suggest that decline at the beginning of the high school period is the result of new pressures to conformity inherent in the tradition. He suggested that there is need for studies in 7th and 8th grades to obtain clarification of major causal factors. Torrance especially emphasised the need for longitudinal studies in this areas.

The individual between 12 to 14 tends to respond to adventure more readily than to reason. During this period gifted children, produce remarkable performances in imaginative, artistic, musical and mechanical fields. He begins to question adult regulations and wants a share in decision making. He feels insecure, however, because of changes in his physical and emotional makeup and a growing strangeness in interpersonal relations (Torrance, 1962).

During the age 14 to 16 much of the imaginative activity seems to be focussed on a future career. Adventure is still the key word for all phases of life for both sexes. The youth is able to see that there are no absolute solutions to some problems, but he has not yet learnt how to apply creatively the principles he has learnt about right or wrong. According to Ligon, he can, with practice, make his emotions creative (Torrance, 1962).

Between 16 and 18 years the individual has the ability to think in terms of abstractions and to translate his social ideas into specific experiences. He can also channel his emotional energy in creative lines. During this period aesthetic interests and skills should be encouraged. Sixteen to eighteen year olds need problems which require creative applications of what has been learnt. Adults must provide 'food for thought' for the adolescents during this age. At times the adults themselves may have to seek creative situations when they find themselves in conflict with this age group of sixteen to eighteen year olds (Torrance, 1962).

Ligon (1957) maintains that children begin developing their imagination during the first year. During the age 2 to 4 years, the child learns about the world through direct experience, and repetition of his experiences in verbal and imaginative play. He thinks over the wonders of nature. His attention span is short, and he shifts activities at random when not directed. He wants to do things for himself. This helps him to develop confidence in his own abilities (Torrance, 1962).

Between 4 and 6 years the child learns the skills of planning for the first time. He begins to enjoy planning, anticipated play and work. He experiments with many roles in his imaginative play. At this age, he starts to become aware of the feelings of others and begins thinking how his actions will affect others. Confidence can be developed during this period through creative arts, new experiences and word games (Torrance, 1962).

Andrews (1930) was considerably more systematic and thorough going than other investigators in his tracing of the development of the imagination during pre-school years. The more creative types of imagination reached a high point from ages three years six months to four years six months and their lowest ebb was reached during the fifth year.

The creative activity of nursery school children has been described and in some instances, recorded and analyzed in terms of their paintings (Alschuler and Hattwick, 1947; McDowell and Howe, 1941), music (Moorhead and Pond, 1942), and block building and clay products (McDowell and Howe, 1941). The children in all these studies were seen at least twice, and in some instances over a period of years. All these studies reported increased elaboration and use of fantasy and imagination with age. Alschuler and Hattwick (1947) analysed each child's art work in relation to his specific school and family experiences, whereas McDowell and Howe

(1941) rated the child's art products on a developmental scale of complexity. Moorhead and Pond (1942) included in their term 'spontaneous music' all of the children's non-verbal activities associated with rhythemical movements. All of these studies reported increased elaboration and use of fantasy and imagination with age.

Markey (1935) observed and described the free play activity and found that imaginative behaviour appeared to be more and of a longer duration among older children. He also found that the total amount of imaginative behaviour increased with age throughout the pre-school period.

Runco and Bahleda (1987) evaluated the relationship of creativity with age using gifted and non-gifted children (5th—8th grades) and found that age accounted for a significant amount of variance in the scores, with older Ss having higher scores than younger subjects.

Piers, Daniels and Quackenbush (1960) selected two groups of students, from the seventh and eighth grades. They were given a battery of Guilford's tests of creativity, and seven scores were obtained on various aspects of originality, ideational fluency and fluency. The findings indicated that mean scores tended to increase with age.

Ahmed (1980) also reported a significant development in the verbal and non-verbal creativity from classes VII to XI.

Raina (1970) studied the relationship between age and total creativity along with its components. Of these, total creativity, originality and elaboration were found to be positively and significantly related with age.

Passi (1972) observed significant developmental trends of creativity scores along grades ninth through eleventh. Similar results were obtained by Lalithamma (1973), Venkata Rami Reddy and Balakrishna Reddy (1984), and Venkata Rami Reddy and Saleena (1988).

Houtz, Sylvia and Tetenbaum (1978) administered a variety of creative thinking and problem-solving tasks to 233 intellectually gifted 2nd to 6th graders at a special school for the gifted in New York city. The tasks were selected to represent conceptual stages of a total creative problem-solving model. Their findings indicate interesting patterns of growth in creative problem-solving abilities. On the creative thinking tasks a plateau in performance appeared from grade 4 on, but on the problem-solving tasks, growth continued through grade 6. Individual variation within the sets of creative thinking and problem-solving tasks was great, suggesting the need to train the gifted in the skills of creativity and problem-solving.

Piers *et al.,* (1960) reported that creativity test scores tended to increase with chronological age. Smolucha and Smolucha (1984) also suggested that artistic creativity matured with age. Flang (1985) found that in divergent thinking, the higher the grades, the better the creativity test responses.

Torrance (1962) studied creativity in school children (Grades I–VI). In the developmental curve for the subjects, the level of originality began in the first grade. The growth was continuous from year to year.

Ogletree (1971) studied elementary school children third through the sixth grade. He found that older children performed better than younger ones. In another investigation Ogletree (1972) analysed creativity scores from school children of different ages and educational levels from 12 European schools. The author found no significant decrements in creativity with age, contrary to American findings. Infact, with each increase in grade level there was an accompanying increase in creativity for most factors.

But as in the case of sex and locality, contradictory findings on the relation between age and creativity could be traced.

Kilpatrick (1900) conducted several tests of imagination on 500 children in grades 1 to 8. He found that younger children were more imaginative than those of fifth and sixth grades, but in the seventh and eighth grades imaginative ability increased.

However, Grippen (1933) observed that creative imagination rarely functions in childhood below the age of five years. Vernon (1948) also reported that constructive imagination did not occur in the child of normal intelligence and emotional development, until age eleven. He based his conclusions upon ability to 'understand fully pictures and to interpret them as a whole'.

Khire (1971) and Badrinath and Satyanarayana (1979) reported that creativity increased upto the age of 13 years whereas Joshi (1974) and Gakhar (1974, 1975) found that creativity increases upto the age of 15 years. Sansanwal and Jarial (1980) observed a consistent increase in the verbal fluency, originality and total verbal creativity of the students from 12 to 16 years of age but beyond the age of 16 years there was a decrease in the above mentioned components of creativity.

Olshin (1965) reported significant positive relationship between age and verbal creativity test scores (older subjects had higher means than younger subjects), but the relationship did not hold for non-verbal tasks.

Similarly Dharmangadan's (1981) study conducted on 300 secondary school children revealed that both 14 year and 15 year old children scored significantly more than 13 year old children. But in the verbal part of the test only 15 year old children scored significantly better than 14 year old children.

Passi (1972) and Thammaprateep (1976) found a negative relationship between age and creativity. Vohra (1975) also observed a negative relationship between nonverbal creativity and age among primary school students. Singh (1978) observed a negative relationship between creativity and age among teacher trainees.

In another study on teacher trainees Singh (1979) classified the subjects as creatives (scoring top 20 per cent) and non-creatives (scoring bottom 20 per cent). The results showed that in the age group from 18–26 years there were more chances to get creative student teachers, whereas the chances of getting creative teachers were less in the age group 27 to 32 years. Similarly Rawat and Agarwal (1977) reported that from 12 to 16 years creativity was negatively related with age in the case of boys, whereas the relationship between these two variables was positive in the case of girls. Raina (1970) also found negative relationship between age and fluency and flexibility. However, the relationship was significant in case of fluency but not with regard to flexibility.

Colvin and Meyer (1906) found a general decline in imagination with age, on the basis of compositions written by children, from grades three through twelve.

Studies with scientific interest concerning creativity by Westerland (1980) have thus far been concentrated on children and teenagers. Though only a few studies with adults and elderly individuals have been done, a decrement with age has been found. The development is partially explained by a slowing in the cognitive process as well as by increasing rigidity with age.

Ruth and Birren (1985) observed a decline in creativity with age, which attributed to reduced speed of information processing, a lower level of complexity and a decreased willingness to risk original solutions.

Mc Cloy (1939) proved that imaginative behaviour correlated more highly with mental age than chronological age.

Lehman (1953) argued that in the same individual, the maximum production rate for creative output of the highest quality occurs earlier than the maximum rate for output of lower quality. He also believed that there was little change in creative production rates in middle age, with a gradual decline in old age. Other studies found that creativity did not decrease with age and that many artists produced their greatest work at an advanced age. Suggestions are given to facilitate creative functioning in the elderly, including communicating the value of creativity in every day life and the concept that creativity does not cease with age. Torrance (1977) also reported that creativity does not decline or cease with age.

Rossman (1931) found that the most active period of productive thinking was 25 to 29 years.

In his study Orcutt (1968) gave a series of creativity and originality tests to 197 children, aged 3, 4 and 5, who were participating in an experimental programme of educational stimulation. He found that in the impersonal situational task, designed to measure conforming and non-conforming tendencies, there were no significant differences between different age groups of children.

A number of tests were administered to 211 university laboratory school children in grades 4 to 12 by Ketcham and Kheiralla (1962). They found that creative ability was normally distributed among the subjects and was not found to increase with age.

Iscoe and Pierce Jones (1963), also found no significant age changes in ideational fluency using the unusual uses tasks with black and white children, 5 to 9 years of age.

Rasool (1977) and Bhargava (1979) also reported that there was no relationship between creativity and age.

According to Passi (1982), there exists a relationship between creativity and age. These two variables are found to have positive as well as negative relationship. This is to say that the creativity increases with age upto a particular age level beyond which it starts decreasing. But what is that optimum age level upto which creativity increases and after which it decreases, is yet to be determined.

III. CREATIVITY AND LOCALITY

In a study by Sharma with 414 male urban and rural 10th graders, creativity was measured by two tests constructed by the author. Intelligence was measured by the Samoohika Mansik Yogyata Pariksha, and ability in fine arts was measured by a subtest from Chatterji's non-language preference record. Creativity was positively affected by the 3 variables and their interactions, except for the interaction of fine arts with culture. A high level of intelligence was considered necessary for the development of creative thinking. On the whole rural boys were more creative than their urban counterparts. The importance of rural environment in promoting creativity was explained by its being less directive, allowing rural inhabitants and interplay of thoughts and ideas. The urban environment was considered oppressive (Sharma, 1971).

Sharma (1972) conducted another study on a sample of 197 students of X class. Of these 86 students were from urban residential backgrounds and 111 were from rural residential backgrounds. Srijanatmaka Pariksha and the Varanh Viprayas Pariksha were the instruments used for data collection. The study revealed that there was a significant difference in the creativity score of urban and rural students favouring the latter.

On the other hand Passi (1972) found urban students to be significantly more creative than rural students.

Singh (1979) analysed the creativity scores of 442 teacher trainees of rural and urban residential backgrounds. On the basis of their creativity scores, the students were divided into two sub-groups: the creative group (those scoring top 20 per cent) and the non-creative group (those scoring bottom 20 per cent). The study revealed that creatives came more from urban residential background than from rural residential background. It was observed that in the creative group 89 per cent of the subjects were of urban background while 11 per cent were of rural background.

Dharmangadan (1981) also observed that urban students scored significantly higher than rural students in flexibility and originality measures of verbal and figural creativity.

Studies conducted by Singh (1977), Singh (1978) and Srivastava (1978) also reported the superiority of urban students over rural students in creativity.

Agarwal and Gupta (1982) observed that locality plays a significant role in developing creative potential among the students and at the same time their findings did not discriminate between the students residing the homes and those residing in hostels.

Singh and Singh (1984) administered a mathematical creativity test and a Hindi adaptation of Thorndike's dimensions of temperament to 120 students of VII and VIII class. ANOVA showed that urban Ss were more active and responsible but less placid than rural Ss. Rural Ss were less sociable, ascendent and reflective but more accepting and impulsive than urban Ss.

However, some studies reported no relationship between locality and creativity. For example, Aaron, Marihal and Malatesha (1969) observed no significant difference in the creativity of students coming from rural and urban areas. Sehgal (1978) also reported similar findings.

The study of Jayaswal (1977) on teacher trainees also reported no significant difference in the creativity scores of the teacher trainees belonging to the urban and rural areas.

According to Singh (1981) and Joshi (1982) also there was no significant difference in the creativity of urban and rural students. Chandrakant (1987) also obtained similar results.

IV. CREATIVITY AND INTELLIGENCE

Are creativity and intelligence same, or distinct but related has been, and continuous to be a controversial issue. There are diverging views on this subject.

That creativity and intelligence might not he perfectly related was suggested as early as in 1898 by Dearborn, even before the standardized intelligence tests were developed. Through the years there have been only sporadic studies comparing performance on tests of intelligence and measurement of imagination or originality (e.g. McCloy and Meier, 1939). But one may have to agree that, for centuries, many assumed that creativity and intelligence were more or less the same.

The subject aroused curiosity and gained importance in leaps and bounds with Guilford's 1950 Presidential address to the American Psychological Association in which he hypothesised that the two may not be the same, but on the other hand there may be low or even negative correlation between the two.

The controversy about the relationship between creativity and intelligence seems to centre around two stand points, viz., *(i)* creativity is a distinct aspect of intellectual functioning which is for all practical purposes independent of conventional intelligence and *(ii)* it depends upon unique cognitive factors which function within the hierarchical structure of intelligence proposed by Vernon (1950) and Foster (1971).

Psychologists like Gallagher (1964), Nichols (1964) and Torrance (1962, 1964) have tried to differentiate the intellectual components of giftedness as determined by IQ tests (convergent thinking) from the qualities of creativity (divergent thinking).

In his tests with adults, Guilford (1962) differentiated convergent thinking (the giving out of factual information, as in standard IQ tests) from divergent thinking (supplying multiple answers to questions which have no 'correct' answer). Fluency (the number of items of a certain kind within a specified time), flexibility (the ability to change the meaning or reinterpret something) and originality are considered the primary components of divergent thinking. These factors also appear to operate in the creative thinking of children (Guilford, 1962; Torrance, 1962).

There are, however, those who argue that the issue of dimensionality is not the crucial in any case. Hudson (1966), for example, maintains that it is not. For him the crucial issue is that a knowledge of IQ seems to be of little help if one is faced with a room full of clever boys, for the one among them with the lowest IQ is almost as likely to be as creative as the one with the highest.

The work of Getzels and Jackson (1962) and Torrance (1964) suggests that in many cases children who are highly creative have IQs considerably below the average for their peers. Hudson (1966) reported essentially the same results for samples of British children.

Torrance (1964) observed that 'If we were to identify children as gifted on the basis of intelligence tests, we would eliminate from consideration approximately 70 per cent of the most creative. This percentage seems to hold fairly well, no matter what measure of intelligence we use and no matter what educational level we study from kindergarten through graduate schools.

The first stand point, viz., creativity is a distinct aspect of intellectual functioning which is for all practical purposes independent of conventional intelligence, was subscribed to by Guilford (1950), Wilson, *et al.* (1954), Yamamoto (1961), Getzels and Jackson (1962), Torrance (1962), Taylor (1964), Wallach and Kogan (1965). They have claimed that creativity and intelligence are two distinct mental abilities each involving a special cluster of skills. This view point derives support from the empirical evidence obtained in the correlational studies, conducted in many countries where low relationship between creativity and intelligence was found (Torrance, 1962; Richards *et al.* 1964; Guilford and Hoepfner, 1966; Raina, 1968; Trivedi, 1969; Passi, 1972; Mehdi, 1973; Patel and Joshi, 1976; Patel, 1978; Sandhu, 1979; Gupta, 1979; Venkata Rami Reddy and Balakrishna Reddy, 1983) and through the factor analytical studies indicating separate factors of the two (Guilford, 1956; Wallach and Kogan, 1965; Cropley, 1966; Kogan 1971; Gakhar and Kaura, 1977). Similar studies by Anderson (1965), Cropley (1967), Thorndike (1963) and Yamamoto (1964a) also indicate that creativity may be viewed as a separate entity from intelligence, but suggest that there may be more number of factors in creativity and that it may not be a unitary trait.

Several studies reported varying degrees of correlation between creativity and conventional intelligence; some of the correlations were significant. Getzels and Jackson (1962), for example, quote correlations ranging from 0.02 (Andrews, 1930) to 0.27 (Welch, 1946), while they themselves obtained correlations ranging from 0.131 to 0.378. Gallagher and Haffman (1964) also reported a low correlation between the two.

Ketcham and Kheiralla (1963) administered a number of tests (Standford Binet, WISC, PMA, Barrons Anagrams, Mednick's RAT and parts of the MTCT) to 211 university laboratory school children in grades 4 to 12. In the elementary school years, the collaboration between creative ability and intelligence ranged from 0.20 to 0.48, depending on the sub-tests used, and a number of them were significant; correlations between creative ability and school achievement ranged from –0.17 to 0.71. Thus, there seems to be a moderate relationship between intelligence and creativity, even in selected groups.

Torrance (1964) reported that in unselected groups of elementary school children the correlation coefficients between creativity as measured by MTCT and intelligence as measured by Standford Binet, California Mental Maturity Test, Kulman Anderson, and Otis Quick Seering were 0.16, 0.25, 0.25 and 0.32 respectively. The correlations tended to be lower for girls than for boys, lower for selected (talented) groups and for individually and orally administered tests. In other words, high scores on the MTCT are usually obtained by children with an IQ of atleast 115 and in a situation where the tests are individually administered and where the examiner encourages the child to think of as many 'original' responses as he can.

Confirmation of Torrance's findings, in whole or in part, has come from the studies of Bowers (1960), Iscoe and Pierce Jones (1964), Olshin (1965) and Bee (1962). Bowers (1960) obtained a low positive correlation (0.26) between various subtests of MTCT and Standford Binet IQs on a group of laboratory school children 9 to 11 years of age. A similar finding was reported for black and white children of the same age who were given Torrance's Unusual Uses Test. However, Olshin (1965) reported a significant relationship between IQ and verbal creativity items on the MTCT, but not for the nonverbal elements, in children of an unspecified age group.

Milgram and Milgram (1976) administered the Wallach and Kogan creativity test battery, a self-report questionnaire of creative activities, and the Milta Intelligence Scale—a group intelligence test—to 145 Israeli high school seniors. Creative activity was related to creative thinking but not to intelligence or school grades. The quantity and quality dimensions of creative activity were as highly related as the dimensions of ideational fluency and rare or unusual responses in creative thinking. Findings support the intelligence—creativity distinction and extend the theoritical position that quantity is a necessary condition for the emergence of unusual responses in creative thinking to the realm of creative performance as well.

Critical questions have been raised by Burt (1962) and Thorndike (1963), especially with respect to the dimensions underlying the various creativity measures. Burt argued that the general intelligence factor would account for the relations found by Getzels and Jackson, pointing out that although the correlations between the creativity and intelligence measures were low, the correlations among the creativity tests themselves were of the same magnitude. Thorndike reanalyzed the Getzels and Jackson data and some of the Guilford data and concluded that pooling measures of creativity into a single composite score was inadvisable since the inter-correlations were so low. But he also suggested that there might be a broad factor distinct from general intelligence, to which the label creativity might be applied, although it is much more loosely formed than the g factor.

Some investigators like Ketcham and Kheiralla (1963) Wallach and Kogan (1965), Wodtke (1964), Yamamoto (1965) have questioned whether creativity as measured by the MTCT is actually independent of intelligence.

In their widely quoted report Getzels and Jackson (1961) labelled as their high IQ group those high school students whose scores on the creative test battery (modified after Guilford) were in the upper 20 per cent, but intellectual scores were below the upper 20 per cent. Although there was a 23 point difference in IQ, the two groups did not differ significantly, in achievement tests. Students who performed equally well (or poorly) in both creative an intelligence tests were not studied. Out of the original unselected group of 292 boys and 241 girls, a group of 26 boys and girls comprised the high creative-low IQ group and another group of 28 youths filled the low creative-high IQ group. These two groups disparate in creativity and intelligence, were then compared on such variables as values, fantasy, career aspirations, family background and environment. From an assessment of such varying measures as IQ, creativity, personality and other tests, plus peer and teacher ratings and parent interviews, the authors concluded that, the high IQs tend to converge on the stereotyped meanings, to perceive personal success by conventional standards, to move toward the model provided by the teacher, to seek out careers which conform to what is expected of them. The high creatives tend to diverge from stereotyped meanings to move away from the model provided by teachers, to seek out careers which do not confirm to what is expected of them.

In fact, Getzels and Jackson's (1962) study has been widely criticised particularly in England, on both methodological and statistical grounds. Foremost among the critics have been Burt (1962, 1964) and Marsh (1964) who concluded that the conventional IQ is still the best single criterion for creative potential. This second point is also supported by McNemar (1964), Wodtke (1964), Marsh (1964) and others. They support the hypothesis that creativity results largely from the operation of 'general ability' rather than a distinct skill labelled as creativity. Support is lent to this contention by Wall (1960) who was specifically concerned with the education of the gifted, and Phatak (1961), Thorndike (1963), Lovell and Shields (1967), Olton *et al.*, (1969), Ginsberg and Whittmore (1968) etc. Joshi (1974) in his study of the intellectually gifted students of age group 12 to 19 years drawn from Gujarat region found that giftedness was an effective contributor to all types of creativity scores.

Cropley (1966) administered a battery of 13 tests, six 'convergent' and seven 'divergent' to 320 Grade seven children and the 'divergent' tests were scored for originally. Correlations were then subjected to principal axis factor analysis. The results indicated that the two largest factors were defined by 'Convergent' tests and 'divergent' tests respectively. These factors were subjected to both orthogonal and oblique rotations and it was found that, although the divergent tests indicated a separate factor, creativity, it showed a significant correlation with the factor defined by the more normal tests of intelligence amounting in this study.

Thorndike (1963) did obtain a factor on which the creativity tests loaded highly, but a substantial portion of variance on this factor was accounted for by the conventional test. He concluded that although creativity tests do tend to intercorrelate significantly there is little evidence that they imply a separate, clearly defined factor of intellect.

In an effort to rigorously assess the test—retest reliability of the MTCT and to determine whether the MTCT are actually independent of traditional measures of intelligence as claimed by Torrance, Wodtke (1964) used unrestricted samples of elementary school children in grades 2 to 5. He obtained low test-retest reliabilities for the sub-test scores. These results agree with the reliabilities reported by Torrance (1962) for his selected groups of laboratory elementary school children, although the reliabilities he obtained with adolescents and adults are reported to be somewhat higher.

Wodtke (1964) concluded, 'until evidence of higher reliability is obtained and until more extensive evidence of predictive validity is available, the use of the test (MTCT) should be confined to research situations ... There is no convincing evidence of the independence of measures of creativity and intelligence and no evidence that intellectual measures do not contribute substantially to such predictions in unselected groups'.

Gakhar and Kaura (1976–77) mentioned that creativity and intelligence though distinguishable from each other, were not found to be distinctly independent of each other. Instead, a small overlap between the two was observed.

A similar conclusion was reached by Yamamoto (1965) after administering the Lorge-Thorndike Intelligence Test and the MTCT to 1288 fifth grade children divided into four groups on the basis of IQ. Corrections for explicit selection and for unreliability of the creativity measures indicated that 'true' correlation might be as high as 0.88.

In their study of creativity, intelligence and personality on 151 fifth grade public school children, Wallach and Kogan (1965) criticised the claims of Torrance and of Getzels and Jackson that creativity was a separate entity different from intelligence when their results actually indicate the opposite, that is, their subtests of creativity were poorly intercorrelated but were moderately correlated with intelligence.

However, borrowing the concept of 'associative flow' from Mednick (1962), Wallach and Kogan (1965) define creativity in terms of uniqueness and productivity, that is, 'the child's ability to generate unique and plentiful associations in a generally task appropriate manner and in a relatively playful context'. Their creative test battery included both verbal (*e.g.*, the names of round things) and visual tasks (*e.g.*, interpretations of various abstract visual patterns). The responses, all oral, were scored for uniqueness (a response given by only a single child in the group) and for productivity (the number of responses). They introduced the creative tasks as 'games', tested each child individualy and imposed no time limits.

From the above well designed investigation, Wallach and Kogan (1965) reported high inter-correlations between their creativity measures (0.40) and a low correlation between overall creativity and intelligence (0.10), there by affirming their definition of creativity as a single entity. Nevertheless, the creativity measures in this study rely heavily on verbal skills. The fact that a low correlation was obtained between these measures and intelligence may, in part, be attributed to the test procedures, which were administered individually and in a game like context.

A wide variety and rapid fluctuations of views regarding the relation between creativity and intelligence since the early work are illustrated by two successive studies by Yamamoto and a study by Wallach and Kogan, all published within about a year of each other. In a 1964 study, the findings of Yamamoto (1964b) concurred with preceding results that the correlation between creativity and intelligence was low.

However, in a 1965 study he concluded that creativity tests do not form a factor independent of general intelligence.

In the same year Wallach and Kogan (1965) claimed that Guilford type creativity measures do not constitute a domain independent of general intelligence, but rather own creativity measures do.

The net results of their efforts seems to be a reaffirmation of Guilford's original hypothesis, albeit with different instruments. The question has not, however, been settled. The variance due to trait and methods factors must be ascertained before a determination among the current views can be made with any certainty (Campbell and Fiske, 1959).

Guilford (1967a) and Dutt, Prem Bountra and Sabhrawal (1977) also report that these two dimensions have curvilinear relationship to each other and it is positive and somewhat substantial.

The relation between creativity and intelligence may not be entirely linear; rather a curvilinear relationship seems to exist between the two. The exact amount of the relationship between intelligence and creativity depends on the type of tests used and the nature of the sample studied (Mehdi, 1977).

Torrance (1967a) summarised the results of studies involving 114 correlations with the figural and 88 with the verbal measures of creative thinking and measures of intelligence. The median coefficient of correlation for the figural measures and intelligence was 0.06 while that for verbal measures was 0.21. Considering the results of various studies, Guilford concludes that high IQ is not a sufficient condition for high divergent production performance, but an above average IQ is an almost necessary condition (Guilford, 1964).

Sharma (1974) conducted a study on 204 students of X grade studying in different secondary schools of Agra city with the objective of finding the relationship between creativity and IQ and found that Intelligent students performed better on creativity tests than those who were low in intelligence. The relationship between creativity and intelligence (r = 0.44) was positive and significant. The rise in intelligence at higher level was not found to be very much helpful to cause significant rise in creativity scores.

Rawat and Agarwal (1977) also found a significant relationship between creativity and intelligence. They found high achievers on the tests of intelligence scored high on tests of creativity also.

Similarly, Singh (1977) observed that creative students scored significantly better than non-creatives in abstract thinking.

Bill (1977) grouped 245 eighth graders by ability on the Standord achievement test and administered the Torrance test of thinking creativity with pictures—Form A, to assess creativity. Children above average in ability scored higher on fluency and flexibility than low, average and superior groups.

Safaya's (1981) study on the relationship between verbal and nonverbal creativity scores and intelligence scores revealed that fluency, flexibility, originality aspects of verbal creativity were positively and significantly related to intelligence. Fluency and originality aspects of nonverbal creativity were positively related to intelligence, where as flexibility and elaboration aspects were negatively related to it. But none of these four correlation coefficients were significant.

In the study carried out by Pestonjee and Usmani (1982) to explore the possible influence of ego strength and intelligence on creativity, it was found that intelligence and ego strength were both important determinants of creativity.

Qureshi (1982) found that fluency, flexibility, originality as well as the total creativity were positively related to intelligence. Gulati (1979) also found that all the components of creativity (fluency, flexibility and originality) were positively and significantly related to intelligence.

The relationship between creativity and intelligence was positive irrespective of the components of creativity—fluency, flexibility or originality—considered (Ashok, 1985).

Significant positive relationship existed between the measures of intelligence and creativity by Singh *et al.* (1977), Sen Gupta, (1982), Ramachandra and Katiyar (1986) and Harnek (1989).

Havoc (1985) studied the relationship between creativity and intelligence at pre-school age. His results indicated that by 4 years of age manifestation of divergent thinking and creativity were identifiable and the relationships between creativity and intelligence were fairly differentiated in Ss, although the presence of convergent thinking in creative attainments was more marked in older sample of subjects.

According to Getzels and Madaus (1969) there are two methodological problems here, which regrettably are not always discriminated . One is the relation between intelligence and creativity represented by measures of recognised creative achievement; the other is the relation between intelligence and creativity represented by measures of divergent thinking. Although the terms 'creativity' and 'divergent thinking' have come to be used synonymously, the distinction as to what is actually being done in a particular study must be borne in mind. A number of studies have dealt with the relation between intelligence and recognized creative achievement (*e.g.*, Mackinnon, 1962; Roe, 1953).

The possibility of substantial relationship between creativity and intelligence at the lower level of intelligence is pointed out by Anderson also (1960).

Research has also led to what is called, "The Threshold Theory'. It is postulated in this theory that a minimum level of intellectual ability is necessary for creativity but creativity and intelligence become independent when that critical level is exceeded (McKinnon, 1962; Taylor, 1964; Vernon, 1964; Barron, 1969).

Beyond a certain IQ (the suggested cut off is 120); there is little or no relationship between intelligence and creativity and that being 'more intelligent' is no guarantee of a corresponding increase in creativity (McClelland, 1958; Sharma, 1971; Passi, 1972; Venkata Rami Reddy and Balakrishna Reddy, 1983).

Some authors (Taylor, 1964; Vernon, 1964) also suggested that creativity and intelligence may become independent only after some critical IQ level has been exceeded.

Anderson (1960) also believed that beyond a certain critical level of IQ, creativity functions independently. This threshold point has been reported above 95th percentile by Meer and Stein (1955) and as an IQ of 120 by Barron (1961), Torrance (1962), Yamamoto (1964b) and Sharma (1971).

However, Cicirelli (1965) and Bennet (1973) found a weak support to this hypothesis. Similar findings have been reported by some others also (Hadden and Lytton, 1968; Lytton and Cotton, 1969; Joshi, 1974; Gakhar and Kaura, 1977).

Taylor and Holland (1962) after reviewing a large number of correlation studies concluded that the greater number of investigations report a positive but low correlation between creativity and intelligence, ranging between 0.20 and 0.40 for general population and almost no relationship at the higher ability levels.

Lewis (1973) found a low correlation between general creativity and intelligence and creativity and academic achievement. Many other studies have reported that scores on creativity correlate poorly with teacher ratings also (Getzels and Jackson, 1962; Holland, 1961; Pegnato and Birch, 1959; and Torrance, 1964).

Child and Croucher (1977) also observed that at higher levels of intelligence the correlation between creativity and intelligence tended to be negligible This was true when they analysed the data in the Yamamoto (1965) model.

Some of the studies found no relation between creativity and intelligence at all (Clark *et al.,* 1965; Cicirelli, 1965; Essenman and Robinson, 1967; Madaus, 1967; Cropley, 1968; Khire, 1971; Lalithamma, 1973; Sharma, 1979; Riqz, 1979; Narayanan, 1984; and Joshi and Joshi, 1986.

Syama Thrimurthy (1987) found that the main effect of intelligence did not have a significant effect on creative thinking ability.

Sansanwal (1987) also found no significant difference between high and low intelligence groups with respect to total creativity or on different components of creativity.

Sansanwal and Jarial (1979) observed to significant difference in the fluency, flexibility, originality and total creativity of students with high and low intelligence.

There is no doubt that creative individuals perform better than the average on intelligence tests, but the correlation between their intelligence and their creativity tends to be low. Mackinnon (1962), for example, reported a correlation of -0.08 between the creative achievement of eminent architects and their performance on the Terman Concept Mastery Test.

Mehdi (1977) found that creativity was significantly negatively related with respect to the rural sample.

Bharadwaj and Sharma (1986) revealed that intelligence in both positively and negatively correlated with originality.

These different view points suggest a need for an extended research effort to answer the question whether creativity and intelligence are distinctly independent of each other.

Lovell and Shields (1967) state, 'divergent thinking can not be accounted for by one dimension; rather the able pupil is creative to different degrees according to the task set him'.

V. CREATIVITY AND PERSONALITY

Research in the field of creative behaviour has shown that creative performance does not depend on certain cognitive characteristics and operations only. Realising the importance of non-cognitive characteristics even. Guilford (1967b) proposed that consideration be given to what motivates individuals interms of needs, interests and attitudes that help the individuals to be productive and creative. Roe (1951) also suggested that personality factors are crucial in the development of creativity.

The personality characteristics of creative children have been studied in a variety of ways—biographical and autobiographical reports of eminent adults, interviews with the mothers and teachers of creative children, interviews with the children themselves, self-administered inventories, and various tests and procedures designed to differentiate the creative child from the less creative one. However, developmental trends have not been studied, indeed most investigations imply that the character traits reported are consistent from early childhood to adulthood. The resulting composite picture of the creative child interms of personality is therefore a blurred and somewhat incongruent one (Arasteh and Arasteh, 1976).

Various authors have argued that creativity is related to unique cognitive factors (Guilford, 1950; Lowenfeld, 1957) and that it is dependent upon certain personality characteristics (Freud, 1949; Barren, 1965; Couch and Keniston, 1960; Mc Guire, 1960).

Creative children have also been described as more 'open-minded', (Long and Henderson, 1965), responsive to stimuli (Greenacre, 1959), autonomous (Smith, 1965), independent and non-conforming (Goertzel and Goertzel, 1960; Northway and Rooks, 1955), honest in terms of living truthfully (Anderson and Anderson, 1965) playful as related to spontaneity, joy and humour (Liberman, 1965; 1966; Torrance, 1962) and have more ability to work (Fine, 1980) than other children.

Dehlavi (1980) investigated the relationship between creativity and creative personality and confirmed the idea that a person with creative abilities would also be expected to have creative characteristics. To explore several personality dimensions of the creative Iranian, a factor analysis of responses to the test, what kind of person are you? Was conducted. The analysis yielded 6 orthogonal factors, *e.g.*, Self strength, Self confidence, Intellectuality etc.

On the basis of personality and attitudinal inventories Reid, King and Wickwire (1959) found seventh grade creative children to be more 'Cyclothymic than Schizothymic' that is 'more sociable, easy going, and warm hearted', rather than withdrawn. From interviews with a fourth grade group of creative children and a control group of comparable group on IQ and age, Weisberg and Springer (1961) concluded that the creative children significantly demonstrated a stronger self image, greater ease of early recall, humor, availability of oedipal anxiety, and uneven ego development.

Maladjustment and loneliness of the creative child were frequently portrayed in the retrospective descriptions of talented individuals (Goertzel and Goertzel, 1960; Greenacre, 1959). Yet, concurrent personality studies of creative children indicate less evidence of maladjustment than among their peers (Liddle, 1958), less anxiety (Flescher, 1963; Meddinus and Love 1965; Reid, King and Wickwire, 1959), less attitudinal rigidity (Fleming and Weintraub, 1962). On the other hand creative children showed greater self-confidence and persistency in goals (Reid, King and Wickwire 1959; Weisberg and Springer, 1961). Even the underachieving, intellectually gifted child, as described by wonderly and Fleming (1965), was found to maintain the same level of self-confidence and personality adjustment as did his better achieving, intellectually creative peers. The investigators attribute this personality equilibrium to a high tolerance for stress. There is also some suggestion that the high achievers have parents who more frequently share activities and ideas and are more affectionate and less restrictive with their children than the parents of low achievers (Morrow and Wilson, 1961).

Several studies on differences between the personality characteristics of high and low creative adolescents have been reported. Bhattacharya (1956) reported that high creatives possessed shallow feeling for life, high sensitivity and ability for prelogical thinking. In a later study he opined that there are two types of creative persons. Of these, one are those who are born creative and the other are those who acquired creativity. While studying the personality characteristics of these two types of persons, he found that the persons belonging to the former type were introverts and the later type were extroverts (Bhattacharya, 1960).

Ray Choudhary (1962, 1965 and 1966) reported that high creatives were distinctly marked by their emotional and temperamental traits than by cognitive and motivational aspects of their personality. They were aggressive, varied in affective life, sensitive to shift in mood tones, tolerant of frustrated experiences, and exhibit signs of intra psychachi conflict about oedipal relationship. Their achievements were found to be determined by super-ego demands and by a need to satisfy narcissitic desires. Further, they were characterised by a preference for, and tolerance for ambiguity, stimulus complexity and structural openness.

After making an extensive study of literature on creativity, Dellas and Gaier (1970) made a summary statement that creative persons are distinguished more by interests, attitudes, values, motives and drives than by intellectual ability. Hudson (1966a) has adopted an extreme position by suggesting that the roots of creativity do not seem to lie in convergent or divergent thinking but rather in the personality and motivational aspect of character.

The most exhaustive studies of children's creativity are those of Weisberg and Springer (1961) and Torrance (1962). Weisberg and Springer found, as mentioned earlier, that highly creative children were rated higher than less creative ones on strength of self-image, ease of early recall, humour, availability of oedipal anxiety and uneven ego development. They considered humour as one of the best discriminators between most divergent and least divergent people. Hudson (1966) also considered 'humour' as a distinguishing characteristic of creative people.

Another great name in this context is of Torrance. He summarised on 84 personality characteristics that have been demonstrated to correlate with creativity of children (Torrance, 1962). Maslow (1972) described a creative person as a self actualising person who has got good psychological health.

Interest of the Indian researchers on the creative child has also been reflected in many investigations. Raina (1968), in his doctoral study on some personality correlates of Indian students found highly creative high school students exhibiting greater achievement, autonomy, dominance, change and endurance than the low creative students.

Paramesh (1970) found the creative children to be neither extroverted nor introverted. They were neither high nor low on neuroticism and anxiety. On the contrary, he found them to be stable in personality organisation and characterised by high theoretical and aesthetic values.

It has been found that creative children, as compared to the non-creative children, tend to be more social, more warm—hearted and less anxious (Reid, King and Wickwire, 1959). They have a reputation for having wild and silly ideas, their work is characterised by the production of ideas 'Off the beaten track', 'outside this world', and by 'humour, playfulness, relative lack of rigidity and relaxation' (Torrance, 1962). They have a wide range of interests and emotional stability and unlike the IQ group creative children are unmindful of teacher's approval (Getzels and Jackson, 1962).

Goyal (1972) emphasised that high creative children at school stage possess a high level of energy, reject repression and supression for the control of their impulses, are more introvert and independent in thought and action, have open minds, can tolerate ambiguity and entertain opposing values.

Aaron and Malatesha (1972) found that high creatives were highly motivated, less modern or radical but more conservative. Bhan (1972) reported that none of the factors of sociability was related significantly to the creative potential. Later in 1973. He reported that in the case of high creatives level of aspiration was high but it was within the productive resources of these individuals. They were self-actualizing and competent enough to maintain harmony between their level of aspiration and creative potential. Lalithamma (1973) found that creativity was positively and significantly correlated with positive self-concept. High creatives had less need for social approval (Rehman and Hussain, 1973). Verma (1973) reported that traits of autonomy, non-conformity, and openness of mind were dominant in high creatives.

Verma (1973) suggested that autonomy, non-conformity and openness of mind could be developed along with the divergent thinking abilities by appropriate plans of school education and help in differentiating potentially creative persons from non-creative persons.

High creatives possessed social boldness, high self sentiment and high guilt proneness (Goyal, 1974). Joshi (1974) reported that creatives were more intelligent, possessed high super ego strength, felt more protected, more radical, had more self sentiment and had high ergic tension. Paramesh and Narayan (1974) observed that high creatives were significantly higher than the low creatives with respect to their interest in persuasive, linguistic, artistic and musical interest areas.

According to Gakhar (1975) creatives possessed high intellectual efficiency, more flexibility, high self acceptance and self-sufficiency. Gopal (1975) investigated the personality variables of creative and non-creative science and engineering students and found that creative students were more reserved, emotionally stable, assertive, sober, expedient, venturesome, self-sufficient and relaxed than their non-creative counterparts.

Chawla (1976) also reported that high creatives were more sober and more intelligent than low creatives. Nair (1976) reported that creatives were characterised by high self-reliance, sense of personal worth, sense of personal freedom, feeling of belongingness, freedom from withdrawing tendencies, freedom from nervous symptoms and freedom from antisocial tendencies. They were also characterised by higher social standards, better social skills, greater involvement in family relations, school relations and community relations. Rao (1976) found that creatives were characterised by more field independence and more integrative complexity.

It was found that creativity was positively and significantly related with introversion (Chauhan, 1977; Srivastava, 1978; Gulati, 1979; Verma, 1980; and Kumar, 1981) while it was negatively related with extroversion (Nagia, 1977 and Bhargava, 1979).

Dasgupta (1977) reported that as compared to low creatives the high creatives suffered more from parental relationship, were more involved and non-conformist in their beliefs and attitudes. Psychotic and neurotic tendencies were more prominent in high creatives, they possessed high self concept (Gupta, 1977 and Singh, 1978), less achievement motivation (Lal and Chilana, 1977); and high intelligence, more social boldness, stronger, self-sentiment and less tension (Mallappa and Upadhyaya, 1977).

Paramesh and Narayanan (1977) reported that creatives had low sociability did not enjoy the company of others experienced difficulty in making friends, were less sympathetic, less cooperative and were less agreeable.

According to Singh, Mathur and Saxena (1977) high creatives felt more secure than non-creatives. High creatives were found to possess rational optimism, high ego strength, realistic and healthy attitude towards life, openness to experience, dedicated persistence, sense of worth, assertiveness, self-confidence and self actualization (Jha, 1975); and they were more conscientious and persistent, more undemonstrative, inactive and phlegmatic than low creatives (Kaur 1978). Creatives were found to be more intelligent, emotionally stable, venturesome, self assured, undisciplined, self-conflict and relaxed (Singh, 1978).

In a factor analytical study of personality variables related to high and low creative thinkers, Nair and Babu (1977) found three factors which characterise the creative group. These were social adequacy feeling, school inadequacy feeling and personal inadequacy feeling.

In another factor analytic study of specific personality characteristics and creativity, creativity was grouped with characteristics like curiosity and initiative, which showed that the personality of a creative child was similar to that of a creative adult (Upadhyacys, 1982).

According to Girijesh Kumar (1978), high creative individuals were more achievement motivated than the low creative individuals.

Srinivasan (1984) investigated the disposition toward originality in 110 male industrial supervisors all of whom were engineers. They were administered a battery of tests that included the unusual uses sub-test of Torrance Tests of Creative Thinking, Roschaech inkblot test, Test of consequence, Thematic apperception, word re-arrangement and Eysenck's Personality Inventory. Results indicated that more creative Ss exhibited qualities of extroversion, had similar degrees of neuroticism as Ss who were less creative and had low psychotic tendencies.

Bhargava (1979) found that creativity was negatively and significantly related to anxiety, extroversion, and was positively and significantly related to independence. Gulati (1979) reported that with respect to different components of creativity, viz., fluency, flexibility and originality, introverts performed better than extroverts. But in some other studies, it was observed that introverts did not differ significantly from extroverts in fluency, flexibility and originality (Jarial, 1980 and Jarial and Sharma, 1981). Artistic aptitude was found to be positively and significantly related to fluency, flexibility and originality (Gulati, 1979). High creatives possessed greater sense of humour, and less conformity than low creatives (Gupta, 1979).

Sansanwal and Jarial reported that creatives were more intelligent, happy go lucky, impulsive lively, gay, enthusiastic, trusting, adaptable, free from jealousy, relaxed, easy to get on with, tranquil, torpid and unfrustrated. They were also outgoing, warm hearted and participating, emotionally mature, stable and realistic about life, enthusiastic, preserving and conscious about their life (Sansanwal and Jarial, 1979).

They were self sufficient, resourceful, preferring their own decisions, self-controlled, self disciplined and had high self-concept (Verma, 1979).

Jyostna (1980) found high creative students tended to be more reserved, critical, more intelligent, more self reliant they had higher super ego strength and were less frustrated than their less creative counterparts.

Kaur (1980) found that creativity was positively and significantly related with positive intelligence self-concept, positive character self-concept, positive aesthetic self-concept, positive adjustment self-concept, positive emotional adjustment self-concept, self-concept intelligence, self-concept character and self-concept social adjustment. Lidhoo and Zargar (1980) found that creativity was negatively related to neuroticism.

Singh (1980) reported that creativity was not related to the level of aspiration and frustration reactions.

Sansanwal and Jarial (1981) found that high creatives scored significantly higher than low creatives in the areas of their positive self-concept of intelligence, character, aesthetic and social adjustment.

Test scores of divergent thinking obtained between 1952 and 1972 were correlated with a variety of personality measures administered since 1980. In this sample of 268 men, divergent thinking was consistently associated with self-reports and ratings of openness to experience, but not with neuroticism, extroversion, agreableness or conscientiousness. Several other personality variables mentioned in the literature were also examined; those that were associated with divergent thinking were also generally correlated with openness. These data suggest that creativity is particularly related to the personality domain of openness to experience (McCrae Robert, 1987).

Goyal (1974), Sharma (1979) and Gakhar and Joshi (1980) explored the personality traits of those students who scored high in fluency, flexibility and originality dimensions of creativity. Of these Goyal (1974) found that flexible students were more guilt prone and less imaginative, while Sharma (1979) reported them as fault finders, imaginative, adventurous, having interests in different activities and thoughts, sensitive to visualise relations and problems, had complex thinking patterns, self-confident, discounted, curious and relaxed. He further reported that the fluent students were good observers, constructives, participating, had interest in various types of activities, sensitive towards observations and problems, adventurous, less contented in deals, relaxed, curious and had a desire to do high acts with sincerity while students were high in originality were independent, had desire to do great and unique things, complex thinkers, self-confident, fault finders, imaginative, dis-contended, curious, relaxed, adventurous, innovative, participating, radical and sensitive. Gakhar and Joshi (1980) reported that highly fluent and flexible students were characterised by high degree of socialization, greater community and low capacity for status, whereas highly original students were characterised by greater self-acceptance, high sense of well being, greater responsibility, emotional balance and stability, high degree of self-sufficiency, extraversion, greater dominance and a high degree of confidence in themselves.

Kundu (1987) observed that creativity was positively related to psychoticism, while the relationship between creativity and extraversion was curvilinear. Dysthemics were found to be more creative than hysterics.

Goyal (1974) and Gopal (1975) studied the personality traits of high creatives studying different subjects. Among them Goyal (1974) reported that science students were characterised by high intelligence, high emotional stability, tough mindedness and better adjustment. These characteristics differentiated this group from the language group. According to Gopal's (1975) study, creative science group was more reserved, assertive, expedient, conservative, group dependent and indisciplined, while engineering students were more reserved, emotionally stable, assertive, sober, expedient venturesome, suspicious, imaginative, shrude experimenting, self sufficient and relaxed.

Babu (1977) conducted a study on a sample of students who were high on creativity as well as on intelligence. This double talented group was found to possess non-anxious disposition, group adjustment, individual adjustment, social conformity, performance anxiety and freedom orientation.

There have been various studies where the personality characteristics of low creatives were studied. In 1968, Raina reported that low creatives were characterised by heterosexuality and greater anxiety.

They possessed high level of aspiration with ambition outstripping the resources of creative personality and they did not maintain harmony between aspiration level and creative potential (Bhan, 1973). Further low creatives had high need for social approval (Rehman and Hussain, 1973).

According to Joshi (1974) low creatives had mental defects; they did not have rigid internal standards, they were not relaxed or secure. They were characterised further by conservatism, poor self-sentiment, and high tension. Gakhar (1975) observed that they had less intellect, less flexibility, low self acceptance and less self-sufficiency.

They had high anxiety (Nair, 1976) and possessed low integrative complexity (Rao, 1976).

Low creatives were high achievement motivated (Lal and Chilana 1977) high in tension (Singh, 1977), less adjusted (Singh, 1979) and felt less secure (Singh, Mathur and Saxena, 1977). Sansanwal and Jarial (1979) found that low creatives were less intelligent, sober, prudent, serious, taciturn, suspicious, self-opiniated, hard to fool, tense, frustrated, driven and wrought. They were dependent on others, more attention seeking, tender minded, more tense, driven and frustrated (Verma, 1979).

Some studies have reported no difference between certain personality characteristics of low and high creatives. Ahmed (1969), for example, found that high and low creatives did not differ on activity, depressive tendencies, emotional instability, introversion and moral values. They did not differ with respect to self-concept (Passi and Lalithamma, 1973) and on ego strength (Verma, 1973) on extraversion and neuroticism (Dutt, *et al.*, 1977), and level of aspiration (Rawat and Garg, 1977).

Paramesh and Narayanan (1977) found that students belonging to high and low levels of creativity did not differ on active, vigorous, impulsive, dominant, stable and reflective traits of temperament.

Vohra (1975) also found no significant relationship between nonverbal creativity and personality characteristics of students. Similarly, Bhoodev Singh (1986) observed no significant effect of personality factors on creativity.

There have been some studies where the adjustment of various levels of creatives were studied. Singh (1975) reported that all components of creativity were positively and significantly related with emotional adjustment, while originality and elaboration were positively and significantly related with social adjustment. According to Gupta (1976) creativity is positively and significantly related to adjustment in social, emotional and educational areas.

Pandit (1976) and Singh (1977) found that high creatives were better adjusted. On the other hand, Sinha and Sharma (1978) reported that high creatives were less adjusted in the home, health and emotional areas of adjustment compared to their low creative counterparts. Kaur (1980) found that high creatives had more problems than low creatives in socio-psychological areas.

Creativity is positively and significantly related to the total social and educational aspects of adjustment but not to the emotional adjustment (Singh, 1980).

According to Singh (1975) fluency was negatively and significantly related to family and social aspects of adjustment, while flexibility was negatively and significantly related to social aspect of adjustment. Kaur (1980) found negative but insignificant relationship between creativity and adjustment. However, Kumari (1975) and Mishra (1977) found that creativity was not related with adjustment.

There are a few studies which have explored the personality characteristics of male and female creatives.

Goyal (1974) reported that female group was characterised by intelligence and venturesome traits. They tended to be the victims of self-conflicts, moralistic and socially precise and socially bold. On the other hand, males were characterised by tough mindedness and suspiciousness.

According to Arora (1976) anxiety was curvilinearly related with creativity in the case of males while it was negatively related with creativity in the case of females. According to Nisha, Singh and Gupta (1976) among males, fluency, original power and ingenious solutions to problems were significantly related to the creative personality. In the case of females fluency and original power were significantly related to creative personality.

Singh (1978) reported that creative males were adventurous while creative females were shy, timid, restrained and threat sensitive. Further, creative males were self-assured, placid, secure, confident, relaxed, tranquil, torpid and unfrustrated whereas creative females were apprehensive, worrying, depressive, troubled, tense, frustrated, driven and overwrought.

Pandey (1980) found that creative male pupil teachers were more good natured, easy going, emotionally expressive, cooperative, unconventional and imaginative than non-creative males whereas female pupil teachers were fault finders, high intelligent, self assured, independent minded, socially bold, ready to try new things, imaginative, and interested in intellectual matters.

There seems to be much similarity in the characteristics of creative persons enlisted by different researchers even through the ideal creative personality differs from culture to culture as indicated by Torrance's cross cultural study (Torrance, 1965).

VI. CREATIVITY AND HOME BACKGROUND

Eventhough there is a general paucity of research in this area and the existing knowledge is insufficient to give a precise idea about the nature of general environmental conditions conducive for creative growth, many factors have been brought to light by a number of recent researches.

Rainer (1979) discussed two traditions in research in psychology that make different assumptions about the relationship between creativity and mental well-being, and between creativity and child-rearing practices of parents. One tradition suggests that most creative people have experienced more intense suffering during childhood than others. The other tradition takes the opposite position that a permissive, non-authoritarian home environment is most conducive to later creativity.

According to Getzels and Jackson (1961) parents and the home atmosphere appear to be more instrumental in fostering or hindering the creative talents of their children than are other determinants.

Saran (1970) concluded that individual development of the child with regard to curiosity, creativity, constructiveness and practical competence depends largely upon the presence of proper environment at home.

In a series of studies Roe (1960) has explored the personality and family background of eminent male scientists, coming from social sciences (Psychology and Anthropology) with those from the exact sciences (biology and physics). The social scientists in contrast to biologists and physicists, indicated that their feelings of family superiority contributed substantially to their development. In summing up the family background of her subjects, Roe states that the parents of the social scientists were seen as overprotective and firm;

and the control, even if not overt, was very evident. More than half of the men in her group reported that they responded to such parental treatment with rebelliousness, and a number of them continued, even in adulthood, to express anger, or disrespect for one or both partners. Open rebellion was not a pattern exhibited by physicists and biologists in their youth; instead they tended to develop a pattern of life requiring little personal interaction with their families, and they showed greater shyness in growing up. Regional was not an important factor in the lives of most of the scientists.

A number of studies have been directed toward the possible influence of early environmental factors on the development of creativity. Getzels and Jackson (1962) found that mothers of high creative children less often than mothers of high IQ children, report worries about the dangers in the world, recollections of insecurity in their own childhood, admiration for conventional qualities in children, vigilance regarding their children's independence.

Drevdahl (1964) testing psychologists, and Mackinnon (1964) testing architects, found that their more creative subjects were given more independence and responsibility during childhood than the average child. Drevdahl (1964), however, noted that creative psychologists reported more than average family pressure for educational achievement.

Research on creative and non-creative 12 years olds by Rainer (1979) indicates that mothers of highly creative subjects behaved more actively when engaged in problem-solving with subjects. Mothers of low creative subjects interacted in a more guarded and cautious manner, yet with more visible demonstrations of positive effect. According to him data on father's attitudes seem to oppose the belief that creative children have permissive, non-authoritarian fathers.

Professional mothers seem to emphasise more independence on the part of their children than non-professional mothers (Van Mering, 1955). According to him, it is reasonable to assume that the children of professional mothers have, therefore, more opportunities to develop creativity, self-confidence and sense of exploration that are regarded as essential for development of creative potential.

A limited environment may also restrict the level of creative performance in children. In Griffiths (1945) descriptive study of pre-school children in Brisbance and London, the Australian children produced more imaginative and colourful drawings than did those in London, presumably because the former had a more varied environment interms of spending more time out-of-doors, visiting the country and seashore, and not living in overcrowded housing.

Dewing and Taft (1973) analysed the characteristics of the parents of creative twelve year olds. On the basis of a battery of creative tests designed to assess divergent thinking and creative performance in real life situations, 394 seventh-grade children were divided into a highly creative group and a less creative (control) group, matched for IQ, sex and school. The attitudes and personality of the parents were also assessed. The more creative parents preferred a complex and stimulating environment for themselves and their children; their were more working mothers in the creative group than in the control group. Mothers of the creative children professed more equalitarian child-rearing attitudes and permitted their children more contact with influences outside the home. Personality characteristics of the parents were more closely related to creativity of like-sex children, especially interms of their creative performance.

Watson (1957) observed the personality of a group of 44 children coming from 'good, loving and strictly disciplined homes' as compared to another group of 34 children in the same community from equally good and loving homes but with considerable permissiveness. Psychological testing and teacher's ratings were used. On the four dimensions of self-control, activity, inner security and happiness, no significant differences were found in the two groups.

In terms of persistence, children from the strict homes tended to be either overly persistent or very easily discouraged. On the four remaining variables, children from permissive homes were significantly higher in terms of exhibiting greater initiative and independence (except perhaps at school tasks), better socialization and cooperation, less inner hostility and friendlier toward others, and showed a higher level of spontaneity, originality and creativity. The author concluded that the results did not differentiate whether parental permissiveness itself led to these personality characteristics in the children or whether such parents tended to have certain hereditary or cultural traits associated with permissive attitudes.

Authoritarianism, including conformity, is considered by Anderson and Anderson (1965) to be the crucial factor in limiting creativity. Children from strongly authoritarian cultures (*e.g.*, Germany and Mexico) supplied story endings which revealed greater defense mechanisms of deception, escape from reality, submission, aggression, and punitive action.

Nichols' study support the above findings. Mothers of over 1000 talented male and female high school seniors were asked to complete the PARI. It was found that mothers who were rated high on authoritarian child rearing attitudes tended to have children who were high in academic performance and low in creativity and originality. The author concluded that "The findings that the children of authoritarian mothers obtained better grades in schools and more favourable ratings by their teachers is not inconsistent with the hypothesis that authoritarian child rearing practices lead to conformity and 'good' behaviour but stifle originality (Quoted from Morrow and Wilson, 1961).

Strauss and Strauss (1968) theorise that children's creativity varies according to the degree to which the child's family role requires conformity to conventional norms. Creativity was measured by the ability to generate ideas which might solve a puzzle presented to family groups. Data for 128 Indian and American families showed that the Indian children had lower scores than the Americans. Sex differences in creativity were greatest in India. The smaller sex differences in American Ss is interpreted as reflecting the greatest freedom and individuality permitted to American girls. It is concluded that individual creativity is likely to increase as societies move toward a less restrictive normative.

Torrance (1971) attempted to programme a task through applications of A.F. Osborn and S.J. Parnes' model of creative problem-solving. 100 graduate students were divided into 5 person groups on the basis of the pattern of their scores on the Runner studies of Attitude patterns. They were ranked on 'control' and 'freedom' orientations. Results support the hypothesis that Ss who had a control orientation would express greater discomfort in creative problem solving and ask for a higher degree of structure than Ss with a freedom orientation.

Louise and Fiebert (1977) predicted an inverse relationship between creativity and parental authoritarianism in 254 children of five and half years of age. Results from 4 tests of creativity and the California F-scale show that creativity scores had correlations of –0.62 with the measure of parental authoritarianism for mothers and –0.65 for fathers.

Some what contradictory results have been obtained by Gallagher (1964) who found that boys and girls who scored high on divergent thinking came mainly from 'parent-oriented' families, as compared to child oriented or home oriented. In particular, fathers who exerted strong control over their son's activities (that is, they stressed achievement more than independence) had sons who performed better on divergent thinking tasks and expressiveness in the classroom than did the sons of fathers who were less controlling. On the other hand, mothers who were rated very high on independence-granting had daughters who were rated high on expressiveness in the classroom as compared to the girls whose mothers were rated low on this variable.

Garber *et al.*, (1979) have examined the effects of varying home environments on creative thinking. 155 pre-school aged children from orthodox and 155 from non-orthodox homes were administered Torrance Tests of Creative Thinking, Figural Form A, and comparisons were made in fluency, flexibility, originality and elaboration. Results indicate that orthodox subjects were significantly more fluent or productive in their creative thinking and were better able to elaborate on a creative idea than were non-orthodox subjects. Flexibility and originality scores were not significantly different for the groups, suggesting a common over riding developmental theme in these areas. The positive influence of the orthodox family structure is discussed in relation to the high scores on fluency and elaboration obtained by the orthodox group.

In her study Asha (1983) observed that in both cases (boys and girls) the children of working mothers scored more on creativity than the other children. Maternal employment seems to have a facilitating influence on the development of creativity.

However, investigations by Heer (1958), Nye and Hoffman (1963) and Blood (1965) reveal that working mothers are generally found to have more marital conflicts than non-working mothers. Since they carry heavy burden, working mothers usually develop tension and this, in turn, results in friction in their children (Rossman and Campbell, 1965; Stolz, 1960; Maccoby, 1958). Families characterised by discord and strained relationships are likely to create serious behavioural problems in children, which may hamper their creative development. According to Van Mering (1955) working mothers insist on more discipline in their children. It is possible that, since creativity flourishes in an atmosphere which permits freedom of thought and action, such a situation may adversely affect the development of creativity.

It is possible that employed mothers who are forced to reduce the amount of time they can spend with their children may fail to give adequate intellectual, emotional and social stimulation. Praugh and Halow (1962) report that the effect of inadequate maternal care and distorted mother-infant relationship are devastating.

Asha (1983) has observed that maternal deprivation in the earlier years of life is supposed to do irreparable damages to the developing child.

Anisworth (1962) reports that maternal deprivation is likely to affect adversely the intellectual and emotional thinking and control process. Lack of emotional warmth and stimulation from mother or inadequate mothering seems to lead to abnormal development.

Dharmangadan (1976) and Olive (1972) obtained a significant correlation between father's occupational status and children's creativity.

Jansevek (1981) administered the Guilford creativity test and DAT to 481 VIII graders. Analysis of variance indicated that parental occupations in teaching, engineering and the technical professions had a positive influence on the creativity of the objects, whereas occupations such as nursing and book keeping had a negative influence. Parental education past elementary school also exerted a positive influence on creativity. Families of creative Ss were better informed, more open to experiences and had higher educational aspirations for their children.

Most of the studies have reported that creatives come from high socio-economic status families (Vohra, 1975; Gupta, 1976; Rawat and Agarwal, 1977; Singh, 1977; Thorat, 1977; Singh, 1978; Srivastava, 1978; Jarial, 1979; Sharma, 1979, 1980; Bhargava, 1979; Ahmed, 1980; and Vijayalakshmi, 1980).

Zargar and Neelam Dhar (1988) attempted to explore the nature and extent of the relationship between creativity and SES, on a sample of 50 boys and 50 girls from different colleges of Srinagar. They found that students belonging to parents of high SES are more creative than those of parents of low SES for both the sexes. According to them students coming from High SES families have all the facilities available to them and also receive high motivation from their parents and enrich experiences boost their creative potential.

These findings are supported by those of Northway and Rookes (1955), Janson (1968), and Strauss and Strauss (1968).

Harnek (1989) conducted a study on a sample of 250, XI class students from three urban schools of Ludhiana and Sangar districts and found significant positive relationship between creativity and high and average SES levels.

Sharma and Jarial (1980) observed that the students of high socio-economic status were superior to those of low socio-economic status on fluency component of creativity.

However, Sharma (1980) found that students from high SES families scored significantly higher than the students from low SES families on originality and total creativity, whereas there was no significant difference between them on fluency and flexibility components of creativity.

Sultan Ahmed and Joshi (1980) analysed the relation between socio-cultural disadvantage and creativity on the one hand and how the school situation affected these various abilities of the students on the other. The investigation was on a sample of 120 students belonging to advantaged and disadvantaged home backgrounds. The schools to which they belonged were of four categories; extremely advantaged schools (EAS), extremely disadavantaged schools (EDS), slightly advantaged schools (SAS) and slightly disadvantaged schools (SDS). It was quite evident from the results that highly enriched background of EDS dominated over the effect of home background while on the contrary advantaged home background prevailed over the effect of slightly advantaged and disadvantaged institutions.

In his study on teacher trainees, Jayaswal (1977) found that family income was positively related to creativity.

Bharadwaj (1981) also found that economic status promoted creativity.

Some of the studies reported that creatives come from average SES. Raina's (1968) study for example, revealed that the high creatives came from the second class socio-economic families and the low creatives from the third class. Similar results were reported by Awasthy (1979).

On the other hand Das (1957), Lalitha (1957), Badrinath and Satyanarayan (1979), Seetharam and Vedanayagam (1979) and Chadha and Sen (1981) reported that there was no significant difference in creativity of students coming from high, average and low SES.

Sharma and Jarial (1980) also reported that the students of high and low SES did not differ significantly in verbal flexibility, originality and total creativity.

Sunil Dutt (1988) also found that the total creativity was not related significantly to SES.

Upadhycys (1982) found that home environment did not significantly related to creativity.

Harnek (1989) found that there is no significant difference in creativity with variation in socio-economic status.

Scores for verbal and non-verbal aspects of divergent thinking appear to differentiate social classes and black and white children. Smith (1965) found that among fifth grade white children in Pittsburgh, the middle-class performed significantly better on verbal tasks, but the lower class excelled on verbal items. In a group of Texas lower-class white and black children 5 to 9 years of age, who were individually given Torrance 'unusual uses' test and the WISC, Iscoe and Pierce-Jones (1964) found that black children generally obtained higher divergent thinking scores, primarily interms of ideational fluency, but the white children got significantly higher IQ scores on the WISC. The surprising superiority of the black child in divergent thinking tasks occurs in a situation in which the black child is not handicapped by white middle-class norms and values. The authors conclude, 'The search for the types of experience that foster originality in children, in a formal educational setting as well as in the environment at large, is a challenge that can not be ignored.

On the other hand, non-cognitive factors concerned with motivation and personality are being recognized as important correlates of creativity, both in children and adults. Even at the pre-school level there are wide individual differences in such motivational factors as non-conformity, freedom of expression, playfulness and curiosity (Liberman, 1965; 1966; Mendel, 1965; Starkweather, 1964; 1965), which are determined to a large extent by the home environment (Dreyer and Wells, 1966; Weisberg and Springer, 1961) and by cultural and social class patterns (Anderson and Anderson, 1965; Reid, King and Wickwire, 1959).

Singh (1977, 1980) studied psychological make-up and sociological background of creative and non-creative student teachers. The studies revealed that high creativity among student teachers tended to go with higher economic value, better personality adjustment, and better family background Low creativity, on the other hand seemed to be associated with higher theoretical value, poorer adjustment, and poorer family background.

This finding is in contrast with the results reported earlier by Das (1957, 1959) and recently by Gupta (1980) who found the two variables to be independent of each other.

Effect of different kinds of schooling was subject to many investigations. Mishra (1986) found that the differences between mean values of students studying in central schools and private schools were significant at 0.05 level on all the components on creativity. It suggests that the students of central school tended to have more degree of creativity than the private school students because of better physical amenities, better teachers, more enriched and comprehensive curricular and co-curricular programmes and lesser number of students in classes and other favourable conditions which tend to promote creativity in students.

Similar findings were reported by Ezekeil (1966), Rastogi, (1967), Chatterjee (1970) and Aaron *et al.,* (1969) who found that students of well equipped and advantaged schools were better on creativity tests than students of ill-equipped schools.

Comparing the creativity scores of students coming from small, average and large families, Jarial (1983) found that the students of small families were significantly superior to the students of average and large families in fluency, flexibility and composite creativity, where as, they did not differ with respect to originality component of creativity.

VII. CREATIVITY AND BIRTH ORDER

The effect of ordinal position of birth on creativity has been explored by some investigators. Most of the research in the area was indirectly focussed on family influences and child rearing practices (Getzels and Dillon, 1973). Significant birth order effects have appeared with substantial consistency, first born males being more creative than later born siblings.

Srivastava (1977) carried out an investigation to find out the impact of birth order and personality types on creative abilities. The study revealed that first borns scored higher on creativity tests compared to later borns.

Jarial (1979) conducted a study to find out the differences in creativity among first borns and later borns, on a sample of 200 students selected from IX and X classes. He found that first borns were superior on different components of verbal creativity.

Jarial (1982) conducted another study to compare the fluency, flexibility, originality and total creativity scores of the students of different birth orders—first, second, third, fourth, fifth, sixth, and seventh—on a sample of 600 male and female students of classes IX, X and XI, studying in various educational institutions of Indore city. The study revealed that *(i)* Students who were first born scored significantly higher than those who were second, third, fourth, fifth, sixth, and seventh borns in originality; they scored better on fluency, and total creativity than third, fourth, fifth and sixth borns; they were better than fourth and fifth borns in flexibility. *(ii)* Second borns were significantly higher than the fourth and fifth borns in fluency; they were better than fifth borns in flexibility, originality and total creativity. *(iii)* Third borns were significantly better than those whose birth order was five with regard to fluency, flexibility, originality and total creativity. *(iv)* Those whose birth order was four scored significantly higher than students whose birth order was five in originality and total creativity measures. *(v)* Seventh borns were significantly higher than fifth borns in flexibility.

Dave (1980) also found that the first born were more creative than those who were later born. Chandrakant (1987) also obtained similar results.

Jarial and Sharma (1980) review 13 studies investigating the relationship between creativity and birth order and concluded that the studies indicated a significant superiority of first borns over the later borns.

Runco and Bahleda (1987) evaluated the relationship of birth order and creativity using 234 gifted and non-gifted children (5th—8th graders), 5 divergent thinking tests, and multivariate procedures to test birth order and its interaction with number of siblings, gender and age. He found that 'only children' had highest divergent thinking test scores, followed by eldest, youngest and then middle children. He also found that subjects with more siblings had higher scores than Ss with one sibling.

Eisenmen (1988) in his study on creativity, birth order and risk taking on 100 first born and 100 later born adult males, found that risk taking and creativity were related and that both were associated with birth order.

Srivastava (1977) conducted an investigation to find out the relationship between creativity and number of siblings. The sample of the study consisted of 543 urban male students of classes IX and X of Varanasi city. The data was collected with the help of the Mehdi's verbal test of creative thinking. The students were divided into 8 birth order groups (1 to 8) on the basis of their birth order positions. In order to find out the effect of family size (number of siblings) they were further divided into three groups: *(a)* slogan group (1-3 siblings); *(b)* average group (4-6 siblings); *(c)* high group (7+ siblings). The findings of the study were: *(i)* There was no significant difference in the creativity scores of the students belonging to different birth order groups. *(ii)* The students belonging to the high group scored significantly higher than the students of slogan group, and *(iii)* There was no significant difference in the creativity scores of the students of slogan and moderate groups, and moderate and low groups.

On the other hand in a study by Srivastava (1977) conducted on a sample of 543 urban and 354 rural children of X class, it was found that birth order of the subjects had no impact on their creativity scores. However, the number of siblings in the family was positively and significantly correlated with creativity scores.

Badrinath and Satyanarayana (1979) also found that students of first, second, third and fourth birth orders did not differ significantly with respect to their creativity scores.

Kaur (1986) reported that creative abilities were found to be independent of birth order.

Datta (1968), Harnek and Manjit (1988), Venkata Rami Reddy and Tulasi Devi also observed similar results.

VIII. APPRAISAL

It may be seen from the brief review of literature presented in the foregoing pages that a number of studies have been carried out on the relation between creativity and other variables. But by and large the results obtained were not unequivocal.

For example, studies on the relation between sex and creativity have yielded three kinds of results: *(i)* boys are superior to girls in creative thinking, *(ii)* girls are superior to boys in creative thinking, and *(iii)* there are no sex differences in creative ability.

The first kind of conclusion that boys are superior to girls in creative thinking was arrived at by Torrance (1961), Kelly (1965), Hutchinson (1967), Middents (1968), Raina (1968, 1969, 1970), Gagneja (1972), Hussain (1976), Agarwal (1977), Awasthy (1979), Dharmangadan (1981), Shukla (1982), Venkata Rami Reddy and Balakrishna Reddy (1984), Chandrakant (1987), Syama Thrimurthy (1987) etc.

Investigations of Yamamoto (1960), Getzels and Jackson (1962), Razik (1964), Mac Gregor and Smith (1965), Ogletree (1968), Walker (1969), Cacha (1971), Passi (1972), Maccoby and Jacklin (1974), Singh (1978), Pandit (1976), Rawat and Garg (1977), Jarial (1981), Pandey (1984), Chadha and Ghose (1985) and Bharadwaj (1985), among others found that girls were superior to boys in creative thinking.

Some other studies however, reported no relation between the two variables (Phatak, 1962; Pogue, 1964; Jackson, 1968; Burns, 1969; Philips and Torrance, 1971; Kloss, 1972; Gakhar, 1974; Thamma Prateep, 1976; Cheek, 1979; Saxena, 1981; Agarwal and Gupta, 1982; Pandey and Pandey, 1984; Dexie, 1985; Bajpai and Ahmed, 1986; Harnek, Gurusagar and Manjeet, 1988).

Not many studies have come to print on the relation between locality and creativity. But even the few studies yielded contradictory results.

It was found by Sharma (1971, 1972) that rural children were more creative than their urban counterparts. However, Passi (1972), Singh (1977, 1978), Dharmangadan (1981), Srivastava (1978), Agarwal and Gupta (1982), Singh and Singh (1984) reported that urban children were better off than rural children. Some others like Aaron, Marihal and Malatesha (1969), Jayaswal (1977), Sehgal (1978), Singh

(1981), Joshi (1982) and Chandrakant (1987) reported that there was no significant difference in the creativity of urban and rural children.

The relation between creativity and intelligence is, probably, the most controversial. Researchers like guilford (1950, 1956), Wilson, *et al,* (1954), Yamamoto (1961), Getzels and Jackson (1962), Torrance (1962), Taylor (1964), Wallach and Kogan (1965), Guilford and Hoepfner (1966), Raina (1968), Trivedi (1969), Passi (1972), Mehdi (1973), Patel and Joshi (1976), Patel (1978), Venkata Rami Reddy and Balakrishna Reddy (1983), etc., contended that creativity was a district aspect of intellectual functioning which was for all practical purposes independent of conventional intelligence.

On the other hand, Burt (1962, 1964), Thorndike (1963), Marsh (1964), Lovell and Shields (1967), Ginsberg and Whittmore (1968), Olton, *et al.,* (1969), Dutt, Prem Bountra and Sabharawal (1973), Sharma (1974), Pestonjee and Usmani (1982), Qureshi (1982), Ashok (1985), etc., observed that creativity and intelligence were not independent.

Studies on the relation between age and creativity also did not yield unequivocal results. Some investigators, especially Torrance (1962, 1964), Yamamoto (1960), Torrance *et al,* (1960), Simpson (1922), Mearns (1941), observed slumps in the development of creativity with age. However, others like piers, Daniels and Quackenbush (1960), Olshin, (1965), Raina (1970), Ogletree (1971, 1972), Ahmed (1980) and Dexie (1985) reported a significant positive relationship between creativity and age.

The relation between personality and creativity was studied by quite a few investigators (Greenacre, 1959; Torrance 1962; Anderson and Anderson, 1965; Liberman, 1965; 1966; Smith, 1965; Ray Choudhary, 1966; Hudson, 1966a; Dellas and Gaier, 1970; Paramesh, 1970; Goyal, 1972; Lalithamma, 1973; Verma, 1973; Goyal, 1974; Chawla, 1976; Nair, 1976; Das Gupta, 1977; Paramesh and Narayanan, 1977; Girijesh Kumar, 1978; Bhargava, 1979; Jyostna, 1980;

Sreenivasan, 1984; Kundu, (1987). Most of the studies reported positive relationship between some personality characteristics and creativity while no relationship was observed in the case of others.

The relationship between creativity and birth order was explored by Srivastava (1977), Dave (1980), Jarial (1979, 1981), Runco and Bahleda (1987) and Eisenman (1988), who found that first borns were more creative than later borns. However, in a few other investigations on this aspect it was found that there was no relation between the two variables (Badrinath and Satyanarayana, 1979; Kaur, 1986; Harnek and Manjit, 1988; Venkata Rami Reddy and Tulasidevi).

The effect of the general home background in terms of the authoritarian or permissiveness of the parents on creativity was the subject of study for some scientists (Watson, 1957; Gallaher, 1964; Anderson and Anderson, 1965; Torrance, 1971; Louise and Febert, 1977; Garber, et al., 1979), while the relation between socio-economic status and creativity was explored by some researchers like Raina (1968), Vohra (1975), Gupta (1976), Rawat and Agarwal (1977), Singh (1978), Srivastava (1978), Jarial (1979), Sharma (1979, 1980), Ahmed (1980), Vijayalakshmi (1980), Sunil Dutt (1988), Zargaa and Neelamdhar (1988), Harnek (1989). The results of these studies, as in the case of other areas were not unequivocal.

3

Statement of the Problem and Hypotheses

Creativity has been recognised as a precious source of emergence, development and survival of man's culture through ages. The functioning of the mind and the nature of human genious has been the centre of attention of psychologists and educationists for centuries. Thinkers belonging to different disciplines such as philosophy, fine arts, literature, psychology, education etc., have often tried to probe into the nature of creativity but got no uniform answer. As is well known each one of these disciplines analyses creativity somewhat differently.

The pace of a nation's progress depends upon identification of the creative talents of its citizens and systematically nourishing such abilities to fruition. It is needless to mention that education has a pivotal role in the identification and nourishing of such creative talents. Research on creativity has been a recent outcome of this realisation. According to Trowbridge (1966) the creative person can contribute something which even the intelligent person cannot.

The physical resources of any nation remain useless until the human resources, through their ingenuity discover how to exploit them. In fact, the resources seem to be vast, pervading and varied. It is man's ability alone that can make miracles out of apparently barren situations. It is man's creative abilities rather than the physical resources that count in making the deserts bloom, in domesticating storms, and in bridling oceans to service.

Ours is the age of science and technology, of discoveries and inventions. The frontiers of knowledge are broadened by creative men. Our dreams are realised by our creativity. Each individual shows in one way or another a special kind of creativeness, or originality, or inventiveness, that has certain peculiar characteristics. But the factors of creativity vary from person to person, both in amount of initial disposition and in the degree to which this potential is realised and developed.

Though creativity is no less important than any other human characteristic for the progress of mankind, research on creativity has been of recent origin due to various reasons, even in advanced countries like USA and UK, not to speak of developing countries like India.

However, today, the focus of the entire world is on this specialised area, 'creativity'. Modern educators are concerned with the identification of the creative abilities so as to nourish them and explore all the possibilities to make use of such unusual productive talents for the development of science, technology, literature, art, music, etc.

But as was mentioned in the previous chapter many of the studies on creativity yielded contradictory results, showing that much is yet to be known about the relationship between creativity and various other factors.

Further, as noted earlier, according to Arasteh and Arasteh (1976) research studies on creativity and the development of talent have proceeded from both childhood and adulthood with an obvious gap in between (i.e.) and adolescent period. Torrance (1964) also observed that of the different educational levels, the high school years have been the most neglected in creativity research.

I. STATEMENT OF THE PROBLEM

Hence, the present investigation was aimed at analysing the creativity of adolescent boys and girls in relation to certain variables like sex, locality, length of schooling (school grade/class, personality traits, mental ability, school-economic status, etc.

II. OBJECTIVES OF THE STUDY

The objectives of the study were:

1. To find out whether boys and girls differ in their creativity.
2. To find out whether children belonging to urban and rural localities differ in their creativity.
3. To examine whether differences in length of schooling (school grade/class) are significantly related to the creativity of children.
4. To examine whether high and low creatives differ with regard to their personality characteristics.
5. To find out whether high creatives and low creatives differ in their mental ability.
6. To find out whether SES differentiates between high and low creativity children.

In addition to the above the relation between creativity and certain familial variables (like type of family, affinity between members of the family, liberty given by parents in doing things, punishment given by parents for mistakes etc.), and certain habits of life like (reading other general books, attitude towards stereotype in work, etc.) was also sought to be analysed.

III. HYPOTHESES

Based upon the above objectives the following hypotheses were formulated for the investigation:

1. There would not be any significant difference between the creativity of boys and girls.
2. There would not be any significant difference between the creativity of the children belonging to rural and urban localities.
3. There would be a significant difference between the creativity of children belonging to different classes.

The above hypotheses were tested separately for each of the four aspects, viz., fluency, flexibility, originality and composite creativity.

Further, to find out whether the relationship between creativity and different variables differed from verbal tests to nonverbal tests, this analysis was carried out separately for the verbal tests, nonverbal tests and both types of tests put together.

4. There would not be any significant difference between the personality characteristics of high creative and low creative children.
5. High creative children would have a higher level of mental ability compared to low creative children.
6. There would not be any significant difference between the socio-economic status of high creative and low creative children.
7. There would not be any significant difference between high creative and low creative children with regard to the frequency with which they study story books, magazines, etc.
8. High creatives would be more unconventional in doing things compared to low creatives.
9. High and low creative children would not differ significantly with regard to the frequency with which they get silly ideas.

10. High creatives and low creatives would not differ with regard to the number of friends they have.
11. Others would find it difficult to adjust with creative children.
12. There would not be any significant difference between high creatives and low creatives with regard to the frequency with which they fall ill.
13. There would be greater affinity between the members of the families of high creative children than that in the case of low creative children.
14. High and low creatives would not differ with regard to the type of family to which they belong.
15. High creatives and low creatives would differ significantly with regard to the liberty given to them by their parents in doing various things.
16. High creatives and low creatives would differ significantly with regard to the frequency with which they are punished for their mistakes.
17. There would not be any significant difference between high creatives and low creatives with regard to their order of birth.

Step-wise multiple regression analysis was also carried out to find out the relative effect of each of the several independent variables and their combined effect on the creativity of the children.

This analysis was also carried out separately for each of the different components of creativity, for the verbal and nonverbal tests and for the two types of tests put together.

Variables Studied

As the problem envisages the investigation of the relation between creativity and variables such as sex, locality, length of schooling (grade/class), intelligence, personality, traits, socio-economic status, etc., a brief description of the variables employed in the study is in order:

I. SEX

In the present investigation boys and girls were included to find out whether there were any significant sex differences in creativity.

II. LOCALITY

Localities were categorised as urban and rural as explained below:

1. ***Urban:*** A locality was considered as urban if it had
   - *(a)* a municipality;
   - *(b)* adequate road and rail connections;
   - *(c)* educational facilities upto collegiate level;
   - *(d)* a large number of government offices;

(*e*) reasonably good facilities for entertainment like cinema houses, theatres, etc.;

(*f*) clubs like the Lions, the Rotary, etc.;

(*g*) atleast one medium-sized industry;

(*h*) a sizable floating population; and

(*i*) business and commercial importance.

2. ***Rural:*** A locality was considered as rural if

(*a*) it did not have modern facilities like—rail and motor transport of considerable frequency, communication facilities like telephone and telegraph protected water supply, hospitals (primary health Centre excepted), and government offices;

(*b*) it was outside a radius of atleast 15 kilometers from the nearest town; and

(*c*) its population was predominantly agricultural.

III. LENGTH OF SCHOOLING (GRADE/CLASS)

Subjects from VIII, IX and X classes were selected for this study, as these classes comprise the terminal stage of secondary education.

Class rather than age was chosen as a measure of development because in a cross sectional study, age differences are confounded by the differences in the date of birth, and in a longitudinal study age differences are confounded with times of measurement (Schaie, 1965). Even if these confoundings were not present, the relation between age and other variables would be purely descriptive and not explanatory (Townsend, 1953). School grade seems to be preferable to age as an index of development in adolescence (Hollender, 1967).

In addition, in the rural communities in India, the date of birth is not correctly recorded and as such the correct age of the pupils cannot be easily ascertained.

Moreover, there is nondetention system in Andhra Pradesh according to which the student will be promoted from class to class irrespective of his achievement provided he puts in a prescribed percentage of attendance. As such, the children in each class will be more or less homogeneous with respect to their age.

IV. PERSONALITY FACTORS

Cattell's High School Personality Questionnaire (HSPQ) form-A was used to measure the personality characteristics of the children. The HSPQ assesses the personality of the respondents on 14 factors.

A brief description of the salient characteristics of the low scorers (Vs) high scorers on the 14 factors measured by the HSPQ is given below[1].

(i) Factor—A

Low Score		**High Score**
Critical	Vs	Good natured, Easygoing
Stands by his own ideas	Vs	Ready to cooperate, likes to participate
Cool, aloof	Vs	Attentive to people
Precise, objective	Vs	Soft hearted, casual
Distrustful, skeptical	Vs	Trustful
Rigid	Vs	Adaptable, careless, "goes along"
Cold	Vs	Warmhearted
Prone to sulk	Vs	Laughs readily
In summary— a low scorer on Factor A is reserved, detached, critical, aloof and stiff.	(while)	a high scorer on this factor is warmhearted outgoing, easygoing and participating.

(ii) Factor—B

Low Score		**High Score**
Low mental capacity	Vs	High general mental capacity

Unable to handle abstract problems	Vs	Insightful, fast-learning, intellectually adaptable
Apt to be less well organised	Vs	Inclined to have more intellectual interests.

(iii) Factor—C

Low Score		**High Score**
Gets emotional when frustrated	Vs	Emotionally mature
Changeable in attitudes and interests	Vs	Stable, constant in interests
Evasive of responsibilities, tending to give up	Vs	Does not let emotional needs obscure realities of a situation, adjusts to facts
Worrying	Vs	Unruffled
Gets into fights and problems situations	Vs	Shows a restraint in avoiding difficulties
This is— a low scorer is affected by feelings, emotionally less stable, easily upset and changeable,	(while)	a high scorer is emotionally stable, mature, faces reality and calm.

(iv) Factor—D

Low Score		**High Score**
Stoical	Vs	Demanding, impatient
Complacent	Vs	Attention getting, showing off
Deliberate	Vs	Excitable, overactive
Not easily jealous	Vs	Prone to jealousy
Self-effecting	Vs	Self-assertive, egotistical
Constant	Vs	Distractible
Not restless	Vs	Shows many nervous symptoms.
In other words— a low scores is undemonstrative, deliberate, inactive, and stodgy,	(while)	a high scorer is excitable, impatient, demanding, overactive and unrestrained.

(v) Factor—E

Low Score		**High Score**
Submissive	Vs	Assertive
Dependent	Vs	Independent minded
Considerate, Diplomatic	Vs	Stern, hostile
Expressive	Vs	Solemn
Conventional, conforming	Vs	Unconventional, rebellious
Easily upset by authority	Vs	Headstrong
Humble	Vs	Admiration demanding
In summary— a low scorer is obedient, mild, easily led, docile and accommodating	(while)	a high scorer is assertive, aggressive, competitive and stubborn.

(vi) Factor—F

Low Score		**High Score**
Silent, introspective	Vs	Talkative
Full of cares	Vs	Cheerful
Concerned, reflective	Vs	Happy-go-lucky
Incommunicative, sticks to inner values	Vs	Frank, Expressive, reflects the group
Slow, cautious	Vs	Quick and alert
This is— a low scorer is sober, taciturn, serious,	(while)	a high scorer is enthusiastic, needless, happy-go-lucky.

(vii) Factor—G

Low Score		**High Score**
Quitting, fickle	Vs	Perservering determined
Frivolous	Vs	Responsible
Self-indulgent	Vs	Emotionally disciplined
Slack, indolent	Vs	Consistently ordered
Undependable	Vs	Conscientious, dominated by sense of duty

Disregards obligations to people	Vs	Concerned about moral standards and rules.
In other words— a low scorer is characterised by low super ego strength or lack of acceptance of group moral standards, disregards rules and is expedient,	(while)	a high scorer has high super ego strength or character, is conscientious, persistent, moralistic, and stoid.

(viii) Factor—H

Low Score		High Score
Shy, withdrawn	Vs	Adventurous, likes meeting people
Retiring in face of opposite sex	Vs	Active, overt interest in opposite sex
Emotionally cautious	Vs	Friendly
Restrained, rule-bound	Vs	Impulsive
Restricted interests	Vs	Emotionaly and artistic interests
Careful, considerate, quick to see dangers	Vs	Carefree, does not see danger signals
That is— a low scorer is shy, timid, restrained and threat-sensitive,	(while)	a high scorer is adventurous, "thick-skinned" and socially bold.

(ix) Factor—I

Low Score		High Score
Unsentimental, expects little	Vs	Fidgety, expecting affection and attention
Self-reliant, taking responsibility	Vs	Clinging, insecure, seeking help and sympathy
Hard (to point of Cynicism)	Vs	Kindly, gentle, indulgent to self and others
Unaffected by "fancies"	Vs	Imaginative in innerlife and in conversation
Acts on practical, logical evidence	Vs	Acts on sensitive institution

Keeps to the point	Vs	Attention seeking, flighty
Does not dwell on physical disabilities	Vs	Hypochondriacal, anxious about self
In summary—a low scorer is tough-minded, rejects illusions.	(while)	a high scorer is tender-minded, sensitive dependent and overprotected.

(x) Factor—J

Low Score		High Score
Likes to go with the group	Vs	Acts individualistically
Likes attention	Vs	Guarded, wrapped up in self
Sinks personality into group enterprise	Vs	Fastidiously obstructive
Vigorous	Vs	Neurasthenically fatigued
Accepts common standards	Vs	Evaluates coldly
In other words—a lower scorer is zestful, likes group actions	(while)	a high scorer is circumspect individualistic, reflective and internally restrained.

(xi) Factor—O

Low Score		High Score
Self confident	Vs	Worrying, anxious
Cheerful, resilient	Vs	Depressed, cries easily
Impenitent, placid	Vs	Easily touched, overcome by moods
Expedient, insensitive to people's approval or disapproval	Vs	Strong sense of obligation, sensitive to people's approval and disapproval
Does not care	Vs	Scrupulous, fussy
Rudely vigorous	Vs	Hypochondriacal and inadequate
No fears	Vs	Phobic symptoms
Given to simple action	Vs	Lonely, brooding

In summary—		
a low scorer is self-assured, placid, secure and complacent,	(while)	a high scorer is apprehensive, self-reproaching, insecure, worrying and troubled.

(xii) Factor Q_2

Low Score		**High Score**
Group dependency	Vs	Self sufficiency
That is— a low scorer is socially group dependent a "joiner" and sound follower,	(while)	a high scorer is self-sufficient, resourceful and prefers own decisions.

(xiii) Factor—Q_3

Low Score		**High Score**
Low self sentiment integration	Vs	High strength of self sentiment.
In other words— a low scorer is uncontrolled, lax, follows own urges and careless of social rules,	(while)	a high scorer is controlled, exacting, will power, socially precise, compulsive, following self image.

(xiv) Factor—Q_4

Low Score		**High Score**
Low ergic tension	Vs	High ergic tension
In other words— a low scorer is relaxed, tranquil, torpid, unfrustrated composed,	(while)	a high scorer is tense, frustrated, driven, over wrought, and fretful.

V. MENTAL ABILITY

Mental ability of the subjects was assessed by Raven's Standard Progressive Matrices, sets, A, B, C, D and E. The following considerations determined the choice of the above instrument for assessing the mental ability:

(i) non availability of a suitable verbal instrument for use with the population under investigation (Evidently, verbal tests that are standardised elsewhere in a language other than the regional language (Telugu) of the population under investigation, would not be suitable for use in the present study);

(ii) the instrument should not ordinarily necessitate any elaborate arrangements for its administration, since the test had to be administered under normal classroom conditions in different localities;

(iii) the instructions should be simple and easy to understand;

(iv) as speed is a factor to which the Ss are not quite used to, a non-speed (power) test may be employed with advantage;

(v) since Raven's Progressive Matrices contains figures, the students find it very interesting. As such, they can be easily motivated.

In the light of the above, Raven's Standard Progressive Matrices was chosen to measure the mental ability of the students.

VI. SOCIO-ECONOMIC STATUS (SES)

The socio-economic status of the students was assessed to find out whether there was any significant difference between the socio-economic status of high creative and low creative children.

VII. FAMILIAL AND PERSONAL CHARACTERISTICS AND HABITS OF LIFE

Torrance (1962), Getzels and Jackson (1962), Lugo and Hershey (1976) and Jha (1978) and many others have pointed out some familial and personal characteristics and habits of life which may be related to the creativity of the children.

Information about a few of them was also collected to examine their relation with creativity.

These variables were:

1. Frequency with which the children studied story books, magazines, etc.
2. The manner in which they would like to do things—conventional/unconventional.
3. The frequency with which the children got odd (silly) ideas.
4. Whether they have many or few friends.
5. Whether others find it difficult or easy to adjust with them.
6. The state of general health of the children.
7. Affinity between the members of their families.
8. Type of family to which the children belonged.
9. Liberty given by the parents to the children in various activities.
10. Frequency with which the children were punished by their parents for their mistakes, and
11. Order of birth.

Information about the above aspects was obtained from a carefully designed personal data sheet, and the association between the creativity of the children and each of the above aspects was analysed.

Reference

1 A detailed description of the different factors can be obtained from Cattell (1970).

5

Method of Investigation

I. DEFINITION OF CREATIVITY

What is creativity? The concept is notoriously difficult to pin down because it had been used synonymously with terms like 'imagination', 'ingenuity', 'spontaneity', 'productivity' 'originality', 'divergent thinking', inventiveness', 'intuition', 'venturesomeness', 'exploration', and 'giftedness'. Child (1973) observed that 'there is no clear, unambiguous and widely accepted definition of creativity'. What Child has said in 1973 is probably equally true even today.

At times imagination is considered as synonymous with creativity. Andrews (1930) defined imagination in children as 'the process by which items of experience are combined to form new products'. Griffiths (1945) differentiated imagination, a mode of thinking concerned with fantasy and day dreams, from imagery, a type of sensory experience in which images arise independent of external stimulation. The term 'creative imagination' has been used by McCloy (1939), Greenacre (1959) and O'Brien, Sibley and Ligon (1953) whereas McDowell and Howe (1941) refer to 'productive imagination'. All these investigators considered newness or originality as the main criterion.

The term 'imagination' and 'fantasy' have been interchangeably used. Both Griffiths (1945) and Singer (1961) equate fantasy with day dreams and imaginative play and the resulting images thereby produced. The term 'imagination' is more often used to describe the process, rather than the product. Singer differentiated early fantasy, characterised by verbal role-taking, from later internalised fantasy, chiefly of a visual type.

Generally considered as an important component of creativity, originality is defined in terms of relative infrequency of a response within a particular group. Guilford (1962) defined originality as 'the production of unusual, farfetched, remote or clever responses ..... presented in terms of the statistical infrequency of a response among members of a certain population that is culturally homogeneous'. Torrance (1962) accepts Guilford's definition with the added proviso that the response 'is relevant to the task, shows intellectual strength or represents some break-away from the obvious, the common place and the banal'.

Doppelt (1964) defined creativity in terms of achievements labeled as creative by 'judges'. To study the judgemental process the author devised a series of 'test' items describing various behaviours which the respondent rates for creativity. All items depict only fictitious events. Scientists, artists and business people will be asked to rate these descriptions and they themselves will be evaluated in an effort to find answers to such questions as *(i)* what kinds of behaviour are considered creative by acceptable judges? *(ii)* Do judges qualified in different areas rate creativity in similar or different ways? *(iii)* Which of the emotions associated with the achievement seem to be related to the creativity ratings? *(iv)* What factors in the backgrounds of the judges are related to ratings made by them.

Whether creativity is to be defined and studied in terms of 'process' or 'product', constitutes a major issue in much research. This issue has been dealt with by Gallagher (1963), Golann (1961), Jackson and Messick (1965), Stein (1962) and

Taylor (1964). Studies of creativity in children have primarily concentrated on the process of creative development.

In general, the most widely applied conceptions of creativity may be classified into three categories, depending on the relative emphasis given to the product or the process or the experience.

Thus some definitions are formulated in terms of a manifest product; it is novel and useful. Mackinnon (1962) for example, suggests that the criterion of creativity is a statistically infrequent response or idea that is adaptive and sustained to fruition.

Other definitions are formulated in terms of an underlying progress; it is divergent yet fruitful. For example, Ghiselin (1952) speaks of creativity as a process of change and development in the psychic life of an individual leading to invention.

Still other definitions are formulated in terms of a subjective experience; it is inspired and immanent. Maslow (1963), for one, insists on the importance of the flesh of insight—the transcendent sensation itself—without reference to whether it will ever result in anything tangible. The salient issue is not 'inspired product', but the 'inspired moment'.

Getzels (1964) has attempted to deal with creativity along somewhat different lines, giving primacy to nature of the problem rather than to the solution. A distinction is made between presented and discovered problem situations, the former involving a problem that is already formulated, the later a problem that still needs formulation. The significant element in creative performance according to Getzels and Csikezentimihalyi (1964) is the envisagement of the creative problem; for it is the fruitful question to which the novel solution is the response.

None of the preceding conceptions of creativity is immune from the objection that each omits some characteristics vital to the others.

Newell and others (1962) have presented an omnibus definition, which states that thinking may be called creative if

1. the product has novelty and value either for the thinker or the culture;
2. the thinking is unconventional;
3. it is highly motivated and persistent, or of great intensity; and
4. the problem was initially vague and undefined, so that part of the task was to formulate the problem itself.

The above statement has the advantage of inclusiveness but like other omnibus conceptions, it has the disadvantage of being and inventory without a unifying rationale.

1. Product Definitions

Guilford (1971) expresses that 'creativity' is an ambiguous word, but when it is used in the phrase 'testing for creativity', its meaning may be restricted to those qualities or traits of individuals that predispose them to produce novel ideas and novel effects.

According to Stein (1960), creation is an activity which brings something 'new' and which has 'utility'. Thus creativity reshapes the horizons of human understanding.

Isrelle and Drevhal (1956) say that 'creativity is an ability to create something new'.

According to Barron (1969), 'creativity means to create something new by assimilating existing principles or things'.

Hutchinson (1949) says 'By creative effort I mean the initiation and execution of some work of literature, art, music or science which is essentially new'.

According to Morgan (1960), 'creativity involves development of something unique by the individual'.

Parnes (1966) defines creative behaviour as that 'which demonstrates both uniqueness and value in its product'.

'Creativity is the capacity of a person to produce compositions, products or ideas which are essentially new or novel and previously unknown to the producer' (Drevdahl, 1956).

According to Mackinnon (1962) the criterion for creativity is a statistically infrequent response or idea that is adaptive and sustained to fruition.

Some consider creativity as a combination of many abilities running through many spheres of human activity. It is manifested in a variety of ways though essentially it is 'the process of bringing something new into birth' (May, 1953).

In their writings on creativity Rogers (1962) and Arnold (1962) insist on a tangible product, such as a poem, a work of art, or scientific theory as an indicator of creativity.

Jha (1978) defined creativity as 'the manifestation of uncommon talent in terms of novel and original products (whether ideas or effects) commanding high professional estimate of their worth'.

'Creative thinking means that the predictions and/or inferences for the individual are new, original, ingenious and unusual. The creative thinker is one who explores new areas and makes new observations, new predictions and new inferences' (Gray, 1954).

According to Wilson, Guilford and Christinsen (1974) creative act is that in which 'something new is produced—an idea or an object including a new form or arrangement of old elements. The new creation must contribute to the solution of some problem'.

According to the Dictionary of Psychology creative thinking means 'the achievement of a new relationship among the parts of experience, which according to Wallas (1926), has four stages; preparation, incubation, inspiration or illumination, and verification. The creative idea comes as a flash of insight or a sudden thought' (Harriman, 1947).

2. Process Definitions

Between the two aspects of creativity—the process of creation and the product of creation—there is no definite opinion as far as the former is concerned because it is almost an inner happening and it differs from individual to individual.

Osborn (1948), the "Father of Brain-storming" and a pioneer of creative education, divides the creative process into the following phases:

Orientation (picking out the problem)

Preparation (gathering relevant material—organisation effort)

Analysis and ideation (seeking possible solutions)

Incubation (a time lag for the mind to synthesise the problem and solution)

Evaluation (putting the pieces together and verifying the solutions through further testing or evaluation).

We should not be deceived by the seeming simplicity of this procedure. It is simple enough to be effective but it is certainly is not automatic. In fact, the creation of new ideas will require tremendous mental effort. Perhaps, that is why it is often said that creativity is "painful". Thomas A. Edison once commented that creativity is 90 per cent perspiration and 10 per cent inspiration.

Simpson (1922) defines creativity as the "....initiative which one manifests by his power to break away from the usual sequence of thought into an altogether different pattern of thought".

Barron (1969) looks at creativity as "energy being put to work in a constructive fashion".

"The creative act is free and independent force, immanently inherent only in a person, a personality. Only something arising in original substance and possessing the power to increase power in the world can be true creativity. .. Creativity is an original act of personalities in the world" (Berdyaev, 1969).

Mednick (1962) defines creative thinking as the process of forming associative elements into new combinations which either meet specified requirements or are in some way useful.

Wallach and Kogan (1965) suggest a basically similar notion; "... greater creativity should be indicated by the ability to produce more associations and to produce more that are unique".

Freud (1949) holds that, "sublimation of repressed unconscious wishes and pregnital and libidinal urges determine creativity".

Fromm (1959) defines the conditions of creativity as the capacity for wonder, the capacity to face incongruity and tension, to orient oneself towards the new, to be aware of experience and to respond fully to such awareness.

According to Mason (1960) creativeness, in the best sense of the word, requires two things: an original concept, or 'idea', and a benefit to some one.

Hallman (1963) has analysed the creative act into five major components.

1 it is a whole act, a unitary instance of behaviour;

2. it terminates in the production of objects or of forms of living which are distinctive;

3. it evolves out of certain mental processes;

4. it co-varies with specific personality transformation; and

5. it occurs within a particular kind of environment.

According to Golann (1961) 'creativity is a normally distributed trait, an intrapsychic process and a style of life'.

Raychaudhuri (1965) indicated that 'the more sophisticated view has located in creativeness, originality, novelty, communication of emotional authenticity, applicability, social acceptance and some sort of combinatorial activity' (Bruner, 1962; Guilford, 1959; Hammer, 1961; Stein and Heinze, 1960).

On the basis of an analysis of the diverse ways of defining creativity and the requirements of a definition for keeping a programme of research focussed on factors affecting creative growth in context, Torrance (1965) describes creativity as 'the process of becoming sensitive to problems, deficiencies, gaps in knowledge, missing elements, disharmonies and so on; identifying the difficulty; searching for solutions, making guesses, or formulating hypotheses about the deficiencies; testing and retesting these hypotheses and possibly modifying and retesting them; and finally communicating the results' (Torrance and Myers, 1970).

Creativity means 'the ability to produce new forms in art or mechanics or to solve problems by novel methods' (Chaplin, 1982).

According to Goldenson (1984) creativity means the ability to apply original ideas to the solution of problems; the development of theories, techniques, or devices; or the production of novel forms of art, literature, philosophy, or science.

According to Arnold (1963) 'creativity involves the rearrangement of past experiences, with possibly some changes into new patterns to satisfy some expressed or implied need'.

According to Passi (1972) 'creativity is a multidimensional (verbal and nonverbal) attribute differentially distributed among people and includes chiefly the factors of seeing problems, fluency, flexibility, originality, inquisitiveness and persistency'.

3. Experience Definitions

As mentioned earlier, Maslow (1963) is a proponent of subjective experience in creativity. He emphasises on the importance of the flash of insight—the transcendent sensation itself—without any reference to whether it will ever result in anything tangible. The important issue is not the 'inspire product' but the 'inspire moment'.

According to Vinake (1952) creativity is 'an integrated harmony between the external world of reality and individual's internalized needs'.

The path of creative insight is often thin and dim. It is not a happening in which some abstraction bursts full blown into consciousness; it is the result of intensive effort at seeking new structures of known information of a long mixing of ideas often 'felt' rather than cognized. It is only the jelling that we 'know' (Marrifield, 1976).

II. INDEX OF CREATIVITY

The critical issue underlying all work in the field of creativity is the criterion problem according to Getzels and Csikszentmihalyi (1964).'

What is an appropriate index of creativity? Getzels and Madaus (1969) observed that the following are some among the most common criteria:

1. ***Achievement or Accomplishment:*** An attempt is made to identify achievements which speak for themselves. At the adult level, for example, the Nobel Prize or some other mark of outstanding accomplishment may be taken as an index that hardly any one would dispute (*e.g.*, Ghiselin, 1952).
2. ***Ratings:*** It is assumed that a person who has an opportunity to observe another person can provide a sound judgement of his inventiveness. Evaluation by peers, supervisors and teachers has been used as a criterion (*e.g.*, Mackinnon, 1964; Drevdahl, 1964).
3. ***Intelligence:*** Performance on intelligence tests is the most widely used and best validated index of mental functioning. Presumably creativity is a mental function,

and a superior IQ may be used as a criterion (*e.g.*, Terman, 1925).

4. ***Personality:*** Characteristics of personality are evaluated in relation to an empirically derived or an a priori profile of the 'creative personality' and the closeness of the fit is used as a criterion (*e.g.*, Cattell and Drevdahl, 1955).

5. ***Creativity Test Scores:*** 'Although attempts to measure aspects of creativity through tests have a long history (Taylor, 1964), the factor analytical studies by Guilford inspired the great variety of so-called creativity tests not only in his terms but in related principles as well.

Thus among the many tests are Mednick's Remote Association Test (Mednick and Mednick, 1964), built on associative theory; Flanagan's Ingenious Solutions to Problems Test (Flanagan, 1958), one of the few attempts at assessing creative thinking through multiple choice items; and the AC Test of Creative Ability (Buhl, 1960), directed especially at problems of engineering. There are numerous other tests, including such older indices as the interpretation of ink blots, block construction and drawing tests. Perhaps the most extensive set of materials for use at all educational levels is the Minnesota Tests of Creative Thinking' (Getzels and Madaus 1969).

III. TESTS FOR MEASURING CREATIVITY DESIGNED BY DIFFERENT AUTHORS

Wallach and Kogan (1965) designed the following tests for measuring creativity:

1. ***Instances Test:*** It is the first of the verbal techniques of the author. In this the child is asked to generate possible instances of a class that is specific in verbal terms.

2. ***Alternate Uses Test:*** It is the second of three verbal techniques. In it the child is to generate possible uses for verbally specified objects.

3. ***Similarities Test:*** In this the child is to generate possible similarities between pairs of verbally specified objects.

4. ***Pattern Meanings Test:*** This is one of the two creativity assessment techniques involving visual rather than verbal stimulus materials.

5. ***Line Meanings Test:*** In this second creativity procedure involving visual stimulus materials, the child is confronted with one or another kind of line drawings and is asked to generate meanings or interpretations relevant to the form of the line in question. The lines were adopted from Tagiuri (1960). Each line is a single continuous unit, in contrast to the discrete elements comprising the patterns in the preceding instrument.

Getzels and Jackson (1962) constructed 5 tests to measure creativity. The tests are briefly described below:

1. ***Word Association Test:*** This test presents the subject with twenty-five words each of which has multiple meanings (*e.g.*, arm, cap, duck, fair, pitch, punch, sack, tender). The student is asked to write as many meanings as he can for each word.

2. ***Uses Test:*** This test presents the subject with the names of five common objects (bricks, pencils, paper, clips, tooth picks, sheet of paper) and asks him to write as many different uses as he can for each object. The idea for this test is derived from two similar tests used by Guilford in his factor analytic studies of cognitive ability.

3. ***Hidden Shapes Test:*** This test is part of Cattell's (1956) Objective—Analytic Test Battery and consists of eighteen geometric figures each of which is followed by four more complex figures. The subject's task is to identify the complex figures in which the simple figure appears.

4. ***Fables Test:*** This test consists of four fables whose last lines are missing. The student is required to supply a moralistic, a humorous and a sad ending for each fable.

5. ***Makeup Problems Test:*** This test consists of four complex paragraphs, each containing many numerical statements about activities such as buying a house, building a swimming pool, and the like. For each paragraph the student is to use the information given to make up as many mathematical problems as he can within the time limit. But the problems must be capable of solution though he is not required to solve the problems.

According to Arasteh and Arasteh (1976) the most systematic assessment of creativity is that made by Torrance and his associates (1960a, 1960b, 1960c, 1961, 1992, 1962a, 1963a, 1964) who have administered the Minnesota Tests of Creative Thinking (MTCT) to several thousand school children. These tests represent a fairly sharp departure from the factor type tests developed by Guilford and his associates (Guilford, Merrifield and Cox, 1961; Merrifield, Guilford and Gershon, 1963), and they differ, too from the battery developed by Wallach and Kogan (1965), which contains measures representing creative tendencies that are similar in nature (Torrance, 1968).

Torrance (1962) grouped the different subtests of the MTCT (Minnesota Tests of Creative Thinking) into three groups:

(a) Verbal tasks using verbal stimuli,

(b) Verbal tasks using nonverbal stimuli, and

(c) Nonverbal tasks.

A brief description of the different sub-tests used by Torrance is given below:

A. Verbal Tasks Using Verbal Stimuli

1. ***Just Suppose Test:*** In the Just Suppose Test the subject is confronted with an improbable situation and asked to

think of all the possible outcomes from the introduction of a new or unknown variable. The verbal statement of the improbable situation is accompanied by a drawing of the situation. Blanks are provided under the verbal statement for responses. For example: 'Just suppose—some one got caught in a big soap bubble and could not out'.

2. ***Imaginative Stories Task:*** The Imaginative Stories Task calls for writing 'the most interesting and exciting story' on a topic related to animals or people having some divergent characteristics. Topics such as the following are suggested: 'The Flying Monkey', 'The Lion that won't Roar', etc. The child may use his own ideas and generate a new topic and write about it.

3. ***Unusual Uses Task:*** The Unusual Uses Task calls for interesting and unusual uses of common objects such as tin cans and book.

4. ***Impossibilities Task:*** The Impossibilities Task was used originally by Guilford and his associates (1951). But Torrance has made a number of modifications of the basic task. In this task the subjects are asked to list as many impossibilities as they can.

5. ***Consequences Test:*** The Consequences Test was also used originally by Guilford and his associates (1951). Torrance has made several modifications in adapting it. He choose three improbable situations and the children were required to list out their consequences.

6. ***Situations Task:*** The Situations Task was modelled after Guilford's (1951) test designed to assess the ability to see what needs to be done. Subjects were given three common problems and asked to think of as many solutions to these problems as they can. For example: 'How would you handle a friend who likes to kid others, but cannot stand to be kidded by them?'

7. ***Common Problems Task:*** This was also an adaptation of one of the Guilford's (1951) tests designed to assess

the ability to see defects, needs and deficiencies. In this task the subjects were given common situations and were asked to think of as many problems as they can that might arise in connection with these situations. For example: 'Getting to school easily in the morning'.

8. ***Mother Hubbard Problem:*** This task was conceived as an adaptation of the 'Situations Task' for oral administration in the primary grades. However, it was found useful in older groups as a group administered task also.

9. ***Improvements Task:*** This was an adaptation of the Apparatus Test of Guilford (1952) which was designed to assess ability to see defects. In this task the subjects are given a list of common objects and are asked to suggest as many ways as they can to improve each object. They are asked not to bother about whether or not it is possible to implement the changes thought of.

10. ***Cow Jumping Problem:*** The Cow Jumping Problem is a companion task for the 'Mother Hubbard Problem' and has been administered to the same groups, under the same conditions. The task is to think of all possible things which might have happened when the cow jumped over the moon.

B. Verbal Tasks Using Nonverbal Stimuli

1. ***Ask and Guess Test:*** It requires the individual first to think of all possible questions about what they see in a given picture, emphasis being on questions which can not be answered by just looking at the picture. Next he is asked to make guesses or formulate hypotheses about the possible causes of the event depicted, and then their consequences—both immediate and remote.

2. ***Product Improvement Task:*** In this task common toys are used and children are asked to think of as many improvements as they can which would make the toy 'more fun to play with'.

3. ***Unusual Uses Task:*** Accompanied with the above (Product Improvement) task, another task (Unusual Uses) is used. In this task the child is asked to think of the cleverest, most interesting and most unusual uses of the given toy—other than as a play thing. These uses could be for the toy as it is, or as it can be changed.

C. Nonverbal Tasks

1. ***Circles and Squares Task:*** In one form, the subject is confronted with a page of forty two circles and asked to sketch objects or pictures which have circle as a major part. In the alternate form, squares are used instead of circles.

2. ***Picture Construction or Shape Task:*** In this task the children are given a piece of coloured paper of a given shape (a triangle or a jelly beam) and a sheet of white paper. The children are required to think of a picture in which the given shape is an integral part. They should paste in wherever they want on the white sheet and add lines with pencil to make any novel picture. They have to think of a name for the picture and white it at the bottom.

3. ***Incomplete Figures Task:*** This is an adaptation of the 'Drawing Completion Test' developed by Kate Franck and used by Barron (1958). An ordinary white sheet is divided into 6 parts (squares), each containing a different stimulus figure. The subjects are asked to sketch some novel object or design by adding as many lines as they can to the six figures.

Following similar procedure tests have been developed by Mehdi (1973), Passi (1979), etc., to be used on Hindi speaking children.

IV. TESTS USED IN THE PRESENT INVESTIGATION TO MEASURE CREATIVITY

As mentioned earlier, the theoretical frame work for development of tests of creativity was provided by empirical studies on the nature of creativity. Especially useful in this context is the distinction Guilford has made between divergent thinking and convergent thinking abilities. Divergent thinking is a kind of mental process in which one thinks in different directions, unlike in convergent thinking, which moves towards responses that suit the known, and accepted as correct. Divergent thinking leads to novel responses to given stimuli. Its unique feature is that scope is provided to produce a variety of responses for any given stimuli.

The creativity of the subjects was measured in the present study with the help of a battery of creativity tests constructed in Telugu (Telugu is the regional language of the people of Andhra Pradesh where this investigation was conducted) by Venkata Rami Reddy. The tests were developed in line with those of Guilford (1962), Getzels and Jackson (1962), Torrance (1962) and Wallach and Kogan (1965). The items in the sub-tests were chosen taking into consideration their familiarity and relevance to the population on which they were to be used. The items were selected in consultation with 6 judges, drawn from the Departments of Psychology and Education, who were conversant with creativity tests.

The battery of creativity tests used consisted of 10 sub-tests. Seven of them were verbal tests while the remaining three were nonverbal tests. A brief description of the tests is presented in the following paragraphs.

1. ***Unusual Uses:*** Basically the Unusual Uses Test which is used in almost all creativity test batteries requires the subjects to redefine the object after thinking about the various ways in which it can be used. Common things like brick, wooden stick, water, and cotton were used as stimuli to let the subject's thinking go in different directions.

2. ***Instances:*** In this test the pupils were given 4 items. For each of the items they were required to tell all things that suit the specific concept under question.

3. ***Similarities:*** The children were provided with 4 pairs of things and they were asked to suggest as many different ways in which the two things in a given pair of objects were similar. They were to generate various similarities between the two objects in each of the four pairs.

4. ***Common Problems:*** This test was designed to assess the ability of the subjects to see defects, needs and deficiencies. This is one of the tests of the factor termed 'sensitivity to problems' by Guilford (1951). The subjects were given 4 common situations and were required to think of as many problems as they can, which they face in each of these situations.

5. ***Impossibilities:*** The impossibilities test is one involving complex restrictions and large potential. The task requires the children to think about all impossibilities (*i.e.*) those which are beyond the capacity of the present dayman-kind.

6. ***Consequences:*** In this test the subjects were confronted with certain hypothetical situations and they were required to think of all possible consequences of these hypothetical situations.

7. ***Product Improvement:*** The Product Improvement task is another complex task, which assesses the ability of the subjects to think of different kinds of defects and ways of improving the given objects. They were given a list of 4 objects and asked to suggest as many ways of improving each of them. They were told not to worry about the practicability of the suggested improvements.

8. ***Pattern Meanings:*** This involved visual rather than verbal stimulus materials. The subjects were given 8 patterns and they were required to generate different possible meanings or interpretations for each of them and list out the different ways in which each looked like.

9. ***Line Meanings:*** This task contained eight figures each of which was a continuous line of a particular sort. The subjects were to think of different interpretations

appropriate to the form of each of the given lines. Each line was a single unit unlike the discrete elements that comprised the patterns in the Pattern Meaning Test.

10. ***Circles:*** In this task the subjects were to construct meaningful figures with the given circles as base by drawing lines inside and/or outside each of them. After completing each figure, they were required to name them.

V. VALIDITY

According to Torrance (1962) 'Perhaps one of the major reasons why research related to the measurement and development of creative thinking did not catch the imagination of educators in the past years lies in the failure of researchers to deal adequately with the difficult problems of criteria and validity'. In the words of Taylor and Holland (1964) 'there is no more crucial problem in creativity than the criterion problem'. In the same vein Arasteh and Arasteh (1976) opined that the crucial problems in creativity research are those of measurement and validity. Torrance (1962) observed that in most cases the theoretical rationale of the instruments developed 'made good sense', but their presumed validity was not convincing. Similarly Shapiro (1972) also commented that the problem of criterion represented the most challenging aspect of all researches into creativity.

Quite interestingly, the most careful jobs of criterion development have been done in connection with personality and life experience studies rather than in efforts to validate measures of the creative thinking abilities!

The gravity of the problem can be seen from the words of Khatena: 'Measures of creativity originating from constructs whose complexities are better recognised than understood, have built in validation problems which the combined efforts of three University of Utah Conferences (Taylor, 1956, 1957, 1959) and the critical and constructive evaluation directions by prominent men in the field (*e.g.*, Mackler and Shontz, 1965; McNemar, 1964; Taylor, 1964;

Wallach and Wing, 1963; Wallach and Kogan, 1965; Yamamoto, 1965) have to date could not resolve (Khatena, 1973).

At the Second Minnesota Conference on Gifted Children, Taylor (1960) listed the obstacles in identifying creative talent as follows:

1. Rarity of the highest type of creative thinking.
2. Failure of the society to recognise creative products until one or two generations after the creation.
3. Tendency in the society to reward recognised creative talents with promotions into positions where the individuals are not able to continue their creative work.
4. The stress of academic programme of non-creative activities.
5. Failure of academic programme to reward creative achievement and divergent thinking.

At the 1959 Utah Conference, Guilford discussed the validation process as a part of the report of the Committee on Predictors of Creativity. He recommended that longitudinal (predictive) validation studies be initiated as quickly as possible. He also recommended Taylor's procedure of working first on the criterion problem and then looking for the measures which should be used to predict them. One may refer to this process as post-current or follow-back validity in contrast to follow-up or predictive validity. Recommendations were also made concerning the desirability of cross-validation, the use of factor or sub-scores rather than just combinations of them, the need for using moderator variables (co-varying factors), and validation procedures other than the regression approach (such as comparing the mean scores of the successful scientists, with the means of the general population from which these scientists originally came). But very little empirical work seems to have come to print in this direction.

The most widely used tests for assessing creativity in children are the MTCT. However, do they measure what they purport to measure and to what extent do they predict later creative ability?

Discussing this aspect Torrance (1962) comments that validity data of the usual kind is difficult to obtain in the case of creativity measures.

As such it is no wonder that different researchers used different procedures to establish validity of their tests. According to Treffinger, *et al.,* (1971) each instrument of creativity mirrored the particular set of beliefs and perceptions of its developer concerning the nature of creativity.

Torrance (1962) gives a variety of 'scattered evidence' for the validity of his tests. He found that his creativity test discriminated industrial arts students rated as highly creative from those rated as least creative, sales-women who sell most from those who sell least, and sales women who work in creative departments from those who work in routine departments. With elementary school children, it was validated in terms of observed behaviour in small group situations, on the basis of peer and teacher nominations, and on the basis of achievement of the traditional kinds.

With regard to the question of prediction of later creative ability mentioned earlier, it was found in a 12 year follow up study of adolescents identified as creatives in 1958 and 1959, that the youths identified as creative during high school tended to become productive adults. Young adults identified as highly creative in high school attained their peak creative achievement, in writing, medical and surgical discovery, dissertation research, musical composition, style of learning and human relations and organisation, more frequently compared to their less creative peers (Torrance, 1972).

Passi (1979) established concurrent validity of his creativity tests by correlating them with intelligence test scores, and achievement test scores.

Schaefer (1968) used teacher evaluation and creativity test scores as criterion measures to differentiate creative high school students in arts and science from a control group. To determine whether Barron-Welsh Art Scale is a good predictor of adolescent creativity, it was administered to the above two criterion groups. In general the creatives achieved higher than the controls.

Schaefer (1969, 1972) also used teacher ratings and creativity test scores to establish the validity of the Biographical Inventory of Creativity.

While discussing the validity of his tests Misra (1986) observed 'we can say that the present tests of scientific creativity measures scientific creativity on the basis of *(i)* the way the tests have been developed and *(ii)* the opinion expressed by nine experts'. He further validated his tests with teachers ratings and obtained rank correlations of 0.35 and 0.44 between teachers' ratings and the creativity test scores.

Mehdi (1973) correlated his creativity tests with teacher ratings. The correlations ranged between 0.32 and 0.40 for verbal tests and between 0.35 and 0.39 for nonverbal tests.

The following types of validity have been established for the battery of creativity tests used in the present study:

1. Construct or Concept Validity

The instrument in the present investigation was constructed in line with those of Torrance (1962), Getzels and Jackson (1962), and Wallach and Kogan (1965) giving due consideration to the relevance and familiarity of the items/objects to the average Indian children of the age group under investigation. The items were scrutinized by 6 judges who were conversant with creativity testing and suggestions given by them were incorporated before including them in the creativity tests designed for the investigation. Thus the test could reasonably be well assumed to have construct validity or concept validity, in the words of Cattell (1969).

2. Concurrent Validity

The scores on the instrument were correlated with those obtained on Raven's Progressive Matrices (RPM) to establish the concurrent validity of the instrument. Taylor and Barron (1964) summarily said 'Most studies suggest that the relation of intelligence tests to creative performance is generally low (0.20 to 0.40) in unselected populations, and is zero or even negative in homogeneous samples at higher levels of intelligence'. Moss and Duenk (1967) reported correlations of 0.19 to 0.28 between both types of IQs and figural creativity, behavioural creativity and total creativity. Wodtke (1964) reported correlations of 0.23 to 0.54 between measures of intelligence and creativity. Torrance (1967a) reviewed 178 studies and obtained a median correlation of 0.20 between creativity and intelligence. According to Passi (1979) correlations between his test and RPM ranged between –0.01 and 0.81 for different sub-tests. The correlation between the creativity as measured by the whole test and verbal intelligence was 0.27, while it was 0.38 for nonverbal intelligence.

In the present case the creativity scores of 90 students selected by a stratified random sampling procedure, approximately evenly distributed between the two sexes, the two localities (urban and rural) and the three classes (VIII, IX and X), were correlated with their scores on the RPM.

The correlation coefficients thus obtained are presented in Table—5.1. It may be seen that in the case of verbal tests, the correlation coefficients for fluency, flexibility, originality and composite creativity scores were 0.42, 0.42, 0.41 and 0.53 respectively. In the case of nonverbal tests the correlation coefficients ranged between 0.38 and 0.46, while for the two types of tests put together the correlations varied between 0.40 and 0.50. The correlation coefficients for the different sub-tests, each considered separately, ranged between 0.16 and 0.89 in the case of verbal tests, while they varied between 0.27 and 0.54 for the nonverbal tests. It is needless to mention that these results are in line with those obtained by other investigators mentioned above.

Table—5.1 Correlation Between Creativity Scores and Scores on Raven's Progressive Matrices (N = 90)

	Fluency	*Flexibility*	*Originality*	*Composite creativity*
Verbal	0.42	0.42	0.41	0.53
Nonverbal	0.46	0.43	0.38	0.46
Verbal and Nonverbal put together	0.44	0.43	0.40	0.50

As pointed out earlier Taylor and Barron (1964) observed that in homogeneous samples at higher levels of intelligence, the correlation between creativity and intelligence would be zero or negative.

To probe into this the creativity scores of a homogeneous group of highly intelligent students was sought to be correlated with their intelligence scores.

Among the 90 students there were 22 who got a score of 40 or above on the RPM. The creativity scores of the 22 students were further analysed to see how they correlated with the scores on the RPM. The results obtained are shown in Table—5.2. It may be seen that all the correlation coefficient were negative.

Table—5.2 Correlation Between Creativity Scores and Scores on Raven's Progressive Matrices for a Homogeneous Group of Highly Intelligent Students (N = 22)

	Fluency	*Flexibility*	*Originality*	*Composite creativity*
Verbal	–0.24	–0.30	–0.32	–0.17
Nonverbal	–0.15	–0.14	–0.14	–0.18
Verbal and Nonverbal put together	–0.26	–0.24	–0.30	–0.28

3. Criterion Validity

Several investigators like Schaefer (1968, 1969, 1972, Mehdi (1973), Misra (1986) used teacher ratings as criteria for validating creative test scores. But the correlation coefficients between the two were not very high. Commenting on the low correlation Mehdi (1973) remarked higher correlations with teacher ratings are usually not obtained due to the unreliability of the ratings'.

Guilford (1954) observed that lack of reliability of ratings was mostly due to lack of clarity of the traits rated, and lack of adequate information on the part of the rater about the traits of the ratees. Therefore the traits should be described properly and care should be taken to see that the raters know the ratees fully well.

The most common errors in rating are error of liniency, error of central tendency, halo effect, etc. These errors occur when the rater is asked to rate a large group of children. For example, when a teacher is rating 40 children he may not know well about all of them, he may be tempted to be linient and give higher rating to many, or he may tend to concentrate his ratings around the mid point, avoiding ratings on either extreme. This effect will be minimised if the teacher is asked to nominate a few of those who are highest and a few who are least on a given trait. According to Nunnally (1959) teacher's ratings of very good and very poor children are more valid. The errors can be further minimised if the meaning of the characteristic rated is properly understood by the rater (Champney, 1941), if the rater is interested in the ratings they make, and have sufficient time to make the ratings (Conrad, 1933).

Keeping these precautions in mind, in line with the procedure adopted by Torrance (mentioned earlier), six teachers of VIII, IX and X classes of a school were explained clearly the meaning of the concept of creativity and were requested to nominate 5 most creative and 5 least creative students from each of their classes, on the basis of the type of their participation in different types of problem situations/ activities in the class in particular, and in the school in general. The six groups of children were administered the creativity tests and their scores were analysed. The results obtained are shown in Tables—5.3, 5.4 and 5.5.

Table—5.3 Means and SDs of the Scores Obtained on Verbal Tests by the High Creative and Low Creative Children as Rated by the Teachers and the Results of the *t* Test

	High Creative	*Low Creative*	*t*
N	30	30	
M	525.15	420.57	5.43*
SD	85.21	62.14	

**t* significant at 0.001 level.

Table—5.4 Means and SDs of the Scores Obtained on Nonverbal Tests by the High Creative and Low Creative Children as Rated by the Teachers and the Results of the *t* Test

	High Creative	*Low Creative*	*t*
N	30	30	
M	164.27	115.21	7.60*
SD	27.59	22.11	

**t* significant at 0.001 level.

It may be seen that the *t* values obtained were 5.43 and 7.60 for the verbal and nonverbal tests respectively. For all the tests put together the *t* value obtained was 6.00. All the *t* values were significant at or above 0.001 level for 58 df. This shows that the creativity tests could discriminate between high creative and low creative children as judged by their teachers on the basis of the type of their participation in different types of problem situations and other activities. This was true for verbal tests, as well as nonverbal tests and also for all the tests put together.

Table—5.5 Means and SDs of the Scores Obtained on the Entire Test Battery (Verbal and Nonverbal Tests Put Together) by the High Creative and Low Creative Children as Rated by the Teachers and the Results of *t* test

	High Creative	*Low Creative*	*t*
N	30	30	
M	689.42	535.78	6.00*
SD	110.24	86.65	

*t significant at 0.001 level.

VI. RELIABILITY

Reliability is especially important for evaluation of the creativity measures. Without information about the reliability of the creativity indices we would not know how to interpret whatever findings we obtain concerning the inter-relationships, because the reliability of a measure, after all, functions as a ceiling or limit upon the extent to which it can reasonably be expected to relate to other variables (Wallach and Kogan, 1965).

Getzels and Jackson (1962) reported internal consistency reliability estimates for their creativity tests ranging between 0.81 and 0.87. The split-half reliability of Wallach and Kogan tests varied between 0.51 and 0.93 for the different components on different sub-tests (Wallach and Kogan, 1965).

The split-half reliability of Passi's tests (Passi, 1979) of creativity ranged between 0.51 and 0.88. He reported the test-retest reliability for the different sub-tests ranging between 0.68 and 0.97. For the whole test battery the reliability coefficient was 0.92. Misra (1986) reported split-half reliability of his tests to range between 0.50 and 0.63.

Torrance and Gowan (1963) found test-retest reliability for the MTCT to vary between 0.65 and 0.70 for the different sub-tests and 0.80 for the whole test. Hoepfner (1967) reported test-retest reliability for MTCT to range between 0.71 and 0.93. Moss and Duenk (1967) obtained reliability estimates varying between 0.68 and 0.83 for this test, while Wodtke (1964) reported reliability coefficients between 0.28 and 0.75 for the verbal creativity test battery.

Mehdi (1973) reported test-retest reliability coefficients for his four verbal tests put together, ranging between 0.90 and 0.96. For the three non-verbal tests put together the reliability coefficients varied between 0.93 and 0.95 for different components of creativity.

The split-half reliability coefficients of the battery of creativity tests used in the present investigation are presented in Table—5.6. It may be seen from the table that the reliability coefficients of verbal tests ranged between 0.78 and 0.83 for the different components of creativity. In the case of the nonverbal tests the reliability coefficients varied between 0.79 and 0.82. The split-half reliability for the different individual sub-tests was between 0.59 and 0.90 in the case of verbal tests, while it was between 0.75 and 0.90 in the case of nonverbal tests.

Table—5.6 Reliability Coefficients of Verbal, Nonverbal and the Entire Test Battery (Verbal and Nonverbal Tests put together (N = 90)

	Fluency	*Flexibility*	*Originality*	*Composite creativity*
Verbal	0.78	0.80	0.83	0.80
Nonverbal	0.82	0.79	0.81	0.82
Verbal and Nonverbal put together	0.80	0.80	0.82	0.81

It may be seen that the reliability coefficients of the tests used in the present study and comparable to those obtained by other investigators.

VII. OTHER INSTRUMENTS USED IN THE STUDY

1. Raven's Standard Progressive Matrices

The mental ability of the students was measured using Raven's Standard Progressive Matrices, sets A, B, C, D and E. Developed by Raven this test is suitable for assessing people with respect to their capacity for observation and clear thinking. One's total score on the test provides an index of his intellectual capacity whatever his nationality (Raven, 1951). It is a culture free test using nonverbal items for measuring the mental ability of the children and as such is widely used even with non-English speaking people (Tuddenham, 1969). Since the test contains only figures, it is highly interesting, and the subjects get easily motivated to take the test. The fact that it is a power test has an added advantage, since speed is a factor to which the subjects are not very much used to.

Raven (1951) has collected extensive standardisation data on the test in England. Rimoldi (1948) got similar norms on children in Argentina, suggesting that the test is culture free. High correlations have been found between scores on RPM and verbal tests (Nunnally, 1959).

As mentioned earlier, since the test contains only figures and can be used on children of any language, it is extensively used in the Indian context. Its validity in terms of correlation with achievement scores ranged between 0.31 and 0.34 (Narayana Rao, 1967). The scores on RPM were correlated with achievement scores of 130 IX class students. The correlation obtained was 0.55. The obtained correlation coefficient was highly significant even at 0.01 level.

2. Cattell's High School Personality Questionnaire, Form—A

Human nature is complex, whether we like it or not. The effective understanding of what at first seems a single symptom or peculiarity of behaviour turns out to require stock taking of the whole personality. Sometimes some researchers and even psychologists fall easily into the mistake of settling on a single test dealing with any one dimension of personality, (*e.g.*) extraversion, self realisation, etc., and from that they try to predict all kinds of behaviour.

But the overwhelming verdict of research findings as well as clinical evidence shows that to predict almost anything effectively, at least a dozen unitary traits generally need to be taken into account (Cattell, 1969).

Keeping this in mind, the personality of the children was assessed in the present study, using Cattell's Junior Senior High School Personality Questionnaire (HSPQ).

The HSPQ covers all the major dimensions of personality which are factor analytically domonstratable in any attempt to describe individual differences comprehensively. It deals with psychologically meaningful and predictively important traits having demonstrable functional unity, such as/are central to any discussion in general psychological theory.

The HSPQ handles the multiplicity of predictions from one test, but not from one score. It helps to obtain scores on fourteen dimensions of personality. These fourteen dimensions which have been confirmed in various experiments (Cattell and Sealy 1965; Coan and Cattell, 1958) cover relatively independent aspects of personality. They represent basic concepts which are understood by psychology, so that insightful understanding of the individual and his development as well as statistical prediction is possible. The above points weighed in favour of selecting the HSPQ for assessing the personality traits of the children.

Having decided to use of the HSPQ, the questionnaire was translated into Telugu, the regional language of the subjects on whom it had to be used. The translation was got checked by 3 judges who were well versed with psychological testing. Terms which were ambiguous were discussed and resolved. The Telugu version thus prepared was administered to a small group of 10 children of VII class. They were asked to answer the items and also check those words which they could not understand. Such of those terms which the children marked were modified or substituted with simpler words.

The scales chosen for the HSPQ were designed to measure source traits of general importance in personality theory—such as ego strength, dominance, surgency, etc., and their primary validity is properly measured directly with regard to these concepts. In other words the scales stand by their concept or construct validity—(*i.e.*) their correlation with pure factors which they are supposed to measure (Cattell, 1969). One of the unique features of the HSPQ and other personality scales developed by Cattell is that each of the items in any factor are selected on the basis of their known correlation with the pure factors (Cattell, Eber and Delhees, 1968). Further the set of factors have been demonstrated to retain their conceptual validities as unitary source traits universally.

Each of the factors was factorially demonstrated to be independent of others. In other words the HSPQ has factorial validity. Further, applied research carried out over the years with the factors has produced constant and substantial correlations of these primary factor scales to a wide array of criteria in educational, clinical, occupational and other areas, establishing its criterion validity (Cattell, 1969). The test-retest reliability of the scale was established on a sample of 30 tenth class students with a time interval of 1 week. It was found to be 0.90.

3. Socio-Economic Status Scale

Different SES scales have been developed by Kuppuswamy (1962), Pareek and Trivedi (1964), Jalota, *et al.*, (1970) and others. But some of these scales (*e.g.*, Kuppuswamy) are constructed to be used on urban samples, while some others (like Pareek and Trivedi) were developed to be used exclusively on rural children. This difficulty is overcome in a scale developed by Venkata Rami Reddy since it was constructed to be used on urban as well as rural children.

It contains all relevant items related to the economic status of the family, occupational level of the parents, level of education of parents, household possessions, etc., which go to determine the social as well as economic status of the family. Thus the scale can be reasonably well assumed to have construct validity.

There is substantial evidence that SES and intelligence are positively correlated (Terman, 1921; 1937; McNemar, 1964; Anastasi, 1958; Tyler, 1965, Herrenstein, 1971). Similarly there is a positive relationship between scholastic achievement and SES according to Curry (1962), Chopra (1966), Srivastava (1967), Fenske (1969), Marjoribanks (1977), Ganapathy and Singh (1981), Sharma (1980), Gupta (1982), Venkata Rami Reddy and Bhaskara Naidu (1988). The scores obtained on the present SES scale were correlated with intelligence test scores and achievement scores. The correlation between SES and achievement scores was 0.50 (N = 90). The correlation coefficient between SES and intelligence was 0.38 (N = 78). Both the correlation coefficient were highly significant even at 0.01 level. The test-retest reliability of the scale was 0.95 with a time interval of two weeks (N = 100).

The above scale was used to measure the socio-economic status of the subjects, as it is especially useful for measuring the SES of both urban and rural children.

4. Personal Data

The data regarding sex, order of birth, etc., and information about some familial and personal characteristics and habits of life was obtained through a carefully designed personal data sheet. The personal data sheet was included at the end of the different instruments which were administered in the present study.

VIII. DESIGN AND SAMPLE

The study was essentially of a 2×2×3 factorial design with 2 sexes (boys and girls) × 2 localities (urban and rural × 3 classes (VIII, IX and X).

Students of VIII, IX and X classes, which comprise the terminal stage of secondary education, belonging to the schools located in Rayalaseema (Andhra Pradesh State is divided into three regions *viz.,* Circar, Rayalaseema and Telangana, for administrative purposes) region of Andhra Pradesh State constituted the population for the study.

The sample for the study was selected by a multistage stratified random sampling procedure. At the outset from among the five Revenue districts which comprise Rayalaseema region, 3 districts were selected at random. The secondary schools located in urban and rural areas of each of the three districts were listed separately, and 5 schools each from urban and rural areas were selected at random from each district thus giving 30 schools (In rural areas all the schools were coeducational. As such coeducational institutions only were selected from urban areas also) from all the 3 districts put together. From the lists of students of each of the schools selected as above, 5 boys and 5 girls were selected at random, from each of the classes (VIII, IX, and X), thus giving a total of 900 subjects for the study, equally distributed between the two sexes, the two localities, and the three classes. The distribution of the sample of the subjects in different sub-groups is presented in Table—5.7.

Table—5.7 Locality—/Sex—/and Class-Wise Distribution of the Sample of Ss Selected for the Study

Class	*Urban*		*Rural*		*Total*
	Boys	*Girls*	*Boys*	*Girls*	
VIII	75	75	75	75	300
IX	75	75	75	75	300
X	75	75	75	75	300
Total	**225**	**225**	**225**	**225**	**900**

IX. SAMPLE CHARACTERISTICS

1. The Ss were boys and girls belonging to the age group 12+ to 16.
2. All the Ss were receiving instruction through the medium of regional language, *viz.*, Telugu.
3. All the children belonged to coeducational institutions.

X. ADMINISTRATION

The Ss were administered the instruments under normal classroom conditions in groups of not exceeding 20 at a time. They were seated comfortably and after establishing proper rapport, they were told about the nature and importance of the investigation, so as to motivate them. Before administering each sub-test, the children were explained what they had to do, with the help of the example given in the instructions for each sub-test.

Each of the 10 sub-tests of the creativity test battery were administered separately, in a game like manner, in line with Wallach and Kogan (1965), without any time limit.

Four of the ten sub-tests were administed in the morning session of the school giving a gap of 15 minutes after the first 2 sub-tests. The next 4 sub-tests were administered in the afternoon session with a small gap of fifteen minutes after two sub-tests. The remaining two sub-tests and Raven's Progressive Matrices were administered in the morning session of the next day with a pause of 15 minutes after the two sub-tests of creativity. Cattell's High School Personality Questionnaire Socio-economic Status Scale and Personal Data sheet were administered in the afternoon session. All these instruments were administered as per the instructions given in the manual, which were explained in Telugu, the religion language of the Ss.

The total time taken to administer all the instruments put together was about 8½ hours including the time taken to give instructions.

At times it happens that the students who are selected at random may not be present on the day of the investigation. Further when the testing takes 4 sessions extending over two days, it is possible that a student who takes the tests in one or two sessions may be absent for the next sessions. To fill up these gaps, a second visit was made to the schools wherever such eventualities have occurred and the tests were administered to the students who were absent during the first administration of the tests. The necessity of a second visit was kept to the minimum by informing the Headmasters/ Headmistresses of the respective schools a few days in advance about the programme, and requesting him/her to see that as far as possible, none of the students selected to serve as Ss for the study was absent during the days of the investigation.

XI SCORING

As there are no right or wrong responses for the creativity test items much care has to be exercised in scoring them. To enhance the objectivity of scoring the usual procedure adopted is to get the responses scored by different scorers, and to see that the liner scorer reliability is high.

According to Guilford (1962), Torrance (1962) and Gage and Berliner (1975) fluency, flexibility and originality are the primary components of divergent thinking. These factors operate in the creative thinking of adults as well as children. The responses of the Ss were scored based upon the following procedure suggested by Guilford (1951), Torrance (1962) and Child (1973) and followed by various investigators like Gakhar (1974), Badrinath and Satyanarayana (1979), Venkata Rami Reddy and Balakrishna Reddy (1983), Venkata Rami Reddy and Balakrishna Reddy (1984), Chadha and Ghose (1985), Misra (1986), Syama Trimurti (1987), Venkata Rami Reddy and Saleena (1988), Venkata Rami Reddy and Vijayakumari, etc.

1. A fluency score was obtained by totalling the number of relevant responses given by the subject. Responses that

were nonsensical or which did not answer the question as posed, were eliminated before counting them.

2. A flexibility score was obtained by categorizing the responses into as many discrete classifications as suggest themselves. Evidently, the subjectivity of the scorer comes into any measure of flexibility so derived; but consensus agreement among different scorers was employed by way of making the final flexibility score more objective.

3. Different authors used different procedures to determine the originality. In this investigation, in line with Guilford (1952) and Torrance (1962) originality was defined in terms of the statistical infrequency of a given responses in a given population. Since originality as defined by statistical infrequency or uncommonness of a response is only relative, each response is original in its own way, though the degree of originality of different response may vary depending upon the statistical infrequency of each of them. Guilford (1952) discriminated five levels of uncommenness, each level representing approximately one fifth of the total responses. Andrews (1930) also rated originality on a 5 point scale on the basis of a frequency tally of the responses of the children in the group. Thus a response given by 20 per cent or less number of Ss of the sample was given an originality score of 5 while a response given by 21 per cent to 40 per cent of the Ss was given a score of 4. Similarly, responses given by 41 per cent to 60 per cent, 61 per cent to 80 per cent and 81 per cent and above were given originality scores of 3, 2, and 1 respectively.

Raven's Progressive Matrices, Cattell's High School Personality Questionnaire, and the Socio-economic Status Scale were scored as per the procedure given in the respective manuals.

XII. ANALYSIS OF DATA

The data was analysed employing appropriate statistical techniques like analysis of variance, *t* test, chi-square test, multiple regression analysis, etc. The usual levels of significance, viz., 0.05, 0.01 and 0.001 were used to test the significance of the obtained statistics. The numerical results were also graphically represented wherever necessary. The results obtained are discussed in the next chapter.

6

Results and Discussion

The results obtained in the study are discussed under three sections. The major hypotheses in this study were concerning the influence of sex (boys and girls), locality of residence (rural and urban) and length of schooling (grades VIII, IX and X) on creativity. An attempt was made to ascertain whether the differences in sex, locality and school grade/class bear any significant relationship with the creativity of the subjects (Ss).

The fluency, flexibility, originality and composite creativity scores (total of the three components) of the Ss were analysed separately for verbal tests and nonverbal tests and also for the total of verbal and nonverbal tests, applying analysis of variance of 2×2×3 (2 sexes × 2 localities × 3 classes) factorial design. The results of this analysis are presented in Section I.

Section II deals with the differentiating characteristics between high creatives and low creatives. The results of multiple, regression analysis of the creativity of the Ss in relation to different variables is presented in Section III.

SECTION—I

Creativity Vs Sex, Locality and Length of Schooling

A. Verbal Tests

1. Fluency

Table—6.1 shows the mean fluency scores and SDs of different subgroups of Ss on the verbal tests. It could be seen from the table that the mean score of boys was 93.28 while that of girls was 90.89. This shows that boys scored a little higher than girls.

It could also be seen from the table that students from urban (U) localities, scored better than those from rural (R) localities. The mean score of urban students was 94.32 while that of rural students was 89.85.

When the students were classified according to the school grade/class to which they belonged, it was found that the mean score of the students of VIII class was the least, while students of X class scored the highest, IX class students falling in between. The mean score of the students of the three classes were—VIII class: 77.74, IX class: 95.06 and X class: 103.47.

Table—6.1 Mean Fluency Scores and SDs of Different Subgroups of Ss Classified According to their Sex, Locality and Class on Verbal Tests

Group		*N*	*M*	*SD*
Boys	(B)	450	93.28	25.45
Girls	(G)	450	90.89	24.69
Rural	(R)	450	89.85	23.87
Urban	(U)	450	94.32	26.08
VIII		300	77.74	20.84
IX		300	95.06	23.38
X		300	103.47	23.76

Note: The following abbreviations are used in the following pages for conveniences:

Boys : B	Rural : R	Sex : S	Class : C
Girls : G	Urban : U	Locality : L	

To examine whether there was any significant difference between the creativity of students belonging to different sexes, different localities and different classes, and to probe into the effect of the interaction between different variables, the creativity scores of the different subgroups of Ss were analysed by applying analysis of variance of 2×2×3 factorial design. The results obtained are shown in Table—6.2.

Table—6.2 Results of ANOVA of the Fluency Scores on Verbal Tests

Source	SS	df	MS	F
S	1281.50	1	1281.50	2.60@
L	4498.00	1	4498.00	9.11**
C	103303.50	2	51651.75	104.68***
S×L	2259.50	1	2259.50	4.58*
S×C	10491.50	2	5245.75	10.63***
L×C	284.50	2	142.25	0.29@
S×L×C	6751.00	2	3375.50	6.84@
Error	438161.50	888	493.42	
Total	**567031.00**	**899**		

Note: 1. *** F significant at 0.001 level
** F significant at 0.01 level
* F significant at 0.05 level
@ F not significant at 0.05 level

2. The same notation is used in all the tables that follow to denote the level of significance of *F*, *t* and X^2 values.

It could be seen from the table that the *F* ratio for sex (S) was 2.60 which was not significant at 0.05 level for 1 and 888 df. This shows that there was no significant difference between the mean fluency scores of boys and girls as measured by the verbal tests. An examination of the mean scores of boys and girls presented in Table—6.1 shows that the mean score of boys was 93.28 while that of girls was 90.89. This shows that the mean score of boys was some what higher than that of girls. However, the difference between the two means was not significant *(See Fig. 1).*

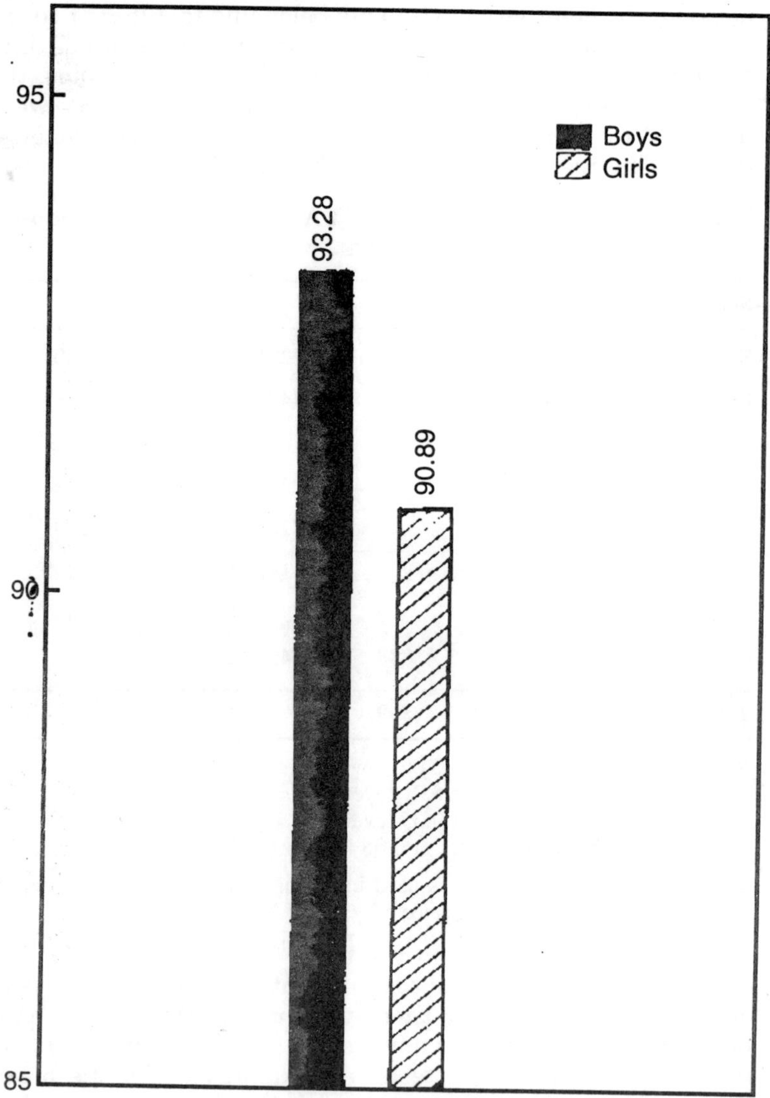

Fig.—1. **Mean Fluency Scores of Boys and Girls on Verbal Tests**

A number of studies have been conducted on sex differences in creativity. As mentioned earlier in Chapter 2, it was found by Pathak (1962), Pogue (1964), Jackson (1968), Burns (1969), Philips and Torrance (1971), Kloss (1972), Gakhar (1974), Thammaprateep (1976), Cheek (1979), Saxena (1981), Agarwal and Gupta (1982), Pandey and Pandey (1984), Dexie (1985), Bajpai and Ahmed (1986), Harnek, Gurusagar and Manjeet (1988) that there were no sex differences in creativity. The above results support the findings of this investigation.

Some other studies like those of Kelly (1965), Hutchinson (1967), Middents (1968), Raina (1968, 1969, 1970), Gagneja (1972), Hussain (1976), Dharmangadan (1981), Venkata Rami Reddy and Balakrishna Reddy (1984), Chandrakant (1987) and Syama Thrimurthy (1987) reported that boys were more creative than girls.

There were yet others who found that girls were more creative than boys (Yamamoto, 1960; Getzels and Jackson, 1962; Razik, 1964; Mac Gregor and Smith, 1965; Ogletree, 1968; Walker, 1969; Cacha, 1971; Passi, 1972; Pandit, 1976; Pandey, 1984; Chada and Ghose, 1985; and Bharadwaj, 1985). The results of the present study are not in line with these findings.

The *F* ratio for locality (L) was 9.11, which was significant at 0.01 level for 1 and 888 df, indicating a significant difference between urban and rural children. The mean score of the Ss belonging to R localities was 89.85 while those hailing from U localities scored 94.32. This shows that urban children were more creative than rural children as measured by the fluency component on the verbal tests *(See Fig. 2)*.

Very often urban environment is more stimulating and conducive for development of creativity. Passi (1972), Singh (1977, 1978), Dharmangadan (1981), Srivastava (1981), Agarwal and Gupta (1982), Venkata Rami Reddy and Balakrishna Reddy (1984) and Singh and Singh (1984) also

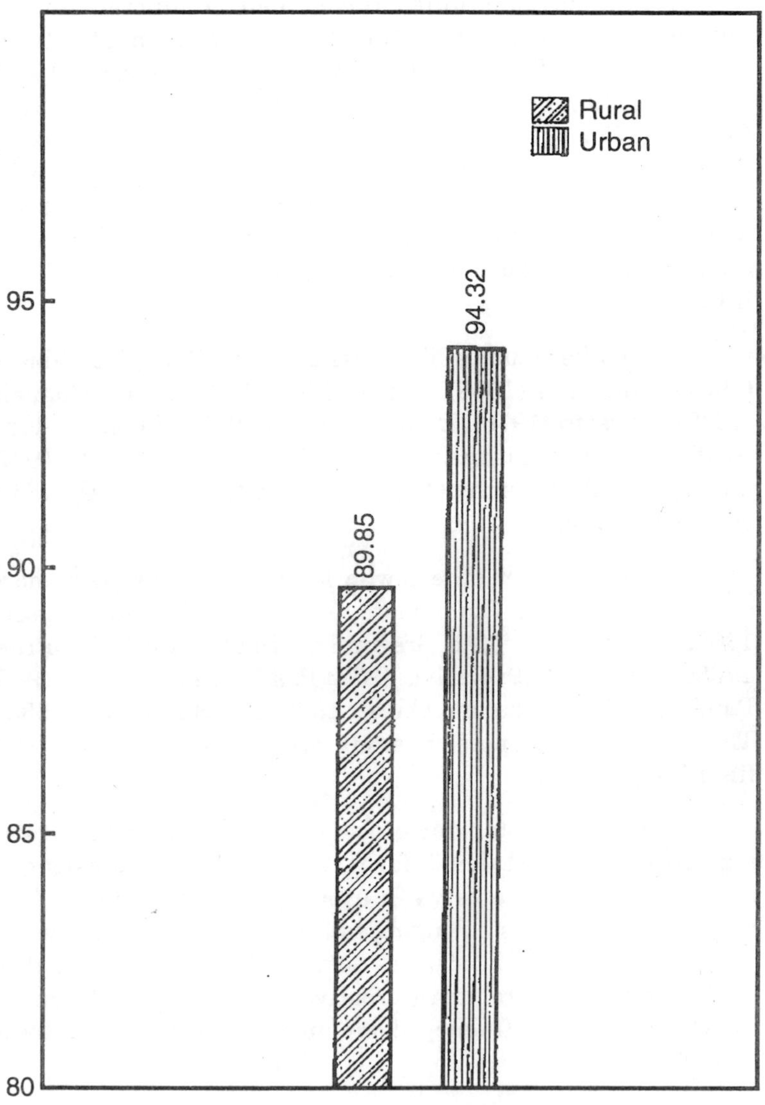

Fig.—2. Mean Fluency Scores of Rural and Urban Students on Verbal Tests

found that urban students are more creative compared to those hailing from rural areas. The results of the present investigation are in line with these findings.

However, some others like Sharma (1971, 1972) found that rural children were more creative than urban children, while Aaron, Marihal and Malatesha (1969), Jayaswal (1977), Sehgal (1978), Singh (1981), Joshi (1982) and Chandrakant (1987) reported no significant difference between the creativity of urban and rural children. The results of the present study do not support the above findings.

With regard to the variable class (C), the *F* ratio of 104.68 was highly significant even at 0.001 level for 2 and 888 df. This shows that there was a significant difference between the creativity of students belonging to different classes.

To find out which class differed significantly from the others, *t* test was applied. The results of this test are shown in Table—6.3 in a concise form, without loss of much information, to conserve space. It may be seen from the table that the mean scores of children belonging to VIII, IX and X class were 77.74, 95.06 and 103.47 respectively, and that each group differed significantly from the others. VIII class students scored the least, while students of X class scored the highest, IX class students falling in between (See Fig. 3).

Table—6.3 Mean Fluency Scores of the Ss Belonging to Different Classes and the Results of the *t* Test on Verbal Tests

VIII	IX	X
77.74	95.06	103.47

Note: 1. The mean scores are arranged in ascending order from left to right.

2. The difference between any two means *underscored* by the same line *is not* significant.
3. The difference between any two means *not underscored* by the same line *is* significant.
4. The level of significance employed is 0.05 level.
5. The same procedure is followed to indicate the results of the *t* test in all the tables that follow.

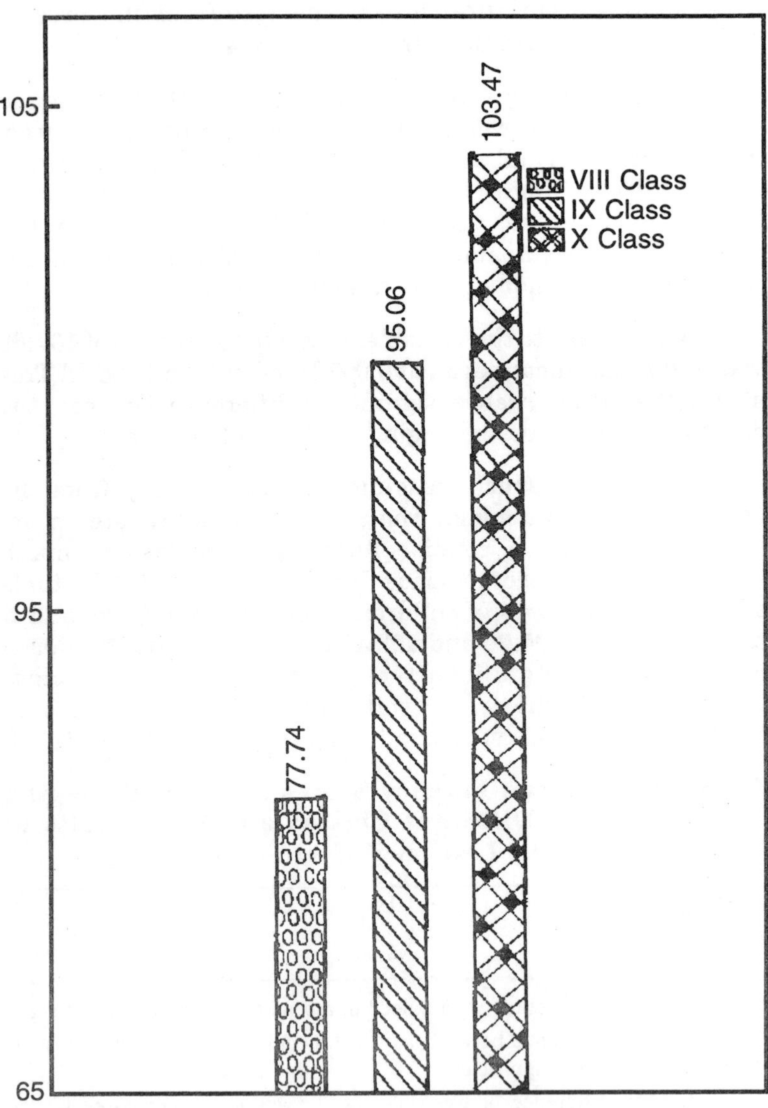

Fig.—3. Mean Fluency Scores of Students Belonging to Different Classes on Verbal Tests

That creativity increases with school grade/class during the high school years has been endorsed by many. Quoting from the Minnesota studies (Yamamoto, 1960; Torrance, *et. al.,* 1960) Torrance (1962) observed that '.... the abilities measured show a decline between sixth and seventh grades, after which there is a fairly steady rise until near the end of the high school period'. A number of other investigators like Piers, Daniels and Quackenbush (1960), Olshin (1965), Ogletree (1971, 1972), Venkata Rami Reddy and Balakrishna Reddy (1984), Ahmed (1969), Dexie (1985) and Venkata Rami Reddy and Salina (1988) also found a significant positive relationship between age and creativity.

However, it may be seen from Table—6.2 that the *F* ratios for the interaction between sex and locality and class and sex were significant. This warrants cautious interpretation of the results of the *F* ratios for main effects.

Table—6.4 Mean Fluency Scores of the Ss Classified According to their Sex and Locality to explain S×L interaction and the Results of the *t* Test

	Table—6.4a	*Table—6.4b*			
	R	U		G	B
Boys	92.63	93.93	Rural	87.08	92.63
	R	U		B	G
Girls	87.08	94.72	Urban	93.93	94.72

Note: 1. As already mentioned (Table—6.1) the following abbreviations are used for convenience.

Boys : B　　Rural : R
Girls : G　　Urban : U

2. For the procedure used to indicate the results of *t* test, please see note under Table—6.3.

It may be seen from Table—6.2 that the *F* ratio for S×L interaction was 4.58, which was significantly at 0.05 level for 1 and 888 df. This indicates that the effect of sex on creativity was not independent of the variations in the locality from which the students hailed and vice versa (Edwards, 1971).

To make a deep probe into this, the mean scores of boys and girls belonging to urban areas and those belonging to rural areas were calculated and analysed separately. The results of this analysis are presented in Table—6.4.

An examination of the mean scores of the Ss classified according to the two variables, sex and locality, presented in Tables—6.4a and 6.4b show that in the case of boys, the mean score of rural students was 92.63 whereas that of urban children was 93.93. This shows that urban children scored somewhat better than their counterparts from rural areas. When *t* test was applied to see whether the difference between the two means was significant it was found that the *t* value was not significant.

In the case of girls, the mean score of rural children was 87.08 while urban children obtained a mean score of 94.72, the difference between the two means was significant.

Considering sex differences, it was found that, in the case of R localities, boys (M = 92.63) scored significantly better than girls (M = 87.08) whereas in the case of U localities, girls (M = 94.72) scored somewhat better than boys (M = 93.93), though the difference between the two means was not significant (See Fig. 4).

This shows how the difference between the creativity of children belonging to urban and rural localities was not similar in the case of boys and girls. Similarly the difference between the creativity of boys and girls was not of the same pattern for urban and rural areas.

There is no gainsaying that the creativity of the children will be stimulated when there is an opportunity for them to participate in a variety of activities, to interact with different kinds of people and to deal with different types of situations.

But because of different types of social customs, taboos, etc., the movements of adolescent girls especially of rural

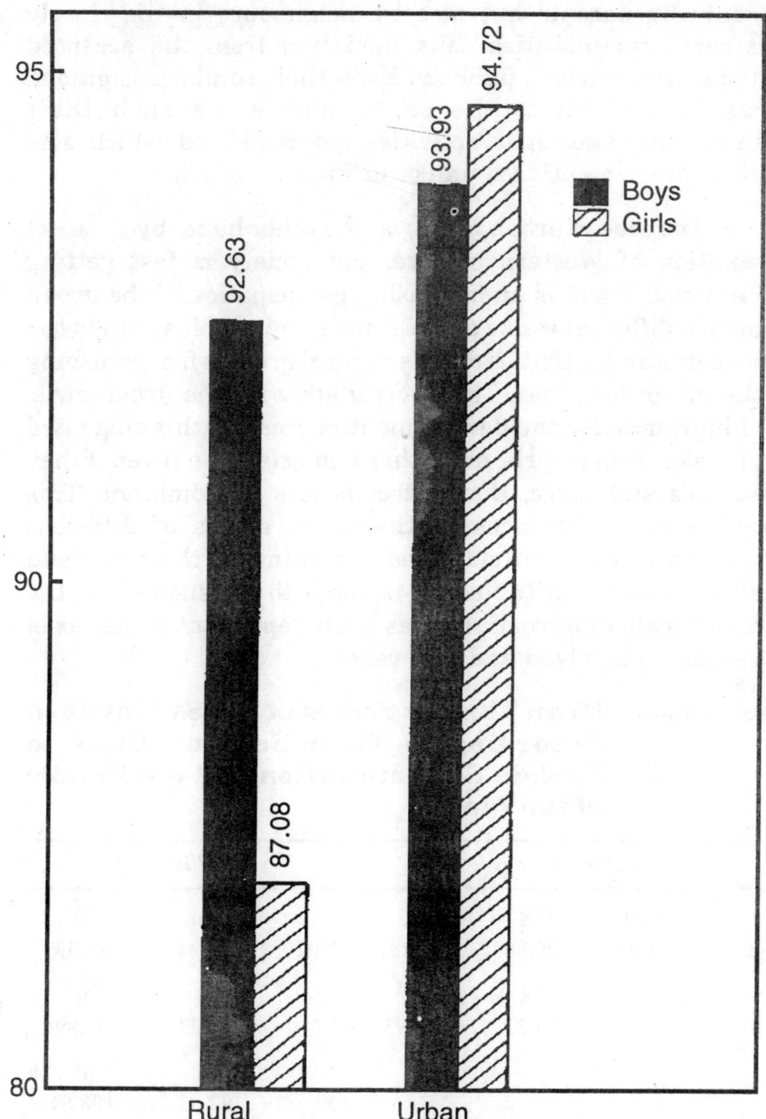

Fig.—4. Mean Fluency Scores of the Students Classified According to Their Sex and Locality (Verbal Tests)

areas are restricted. Their activities are closely supervised not only by parents but also by neighbours in the closely knit rural communities. Any deviation from the accepted customs are criticised publicly. Even their thinking is guided so as to confirm to the social norms. As such their environment, and their activities get restricted which sets limits to their creativity, unlike in the case of boys.

In the case of urban areas, on the other hand, by virtue of percolation of Western culture, the society is fast getting modernised. There is an increasing participation of the urban women in different walks of life. Hence, the sex bias seen in the movements and activities of girls in rural areas is fast vanishing in the urban localities. Thus, fortunately for the urban girls, the hindrances for the development of creative thinking cited in the case of rural girls, are either non existent or even if they exist here and there, their effect is less predominant. This explains the differences in the mean scores of different subgroups of children classified according to their sex and locality presented in Tables—6.4a and 6.4b and shows how, the effect of locality on creativity was not independent of the sex of the students involved and vice versa.

Table—6.5 Mean Fluency Scores of the Ss Classified According to Their Sex and Class to Explain S×C Interaction and the Results of the *t* test

	Table—6.5a				*Table—6.5b*	
	VIII	IX	X		B	G
Boys	74.94	95.89	108.81	VIII	74.94	80.53
	VIII	IX	X		G	B
Girls	80.53	94.23	97.93	IX	94.23	95.89
					G	B
				X	97.93	108.81

Note: Please see note under Table—6.3.

The *F* ratio 10.63 for S×C interaction, which was significant at 0.01 level, indicates that the effect of sex was not independent of the class to which the students belonged and vice versa. To probe into this the mean scores of the Ss classified according to the two variables (sex and class) were further analysed as in the earlier case.

An observation of the mean scores of different subgroups of Ss classified according to the variables sex and class presented in Tables—6.5a and 6.5b explains the situation. It could be observed from Table—6.5a that in the case of boys, the mean scores of students of VIII, IX and X classes were 74.94, 95.89 and 108.81 respectively, when *t* test was applied it was found that each mean differed significantly from the others. There was a significant improvement in the creativity of boys from class to class. In the case of girls the mean scores of Ss belonging to VIII, IX and X classes were: 80.53, 94.23 and 97.93 respectively. It may be seen that there was progressive improvement in the creativity of girls also from class to class. But the results of *t* test show that, there was no significant improvement from class IX to X in the case of girls (See Fig. 5).

It may be noticed from Table—6.5a that eventhough there was progressive improvement of the creativity scores of the children from class to class, the improvement from class VIII to IX was at variance from the improvement that could be seen from class IX to X. For example in the case of boys the improvement from Class VIII to IX was 20.95 points, while the improvement from IX to X class was only 12.92 points. Similar trend could be seen in the case of the mean scores of girls also.

According to Sullivan (1953) and Torrance (1962) creativity gets hampered whenever there is stress on the child. The stress may be in the form of adjusting to a new environment, transition from one school to another, transaition from one society to another, or over emphasis on achievement in the school. In Andhra Pradesh where this investigation was conducted a system of education called 'nondetention system' is practised. According to this system, the students get automatically promoted to the next higher

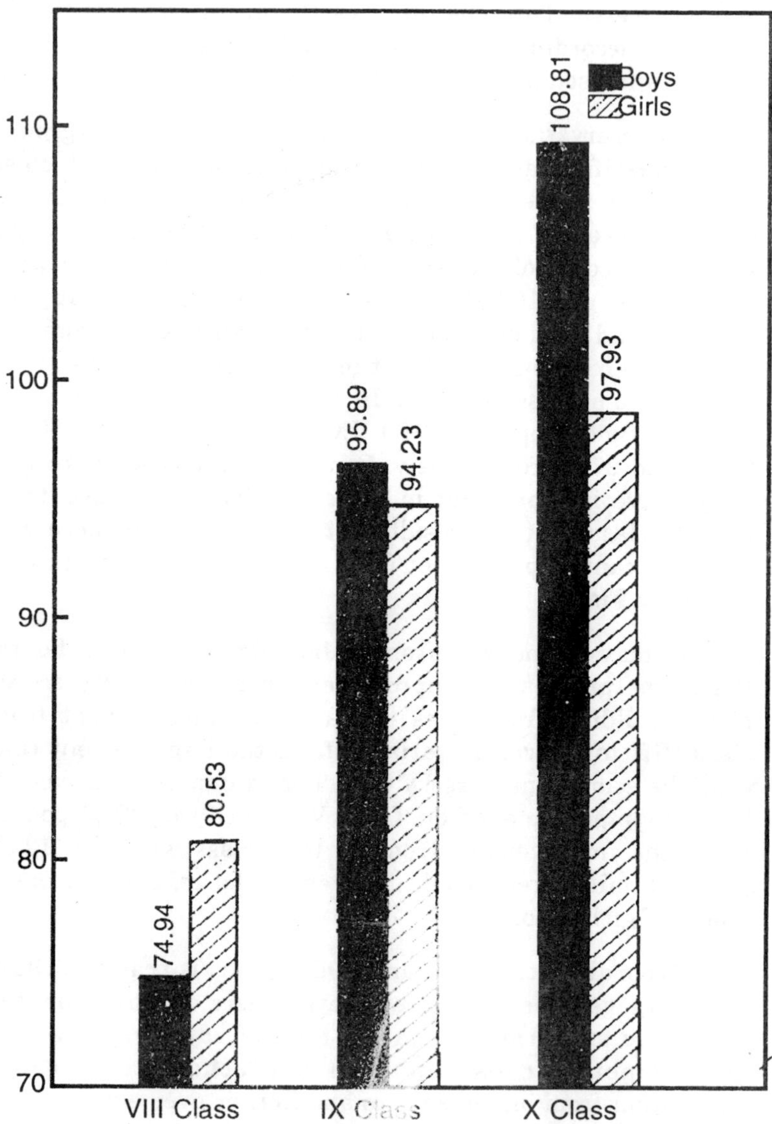

Fig.—5. **Mean Fluency Scores of the Students Classified According to their Sex and Class (Verbal Tests)**

class irrespective of their performance in the annual and other examinations, provided they put in a prescribed minimum percentage of attendance. However, the students can be detained in the VII and X classes if they do not get the minimum prescribed marks in the public examination conducted at the end of these classes. It has been observed by many that the system has affected the motivation of the children to study, since the marks obtained in the periodical tests are not going to matter for their promotion. The parents also do not evince adequate interest in the progress of the child (which is the terminal stage of secondary education in the Indian context).

But at the X class level (Editor, Educational India, 1977; Editor, The Educational Review, 1971; Venkata Rao, 1971; Through different States, 1972; Venkata Rami Reddy and Bhaskar Naidu, 1982; 1988; Venkata Rami Reddy and Salina, 1988) very often, there is mounting pressure on the child to achieve well, since he has to obtain a prescribed minimum to pass the public examination at the end of this class, which becomes the passport to get certain types of employment or for entry into the Junior Colleges, the stepping stones for higher education. This pressure on studies and emphasis on achievement, naturally curbs creative thinking (Torrance, 1962; Venkata Rami Reddy and Salina, 1988). Thus the growth from IX to X class is not much, and sometimes it is not significant. It has been observed in some studies that there is a slight fall in the creative thinking of the children at the X class level.

This type of pressure on achievement at the X class level is more in the case of girls since a fail in the examination, more often than not, leads to discontinuance of education of the girl leading to her marriage, which many of the girls shun at that age. This emphasis on achievement and anxiety about possible failure would indeed have a serious negative effect on the creativity of the children.

An examination of the mean scores of girls belonging to the three classes shows that there was an improvement of

13.70 points from VIII to IX class, while the improvement from IX to X class was only 3.70 points, which was not significant.

When the mean scores of Ss belonging to different classes were considered separately for each of the sexes (Table—6.5b) it was found that in the case of VIII class, girls (M = 80.53) scored significantly better than boys (M = 74.94) whereas in the case of X class boys (M = 108.81) scored significantly better than girls (M = 97.93). The difference between the two means was not significant in the case of IX class students.

An interesting trend of results may be seen in Table—6.5b. The mean scores of boys and girls at the VIII class level were 74.94 and 80.53 respectively. In the case of IX class, the mean scores were 95.89 and 94.23 respectively. At the X class level their mean scores were 108.81 and 97.93 respectively. It may be seen from the above values that at the VIII class level girls achieved better than boys, the difference being 5.59 points. At the IX class level boys achieved better than girls but the difference was only 1.66 points. But at the X class level boys achieved far better than girls, the difference between the scores being 10.88 points.

This shows that at the VIII class level girls performed better, while by the time they came to X class boys outperformed the girls. That girls did better at the VIII class level (12 to 13 years) may be because of their earlier maturity but gradually, by the time they come to X class (14 to 15 years), boys overcome the girls.

This shows how the difference between the mean scores of children belonging to different classes was not of the same order for boys and girls. Similarly, the difference between the creativity of boys and girls was not of the same pattern for different classes. This explains the significant interaction effect between sex and class.

The *F* ratio of 0.29 for L×C interaction effect was not significant at 0.05 level. This indicates that the effect of locality was independent of the class to which the students belonged and vice versa.

The *F* ratio for the three factor interaction (S×L×C) was 6.64 which was significant at 0.01 level. This shows that the effect of any two variables taken at a time was not independent of the level of the third variable involved.

2. Flexibility

Table—6.6 shows the mean flexibility scores of different subgroups of Ss on the verbal tests. It may be seen from the table that as in the case of fluency, for flexibility also boys scored better than girls. The mean score of boys was 60.67 while that of girls was 59.01.

Table—6.6 Mean Flexibility Scores and SDs of Different Subgroups of Ss Classified According to Their Sex, Locality and Class on Verbal Tests

Group	*N*	*M*	*SD*
Boys	450	60.67	13.93
Girls	450	59.01	13.82
Rural	450	59.06	13.06
Urban	450	60.61	13.08
VIII	300	52.45	11.62
IX	300	60.80	13.06
X	300	66.26	12.54

In the case of the locality variable also, U students (M = 60.61) scored some what better than R students (M = 59.06) as in the case of the fluency component.

The mean scores of VIII, IX and X class students were 52.45, 60.80 and 66.26 respectively. This shows that VIII class students scored the least while students of X class scored the highest.

To examine whether these differences between the mean scores of different subgroups of Ss were significant, the flexibility scores were further analysed by analysis of variance as in the case of the fluency component. The results obtained are shown in Table—6.7.

Table—6.7 Results of ANOVA of the Flexibility Scores on Verbal Tests

Source	*SS*	*df*	*MS*	*F*
S	568.25	1	568.25	3.79[@]
L	588.00	1	588.00	3.92*
C	28999.25	2	14499.63	96.73***
S×L	1526.50	1	1526.50	10.18**
S×C	1755.00	2	877.50	5.85**
L×C	241.50	2	120.75	0.80[@]
S×L×C	1063.50	2	531.75	3.55*
Error	133108.30	888	149.90	
Total	**167850.30**	**899**		

Note: Please see note under Table—6.2.

It could be seen from the table that the *F* ratio for sex was 3.79 which was not significant at 0.05 level for 1 and 888 df. This indicates that as in the case of fluency there was no significant difference between boys and girls with regard to the flexibility score as measured by the verbal tests.

The *F* ratio for locality (*F* = 3.92) was significant at 0.05 level. An observation of the mean scores presented in Table—6.6 reveals that U students (M = 60.61) scored better than R students (M = 59.06) on this component as was the case with fluency.

Considering the class of the students, the F ratio obtained was 96.73 which was highly significant even at 0.001 level, indicating a significant difference between the flexibility scores of the Ss belonging to different classes.

Table—6.8 Mean Flexibility Scores of the Ss Belonging to Different Classes and the Results of the *t* Test on Verbal Tests

VIII	IX	X
52.45	60.80	66.26

Note: Please see note under Table—6.3.

To find out which class differed significantly from the others, *t* test was applied as in the earlier case. The results of this analysis are presented in Table—6.8. It could be observed from the table that the mean scores of the students of VIII, IX and X classes were 52.45, 60.80 and 66.26 respectively. Each mean differed significantly from the others. Students of X class scored the highest while VIII class students scored the least.

However, as mentioned earlier, these results based upon the *F* ratios for the main effects should be interpreted cautiously in view of the significant interactions between sex, locality and class.

The *F* ratio for the interaction between sex and locality (S×L) was significant at 0.01 level. This implies as pointed out in the previous section, that the effect of sex on the flexibility scores of the Ss was not independent of the locality to which they belonged. Conversely the effect of the locality on the flexibility scores was not independent of the sex of the students considered.

An examination of the mean scores of the students classified according to the two variables, sex and locality presented in Table—6.9 explains the situation. It may be seen from Table—6.9a that in the case of boys, children from R localities scored a little higher than those belonging to U areas. The difference between the means, however, was not significant. In the case of girls, on the other hand, urban children scored significantly better than rural children.

Table—6.9 Mean Flexibility Scores of the Ss Classified According to Their Sex and Locality to Explain S×L Interaction and the Results of the *t* Test

Table—6.9a			*Table—6.9b*		
	U	R		G	B
Boys	60.14	61.20	Rural	56.93	61.20
	R	U		B	G
Girls	56.93	61.08	Urban	60.14	61.08

Note: Please see note under Table—6.3.

Considering sex differences, it may be seen from Table—6.9b that, in the case of rural children boys scored significantly better than girls. In the case of children from urban localities, on the other hand, girls tended to score somewhat better than boys. The difference between the means, however, was not significant.

This shows that locality differences were not independent of the sex of the students, and that sex differences were not independent of the locality from which the students hailed.

It may be noticed from Table—6.4 that similar results were obtained in the case of fluency also.

The *F* ratio (5.85) for the interaction between sex and class was also significant at 0.01 level. An examination of the mean scores of the Ss classified according to the two variables (Table—6.10) shows that irrespective of their sex, students of VIII class were the least scorers, while students of X class scored the highest. It may be seen from the table, however, that though the direction of difference between means was the same for both the sexes, the magnitude of difference from class to class was not of the same order for boys and girls. For example, there was a difference of 9.83 points from VIII to IX class, and a difference of 7.39 points from IX to X class in the case of boys. Considering the differences from class to class in the case of girls. it may be seen that the difference between VIII and IX class was 6.88 while it was only 3.52 between IX and X class. This shows that the magnitude of difference from class to class was not similar for boys and girls. A similar phenomenon was observed in the case of fluency component also as discussed earlier.

Table—6.10 Mean Flexibility Scores of the Ss Classified According to Their Sex and Class to Explain S×C Interaction and the Results of the *t* Test

	Table—6.10a				*Table—6.10b*	
	VIII	IX	X		B	G
Boys	51.65	61.48	68.87	VIII	51.65	53.25
	VIII	IX	X		G	B
Girls	53.25	60.13	63.65	IX	60.13	61.48
					G	B
				X	63.65	68.87

Note: Please see note under Table—6.3.

Further, considering sex differences separately, for each class, it may be seen from the second part of the table that girls tended to score higher than boys in the case of VIII class children, though the difference between the two means was not significant. But by the time they reach X class boys performed significantly better than girls. This explains the significant interaction between sex and locality.

The *F* ratio (0.80) for the interaction between locality and class was not significant at 0.05 level. This shows that the locality effect on the creativity of the children was independent of the class to which they belonged and vice versa.

The *F* ratio (3.55) for the three factor interaction was significant at 0.05 level indicating that the interaction between any two variables taken at a time was not independent of the level of the third variable.

It may be seen from Tables—6.1 and 6.2; and 6.6. and 6.7 that similar results were obtained on these two components of creativity, *viz.*, fluency and flexibility.

3. Originality

The mean originality scores and SDs of the different subgroups of Ss are shown in Table—6.11. An examination of the table shows that the mean score of boys was 321.92 while that of girls was 315.80.

Table—6.11 Mean Originality Scores and SDs of Different Subgroups of Ss Classified According to Their Sex, Locality and Class on Verbal Tests

Group	*N*	*M*	*SD*
Boys	450	321.92	105.48
Girls	450	315.80	105.34
Rural	450	310.43	103.24
Urban	450	482.64	144.52
VIII	300	273.39	91.64
IX	300	337.34	107.24
X	300	345.86	101.62

When the students were classified as urban and rural based upon the locality to which they belonged, it was found that those from U localities scored better than those from R localities. The mean scores of R and U children were 310.43 and 482.64 respectively.

With regard to the performance of the Ss belonging to different classes, the mean scores of students of VIII, IX and X classes were 273.39, 337.34 and 345.86 respectively.

As in the earlier cases the originality scores were further analysed by ANOVA. The results obtained in this analysis are shown in Table—6.12.

Table—6.12 Results of ANOVA of the Originality Scores on Verbal Tests

Source	*SS*	*df*	*MS*	*F*
S	8440.00	1	8440.00	0.85@
L	63992.00	1	63992.00	6.48*
C	941264.00	2	470632.00	47.69***
S×L	52000.00	1	52000.00	5.27*
S×C	108368.00	2	54184.00	5.49*
L×C	6592.00	2	3296.00	0.33@
S×L×C	66824.00	2	33412.00	3.39*
Error	8761832.00	888	9866.93	
Total	**10009310.00**	**899**		

Note: Please see note under Table—6.2.

It could be seen from the table that the *F* ratio for sex was 0.85 which was not significant at 0.05 level. This shows that there was no significant difference between the originality of boys and girls as measured by the verbal tests.

With regard to the variable locality, the F ratio was 6.48 which was significant at 0.05 level. The mean score of rural children was 310.43 while it was 482.64 in the case of urban children. This shows that the students belonging to U localities scored significantly better than the students of R localities.

The *F* ratio for class was also significant (F = 47.69, significant at 0.001 level for 2 and 888 df). This shows that there was a significant difference between the originality scores of students belonging to different classes.

To find out students of which class differed significantly from the others, *t* test was applied. The results of this analysis are presented in Table—6.13. It may be seen from the table that VIII class students scored the least (M = 273.39) and differed significantly from students of IX and X classes. The difference between IX and X class students was, however, not significant *(See Fig. 6)*.

Table—6.13 Mean Originality Scores of the Ss Belonging to Different Classes and the Results of the *t* Test

VIII	IX	X
273.39	337.34	345.86

Note: Please see note under Table—6.3.

It may be noticed from Table—6.12 that the *F* ratio for the interaction between sex and locality and that between sex and class were significant, setting limits to the conclusions that can be drawn on the basis of the *F* ratios for main effects.

The *F* ratio for the S×L interaction was 5.27, which was significant at 0.05 level. This indicates, as mentioned earlier, that the effect of sex was not independent of the locality of the students involved and vice versa.

Table—6.14 Mean Originality Scores of the Ss Classified According to Their Sex and Locality to Explain S×L Interaction and the Results of the *t* Test

Table—6.14a			*Table—6.14b*		
	R	U		G	B
Boys	321.09	322.76	Rural	299.77	321.09
	R	U		B	G
Girls	299.77	331.84	Urban	322.76	331.84

Note: Please see note under Table—6.3.

To probe into this the mean scores of the Ss classified according to their sex and locality were further analysed as in the case of fluency and flexibility components. The results obtained are shown in Table—6.14.

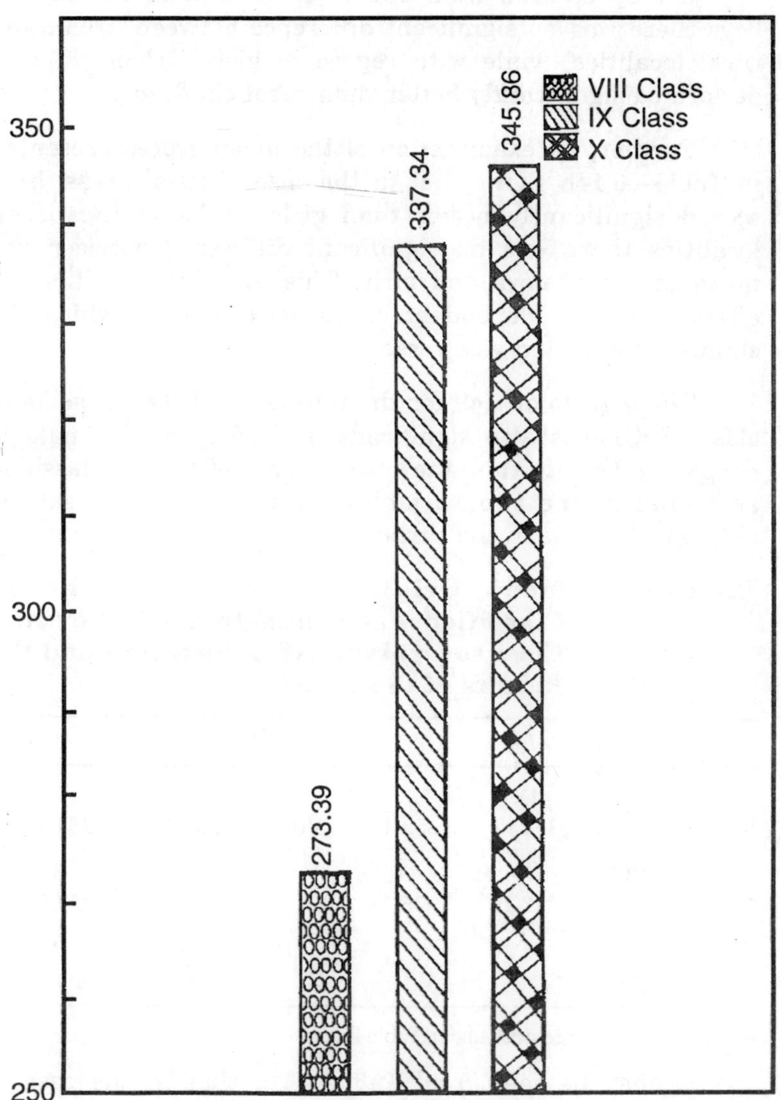

Fig.—6. Mean Originality Scores of Students Belonging to Different Classes on Verbal Tests.

It may be seen from Table—6.14a that in the case of boys there was no significant difference between urban and rural localities, while with regard to girls, urban children performed significantly better than rural children.

Further, an examination of the mean scores presented in Table—6.14b shows that in the case of rural areas, boys scored significantly better than girls, while in the urban localities there was no significant difference between the mean scores of boys and girls. This explains how the sex effect was not independent of the locality from which the children hailed and vice versa.

The *F* ratio of 5.49 for the interaction between sex and class (S×C) was also significant at 0.05 level. To make a deeper probe into this, the mean scores of the Ss classified according to the two variables were further analysed by applying *t* test as in the earlier cases.

Table—6.15 Mean Originality Scores of the Ss Classified According to Their Sex and Class to Explain S×C Interaction and the Results of the *t* Test

Table—6.15a				*Table—6.15b*		
	VIII	IX	X		B	G
Boys	264.43	337.91	363.43	VIII	264.43	282.35
	VIII	X	IX		G	B
Girls	282.35	328.29	336.77	IX	336.77	337.91
					G	B
				X	328.29	363.43

Note: Please see note under Table—6.3.

It may be seen from Table—6.15 that in the case of boys, those belonging to X class scored the highest, while VIII class children scored the least. Each mean differed significantly from the others. In the case of girls, on the other hand, there was no significant difference between IX and X classes.

Considering the differences between boys and girls, it may be seen from Table—6.15b that, as in the case of fluency and flexibility, girls tended to score better than boys on this component also at the VIII class level. But at the X class level, boys out performed girls.

The *F* ratio 0.33 for L×C interaction was not significant at 0.05 level indicating independence of the locality and class effects on the originality scores of the students.

The S×L×C interaction effect was significant (F = 3.39, significant at 0.05 level for 2 and 888 df). As mentioned earlier, this indicates that the effect on the interaction between any two variables taken at a time was not independent of the level of the third variable.

4. Composite Creativity Score

Generally one's creative thinking is judged on the basis of the composite creativity score obtained on all the different components of creativity, since it is considered to be the true index of total creative potential and a more stable measure (Deshmukh, 1984). Thus an attempt was made to analyse the composite creativity scores of the Ss to see the effect of different variables of it.[1]

Table—6.16 shows the mean composite creativity scores and SDs of different subgroups of Ss while in Table—6.17 the results of ANOVA of the scores are presented. It could be seen from Table—6.16 that boys obtained a mean score of 475.51, while girls got a mean score of 466.40. From Table—6.17 it may be seen that the *F* ratio for sex was 1.08 which was not significant at 0.05 level for 1 and 888 df. This shows that there was no significant difference between boys and girls with regard to their composite creativity.

When the students were classified depending upon the class to which they belonged the mean scores of the three groups were—VIII class: 403.93, IX class: 493.98 and X class: 514.96 respectively. The difference between the means was significant at 0.001 level (F = 60.63), warranting further analysis by *t* test. It may be seen from Table—6.18 that students of VIII class scored significantly less than those from IX and X classes. There was no significant difference, however, between the mean scores of IX and X classes.

Table—6.16 Mean Composite Creativity Scores and SDs of Different Sub-Groups of Ss Classified According to Their Sex, Locality and Class on Verbal Tests

Group	*N*	*M*	*SD*
Boys	450	475.51	141.92
Girls	450	466.40	140.71
Rural	450	459.27	137.19
Urban	450	482.64	144.52
VIII	300	403.93	121.50
IX	300	493.98	140.18
X	300	514.96	136.37

Table—6.17 Results of ANOVA of the Composite Creativity Scores on Verbal Tests

Source	*SS*	*df*	*MS*	*F*
S	18656.00	1	18656.00	$1.08^{@}$
L	122832.00	1	122832.00	7.13^{**}
C	2087776.00	2	1043888.00	60.63^{***}
S×L	108400.00	1	108400.00	6.29^{*}
S×C	222896.00	2	111448.00	6.47^{**}
L×C	9504.00	2	4752.00	$0.28^{@}$
S×L×C	132976.00	2	66488.00	3.86^{*}
Error	15[illegible]8300.00	888	17216.56	
Total	**17991340.00**	**899**		

Note: See note under Table—6.2.

With regard to the locality variable, urban students (M = 482.64) scored significantly better than rural students (M = 459.27). The difference was significant at 0.01 level (F = 7.13).

Table—6.18 Mean Composite Creativity Scores of Ss Belonging to Different Classes and the Results of the *t* Test on Verbal Tests

VIII	IX	X
403.93	493.98	514.96

Note: Please see note under Table—16.3.

An examination of the F ratios obtained for the different two factor interaction effects shows that except the L×C interaction, the other two factor interaction effects were significant at or above 0.05 level warranting careful interpretation of the results based upon the F ratios for the main effects.

Table—6.19 Mean Composite Creativity Scores of the Ss Classified According to Their Sex and Locality to Explain S×L Interaction and the Results of the *t* Test

Table—6.19a			*Table—6.19b*		
	R	U		G	B
Boys	474.80	476.21	Rural	443.75	474.80
	R	U		B	G
Girls	443.75	489.06	Urban	476.21	489.06

Note: Please see note under Table—6.3.

The S×L interaction effect (F = 6.29) was significant at 0.05 level. A further analysis of the mean scores of the Ss classified on the basis of the above two variables showed that there was no significant difference between the creativity of urban boys and rural boys. But in the case of girls urban children scored significantly better than those from rural areas (Table—6.19a).

It may also be seen from the second part of the table that boys performed better than girls in the case of rural areas, while in urban localities the difference between the two sexes was not significant (Table—6.19b).

The significant S×C interaction indicates that the effect of sex was not independent of the class to which the students belonged and vice versa. To make a deeper probe into this aspect, the mean scores of the students classified according to the two variables were calculated and analysed as in the earlier cases.

Table—6.20 Mean Composite Creativity Scores of the Ss Classified According to Their Sex and Class to Explain S×C Interaction and the Results of the *t* Test

Table—6.20a				*Table—6.20b*		
	VIII	IX	X		B	G
Boys	391.00	495.34	540.18	VIII	391.00	416.85
	VIII	X	IX		G	B
Girls	416.85	489.73	492.93	IX	492.93	495.34
					G	B
				X	489.73	540.18

Note: Please see note under Table—6.3.

The Table—6.20a shows that in the case of boys, the mean score of VIII class students was the lowest, while that of the X class students was the highest and each mean differed significantly from the others. In the case of girls, VIII class students scored the least and differed significantly from the others; the difference between the mean scores of IX and X class students was not significant at 0.05 level.

Considering sex differences, it may be seen from Table—6.20b that there was no significant difference between the mean scores of boys and girls in the case of VIII and IX classes. In the case of X class, however, boys scored significantly better than girls. This shows that class and sex effects were not independent of each other.

The effect of the interaction between locality and class (F = 0.28) was not significant at 0.05 level indicating that the effect of locality on the creativity of the Ss was independent of the class to which they belonged and vice versa.

The F ratio (3.86) for S×L×C interaction, which was significant at 0.05 level for 2 and 888 df, shows that the effect of any two variables taken at a time was not independent of the level of the third variable.

Summary

It may be observed from the above analysis that though boys achieved better than girls, the difference between the means was not significant. This was true for all the components—fluency, flexibility and originality and also for composite creativity. Urban children scored significantly better than rural children. This was also true for all the components of creativity as well as for the composite creativity score. There was progressive improvement in the creativity of the children from VIII class to X class. However, the improvement from IX class to X class was not as much as that from VIII class to IX class, and was not significant in the case of originality and composite creativity scores.

Further, the interaction effect between sex and locality and that between sex and class were significant setting limits to the conclusions that can be drawn from the F ratios for the main effects. This was also true for all the components: fluency, flexibility and originality and also for the composite creativity score.

B. Nonverbal Tests

Though some investigations like Mednick (1962), Torrance (1962), Torrance and Gowan (1963), Starr and Nicholl (1975) have observed that verbal and nonverbal creativity emerged as distinct factors, very few studies have been conducted to analyse the effect of different variables on nonverbal creativity.

Studies using verbal and nonverbal tests of creativity mostly tried to analyse the relation between verbal intelligence/nonverbal intelligence on the one hand and verbal creativity/nonverbal creativity on the other (Rittmyer, 1968; Dewing, 1970).

Smith tried to see whether SES of the children had a differential effect on their performance in verbal and non-verbal creativity tests, and found that middle class, children performed better on verbal tests while lower class children did better on nonverbal tests. Similarly, Gupta (1978) analysed the performance of children from private and government schools on verbal and nonverbal tests. He found that children from private schools did better on both the types of tests.

Is there effect of sex, locality and length of schooling (school grade/class) on the creativity of the children similar for verbal and nonverbal tests? To probe into this the creativity scores of different subgroups of Ss as measured by the nonverbal tests were analysed. The results of this analysis are presented in the following pages.

1. Fluency

Table—6.21 shows the mean fluency scores of different sub-groups of Ss on the nonverbal tests. It could be observed from the table that the mean scores of boys and girls were 25.63 and 24.12 respectively. It is evident from these mean scores that as in the case of verbal tests, on nonverbal tests also boys seem to perform better than girls.

When the Ss were classified according to the locality to which they belonged, those R localities scored higher than those from U localities. The mean score of R students was 25.15 while that of U students was 24.60.

Considering the school grade/class to which the students belonged the mean fluency scores of students of VIII, IX and X classes were: 23.04, 26.58 and 25.00 respectively.

Table—6.21 Mean Fluency Scores and SDs of Different Subgroups of Ss Classified According to Their Sex, Locality and Class on Nonverbal Tests

Group	*N*	*M*	*SD*
Boys	450	25.63	6.46
Girls	450	24.12	6.12
Rural	450	25.15	6.28
Urban	450	24.60	6.37
VIII	300	23.04	5.83
IX	300	26.58	6.62
X	300	25.00	6.02

To examine the effect of sex, locality and school grade on the fluency scores of the students as measured by the non-verbal tests, the scores of different subgroups of the Ss were further analysed by a 2×2×3 factorial design as in the case of verbal tests. Table—6.22 shows the results of this analysis.

Table—6.22 Results of ANOVA of the Fluency Scores on Nonverbal Tests

Source	SS	df	MS	*F*
S	507.75	1	507.75	14.41***
L	67.25	1	67.25	1.91@
C	1890.62	2	945.31	26.82***
S×L	780.25	1	780.25	22.14***
S×C	1003.00	2	501.50	14.23***
L×C	377.62	2	188.81	5.36**
S×L×C	194.37	2	97.19	2.76@
Error	31293.19	888	35.24	
Total	**36114.06**	**899**		

Note: Please see note under Table—6.2.

It could be seen from the table that the F ratio (14.41) for sex was significant at 0.001 level. From Table—6.21 it may be seen that boys (M = 25.63) scored significantly better than girls (M = 24.12) with regard to nonverbal fluency.

The *F* ratio of 1.91 for locality was not significant at 0.05 level for 1 and 888 df, indicating no significant difference between the children belonging to the two localities.

The *F* ratio for class was 26.82 significant at 0.001 level. This shows a significant difference between students belonging to different classes. To findout students of which class differed significantly from the others, *t* test was applied and the results of this test are shown in Table—6.23.

Table—6.23 Mean Fluency Scores of the Ss Belonging to Different Classes and the Results of the *t* Test on Nonverbal Tests

VIII	X	IX
23.04	25.00	26.58

Note: Please see note under Table—6.3.

It could be seen from the table that students of each class differed significantly from the others. The mean scores of the three classes, VIII, IX and X, were 23.04, 26.58 and 25.00 respectively. It may be seen that VIII class students were the least scores. Students of IX class performed better than those belonging to X class.

As mentioned earlier, slumps in creativity occur whenever there is stress of the child in some form or other like undue emphasis on achievement in examinations, adjusting to a new environment, transition from elementary school to high school or transition from one type of society to another. In the words of Torrance (1962) 'the various declines may be explained interms of reaction to new stresses encountered at each new stage of development or each transitional state in education'. Sullivan (1953) is also of the opinion that creativity gets hampered whenever there is pressure of some sort or the other on the child. It is an accepted fact that over emphasis on academic achievement (convergent thinking) adversely affects creativity of the child.

As mentioned earlier, in Andhra Pradesh, where this investigation was conducted, there is a great stress, on the child, that too imposed on him all of a sudden, at the X class level because of the nondetention system. This would have affected the creativity of the X class children.

An examination of the *F* ratios obtained for the various two factor interaction effects shows that all the two factor interaction effects were significant at or above 0.01 level setting limits to the conclusions that can be arrived as based upon the *F* ratios for the main effects.

The *F* ratio for S×L interaction was 22.14 which was significant at 0.001 level. To probe into this, the mean scores of the Ss classified according to the two variables (sex and locality) were further analysed. The results obtained are presented in Table—6.24.

Table—6.24 Mean Fluuency Scores of the Ss Classified According to Their Sex and Locality to Explain S×L, Interaction and the Results of the *t* Test

	Table—6.24a			*Table—6.24b*	
	U	R		G	B
Boys	24.42	26.83	Rural	23.47	26.83
	R	U		B	G
Girls	23.47	24.78	Urban	24.42	24.78

Note: Please see note under Table—6.3.

From Table—6.24a it could be seen that in the case of boys, the mean score of R students was significantly higher than that of U students, whereas in the case of girls U students scored better than R students.

Considering sex differences separately for rural and urban areas, it was found that in the case of R localities boys (M =

26.83) scored significantly better than girls (M = 23.47) while in the case of U localities there was no significant difference between boys and girls. Thus sex differences were not independent of the locality to which the students belonged and locality differences were also not independent of the sex of the students involved. This explains the significant S×L interaction.

The *F* ratio, 14.23, for S×C interaction was also significant at 0.01 level for 2 and 888 df. From Table—6.25a it could be seen that in the case of boys the mean fluency scores of VIII, IX and X class students were 22.92, 28.82 and 25.14 respectively and that each mean significantly differed from the others. In the case of girls, VIII class students scored the least and differed significantly from X class students. The difference between VIII and IX class students or that between IX and X class students was not significant.

Table—6.25 Mean Fluency Scores of the Ss Classified According to Their Sex and Class to Explain S×C Interaction and the Results of the *t* Test

	Table—6.25a				*Table—6.25b*	
	VIII	X	IX		B	G
Boys	22.92	25.14	28.82	VIII	22.92	23.16
	VIII	IX	X		G	B
Girls	23.16	24.35	24.87	IX	24.35	28.82
					G	B
				X	24.87	25.14

Note: Please see note under Table—6.3.

Considering sex differences, separately for the different classes, in the case of VIII class girls scored some what better than boys though the difference between two means was not significant. In the case of IX class, boys scored better than girls. There was no significant difference between the two sexes in the case of the X class.

The *F* ratio for L×C interaction was also significant at 0.01 level. From Table—6.26a it could be seen that in the case of R localities, VIII class students scored least and differed significantly from those belonging to IX and X class students. In the case of urban areas, on the other hand, IX class students scored the highest and differed significantly from the others. Other differences between means were not significant.

Table—6.26 Mean Fluency Scores of the Ss Classified According to Their Locality and Class to Explain L×C Interaction and the Results of the *t* Test

	Table—6.26a				*Table—6.26b*	
	VIII	IX	X		U	R
Rural	23.31	26.07	26.07	VIII	22.77	23.31
	VIII	X	IX		R	U
Urban	22.77	23.93	27.10	IX	26.07	27.10
					R	U
				X	23.93	26.07

Note: Please see note under Table—6.3.

Considering locality differences separately for each class, it may be seen from Table—6.26b that there was no significant difference between urban and rural areas in the case of VIII and IX classes while in the case of X class urban students scored significantly better than their counterparts from rural areas.

This shows that differences between the creativity of students belonging to different classes were not similar for urban and rural areas. Similarly, urban rural differences were of different patterns for the children belonging to different classes. This explains the significant L×C interaction effect.

The *F* ratio of 2.76 for S×L×C interaction was not significant at 0.05 level, indicating that the effect of any two variables taken at a time was independent of the level of the third variable.

2. Flexibility

Table—6.27 shows the mean scores of different subgroups of Ss for the flexibility component while the results of ANOVA of the scores are presented in Table—6.28. It may be seen from these tables that boys scored significantly better than girls (F = 18.04, significant at 0.001 level for 1 and 888 df).

Similarly, rural students scored significantly better than urban students (F = 5.07, significant at 0.05 level).

Table—6.27 Mean Flexibility Scores and SDs of Different Subgroups of Ss Classified According to Their Sex, Locality and Class on Nonverbal Tests

Groups	*N*	*M*	*SD*
Boys	450	21.25	4.38
Girls	450	20.05	4.41
Rural	450	20.97	4.28
Urban	450	20.33	4.56
VIII	300	19.42	4.17
IX	300	21.51	4.71
X	300	21.03	4.12

Table—6.28 Results of ANOVA on the Flexibility Scores on Nonverbal Tests

Source	SS	df	MS	*F*
S	325.19	1	325.19	18.04***
L	91.50	1	91.50	5.07*
C	719.06	2	359.53	19.94***
S×L	195.09	1	195.09	10.82**
S×C	286.56	2	143.28	7.95***
L×C	40.59	2	20.29	1.13@
S×L×C	61.53	2	30.76	1.71@
Error	16009.22	888	18.03	
Total	**17728.75**	**899**		

Note: Please see note under Table—6.2.

The significant *F* ratio of 19.94 for the variable class, shows that there was a significant difference between the students of different classes with regard to their flexibility score. An examination of the results of the *t* test presented in Table—6.29 shows that students of VIII class were the least scorers and differed significantly from the students of IX and X classes. There was no significant difference between the mean scores of the later two classes. The mean scores of VIII, IX and X classes were 19.42, 21.51 and 21.03 respectively.

Table—6.29 Mean Flexibility Scores of the Ss Belonging to Different Classes and the Results of the *t* Test on Nonverbal Tests

VIII	X	IX
19.42	21.03	21.51

Note: Please see note under Table—6.3.

However, in view of the significant *F* ratios for the S×L and SxC interaction effects, these results based upon the *F* ratios for the main effects should be interpreted cautiously.

Table—6.30 Mean Flexibility Scores of the Ss Classified According to Their Sex and Locality to Explain S×L Interaction and the Results of the *t* Test

Table—6.30a			*Table—6.30b*		
	U	R		G	B
Boys	20.47	22.04	Rural	19.90	22.04
	R	U		G	B
Girls	19.90	20.20	Urban	20.20	20.47

Note: Please see note under Table—6.3.

The results obtained from a further analysis of the mean scores of the Ss classified according to the relevant variables are presented in Tables—6.30 and 6.31.

In the case of boys, rural students scored significantly better than urban students. There was no significant difference between the children belonging to the two localities in the case of girls.

Boys scored better than girls in the case of R, areas, while there was no significant difference between boys and girls in the case of U localities.

Table—6.31 Mean Flexibility Scores of the Ss Classified According to Their Sex and Class to Explain S×C Interaction and the Results of the *t* Test

Table—6.31a						
	VIII	X	IX		G	B
Boys	19.75	21.11	22.89	VIII	19.09	19.75
	VIII	IX	X		G	B
Girls	19.09	20.12	20.94	IX	20.12	22.89
					G	B
				X	20.94	21.11

(The right part, from the VIII/IX/X column onward, is headed *Table—6.31b*.)

Note: Please see note under Table—6.3.

Considering the interaction effect of sex and class, it was found that among boys VIII class students scored the least while IX class students scored the highest and each group differed significantly from the others. In the case of girls also VIII class students scored the least, and differed significantly from others. But the difference between IX and X class students was not significant.

Considering sex differences, there was no significant difference between boys and girls in the case of VIII and X classes, but in the case of IX class boys scored significantly better than girls.

The *F* ratio (1.13) for the L×C interaction and that for the three factor interaction (*F* = 1.71) were not significant at 0.05 level.

3. Originality

Tables—6.32 and 6.33 show the mean scores and results of ANOVA respectively for the originality component. It could be observed from these tables that as in the case of fluency and flexibility; with regard to originality component also, boys scored significantly better than girls. Rural children performed significantly better than their urban counterparts.

Table—6.32 Mean Originality Scores and SDs of Different Subgroups of Ss Classified According to Their Sex, Locality and Class on Nonverbal Tests

Group	*N*	*M*	*SD*
Boys	450	97.06	26.88
Girls	450	92.37	26.97
Rural	450	97.26	26.44
Urban	450	92.16	27.37
VIII	300	86.56	24.77
IX	300	103.21	28.34
X	300	94.38	25.22

Table—6.33 Results of ANOVA of the Originality Scores on Nonverbal Tests

Source	*SS*	*df*	*MS*	*F*
S	4960.50	1	4960.50	7.59**
L	5852.00	1	5852.00	8.96**
C	41651.00	2	20825.50	31.89***
S×L	4539.00	1	4539.00	6.95**
S×C	10821.00	2	5410.50	8.28***
L×C	7828.50	2	3914.25	5.99**
S×L×C	1898.50	2	949.25	1.45@
Error	579957.00	888	653.10	
Total	**657507.50**	**899**		

Note: Please see note under Table—6.2.

Considering the class of the Ss, VIII class students were the least scorers, as in the case of the other components, while IX class students got the highest score. Each mean differed significantly from the others (Table—6.34).

Table—6.34 Mean Originality scores of the Ss Belonging to Different Classes and the Results of the *t* Test on Nonverbal Tests

VIII	X	IX
86.56	94.38	103.21

Note: Please see note under Table—6.3.

As observation of the *F* ratios for the two factor interactions reveals that all the two factor interactions were significant at or above 0.01 level indicating that the effect of any one variable was not independent of the level of the others, warranting further analysis of the mean scores of the Ss classified according to the different variables.

It may be seen from Tables—6.35 and 6.36 that similar results as those obtained on flexibility were obtained in the case of originality also. In the case of boys rural students performed better than urban students. There was no significant difference between urban and rural children in the case of girls (Table—6.35a).

Table—6.35 Mean Originality Scores of the Ss Classified According to Their Sex and Locality to Explain S×L Interaction and the Results of the *t* Test

Table—6.35a			*Table—6.35b*		
	U	R		G	B
Boys	92.27	101.86	Rural	92.67	101.86
	U	R		G	B
Girls	92.06	92.67	Urban	92.06	92.27

Note: Please see note under Table—6.3.

Considering sex differences boys scored better than girls in rural areas. The difference between the two sexes was not significant in the case of urban localities (Table—6.35b).

Table—6.36 Mean Originality Scores of the Ss Classified According to Their Sex and Class to Explain S×C interaction and the Results of the *t* Test

	Table—6.36a				*Table—6.36b*	
	VIII	X	IX		G	B
Boys	87.39	93.44	110.35	VIII	85.72	87.39
	VIII	X	IX		G	B
Girls	85.72	95.31	96.07	IX	96.07	110.35
					B	G
				X	93.44	95.31

Note: Please see note under Table—6.3.

Considering S×C interaction, Table—6.36 shows that in the case of boys those from VIII class scored least, while those belonging to IX class were the highest scorers. Each group differed significantly from the others. Among girls, though the trend of the mean scores was the same, there was no significant difference between IX and X class students (Table—6.36a). There was a significant difference between boys and girls in the case of IX class only but not in the case of VIII and X classes (Table—6.36b).

Similarly, it may be seen from Table—6.37a that differences between the mean scores of different classes were not similar for rural and urban children, and that locality differences were not similar for children belonging to different classes.

There results show that the class effect was not of the same order for urban and rural localities. Similarly, locality differences were not similar for students of different classes. This explains the significant interaction between locality and class.

The *F* ratio for the three factor interaction was not significant. This shows that the effect of any two variables taken at a time was independent of the level of the third variable.

Table—6.37 Mean Originality Scores of the Ss Classified According to Their Locality and Classes to Explain L×C Interaction and the Results of the *t* Test

Table—6.37a				*Table—6.37b*		
	VIII	X	IX		U	R
Rural	88.61	100.76	102.42	VIII	84.50	88.61
	VIII	X	IX		R	U
Urban	84.50	87.99	104.00	IX	102.42	104.00
					U	R
				X	87.99	100.76

Note: Please see note under Table—6.3.

4. Composite Creativity Score

Table—6.38 shows the mean composite creativity scores of different subgroups of Ss on the nonverbal tests and Table—6.39 shows the results of ANOVA of the scores. It may be seen from the two tables that boys (M = 143.83) scored significantly better than girls (M = 136.09), and that R children (M = 143.17) performed significantly better than U children (M = 136.75). VIII class students got the least score while students of the IX class scored the highest (see Fig. 7). Each group differed significantly from the others (Table—6.40).

Table—6.38 Mean Composite Creativity Scores and SDs of Different Subgroups of Ss Classified According to Their Sex, Locality and Class on Nonverbal Tests

Group	*N*	*M*	*SD*
Boys	450	143.83	36.78
Girls	450	136.09	36.88
Rural	450	143.17	36.02
Urban	450	136.75	37.74
VIII	300	128.99	34.14
IX	300	150.75	39.36
X	300	140.14	34.10

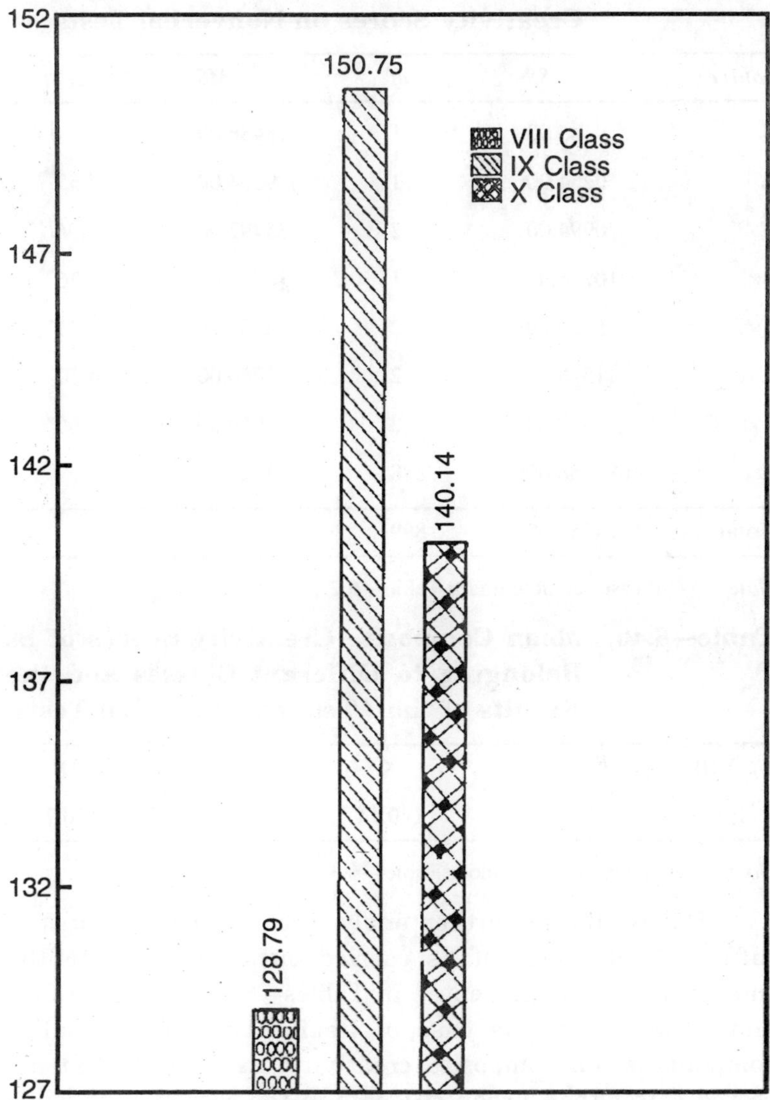

Fig.—7. Mean Composite Creativity Scores of Students Belonging to Different Classes on Nonverbal Tests.

Table—6.39 Results of ANOVA of the Composite Creativity Scores on Nonverbal Tests

Source	*SS*	*df*	*MS*	*F*
S	13486.00	1	13486.00	11.00**
L	9254.00	1	9254.00	7.55**
C	70994.00	2	35497.00	28.96***
S×L	10734.00	1	10734.00	8.76**
S×C	25762.00	2	12881.00	10.51***
L×C	11520.00	2	5760.00	4.70**
S×L×C	3920.00	2	1960.00	1.60@
Error	1088488.00	888	1225.77	
Total	**1234158.00**	**899**		

Note: Please see note under Table—6.2.

Table—6.40 Mean Composite Creativity Scores of Ss Belonging to Different Classes and the Results of the *t* Test on Nonverbal Tests

VIII	X	IX
128.99	140.14	150.75

Note: Please see note under Table—6.3.

The results of further analysis of the mean scores of different subgroups of Ss carried out to probe into the interaction effects presented in Tables—6.41, 6.42, and 6.43 show that as in the case of flexibility and originality components, on composite creativity also, rural students scored better than urban students in the case of boys while there was no significant difference between girls belonging to the two localities. In the case of rural areas boys performed better than girls. With regard to urban localities, however, sex differences were not significant (Table—6.41)

Table—6.41 Mean Composite Creativity Scores of the Ss Classified According to Their Sex and Locality to Explain S×L Interaction and the Results of the *t* Test

	Table—6.41a			*Table—6.41b*	
	U	R		G	B
Boys	137.17	150.49	Rural	135.84	150.49
	R	U		G	B
Girls	135.84	136.34	Urban	136.34	137.17

Note: Please see note under Table—6.3.

Table—6.42 Mean Composite Creativity Scores of the Ss Classified According to Their Sex and Class to Explain S×C Interaction and the Results of the *t* Test

	Table—6.42a				*Table—6.42b*	
	VIII	X	IX		G	B
Boys	130.12	139.28	162.77	VIII	127.87	130.12
	VIII	IX	X		G	B
Girls	127.87	139.40	141.00	IX	139.40	162.77
					B	G
				X	139.28	141.00

Note: Please see note under Table—6.3.

Table—6.43 Mean Composite Creativity Scores of the Ss Classified According to Their Locality and Class to Explain L×C Interaction and the Results of *t* Test

	Table—6.43a				*Table—6.43b*	
	VIII	X	IX		U	R
Rural	131.67	147.98	149.88	VIII	126.35	131.65
	VIII	X	IX		R	U
Urban	126.35	132.30	152.29	IX	149.88	152.29
					U	R
				X	132.30	147.98

Note: Please see note under Table—6.3.

Considering S×C interaction, among boys VIII class students least, and IX class students scored highest. Each mean differed significantly from the others. In the case of girls, on the other hand, the difference between IX and X classes was not significant. Sex differences were significant only in the case of IX class (Table—6.42).

It may be seen from Table—6.43, where the mean scores of different subgroups of Ss classified according to their class and locality are presented, that in both rural and urban localities, VIII class students obtained the lowest mean scores while IX class students scored the highest. VIII class students differed significantly from others in the case of rural areas, while in the case of urban children IX class students differed significantly from the others. Other differences between means were not significant. Considering locality differences, the difference between urban and rural areas was significant only in the case of X class students (Table—6.43b).

The *F* ratio, 1.60 for the three factor S×L×C interaction was not significant at 0.05 level. This shows that the interaction between any two variables taken at a time was independent of the level of the third variable.

Summary

It may be seen from the above analysis that boys performed better than girls on the nonverbal tests. This was true for all the components of creativity and also for the composite creativity score. Further, rural students obtained higher scores than their urban counterparts. This was true for flexibility, originality and composite creativity score. In the case of fluency, though rural children scored better than urban children the difference between the means was not significant.

VIII class students scored the least while IX class obtained the highest score, X class students falling in between. This was true for all the components of creativity.

The interaction effect between sex and locality and that between sex and class were significant for all the components.

The class X locality effect was significant in the case of fluency, originality and composite creativity score.

A comparison of the results obtained on verbal and non-verbal tests shows some interesting features.

Sex differences were significant in the case of nonverbal tests, boys scoring better than girls. In the case of verbal tests also the mean score of boys was higher than that of girls on all the components without any exception, but the differences between the mean scores were not significant.

With regard to the locality variable, interestingly rural children performed better than urban children, while on verbal tests urban students scored better than their counterparts from rural areas.

Considering class differences substantial improvement was seen from class VIII to IX in the case of both types of tests. There was only marginal improvement from IX class to X class in the case of verbal tests. But in the case of nonverbal tests there was, on the whole, a drop in the creativity at the X class level, subject to small variations for different subgroups of Ss, lending support to the observation of Torrance (1962) and Sullivan (1953) that creativity slumps in certain situations.

As mentioned earlier different investigators like Torrance (1962), Torrance and Gowan (1963), Starr and Nicholl (1975) have pointed out that nonverbal creativity is distinct from verbal creativity. Yet research investigations on nonverbal creativity, or on the relative effect of different variables on verbal and nonverbal creativity are rare to find, to help make a comparison of the results of this study with those of others.

Anderson (1968) has pointed out that certain psychological characteristics like 'slight dominance of hippocampal or cortical inhibitary activity over reticular or cortical arousal activity' are necessary for nonverbal creativity.

Is there any urban rural difference in this characteristic? If so can it be a possible source of variation in the performance of urban and rural children on the nonverbal tests, in contrast to their performance on verbal tests? Or, are there any special features in the rural environment more conducive for development of nonverbal creativity rather than verbal creativity?

It has been pointed out earlier that because of the non-detention system there is an overemphasis on achievement in the examinations at the X class level, which has a negative effect on creativity. In this negative effect on creativity more in the case of nonverbal tests than in the case of verbal tests?

Do the psychological characteristics mentioned earlier which are necessary for nonverbal creativity fluctuate with age? Or with stress and anxiety? If so is it possible that these fluctuations have resulted in the decline in the creativity at the X class level? Further studies may have to be conducted to probe into these aspects.

It may also be noticed that more or less similar results were obtained on all the components of creativity. This is true for verbal as well as nonverbal tests. This is a common phenomenon observed in almost all studies using Torrance and Guilford type of tests. As mentioned by Starr and Nicholl (1975) this is 'to some extent a reflection of the method of scoring in which the same activities are scored for different dimensions'.

C. Verbal and Nonverbal Tests

In this section the analysis of the scores obtained by the Ss on all the 10 subtests (7 verbal and 3 nonverbal) put together is presented.

1. Fluency

The means and SDs of fluency scores of the different subgroups of Ss are presented in Table—6.44. It may be seen from the table that the mean fluency score of boys

(M = 119.21) was higher than that of girls (M = 115.01). Considering the locality variable the mean scores of R and U children were 115.13 and 119.09 respectively. This indicates the superiority of the urban children. With regard to the class of the students, VIII class children were the least scorers while X class children obtained the highest mean score.

Table—6.44 Mean Fluency Scores and SDs of Different Subgroups of Ss Classified According to Their Sex, Locality and Class (on All the Tests—Verbal and Nonverbal put together)

Group	*N*	*M*	*SD*
Boys	450	119.21	29.11
Girls	450	115.01	29.28
Rural	450	115.13	27.61
Urban	450	119.09	30.72
VIII	300	101.14	25.05
IX	300	121.76	27.43
X	300	128:44	28.04

When the scores of the different subgroups of Ss were further analysed employing ANOVA of a 2×2×3 factorial design, as in the earlier cases, it was found that the *F* ratio (5.76) for sex was significant at 0.05 level (Table—6.45) for 1 and 888 df, indicating that there was a significant difference between boys and girls with regard to their fluency component of creativity. From Table—6.44 it is evident that boys scored significantly better than girls on this component.

The significant *F* ratio (5.15) for locality, and the mean scores of rural and urban children (Table—6.44) shows that urban children (M = 119.09) fared significantly better than rural children (M = 115.13).

The *F* ratio (88.12) for class was highly significant even at 0.01 level. From Table—6.46 it may be seen that X class children scored the highest while VIII class children scored the least. The mean scores of VIII, IX and X classes were 101.14, 121.76 and 128.44 respectively. Each class differed significantly from the others.

Table—6.45 Results of ANOVA of the Fluency Scores (on All the Tests—Verbal and Nonverbal put together)

Source	*SS*	*df*	*MS*	*F*
S	3974.00	1	3974.00	5.76*
L	3549.00	1	3549.00	5.15*
C	121529.00	2	60764.50	88.12***
S×L	5372.00	1	5372.00	7.79**
S×C	13060.00	2	6530.00	9.47***
L×C	401.00	2	200.50	0.29@
S×L×C	11103.00	2	5551.50	8.05***
Error	612328.00	888	689.56	
Total	**771316.00**	**899**		

Note: Please see note under Table—6.2.

Table—6.46 Mean Fluency Scores of Ss Belonging to Different Classes and the Results of the *t* Test (on All the Tests—Verbal and Nonverbal put together)

VIII	IX	X
101.14	121.76	128.44

Note: Please see note under Table—6.3.

It may be seen from Table—6.45 that the S×L and S×C, interaction effects were significant at or above 0.01 level. Hence, as mentioned earlier the results based upon the *F* ratios for the main effects are limited in scope and should be interpreted cautiously.

The F ratio for S×L, interaction was 7.79 which was significant at 0.01 level. Hence, the mean score of the Ss classified according to the two variables (sex and locality) were further analysed as in the earlier cases. The results obtained are presented in Table—6.47. From Table—6.47a it could be seen that in the case of boys R students (M = 119.67) tended to fare better than U students (M = 118.76). But the difference between the means was not significant. On the other hand in the case of girls U students (M = 119.44) scored significantly better than R students (M = 110.58).

Table—6.47 Mean Fluency Scores of the Ss Classified According to Their Sex and Locality to Explain S×L Interaction and the Results of the *t* Test

	Table—6.47a			*Table—6.47b*	
	U	R		G	B
Boys	118.76	119.67	Rural	110.58	119.67
	R	U		B	G
Girls	110.58	119.44	Urban	118.76	119.44

Note: Please see note under Table—6.3.

Considering sex differences separately for R and U areas it was found (Table—6.47b) that in the case of R localities boys (M = 119.67) scored significantly better than girls (M = 110.58), while in the case of U localities there was no significant difference between the two sexes. This shows that sex differences were not independent of the locality to which the students belonged and conversely locality differences were not independent of the sex of the students considered.

The F ratio of 9.47 for S×C interaction was significant at 0.001 level for 2 and 888 df. From Table—6.48a it could be seen that in the case of boys VIII class students were the least scorers while X class students were the highest scorers. Each class differed significantly from the others.

Table—6.48 Mean Fluency Scores of the Ss Classified According to their Sex and Class to Explain S×C Interaction and the Results of the *t* Test

Table—6.48a				*Table—6.48b*		
	VIII	IX	X		B	G
Boys	98.18	124.79	134.67	VIII	98.18	104.09
	VIII	IX	X		G	B
Girls	104.09	118.74	122.20	IX	118.74	124.79
					G	B
				X	122.20	134.67

Note: Please see note under Table—6.3.

In the case of girls also a similar pattern of results was obtained. However, the difference between IX and X class students was not significant. Considering sex differences separately for the different classes, in the case of VIII class, girls scored significantly better than boys while in the case of X class boys scored significantly better than girls. There was no significant difference between boys and girls in the case of IX class (Table—6.48b).

It may be noticed that similar results were obtained in the case of the fluency component on verbal tests also.

The *F* ratio 0.29 for L×C interaction was not significant at 0.05 level. This indicates that the locality effects on creativity of the children was independent of the class to which the students belonged and vice versa.

The *F* ratio (8.05) for the three factor interaction was significant at 0.001 level indicating that the effect of any two variables taken at a time was not independent of the level of the third variable involved.

2. Flexibility

The means and SDs of the flexibility scores of the different subgroups of Ss are shown in Table—6.49, while the results of ANOVA of the scores is presented in Table—6.50.

It could be inferred from the two tables that though the mean score of boys (M = 82.52) was higher than that of girls (M = 80.15), the difference between the two means was not significant at 0.05 level. Similarly, with regard to the locality variables, though urban children (M = 81.57) scored somewhat better than rural children (M = 81.10), the difference between the two groups was not significant.

Table—6.49 Mean Flexibility Scores and SDs of Different Subgroups of Ss Classified According to Their Sex, Locality and Class (on All the Tests—Verbal and Nonverbal put together)

Group	*N*	*M*	*SD*
Boys	450	82.52	20.47
Girls	450	80.15	20.21
Rural	450	81.10	22.12
Urban	450	81.57	19.55
VIII	300	72.26	15.47
IX	300	84.13	25.92
X	300	87.61	16.33

Table—6.50 Results of ANOVA of the Flexibility Scores (on All the Tests—Verbal and Nonverbal put together)

Source	*SS*	*df*	*MS*	*F*
S	1258.00	1	1258.00	3.25[@]
L	49.00	1	49.00	0.13[@]
C	38881.00	2	19440.50	50.30[***]
S×L	4147.00	1	4147.00	10.73[**]
S×C	1869.50	2	934.75	2.42[@]
L×C	322.00	2	161.00	0.42[@]
S×L×C	2526.00	2	1263.00	3.27[*]
Error	343210.00	888	386.50	
Total	**392262.50**	**899**		

Note: Please note under Table—6.2.

The *F* ratio of 50.30 for class was significant at 0.001 level for 2 and 888 df indicating variation between the flexibility scores of children belonging to different classes.

From Table—6.51 it may be seen that as in the earlier cases students of VIII class scored the least while students of X class obtained the highest mean score. Each group differed significantly from the others.

Table—6.51 Mean Flexibility Scores of Ss Belonging to Different Classes and the Results of the *t* Test (on All the Tests—Verbal and Nonverbal put together)

VIII	IX	X
72.26	84.13	87.61

Note: Please see note under Table—6.3.

However, as mentioned earlier, these results based upon the *F* ratios for the main effects are limited in scope by virtue of the significant *F* ratios for the interaction effects.

Table—6.52 shows the mean scores of different subgroups of Ss classified according to their sex and locality and the results of *t* test.

It may be seen from the table that in the case of boys, R students scored significantly better than U students, whereas in the case of girls, U students scored significantly better the R students. Boys scored significantly better than girls in the rural areas while there was no significant difference between the two sexes in urban localities (Table—6.52).

The other two factor interaction effects between sex and class and locality and class were not significant at 0.05 level indicating that the effect of sex was independent of the variations in the class of the students and vice versa. Similarly, the effect of locality was also independent of the class to which the students belonged and vice versa.

The *F* ratio of 3.27 of the three factor (S×L×C) interaction effect was, however, significant at 0.05 level indicating that the interaction between any two variables taken at a time was not independent of the level of the third variable.

Table—6.52 Mean Flexibility Scores of the Ss Classified According to Their Sex and Locality to Explain S×L Interaction and the Results of the *t* Test

Table—6.52a			*Table—6.52b*		
	U	R		G	B
Boys	80.60	84.43	Rural	77.77	84.43
	R	U		B	G
Girls	77.77	82.53	Urban	80.60	82.53

Note: Please see note under Table—6.3.

3. Originality

The mean originality scores and SDs of different subgroups of Ss are presented in Table—6.53, while Table—6.54 shows the results of ANOVA of the scores. It could be seen from the tables that boys (M = 419.04) scored somewhat better than girls (M = 408.08), the difference between the means was however, not significant at 0.05 level.

Table—6.53 Mean Originality scores and SDs of Different Subgroups of Ss Classified According to their Sex, Locality and Class (on all the tests—Verbal and Nonverbal put together)

Group	*N*	*M*	*SD*
Boys	450	419.04	122.48
Girls	450	408.48	122.91
Rural	450	407.55	121.05
Urban	450	419.98	124.23
VIII	300	359.14	104.39
IX	300	441.42	128.09
X	300	440.73	116.05

Table—6.54 Results of ANOVA of the Originality Scores (on All the Tests—Verbal and Nonverbal put together)

Source	*SS*	*df*	*MS*	*F*
S	25088.00	1	25088.00	1.88@
L	34768.00	1	34768.00	2.60@
C	1342672.00	2	671336.00	50.25***
S×L	88576.00	1	88576.00	6.63*
S×C	92848.00	2	46424.00	3.47*
L×C	36768.00	2	18384.00	1.37@
S×L×C	90400.00	2	452.00	3.38*
Error	11863540.00	888	13359.84	
Total	**13574660.00**	**899**		

Note: Please see note under Table—6.2.

The *F* ratio 2.60 for locality was also not significant at 0.05 level, though the children from urban localities (M = 419.98) tended to score better than those from rural localities (M = 407.55).

The *F* ratio for class (50.25) was highly significant even at 0.001 level for 2 and 888 df. To findout students of which class differed significantly from the others *t* test was applied as in the earlier cases. It may be seen from Table—6.55 that VIII class students, the youngest of the three groups got the lowest mean score and differed significantly from the other two classes. The difference between the mean scores of IX and X classes was not significant.

An observation of the *F* ratios for the two factor interactions shows that the S×L interaction and S×C interaction were significant at 0.05 level, warranting careful interpretation of the results derived from the *F* ratios for the main effects.

Table—6.55 Mean Originality Scores of Ss Belonging to Different Classes and the Results of the *t* Test (on All the Tests—Verbal and Nonverbal put together)

VIII	X	IX
359.14	440.73	441.42

Note: Please see note under Table—6.3.

Considering S×L, Interaction, it may be seen from Table—6.56 that in the case of boys there was no significant difference between the mean scores of urban and rural children, whereas in the case of girls U students scored significantly better than R students (Table—6.56a).

Table—6.56 Mean Originality Scores of the Ss Classified According to Their Sex and Locality to Explain S×L Interaction and the Results of the *t* Test

	Table—6.56a			*Table—6.56b*	
	U	R		G	B
Boys	415.34	422.75	Rural	392.35	422.75
	R	U		B	G
Girls	392.35	424.62	Urban	415.34	424.62

Note: Please see note under Table—6.3.

Considering sex differences, it may be seen that boys scored significantly better than girls in R areas while there was no significant difference between boys and girls in the case of urban areas (Table—6.56b).

With regard to S×C interaction effect, it may be seen from Table—6.57, that irrespective of the sex of the Ss VIII class students scored the least and differed significantly from the other groups. Table—6.57 shows sex difference separately for the students of each class. It may be observed that sex differences were significant only in the case of X class students, but not in the case of VIII and IX classes.

The *F* ratio of 1.37 for the L×C interaction was not significant showing that the locality and class effects were independent of each other.

Table—6.57 Mean Originality Scores of the Ss Classified According to Their Sex and Class to Explain S×C Interaction and the Results of the *t* Test

Table—6.57a				*Table—6.57b*		
	VIII	X	IX		B	C
Boys	351.39	457.75	477.99	VIII	351.39	366.89
	VIII	X	IX		G	B
Girls	366.89	423.71	441.51	IX	441.51	477.99
					G	B
				X	423.71	457.75

Note: Please see note under Table—6.3.

The *F* ratio 3.38 for the three factor interaction, however, was significant indicating that the effect of any two variables taken at a time was not independent of the variations in the level of the third variable.

4. Composite Creativity Score

Table—6.58 shows the means and SDs of the composite creativity scores of different subgroups of Ss. It could be seen from the table that the mean score of boys was 618.94 while it was 603.94 for girls (See Fig. 8). These mean scores coupled with the results of ANOVA presented in Table—6.59 show that there was no significant difference between the composite creativity of boys and girls.

In the case of the locality variable also, though students of U localities (M = 618.90) tended to score better than those from rural areas (M = 603.46), the difference between the means was not significant (See Fig. 9).

With regard to the differences between students belonging to different classes it may be observed from Table—6.60 that as in the case of originality VIII class students scored the least and differed significantly from IX and X class children *(See Fig. 10)*.

Table—6.58 Mean Composite Creativity Scores and SDs of different Sub-Groups of Ss Classified According to Their Sex, Locality and Class (on All the Tests—Verbal and Nonverbal put together)

Group	*N*	*M*	*SD*
Boys	450	618.94	165.15
Girls	450	603.42	166.36
Rural	450	603.46	160.58
Urban	450	618.90	170.78
VIII	300	532.26	140.64
IX	300	645.79	171.07
X	300	655.49	155.46

Table—6.59 Results of ANOVA of the Composite Creativity Scores (on All the Tests—Verbal and Nonverbal put together)

Source	*SS*	*df*	*MS*	*F*
S	54240.00	1	54240.00	2.27@
L	53632.00	1	53632.00	2.24@
C	2816736.00	2	1408368.00	58.87***
S×L	213088.00	1	213088.00	8.91**
S×C	197216.00	2	98608.00	4.12*
L×C	23552.00	2	11776.00	0.49@
S×L×C	180768.00	2	90384.00	3.78*
Error	21242720.00	888	23921.98	
Total	**24781950.00**	**899**		

Note: Please see note under Table—6.2.

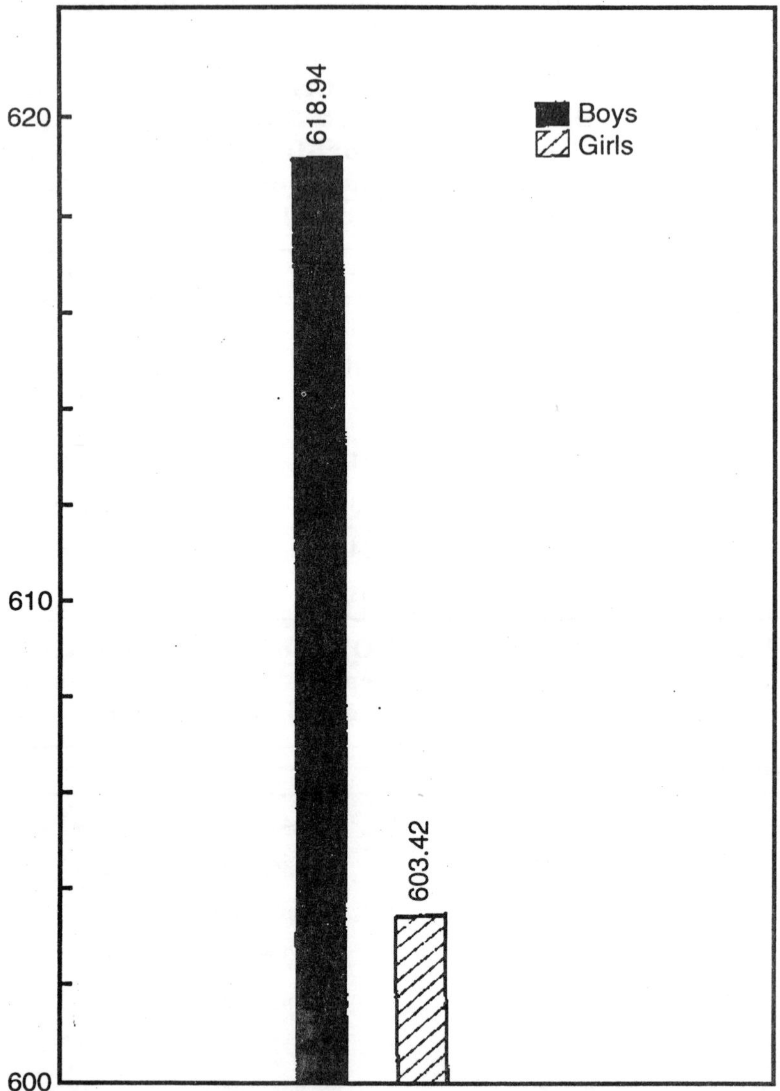

Fig.—8. Mean Composite Creativity Scores of Boys and Girls on Verbal and Nonverbal Tests Put Together.

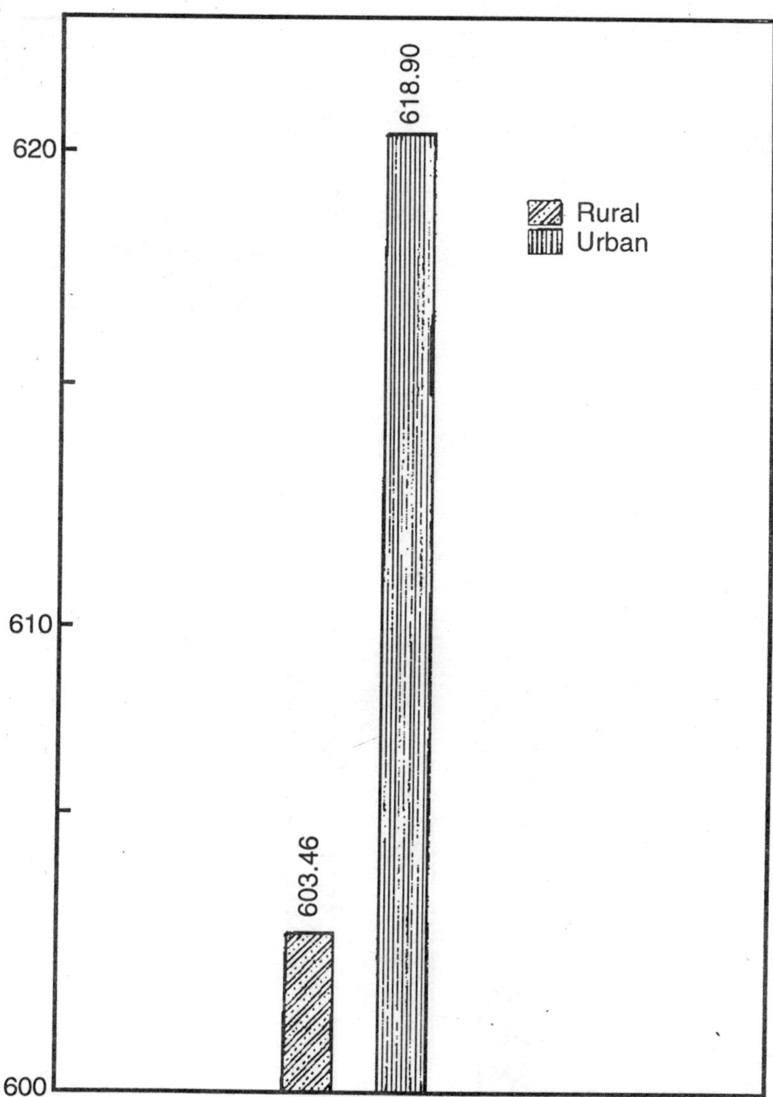

Fig.—9. **Mean Composite Creativity Scores of Rural and Urban Students on Verbal and Nonverbal Tests Put Together.**

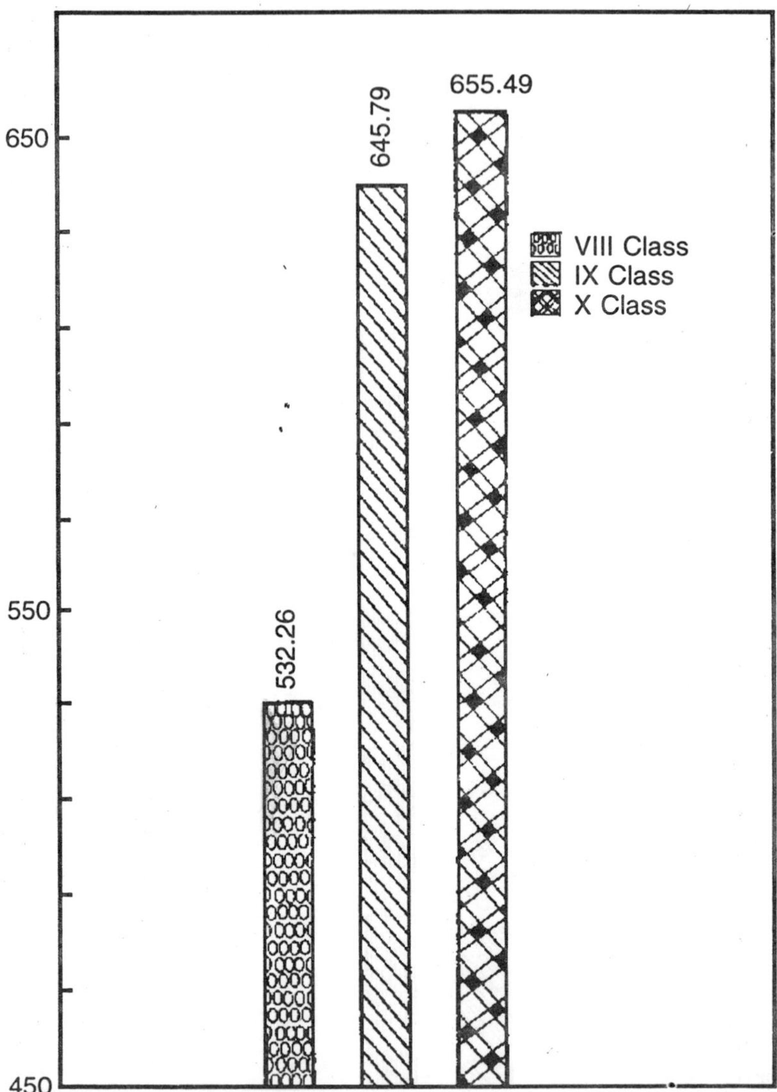

Fig.—10. Mean Composite Creativity Scores of Students Belonging to Different Classes on Verbal and Nonverbal Tests Put Together.

Table—6.60 Many Composite Creativity Scores of Ss Belonging to Different Classes and the Results of the *t* Test (on All the Tests—Verbal and Nonverbal put together)

VIII	IX	X
532.26	645.79	655.49

Note: Please see note under Table—6.3.

A further analysis of the mean scores of the Ss categorised according to the different variables presented in Tables—6.61 and 6.62 to probe into the significant interaction effects showed that in the case of boys, urban rural differences were not significant, while in the case of girls children from U localities scored better than those from R localities. In the case of R areas boys performed better than girls while in the case of U areas sex differences were not significant (Table—6.61).

Table—6.61 Mean Composite Creativity Scores of the Ss Classified According to their Sex and Locality to Explain S×L, Interaction and the Results of the *t* Test

	Table—6.61a			*Table—6.61b*	
	U	R		G	B
Boys	611.28	626.61	Rural	580.31	626.61
	R	U		B	G
Girls	580.31	626.52	Urban	611.28	626.52

Note: Please see note under Table—6.3.

Considering S×C interaction, it may be seen from Table—6.62 that VIII class students obtained the lowest mean score and differed significantly from others in the case of boys as well as girls. An examination of the mean scores of boys and girls presented in Table—6.62 shows that boys (M = 680.20) scored better than girls (M = 630.79) in the case of X class students. In the case of the other two classes there was no significant difference between the mean scores of boys and girls.

Table—6.62 Mean Composite Creativity Scores of the Ss Classified According to Their Sex and Class to Explain S×C Interaction and the Results of the *t* Test

	Table—6.62a				*Table—6.62b*	
	VIII	IX	X		B	G
Boys	520.91	655.73	680.20	VIII	520.91	543.62
	VIII	X	IX		G	B
Girls	543.62	630.79	635.85	IX	635.85	655.73
					G	B
				X	630.79	680.20

Note: Please see note under Table—6.3.

Summary

It may be observed from the above results that though boys tended to score some what better than girls, the difference between the creativity of boys and girls as measured by the verbal and nonverbal tests put together, was not significant. This was true for flexibility, originality and composite creativity scores. In the same vein, urban children obtained higher scores than their counterparts from rural areas. But the differences were not significant in the case of flexibility, originality and composite creativity score.

The interaction effects between sex and locality were significant for all the components of creativity and also for composite creativity score. The SxC interaction was also significant for fluency, originality and composite creativity scores.

An examination of the results obtained on the verbal, nonverbal and all the tests put together shows that boys tended to score better than girls in all cases. But the difference between the mean scores of boys and girls was significant only in the case of nonverbal tests, and for the fluency component on verbal and nonverbal tests put together.

As mentioned earlier, an interesting phenomenon observed is with regard to the locality effect on the creativity of the children as measured by different types of tests. Urban children scored better than their rural counterparts in the case of verbal tests. Contrarily, in the case of nonverbal tests rural children outperformed those from urban areas.

There was progressive improvement in the creativity of the Ss from class to class as measured by verbal tests, though the improvement from IX class to X class was not as much as that from VIII class to IX class. But with regard to creativity as measured by nonverbal tests there was a slight decline at the X class level. As suggested earlier further investigations may be carried out to probe into these aspects.

SECTION—II

Differentiating Characteristics of High Creatives and Low Creatives

Traditionally attempts at fostering creativity revolved round identifying personality and other characteristics of highly creative individuals, and trying to inculcate those characteristics among the subjects.

Torrance (1962), Getzels and Jackson (1962) and others have suggested a number of familial and personality characteristics and habits of life which may be associated with high creativity. Getzels and Jackson (1962) in their well known study on creativity and intelligence tried to see whether certain characteristics differentiated their high creative (but not high intelligent) group of children from their high intelligent (but not high creative) group of children.

An attempt was made in the present investigation to identify differentiating characteristics of high creatives and low creatives.

The first step in this process was, to identify a group of high creatives and a group of low creatives. For the purpose of this investigation those whose total creativity score (composite creativity score, as measured by all the ten tests put together) was above M + 1 SD were taken as high creative group while those whose total creativity score was less than M –1 SD were treated as low creative group, and an attempt was made to see whether these two groups differed in their personality and familial characteristics and certain habits of life.

1. Personality

According to Cattell (1969) 'If we are referring to sustained deeper forms of creativity in the general life situation, then personality is of predominant importance'. In line with this thinking research on creative persons has been vigorously pursued through personality selection by investigators like Drevdahl (1954), Cattell (1963), Getzels and Jackson (1962), Jones (1964), Taylor and Barron (1963), Scheier (1965), Cross, Cattell and Butcher (1967), Cattell and Butcher (1968), Vohra (1975), Gakhar and Joshi (1980), Kaur (1980), Singh (1980), Kundu (1987), etc. There have been contradictory findings in this area as well, as in the case of other aspects related to creativity.

Do the high and low creative adolescents differ in their personality traits? To probe into this the personality scores, as measured by the HSPQ of the high creative and low creative groups were analysed. In the whole group of 900 children who served as sample of Ss for the present study, 143 scored above M+ 1 SD, and were treated as high creatives, while 135 scored below M– 1 SD and were considered as low creatives. The HSPQ yields scores on 14 factors (Factors A, B, C, D, E, F, G, H, I, J, O, Q_2, Q_3, and Q_4. The mean scores[2] of high creatives and low creatives on these 14 personality factors are presented in Table—6.63.

Factor A: It may be seen from the table that for factor A, the mean score of the high creative group was 10.92 while that of the low creative group was 11.37. The difference between the two means was tested for significance by applying *t* test as in the earlier cases. It may be seen from the last column of the table that the *t* value for this factor was 2.25 which was significant at 0.05 level, indicating a significant difference between the high and low creative children with regard to their personality as measured by this factor. It may be noted that the personality score of high creatives was less than that of the low creatives on this factor.

Table—6.63 Mean Personality Scores of High Creative and Low Creative Children and the Results of *t* Test (Whole Group)

Personality factors	*High creative (N = 143)*		*Low creative (N = 135)*		*t*
	Mean	*SD*	*Mean*	*SD*	
Factor A	10.92	2.68	11.37	2.82	2.25*
Factor B	6.52	1.71	4.89	2.30	9.60***
Factor C	11.84	3.21	11.40	3.08	2.06*
Factor D	9.66	2.99	10.34	2.67	3.39***
Factor E	7.95	2.86	9.16	3.30	5.71***
Factor F	9.95	2.82	9.25	2.98	3.42***
Factor G	11.65	2.86	10.73	3.16	4.40***
Factor H	11.99	3.33	10.61	2.93	6.50***
Factor I	11.57	2.58	11.01	3.04	2.77**
Factor J	9.18	2.82	8.76	2.60	2.15*
Factor O	8.43	2.63	9.44	2.98	5.06***
Factor Q_2	9.80	2.19	9.18	2.83	3.28**
Factor Q_3	12.89	2.97	11.32	3.40	7.32***
Factor Q_4	8.87	3.13	8.78	2.81	0.43@

Note: Please see note under Table—6.2.

A person who gets a low score on this trait is, cool, aloof, likes working alone, prefers things or words to people, favours thinking quality in companionship. He is precise, critical and introspective. He is more penetrating in his evaluation of people and things and more inventive (Cattell, 1969). A high score on this factor, on the other hand, indicates qualities like easygoing, casual, careless and attentive to people than things or words. There is no gainsaying the characteristics of a low scorer on this factor cited above, are more congenial for creative work than those of a high scorer.

Cattell and Butcher (1968) prepared a profile of personality factors for the creative person on the basis of studies on several samples of adults. It has been found by them that creatives score lower than the mean for the general population on this factor. The results of the present study corroborate the findings of Cattell and Butcher.

Factor B: In the case of factor B, the high creative group obtained a mean score of 6.52 while the mean score of the low creative group was 4.89. The difference between the two means was significant. This shows that high creatives scored higher than the low creatives on this factor.

Factor B on the HSPQ is related to general intelligence. It has been, found by many, as reported in the previous chapter that there is a significant relationship between creativity and intelligence though high intelligence does not guarantee high creativity. It is no wonder therefore, that the high creative group exhibited a higher level of intelligence than the low creative group.

It has been observed further that those who score high on factor B are insightful, fast learning, intellectually adaptable, inclined to have more intellectual interests. In contrast those who score low on this factor are characterised by low mental capacity and inability to handle abstract problems (Cattell, 1969). Evidently high general mental capacity, insightfulness, and intellectual interests are necessary for creative work.

It may be mentioned in this context that in the present investigation also the high creative group obtained a higher score on Raven's Progressive Matrices compared to the low creative group.

Factor C: With regard to factor C also high creatives got a significantly higher mean score than low creatives, as in the case of Factor B.

This factor is concerned with ego strength and emotional stability. A person who scores high on factor C tends to have higher ego strength. He is emotionally mature, calm, unruffled and shows restraint in avoiding difficulties. In contrast, those who score low on this factor are characterised by ego weakness and emotional instability. They are easily upset, changeable in attitudes and interests, and have a tendency to give up easily. They show more than average number of generalised neurotic responses. A low factor C is seen in a wide range of neurosis and some psychoses. According to Cattell this factor is the core of frustration tolerance.

There is no gainsaying emotional maturity, calm and unruffled nature, and more than any thing else, perseverance and frustration tolerance and essential for creative thinking. Neurotic tendency indeed, hampers rather than helps creativity.

Ray Chowdary (1962, 1965, 1966) also reported that his high creative Ss were more frustration tolerant than low creatives. Ried, King and Wickwire (1959) and Nair (1976) observed that high creatives were more persistent. Cattell and Butcher (1968) found from their studies on a number of samples of creative individuals that high creatives scored far higher on this factor than the average.

Factor D: High scorers on factor D of the HSPQ are excitable, impatient, showing off, distractible and show many nervous symptoms. Degan (1952), Lorr, *et al.,* (1953), Wittenborn (1951) found that high scorers on this factor tend to be characterised by restless overactivity and distractibility. They are also impulsive. Low scorers on this factor, on the other hand and stoical, complacent, constant and not restless. A low score rather than a high score on this factor is evidently more conducive for creative work.

The results of the present investigation, where high creatives (M = 9.66) got a significantly lower score on his factor compared to the low creatives (M = 10.34), corroborate this view.

Factor E: On factor E also a low score seems to favour creativity since the high creative group scored lower on this factor (M = 7.95) compared to the low creative group (M = 9.16). The *t* value of 5.71 for the significance of the difference between the two means was significant at 0.001 level.

Factor E on the HSPQ is related to submissiveness Vs dominance. High creatives on this factor are assertive, aggressive, stern, hostile, rebellious and head strong, while low scorers and submissive, obedient, mild, accommodating, and considerate. The first set of characteristics like stubbornness, hostility, head strong nature are not as conducive for creativity as mildness, calmness, etc.

Cattell (1969) points out that 'high dominance may lead to disobedience, head strong self will, independence and creativity of mind, and sometimes antisocial behaviour. But the more direct expressions are often controlled, and in 'sublimated' form the trait is not always rated undesirable. For example good sports performance and independence and creativity in arts and sciences and associated with dominance'.

From the results of the present study, however, creativity seems to be associated with submissiveness rather than dominance. An examination of the results of a similar analysis of the personality characteristics of high creative and low creative children belonging to different subgroups like boys, girls, urban, rural, etc., presented in the foregoing pages shows that in all subgroups, irrespective of the sex, locality, or class/grade of the Ss, children who were high in creativity got a lower score on this trait compared to those who were low in creativity.

In the step-wise multiple regression analysis carried out to probe into the relative effect of the different independent variables on creativity of the children also, it was found that this was one of the important factors that had a significant bearing on creativity, and that the partial r's obtained were negative, indicating a negative correlation between this factor and creativity of the children.

Factor F: It may be seen from the table that with regard to factor F, high creatives got a significantly higher mean score than low creatives. A person who scores high on this factor tends to be enthusiastic, cheerful, expressive, quick and alert. All these traits indeed facilitate one's creativity, rather than traits like sober, taciturn, serious, incommunicative, slow, cautious and sticking to inner values, which are characteristic of a low scorer on this factor.

According to Cattell (1969) desurgent individuals (low scorers on this factor) have generally been brought up with more severe, exacting standards and different conditions. This type of child rearing curbs creativity (Watson, 1957; Anderson and Anderson, 1965; Torrance, 1971).

Factor G: Factor G of the HSPQ is related to super ego strength. The G+ person (one who scores high on this factor), has a high super ego strength, is perseverent, conscientious, moralistic, dominated by sense of duty, and emotionally disciplined, while a G– person (the person who scores low on this factor), tends to be fickle, quitting, frivolous and slack. Needless to emphasise the first set of characteristics, rather than the second, help one's creative ability.

A number of studies indicate that the score on this factor determines 'success in a variety of performances requiring persistence, freedom from oscillation and good organisation of thinking'. Cattell, 1969, Joshi (1974) also found that high creatives had a higher super ego strength.

In the present investigation high creatives got a significantly higher mean score (M = 11.65) on this factor compared to the low creatives (M = 10.73) corroborating the above findings. Cattell and Butcher's (1968) personality profile of creative individuals shows that the creatives scored higher than the average on factors D and E, and lower than the average on factors F and G. But in the present investigation it was found that high creatives scored lower than the low creatives on factors D and E, and higher than the low creatives on factor F and G. The contradiction between these results may be because Cattell and Butcher's profile of creatives was based on studies on creative adults while the present investigation is on adolescents.

Factor H: With regard to factor H also high creative children obtained a higher mean score than low creative children. The person who scores high on this factor tends to be adventurous and socially bold; likes meeting people, is active, friendly and impulsive and has emotional and artistic interests, which are likely to make him more creativity prone, compared to qualities like timid, restrained, rule bound, threat sensitive and restricted interests, which are characteristic of low scorers on this factor.

Factor I: It has been found that an I+ individual (one who scores high on the factor I), shows a definite dislike for crude people and rough occupations. He has a taste for romantic travel and new experiences. He is imaginative and has an aesthetic mind and a love of dramatics. Artists score high on this factor (Cattell, 1969). This shows that an I+ is prone to be more creative. This is substantiated by the results of this investigation, where high creative got a higher mean score than low creatives.

Factor J: The J+ individual has been found to act individualistically, he prefers to do things on his own, is intellectually fastidious, and reflective, thinks over his mistakes and ways to avoid them. He has fewer friends. These are unmistakably the qualities required for creative thinking. It may be seen from Table—6.63 that high creatives scored higher on this factor compared to low creatives, who are characterised by qualities like going with the group, sinking personality into group enterprise, accepting common standards, etc., which are quite the opposite of divergent thinking and creative behaviour.

An examination of the profile of the creatives shows that, on factors H, I, J, creative individuals scored higher than the average (Cattell and Butcher, 1968). These results corroborate the findings of the present study.

Factor O: On factor O high creatives scored significantly lower (M = 8.43) than low creatives (M = 9.44) as in the case of factors A, D, and E. The person who scores high on this factor tends to be apprehensive, self-reproaching, insecure, worrying, troubled, depressed, overcome by moods, sensitive to people's approval or disapproval. He has a sense of inferiority and is easily down hearted. On the other hand persons who score low on this factor are self-assured, self-confident, cheerful, resilient, impenitent and insensitive to people's approval or disapproval which are more conducive for one to be creative.

Clinically, high factor O score was found in every one of forty profiles of clinical interest (prepared on the basis of scores on four thousand cases), including various forms of neurosis, psychosis, character disorder, etc. Occurrence of a high O in neurotics has been established beyond doubt (Cattell, 1969).

Evidently the characteristics cited earlier and neurotic tendency do not help creative thinking. Cattell and Butcher (1968) also observed that their creatives scored lower than the average on this factor.

Factor Q_2 : A person who scores high on factor Q_2 is self sufficient, resourceful, resolute and accustomed to making his own decisions, whereas a low scorer tends to be group dependent, goes with the group, strongly values social approval and is conventional, which are evidently not the qualities of a creative individual. Scientists, executives and other individuals, who think much on their own, turn out to be above average on this factor (Cattell, 1969).

Evidently high creative children should score higher on this factor than low creative children. The results of this study are in the expected direction. Gakher (1975), Gopal (1975) and Nair (1976) found that high creatives were characterised by greater self sufficiency. They had a lesser need for social approval (Rehman and Hussain, 1973). Cattell and Butcher's

(1968) profile of creatives also shows that creative individuals were characterised by a high score on this factor. These results support the findings of the present investigation.

Factor Q_3: The mean score of the high creative group on factor Q_3 was 12.89, while that of the low creative group was 11.32. The difference between the two means was significant at 0.001 level. Thus a high score on this factor seems to favour creativity.

High scorers on this factor have a high strength of self sentiment, they are self controlled, exacting, socially precise, compulsive and ambitious to do well, while Q_3- is essentially an untutored, unreflective emotionality. One who scores at the high end of this factor, a Q_3+, is a problem raiser and solution offerer in group situations. High Q_3 is found to be associated with success in mathematical, mechanical and production organisational activities. These observations corroborate the findings of the present study where high creatives were found to score higher on this factor compared to their low creative counterparts.

Goyal (1974) and Joshi (1974) also observed that high creatives had a higher self sentiment than low creatives. From the profile of creatives prepared by Cattell and Butcher also it may be seen that the creatives were characterised by a high score on this factor.

Factor Q_4: From Table—6.63, it may be seen that in the case of factor Q_4, the mean scores of the high creative group was 8.87 while that of the low creative group was 8.78. The difference between the two means was not significant ($t = 0.43$). Figure 11 shows the mean personality score of high creatives and low creatives on the different factors.

A similar analysis of the personality scores of high creative and low creative children was carriedout for the different subgroups of Ss. It may be seen from Table—6.64 that in the case of boys there were 74[3] who were high creative while 69 were low creative. The mean score of high creative children on personality factor A was 10.51 while that of low creative children was 11.07. The difference between the two means was significant at 0.05 level. As in the case of the whole group the high creative group obtained a lower mean score on this factor compared to the low creative group.

Table—6.64 Mean Personality Scores of High Creative and Low Creative Boys and the Results of *t* Test

Personality factor	*High creative (N = 74)*		*Low creative (N = 69)*		*t*
	Mean	*SD*	*Mean*	*SD*	
Factor A	10.51	2.49	11.07	2.70	2.07*
Factor B	6.45	1.83	4.88	2.39	6.41***
Factor C	12.08	2.91	10.93	3.07	3.98***
Factor D	9.74	3.03	10.45	2.37	2.57*
Factor E	8.50	2.96	9.80	3.16	4.43***
Factor F	10.09	2.51	9.16	2.87	3.40***
Factor G	11.70	2.96	11.36	2.96	1.18@
Factor H	12.14	3.33	10.57	2.47	5.52***
Factor I	10.97	2.51	10.77	2.81	0.75@
Factor J	9.04	2.85	8.91	2.84	0.45@
Factor O	8.00	2.44	9.71	3.03	6.17***
Factor Q_2	9.99	2.18	9.49	2.75	1.87@
Factor Q_3	13.12	2.99	10.96	3.32	7.78***
Factor Q_4	8.54	3.28	8.93	2.69	1.34@

Note: Please see note under Table—6.2.

On factor B, which is concerned with mental ability, high creative boys obtained a higher score than low creative boys. On factor C also higher personality scores were obtained by high creative children as in the case of the whole group. On factors D and E, low creative children got higher personality score than high creative children. These results are also in line with those obtained in the case of the whole group. On factor F high creative children obtained higher personality score than the low creative children. These results are also akin to those obtained in the case of the whole group.

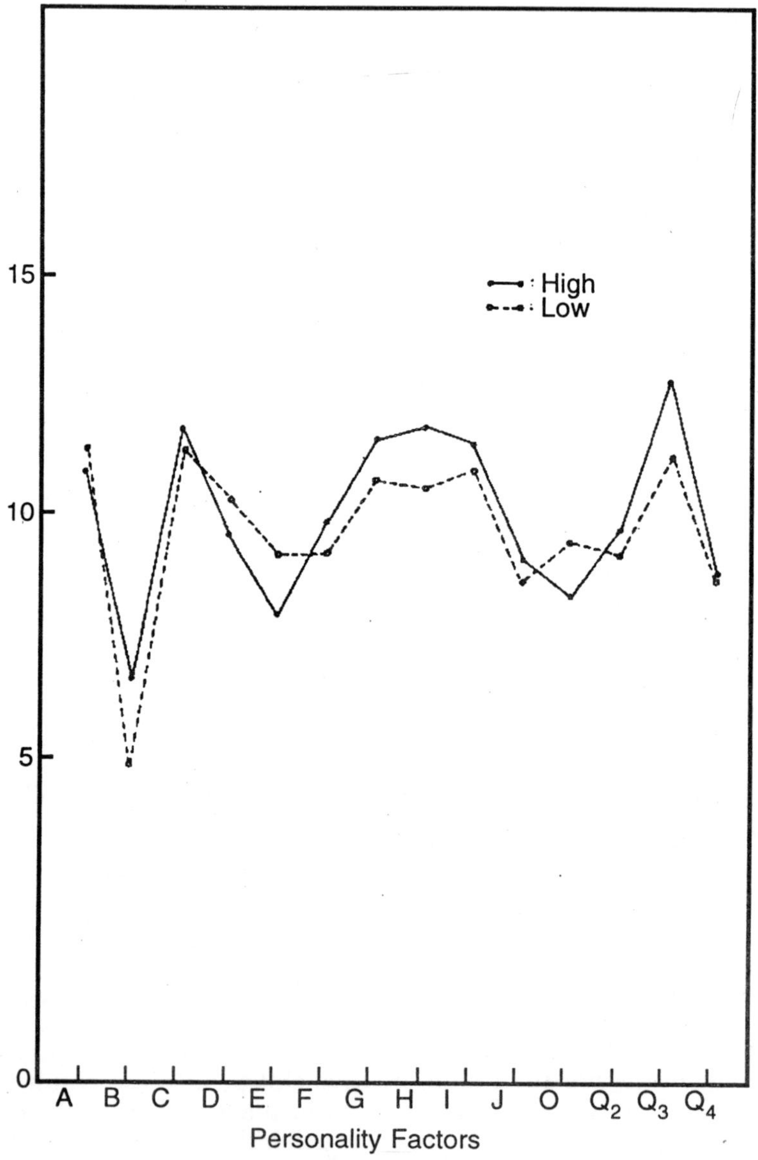

Fig.—11 Mean Personality Scores of High Creative and Low Creative Children (Whole Group)

With regard to factor G, though high creative boys obtained a higher score than low creative boys as in the case of the whole group, the difference between the means was not significant. The mean score of the high creative group on this factor was 11.70, while that of the low creative group was 11.36. The *t* value for the difference between means was 1.18, not significant at 0.05 level. Similarly in the case of factors I, J, and Q_2 though high creative boys obtained higher mean scores than low creative boys as in the case of the whole group, the difference between the means was not significant.

When a group of high creatives and low creatives were selected among girls and the personality scores of these two groups were analysed, the results are shown in Table—6.65 were obtained.

It may be seen from the table that the difference between the mean score of high creative and low creative girls were significant in the case of factor B, D, E, G, H, I, J, Q_2, Q_3, and Q_4. The trend of results was the same as that obtained for the whole group and also that for boys. For example, on factors D and E high creatives obtained a lower personality score compared to low creatives in the case of boys. Similar results were obtained in the case of girls also.

The difference that could be seen between the pattern of results obtained for boys and girls was only on factor C and factor Q_4. On factor Q_4 high creative girls obtained a significant higher personality score than low creative girls. In the case of boys high creatives tended to obtain somewhat lower personality score than low creatives though the difference between the means was not significant.

On factor C, high creative boys obtained a higher personality score than low creative boys. In the case of girls high creatives obtained somewhat lower score than low creatives. The difference between means was, however, not significant.

It may be concluded, therefore, that the overall pattern of results obtained with regard to personality difference between high creative girls and low creative girls was similar to that obtained in the case of boys.

Table—6.65 Mean Personality Scores of High Creative and Low Creative Girls and the Results of *t* Test

Personality factors	*High creative (N = 60)*		*Low creative (N = 68)*		*t*
	Mean	*SD*	*Mean*	*SD*	
Factor A	11.38	2.74	11.72	2.87	1.18@
Factor B	6.59	1.61	4.85	2.24	7.25***
Factor C	11.55	3.43	11.85	2.96	0.99@
Factor D	9.76	2.75	10.34	2.97	1.99*
Factor E	7.35	2.76	8.66	3.18	4.41***
Factor F	9.76	3.17	9.35	3.16	1.31@
Factor G	11.50	2.65	10.22	3.24	4.31***
Factor H	11.97	3.26	10.71	3.36	4.02***
Factor I	12.38	2.47	11.21	3.18	4.04***
Factor J	9.38	2.82	8.66	2.34	2.58**
Factor O	9.02	2.66	9.26	2.96	0.86@
Factor Q_2	9.59	2.24	8.85	2.81	2.69**
Factor Q_3	12.71	2.99	11.75	3.42	3.11**
Factor Q_4	9.23	2.99	8.47	2.82	2.57*

Note: Please see note under Table—6.2.

Table—6.66 shows the mean personality scores of high creative and low creative rural children, while Table—6.67 shows the mean personality scores of high creative and low creative urban children. Similarly, the results obtained in the case of high and low creatives among VIII, IX and X class students are presented in Tables—6.68, 6.69, and 6.70 respectively.

Table—6.66 Mean Personality Scores of High Creative and Low Creative Rural Children and the Results of *t* Test

Personality factors	*High creative (N = 69)*		*Low creative (N = 67)*		*t*
	Mean	*SD*	*Mean*	*SD*	
Factor A	10.90	2.63	11.79	2.60	3.22**
Factor B	6.01	1.81	4.79	2.67	4.76***
Factor C	12.14	3.20	11.40	3.19	2.42*
Factor D	9.13	3.06	10.52	2.61	4.82***
Factor E	8.16	3.34	9.10	2.88	3.13**
Factor F	9.65	2.79	9.28	2.84	1.28@
Factor G	12.14	2.94	11.03	3.21	3.70***
Factor H	12.29	3.31	11.04	2.87	4.13***
Factor I	12.22	2.31	11.22	2.96	3.56***
Factor J	9.26	3.11	8.43	2.44	2.90**
Factor O	8.10	2.83	9.15	2.81	3.63***
Factor Q_2	9.94	2.19	8.81	2.88	4.15***
Factor Q_3	13.46	3.02	10.69	3.48	8.97***
Factor Q_4	8.62	3.08	8.25	2.81	1.25@

Note: Please see note under Table—6.2.

Table—6.67 Mean Personality Scores of High Creative and Low Creative Urban Children and the Results of *t* Test

Personality factors	*High creative (N = 74)*		*Low creative (N = 71)*		*t*
	Mean	*SD*	*Mean*	*SD*	
Factor A	10.86	2.65	10.97	2.92	$0.38^{@}$
Factor B	6.97	1.49	4.96	1.91	9.28^{***}
Factor C	11.55	3.09	11.30	2.99	$0.89^{@}$
Factor D	10.00	2.92	10.04	2.79	$0.15^{@}$
Factor E	7.68	2.36	9.13	3.63	5.03^{***}
Factor F	9.97	2.78	9.18	3.15	2.76^{**}
Factor G	11.30	2.62	10.41	3.08	3.17^{**}
Factor H	11.92	3.26	10.34	2.98	5.39^{***}
Factor I	11.27	2.82	10.82	3.07	$1.59^{@}$
Factor J	9.27	2.69	9.06	2.68	$0.78^{@}$
Factor O	8.70	2.37	9.80	3.06	4.01^{***}
Factor Q_2	9.69	2.04	9.55	2.68	$0.55^{@}$
Factor Q_3	12.57	2.92	11.94	3.13	2.16^{*}
Factor Q_4	9.09	3.15	9.21	2.72	0.41^{*}

Note: Please see note under Table—6.2.

Table—6.68 Mean Personality Scores of High Creative and Low Creative VIII Class Children and the Results of *t* Test

Personality factors	*High creative (N = 49)*		*Low creative (N = 48)*		*t*
	Mean	*SD*	*Mean*	*SD*	
Factor A	11.35	2.76	11.19	2.74	$0.43^{@}$
Factor B	5.90	2.18	4.90	2.70	3.16^{**}
Factor C	11.55	2.69	11.27	3.22	$0.80^{@}$
Factor D	10.35	3.62	10.36	2.58	$0.02^{@}$
Factor E	7.94	2.93	9.48	2.62	4.55^{***}
Factor F	10.10	2.74	9.04	2.75	3.15^{***}
Factor G	10.80	3.05	10.50	2.99	$0.84^{@}$
Factor H	11.47	3.00	10.90	2.71	$1.67^{@}$
Factor I	12.20	2.38	10.38	2.73	5.63^{***}
Factor J	8.39	2.31	8.33	2.66	$0.17^{@}$
Factor O	9.59	2.64	9.44	2.37	$0.48^{@}$
Factor Q_2	8.65	2.60	9.00	2.89	$1.03^{@}$
Factor Q_3	12.24	2.95	11.19	3.16	2.98^{**}
Factor Q_4	9.12	2.46	8.85	3.33	$0.77^{@}$

Note: Please see note under Table—6.2.

Table—6.69 Mean Personality Scores of High Creative and Low Creative IX Class Children and the Results of *t* Test

Personality factors	*High creative (N = 45)*		*Low creative (N = 44)*		*t*
	Mean	*SD*	*Mean*	*SD*	
Factor A	11.40	2.73	11.41	2.71	0.03@
Factor B	6.53	1.87	4.70	1.73	6.43***
Factor C	11.82	3.13	11.89	2.76	0.18@
Factor D	9.58	2.80	10.32	3.06	2.04*
Factor E	7.18	2.50	8.75	3.52	4.27***
Factor F	9.31	2.76	8.68	2.98	1.75@
Factor G	11.62	2.59	11.09	2.97	1.50@
Factor H	12.04	2.98	10.34	3.17	4.58***
Factor I	11.69	3.03	10.64	3.08	2.84**
Factor J	9.24	2.93	8.68	2.20	1.66@
Factor O	8.56	2.87	9.64	3.68	2.81**
Factor Q_2	9.51	1.70	9.30	2.36	0.71@
Factor Q_3	12.56	2.97	12.02	4.15	1.33@
Factor Q_4	8.40	3.29	8.73	2.72	0.89@

Note: Please see note under Table—6.2.

Table—6.70 Mean Personality Scores of High Creative and Low Creative X Class Children and the Results of t Test

Personality factors	High creative (N = 51)		Low creative (N = 48)		t
	Mean	SD	Mean	SD	
Factor A	10.67	2.36	11.69	2.97	3.10**
Factor B	6.96	1.27	5.40	1.91	6.15***
Factor C	11.94	3.58	10.48	2.57	4.15***
Factor D	9.53	2.90	10.65	2.73	3.31***
Factor E	8.08	2.91	8.40	3.38	0.88@
Factor F	10.12	2.58	9.29	2.47	2.58**
Factor G	11.88	3.03	10.81	3.12	3.03**
Factor H	12.31	3.44	10.38	3.00	5.38***
Factor I	11.29	2.68	11.67	2.47	1.15@
Factor J	9.29	2.97	9.65	2.28	1.08@
Factor O	7.86	2.27	9.25	2.99	4.25***
Factor Q_2	10.16	2.37	9.19	2.23	3.18**
Factor Q_3	13.25	3.07	12.31	3.20	2.64**
Factor Q_4	9.20	3.13	9.42	2.67	0.64@

Note: Please see note under Table—6.2.

An examination of the results presented in Tables—6.63 to 6.70 shows a similar trend of results with regard to the personality scores of high creatives Vs low creatives, irrespective of the sex, locality or class of the Ss. That in the case of some of the subgroups the *t* values were not significant, though the direction of the difference between the mean scores was the same as that in the case of the whole group, may be because of the smaller number of high creatives and low creatives in the subgroups in contrast to the number of high creatives and low creatives in the whole group.

2. Intelligence (Mental Ability)

There is no gain saying the controversy, intelligence Vs creativity, is that which sparked off research work in the area of creativity. Even 40 years after the happy moment for psychological research, when Guilford hypothesised a distinction between intelligence and creativity, the controversy between the two is yet to be completely resolved. As a matter of fact this is the one area which attracted the greatest attention of researchers. Yet, there are as many questions in this area, as those to which answers seem to have been found.

Do the high and low creatives differ in their intelligence? To probe into this the mental ability scores of the two groups of children were analysed. Table—6.71 shows the means and SDs of the high creative and low creative groups of children on Raven's Progressive Matrices.

It may be seen from the table that considering the whole group of Ss, the mean mental ability score of the high creative group was 37.68 while that of the low creative group was 21.94 (See Fig. 12). *t* test was applied to see whether the difference between the two means was significant. The *t* value obtained was 41.81 which was highly significant even at 0.001 level for 276 df.

Considering different subgroups, it could be observed from the table that the mean mental ability scores of high creative boys was 39.00 while that of low creative boys was

Table—6.71 Mean Mental Ability Scores of Different Subgroups of High Creative and Low Creative Children and the Results of *t* Test

	High creative			Low creative			t
	N	*Mean*	*SD*	*N*	*Mean*	*SD*	
Whole group	143	37.68	10.68	135	21.94	9.03	41.81***
Boys	74	39.00	10.94	69	22.12	9.90	31.28***
Girls	66	35.45	10.90	68	21.54	8.32	25.94***
Rural	69	34.48	11.33	67	21.58	8.98	23.61***
Urban	74	39.82	9.59	71	22.17	9.29	34.59***
VIII	49	28.73	10.61	48	20.40	7.99	13.47***
IX	45	36.53	12.34	44	21.20	10.40	21.45***
X	51	40.57	9.57	48	28.50	9.14	19.62***

Note: Please see note under Table—6.2.

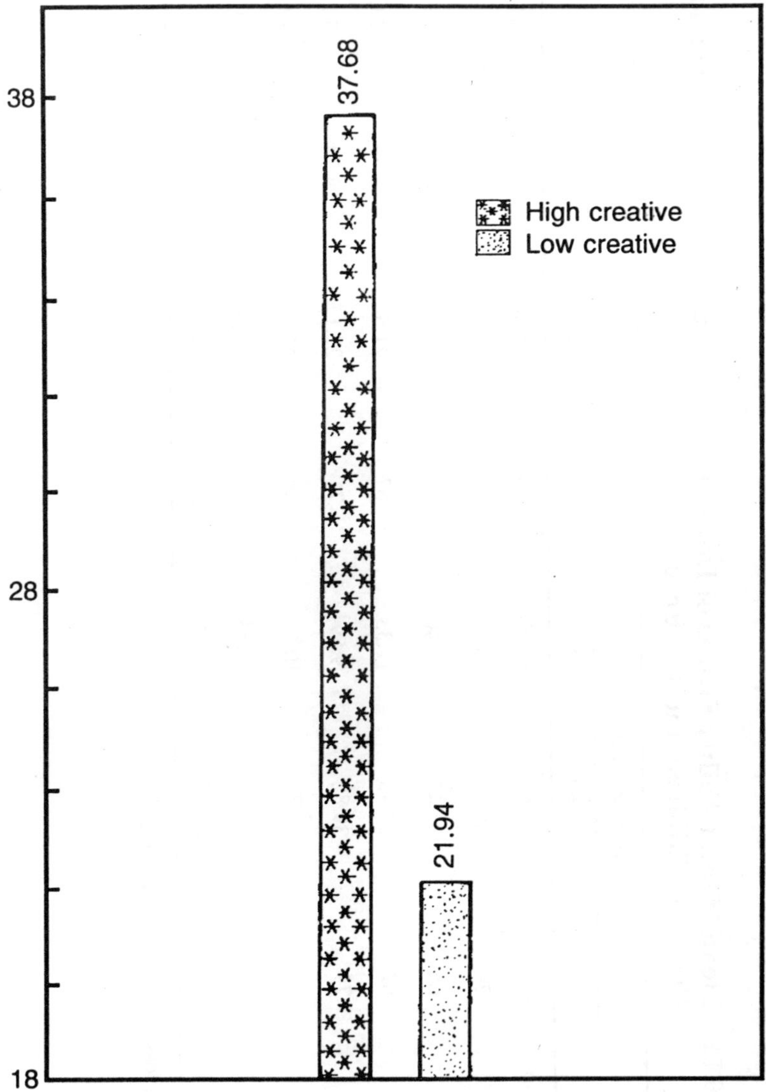

Fig.—12 Mean Metal Ability Scores of High Creative and Low Creative Children (Whole Group).

22.12. The difference between these two means was also significant at 0.001 level ($t = 31.28$). The mean intelligence scores of high and low creative girls were 35.45 and 21.54 respectively. The difference between these two means also was significant at 0.001 level.

When the Ss were classified as per the locality to which they belonged, in the case of rural children the mean score of the high creative group was 34.48 while it was 21.58 for the low creative group. The difference between the two means ($t = 23.61$) was significant at 0.001 level. Similar results were obtained in the case of children hailing from urban localities. This shows that high creatives were more intelligent than low creatives irrespective of their locality or sex.

Similar results were obtained when the children were classified according to their class/school grade.

It may be concluded therefore, that irrespective of their sex, locality or class in which they were studying, high creative children were significantly more intelligence than low creative children.

The results of the present study fall in line with those of Phatak (1961, 1962), Raina (1968), Trivedi (1969), Passi (1972), Sharma (1971), Sharma (1972, 1974), Azmi (1974), Bedi (1974), Goyal (1974), Joshi (1974), Kumari (1975), Dhaliwal and Saini (1976), Dutt *et al.,* (1977), Gakhar and Kaura (1977), Singh, Mathur and Saxena (1977), Singh (1978), Patel and Joshi (1976), Badrinath and Satyanarayana (1979), Gulati (1979), Gupta (1979), Jarial (1979), Sandhu (1979), Jarial and Sharma (1980), Gakhar *et al.,* (1980), Chadha and Sen (1981) and Venkata Rami Reddy and Balakrishna Reddy (1983).

3. Socio-Economic Status

Not many studies have been reported on the relation between socio-economic status and creativity. Hence an attempt was made to see whether high and low creatives differed in the socio-economic status.

As in the case of personality and intelligence, the SES scores of the high creative and low creative groups of children were analysed by applying t test. The mean SES scores of high creatives and low creatives are shown in Table—6.72 along with the results of the t test.

Considering the whole group of Ss, the mean SES score of the high creatives was 24.90 while that of the low creatives was 17.03 (See Fig. 13). The difference between the two means was significant at 0.001 level for 276 df. This shows that high creative children belonged to a high socio-economic strata compared to those who were low in creativity.

Considering different subgroups, in the case of boys the mean SES scores of the high creatives was 21.51 while that of low creatives was 18.68. The difference between these two means was also significant at 0.001 level (t = 5.56), showing that high and low creatives differed significantly with regard to their SES.

In the case of girls the mean SES scores of high and low creative Ss were 28.20 and 16.18 respectively. The difference between these two means also was significant at 0.001 level.

When the Ss were classified as per the locality to which they belonged, in the case of children belonging to rural areas, the mean SES score of the high creative group was 20.61 while that of the low creative group was 15.73. The difference between the two means was significant at 0.001 level indicating that Ss belonging to the high creative group were higher in their SES than those belonging to the low creative group. This was true in the case of children belonging to urban localities also.

Similar results were obtained when the children were classified according to the class to which they belonged.

Families belonging to higher socio-economic strata provide better facilities at home. Children from these families may have more opportunities to read general books,

Table—6.72 Mean SES Scores of Different Subgroups of High Creative and Low Creative Children and the Results of t Test

	High creative			*Low creative*			t
	N	*Mean*	*SD*	*N*	*Mean*	*SD*	
Whole group	143	24.90	10.36	135	17.03	7.77	21.81***
Boys	74	21.51	10.45	69	18.68	8.13	5.56***
Girls	66	28.20	8.84	68	16.18	7.32	24.46***
Rural	69	20.61	9.77	67	15.73	7.07	9.81***
Urban	74	27.41	8.71	71	18.41	8.36	18.71***
VIII	49	24.35	8.81	48	17.12	6.25	12.97***
IX	45	24.56	10.36	44	16.23	8.47	12.81***
X	51	24.24	10.42	48	17.94	7.19	10.58***

Note: Please see note under Table—6.2.

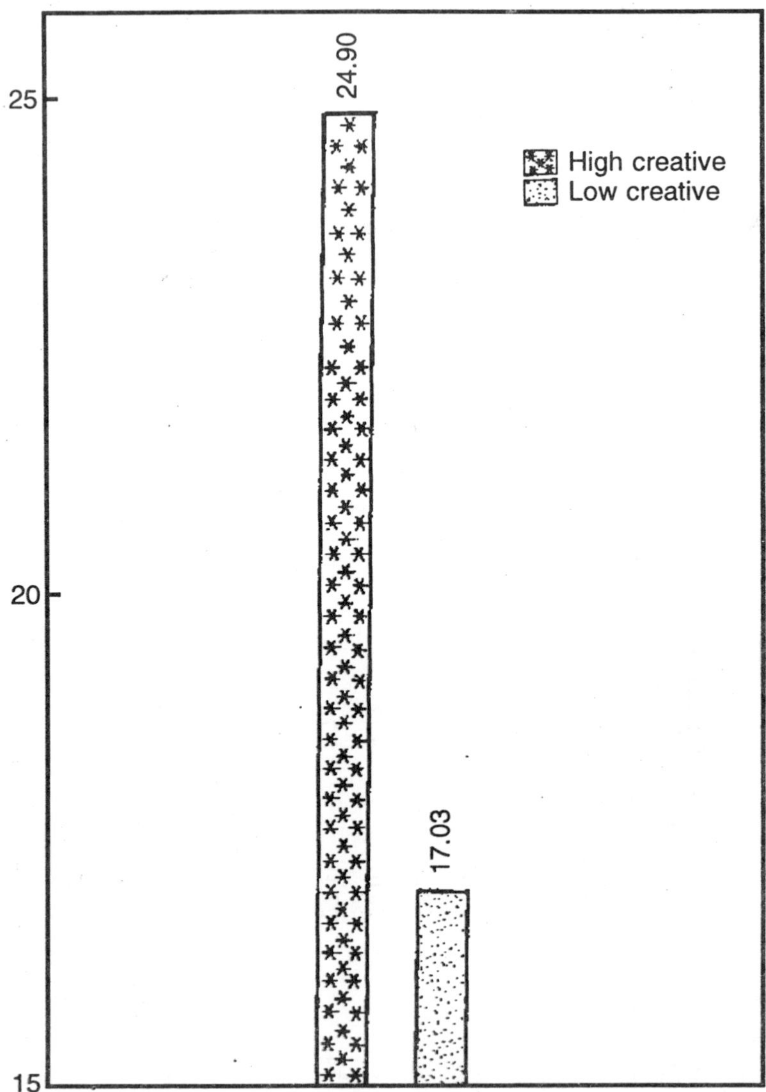

Fig.—13 Mean SES Scores of High Creative and Low Creative Children (Whole Group).

magazines, etc. In other words the children from higher socio-economic strata may have a more stimulating environment, which helps development of creative thinking.

It may also be mentioned in this context that it has been found in the present investigation, that there is a significant association between the habit of reading magazines, story books etc., among the children and their creativity.

It may be concluded from the above results that high creative children belonged to a higher socio-economic status compared to low creative children. This was true irrespective of the sex of the children or the locality from which they hailed or the class/grade to which they belonged.

The results of the present study corroborate the findings of Vohra (1975), Gupta (1976), Rawat and Agarwal (1977), Singh (1977), Thorat (1977), Singh (1978), Srivastava (1978), Jarial (1979), Sharma (1979, 1980), Bhargava (1979), Ahmed (1980), Vijayalakshmi (1980), and Singh (1980) who reported that creatives come from families belonging to higher socio-economic strata.

4. Familial and Personal Characteristics and Habits of Life

As mentioned in Chapter 3 and 4 Torrance (1962), Getzels and Jackson (1962), Lugo and Hershey (1976), Jha (1978) have pointed out certain familial and personal characteristics and habits of life which may have an influence on the development of creativity among children. To probe into this certain questions related to these aspects were included in the personal data sheet. The present section deals with finding out whether these familial and personal characteristics differentiate high creatives and low creatives. For example does the habit of reading magazines, story books, etc., differentiate high creatives and low creatives. In other words does the incidence of frequent reading of magazines, etc., occur more in high creative children than low creative children?

I. To probe into this the following question was given to the students: "Do you read magazines, story books, etc? Frequently/Occasionally/Rarely or Never".

As mentioned earlier in the whole sample of 900 children, there were 143 who were high creatives and 135 who were low creatives. Out of them 39 marked frequently for the above question (Table—6.73). 26 of the 39 who marked frequently for the above question fell in the high creative group while the remaining 13 fell in the low creative group. Thus the incidence of frequent reading of magazines, etc., seems to be more among the high creatives rather than among low creatives. It may also be seen from the table that our of the 58 who marked rarely or never for this question, 40 (68.97 per cent) fell in the low creative group while 18 (31.03 per cent) fell in the high creative group. This shows that rarity of reading magazines etc., seems to be more prominent in the low creative group.

In line with Getzels and Jackson (1962) who in their famous study 'creativity and intelligence' tried to analyse the incidence of certain characteristics in their high creatives in contrast to their high intelligents, X^2 test in contingency tables was applied to the above data. The obtained X^2 value was 14.06, significant at 0.001 level for 2 df.[4] This shows that there was a significant difference between high creatives and low creatives with regard to their habit of reading magazines, story books, etc. Frequent reading of magazines, etc., was characteristic of high creatives rather than low creatives.

Similar analysis was carried out for different subgroups of Ss like boys, girls, etc. It may be seen from the table that among the high and low creative boys 17 read magazines, story books, etc., frequently, while 21 read rarely or never. The remaining 105 marked 'occasionally' for the above question. Among the 17 boys who read magazines etc., frequently, 12 (70.59 per cent) fell in the high creative group, while 5 (29.41 per cent) fell in the low creative group. Out of the 21 boys who read story books, etc., rarely or never, 28.57

Table—6.73 Number of Percentage (given in parentheses) of High Creative and Low Creative Ss Giving Different Responses for the Question: "Do you Read Magazines, Story Books, etc? Frequently/Occasionally/Rarely or Never" and the Results of X^2 Test

Group		*High creative*	*Low creative*	*Total*	X^2 *(df = 2)*
1	*2*	*3*	*4*	*5*	*6*
	Frequently	26 (66.67)	13 (33.33)	39	
Whole group	Occasionally	99 (54.70)	82 (45.30)	181	14.06***
	Rarely or Never	18 (31.03)	40 (68.97)	58	
	Frequently	12 (70.59)	5 (29.41)	17	
Boys	Occasionally	56 (53.33)	49 (46.67)	105	7.04*
	Rarely or Never	6 (28.57)	15 (71.43)	21	
	Frequently	14 (63.64)	8 (36.36)	22	
Girls	Occasionally	43 (53.09)	38 (46.91)	81	7.37*
	Rarely and Never	9 (29.03)	22 (70.97)	31	
	Frequently	11 (57.89)	8 (42.11)	19	
Rural	Occasionally	51 (56.04)	40 (43.96)	91	7.31*
	Rarely and Never	7 (26.92)	19 (73.08)	26	

(Contd...)

Table—6.73 (Contd...)

1	*2*	*3*	*4*	*5*	*6*
	Frequently	14 (56.04)	5 (43.96)	19	
Urban	Occasionally	50 (53.19)	44 (46.81)	94	9.09*
	Rarely or Never	10 (31.25)	22 (68.75)	32	
	Frequently	8 (53.33)	7 (46.67)	15	
VIII	Occasionally	36 (54.55)	30 (45.45)	66	2.85@
	Rarely and Never	5 (31.25)	11 (68.75)	16	
	Frequently	10 (71.43)	4 (28.57)	14	
IX	Occasionally	26 (47.27)	29 (52.73)	55	2.92@
	Rarely and Never	9 (45.00)	11 (55.00)	20	
	Frequently	8 (57.14)	6 (42.86)	14	
X	Occasionally	40 (58.82)	28 (41.18)	68	9.44*
	Rarely or Never	3 (17.65)	14 (82.35)	17	

per cent fell in high creative group while 71.43 per cent fell in the low creative group.

X^2 test was applied as in the earlier case to see the significance of the difference between the two groups. The X^2 value obtained was significant at 0.05 level ($X^2 = 7.04$) for 2 df. This shows that as in the case of the whole group of Ss, among boys also there was a significant difference between high creative and low creative children with regard to the frequency with which they read other books. Similar results were obtained in the case of girls ($X^2 = 7.37$ significant at 0.05 level).

When the children were classified as rural and urban depending upon the locality to which they belonged the X^2 values obtained were 7.31 and 9.09, both of which were significant at 0.05 level. This shows that there was a significant difference between high creatives and low creatives with regard to the frequency of their reading of other general books, irrespective of the locality to which they belonged.

Does the relation hold good irrespective of the school grade/class to which the children belonged? An examination of Table—6.73 shows that the X^2 value was significant in the case of X class students. But in the case of students of VIII and IX classes the X^2 values obtained were not significant at 0.05 level for 2 df, though the trend of results was in the expected direction (i.e.) larger percentage of high creatives and smaller percentage of low creatives marked 'frequently', and smaller percentage of high creatives and larger percentage of low creatives marked 'rarely or never' for the question. Will it be that the maturity of the students of VIII and IX classes is not enough for their creative thinking to be stimulated by mere reading of story books, magazines etc. However, it may be mentioned in this context that it was found in another study that when the children were told stories selected from children's magazines, and guided to think of the various possibilities for a situation to occur or not to occur, etc., their creativity scores increased significantly as measured by a post test (Venkata Rami Reddy and Vijayakumari).

Magazines contain different types of stories depicting various situations. Though imaginary and fictious, they provide the children with opportunity to think about various objects, places, events, situations, etc., which help in the development of their divergent thinking.

It may be concluded from the above analysis that generally speaking high creatives and low creatives differed with regard to the frequency with which they read magazines, story books, etc.

II. It has been suggested by many that the creatives are likely to be unconventional. They would like to break new ground. According to Torrance (1962) their work is characterised by the production of ideas off the beaten track, outside the mold. They enjoy the risk and uncertainty of the unknown (Getzels and Jackson, 1962). To probe into the substainability of this contention, the following question was included in the personal data sheet: "When a work is given, how do you prefer to do it? Like others/in a new way".

The responses given by the high creative and low creative groups of Ss for this question are shown in Table—6.74. It may be seen that among the 77 who marked 'like others' for this question 30 (38.96 per cent) fell in the high creative group while 47 (61.04 per cent) fell in the low creative group. Among those who preferred to do things in a new way 113 (56.22 per cent) belonged to the high creative group while 88 (47.38 per cent) belonged to the low creative group. X^2 test was applied as in the earlier case to see the significance of the difference between the two groups. The X^2 value obtained was 6.64, significant at 0.05 level for 1 df.

It may be seen from the table that between high creatives and low creatives, relatively larger percentage of those who marked 'like others' fell in the low creative group than in the high creative group. Among those who marked 'in a new way', larger percentage were in the high creative group than in the low creative group. It may be concluded,

Table—6.74 Number and Percentage (given in parantheses) of High Creative and Low Creative Ss Giving Different Responses for the Question: "When a Work is Given, How Do You Prefer to Do it? Like Others/or in a New Way" and the Results of the X^2 Test

Group		*High creative*	*Low creative*	*Total*	X^2 *(df = 1)*
1	*2*	*3*	*4*	*5*	*6*
Whole group	Like others	30 (38.96)	47 (61.04)	77	6.64*
	In a new way	113 (56.22)	88 (47.38)	201	
Boys	Like others	15 (34.88)	28 (65.12)	43	7.00*
	In a new way	39 (59.00)	41 (41.00)	100	
Girls	Like others	15 (46.88)	17 (53.12)	32	0.10@
	In a new way	51 (50.00)	51 (50.00)	102	

(Contd...)

Table—6.74 (Contd...)

1	*2*	*3*	*4*	*5*	*6*
Rural	Like others	17 (38.64)	27 (61.36)	44	$3.81^{@}$
	In a new way	52 (56.52)	40 (43.48)	92	
Urban	Like others	13 (38.24)	21 (61.76)	34	$2.91^{@}$
	In a new way	61 (54.95)	50 (45.05)	111	
VIII	Like others	7 (26.92)	19 (73.08)	26	7.91^{**}
	In a new way	42 (59.15)	29 (40.85)	71	
IX	Like others	12 (40.00)	18 (60.00)	30	$2.02^{@}$
	In a new way	33 (55.93)	26 (44.07)	59	
X	Like others	11 (44.00)	14 (56.00)	25	$0.76^{@}$
	In a new way	40 (54.05)	34 (45.95)	74	

therefore, that the tendency to do things in a new way was related to the creativity of the Ss.

Similar trend of results could be seen in all the subgroups. But the X^2 value was significant only in the case of boys and VIII class children. In other cases the X^2 was not significant at 0.05 level.

III. Do high creative children get silly ideas more often than others? According to Torrance (1962), creative children have a reputation for having wild or silly ideas. Teachers and peers also agree on this point. To probe into this the question "Do you get silly ideas? Frequently/ Occasionally/Rarely" was given and the responses of the Ss for this item were analysed. Table—6.75 shows the results of this analysis.

It could be seen from the table that out of the 22 students who marked 'frequently' for this question, 50 per cent belonged to high creative group and 50 per cent belonged to the low creative group. Similarly, there was not much difference between the percentage of high creatives and low creatives who rarely got silly ideas. The X^2 value was evidently not significant.

Similar results were obtained in the case of all subgroups except for children from urban localities.

It may be concluded therefore, that the creativity of the children does not seem to be associated with the frequency with which they got silly ideas. These results are not in line with those reported by Torrance (1962).

IV. Torrance has pointed out that "although their humour and playfulness may win some friends for them, it does not always make them 'easier to live with'. In fact, it may make their behaviour even more unpredictable than otherwise and this probably makes their presence in a group upsetting". Torrance also found that many highly creative children find quite early that the use of their creative talents alienates them from their friends. Buhl (1961) supports these findings.

Table—6.75 Number and Percentage (given in parantheses) of High Creative and Low Creative Ss Giving Different Responses for the Question: "Do You Get Silly Ideas? Frequently/Occasionally/Rarely" and the Results of X^2 Test

Group		*High creative*	*Low creative*	*Total*	X^2 *(df = 2)*
1	2	3	4	5	6
	Frequently	11 (50.00)	11 (50.00)	22	
Whole	Occasionally	82 (48.24)	88 (51.76)	170	2.26@
	Rarely	50 (58.14)	36 (41.86)	86	
	Frequently	6 (46.15)	7 (53.85)	13	
Boys	Occasionally	45 (48.39)	48 (51.61)	93	2.19@
	Rarely	23 (62.16)	14 (37.84)	37	
	Frequently	5 (55.56)	4 (44.44)	9	
Girls	Occasionally	36 (46.15)	42 (53.83)	78	0.73@
	Rarely	25 (53.19)	22 (46.81)	47	

(*Contd...*)

Table —6.75 (Contd...)

1	2	3	4	5	6
	Frequently	6 (66.67)	3 (33.33)	9	
Rural	Occasionally	42 (51.22)	40 (48.78)	82	1.22@
	Rarely	21 (46.67)	24 (53.33)	45	
	Frequently	6 (46.15)	7 (53.85)	13	
Urban	Occasionally	39 (42.86)	52 (57.14)	91	8.92@
	Rarely	29 (70.73)	12 (29.27)	41	
	Frequently	5 (83.33)	1 (16.67)	6	
VIII	Occasionally	29 (46.77)	33 (53.23)	62	2.95@
	Rarely	15 (51.72)	14 (48.28)	29	
	Frequently	4 (26.67)	11 (73.33)	15	
IX	Occasionally	28 (54.90)	23 (45.10)	51	4.14@
	Rarely	13 (56.52)	10 (43.48)	23	
	Frequently	5 (45.45)	6 (54.55)	11	
X	Occasionally	26 (48.15)	28 (51.85)	54	1.13@
	Rarely	20 (58.82)	14 (41.18)	34	

To probe into this point of view, the following two questions were included in the personal data sheet: "Do you have many friends?: Yes/No", and "Do others feel that it is difficult to adjust with you?: Many/Some/None or very few". An analysis of the responses of the different subgroups of Ss for these two questions is presented in Tables—6.76 and 6.77.

It may be seen from Table—6.76 that in the case of the whole group, 252 pointed out that they had many friends, while only 26 felt that they had few friends. Out of the 252 who said they had many friends 50.79 per cent were high creatives while 49.21 per cent were low creatives. Evidently there is not much difference between these percentages. Among the 26 Ss who did not have many friends 57.69 per cent were high creatives while 42.31 per cent were low creatives. The chi-square test yielded a X^2 value of 0.45 which was not significant at 0.05 level for 1 df. Similar results were obtained in the case of all the subgroups of Ss.

This shows that high creatives and low creatives did not differ with regard to the number of friends they have. These results do not corroborate the observations of Torrance (1962) cited earlier.

V. Table—6.77 shows the analysis of the responses of the Ss to the question whether others find it difficult to adjust with them. It may be seen from the table that in the case of the whole group of high creatives and low creatives 40 pointed out that many find it difficult to adjust with them. Out of them 17.50 per cent were high creatives while 82.50 per cent were low creatives. Out of the 150 Ss who mentioned that none or very few feel difficult to adjust with them, 60 per cent were high creatives while 40 per cent were low creatives. This shows that greater percentage of low creatives than high creatives mentioned that many find it difficult to adjust with them. In contrast lesser percentage of low creatives than the high creatives mentioned that very few find it difficult to adjust with them. Similar results were

Table—6.76 Number and Percentage (given in parantheses) of High Creative and Low Creative Ss Giving Different Responses for the Question: "Do You Have Many Friends?: Yes/No" and the Results of X^2 Test

Group		*High creative*	*Low creative*	*Total*	X^2 (*df* = *1*)
1	2	*3*	*4*	*5*	*6*
Whole	Yes	128 (50.79)	124 (49.21)	252	0.45@
	No	15 (57.69)	11 (42.31)	26	
Boys	Yes	68 (51.52)	64 (48.48)	132	0.04@
	No	6 (54.55)	5 (45.45)	11	
	Yes	58 (48.33)	62 (51.67)	120	0.39@
	No	8 (57.14)	6 (42.86)	14	

(Contd...)

Table—6.76 (Contd...)

1	2	3	4	5	6
Rural	Yes	63 (51.64)	59 (48.36)	122	0.39@
	No	6 (42.86)	8 (57.14)	14	
Urban	Yes	67 (49.63)	68 (50.37)	135	1.55@
	No	7 (70.00)	3 (30.00)	10	
VIII	Yes	47 (51.65)	44 (48.35)	91	0.76@
	No	2 (33.33)	4 (66.67)	6	
IX	Yes	39 (45.56)	43 (52.44)	82	3.76@
	No	6 (85.71)	1 (14.29)	7	
X	Yes	48 (53.33)	42 (46.67)	90	1.31@
	No	3 (33.33)	6 (66.67)	9	

Table—6.77 Number and Percentage (given in parantheses) of High Creative and Low Creative Ss Giving Different Responses for the Question: "Do Others Feel that it is Difficult to Adjust with you? Many/Some/None or Very Few" and the Results of X^2 Test

Group		*High creative*	*Low creative*	*Total*	X^2 $(df = 2)$
1	2	*3*	*4*	*5*	*6*
	Many	7 (17.50)	33 (82.50)	40	
Whole	Some	46 (52.27)	42 (47.73)	88	22.87***
	None or very few	90 (60.00)	60 (40.00)	150	
	Many	5 (21.74)	18 (78.26)	23	
Boys	Some	19 (45.24)	23 (54.76)	42	13.78**
	None or very few	50 (64.10)	28 (35.90)	78	
	Many	2 (11.76)	15 (88.24)	17	
Girls	Some	26 (56.52)	20 (43.48)	46	11.05**
	None or very few	38 (53.52)	33 (46.48)	71	

(Contd...)

Table—6.77 (Contd...)

1	*2*	*3*	*4*	*5*	*6*
	Many	6 (21.43)	22 (78.57)	28	
Rural	Some	21 (52.50)	19 (47.50)	40	12.98**
	None or very few	42 (61.76)	26 (38.24)	68	
	Many	1 (9.09)	10 (90.91)	11	
Urban	Some	24 (48.98)	25 (51.02)	49	9.31**
	None or very few	49 (57.65)	36 (42.35)	85	
	Many	4 (20.00)	16 (80.00)	20	
VIII	Some	18 (56.25)	14 (43.75)	32	9.49**
	None or very few	27 (60.00)	18 (40.00)	45	
	Many	3 (25.00)	9 (75.00)	12	
IX	Some	7 (33.33)	14 (66.67)	21	8.82*
	None or very few	25 (62.50)	21 (37.50)	56	
	Many	1 (16.67)	5 (83.33)	6	
X	Some	20 (54.05)	17 (45.95)	37	3.11@
	None or very few	30 (53.57)	26 (46.43)	56	

obtained in all the subgroups. The X^2 values were significant for all subgroups except in the case of X class children.

The results show that it is the low creatives, who feel that many find it difficult to adjust with them rather than the high creatives contradicting the observation of Torrance (1962).

The contradiction between the results of the two studies may be because Torrance's study was on the personality characteristics of high creative children in contrast to those of 'low creative but equally intelligent' children. In the present study no attempt was made to equate the two groups with regard to their intelligence. Further probing into this aspect seems to be warranted.

VI. Is there any significant association between the general health of the children and their creativity? In other words, do high creatives suffer from chronic ill health of some sort or other as is believed by some?

To probe into this, the responses of the Ss to the question "Do you suffer from illness? Frequently/Occasionally/ Rarely" were analysed. Table—6.78 shows the results of this analysis.[5]

It may be seen from the table that in the case of the whole group, 13 children mentioned that they frequently suffered from illness. Out of them 38.46 per cent were high creatives while 61.54 per cent were low creatives. This shows that larger percentage of low creatives than high creatives suffered from frequent illness. In contrast larger percentage of high creatives than low creatives mentioned that they rarely suffered from illness.

X^2 test was applied to see the significance of the difference between the two groups. The X^2 value obtained was 21.09 which was highly significant even at 0.001 level for 2 df.

Similar trend of results could be seen in the case of all the subgroups. The X^2 value was significant in all the cases except VIII class and X class children.

Table—6.78 Number and Percentage (given in parentheses) of High Creative and Low Creative Ss Giving Different Responses for the Question: "Do You Suffer from Illness? Frequently/Occasionally/Rarely" and the Results of X^2 Test

Group		*High creative*	*Low creative*	*Total*	X^2
1	2	*3*	*4*	*5*	*6*
	Frequently	5 (38.46)	8 (61.54)	13	21.09***
Whole	Occasionally	66 (40.99)	95 (59.01)	161	(df = 2)
	Rarely	72 (69.23)	32 (30.77)	104	
	Frequently	2 (50.00)	2 (50.00)	4	8.62*
Boys	Occasionally	40 (43.01)	53 (56.99)	93	(df = 1)
	Rarely	32 (69.57)	14 (30.43)	46	
	Frequently	3 (33.33)	6 (66.67)	9	12.00**
Girls	Occasionally	24 (36.36)	42 (63.64)	66	(df = 2)
	Rarely	39 (66.10)	20 (33.90)	59	

(Contd...)

Table—6.78 (Contd...)

1	2	*3*	*4*	*5*	*6*
	Frequently	2 (22.22)	7 (77.78)	9	8.92*
Rural	Occasionally	34 (44.16)	43 (55.84)	77	(df = 2)
	Rarely	33 (66.00)	17 (34.00)	50	
	Frequently	3 (75.00)	1 (25.00)	4	14.27***
Urban	Occasionally	33 (37.50)	55 (62.50)	88	(df = 1)
	Rarely	38 (71.70)	15 (28.30)	53	
	Frequently	1 (20.00)	4 (80.00)	5	1.64@
VIII	Occasionally	31 (48.44)	33 (51.56)	64	(df = 1)
	Rarely	17 (60.71)	11 (39.29)	28	
	Frequently	2 (66.67)	1(33.33)	3	12.72**
IX	Occasionally	16 (32.65)	33 (67.35)	49	(df = 1)
	Rarely	27 (72.97)	10 (27.03)	37	
	Frequently	3 (42.86)	4 (57.14)	7	
X	Occasionally	23 (44.23)	29 (55.77)	52	3.25@
	Rarely	25 (62.50)	15 (37.50)	40	(df = 2)

This shows that creative children do not suffer from chronic ill health. The less creatives seem to fall ill more frequently.

VII. Has close affinity between the members of the family of the children any thing to do with their creativity? In one of the most thorough going studies of factors affecting creativity of the children, Weisberg and Springer (1961) observed that, "the family unit of the creative children is not an overly close one, there is little clinging to one another".

To examine this phenomenon, the responses of the Ss to the question "Is there close affinity between the members of your family?: Yes/No". Were analysed. It may be seen from Table—6.79 that larger percentage of those who said 'Yes' to the above question were from high creative group than from the low creative group. In contrast, among those who responded that there was no close affinity between the members of the family, larger percentage were from low creative group than from the high creative group.

X^2 test of homogeneity was applied as in the earlier cases, to see whether the two groups were homogeneous with regard to the affinity between the members of their families. The obtained X^2 value (21.24) was highly significant. An examination of the table shows that similar results were obtained in the case of all subgroups. All the X^2 values were significant except that for boys. In the case of boys also the pattern of results was the same, *viz.,* among those who mentioned that there was a close affinity between the members of the family, many were from the high creative group compared to those from the low creative group. Among those who said that there was no close affinity between the members of the family, many were from low creative group. But the X^2 value was not significant.

From these results it may be concluded that high creatives and low creatives differed with regard to the affinity between the members of their families. High creatives were

Table—6.79 Number and Percentage (given in parentheses) of High Creative and Low creative Ss Giving Different Responses for the Question: "Is there Close Affinity Between the Members of Your Family? Yes/No" and the Results of X^2 Test

Group		*High creative*	*Low creative*	*Total*	X^2 *(df = 1)*
1	2	3	4	5	6
Whole	Yes	134 (57.51)	99 (42.49)	233	21.24^{***}
	No	9 (20.00)	36 (80.00)	45	
Boys	Yes	68 (54.84)	56 (45.16)	124	$3.57^{@}$
	No	6 (31.58)	13 (68.42)	19	
Girls	Yes	63 (58.33)	45 (41.67)	108	18.36^{***}
	No	6 (11.54)	23 (83.46)	26	

(Contd...)

Table—6.79 (Contd...)

1	*2*	*3*	*4*	*5*	*6*
Rural	Yes	64 (57.66)	47 (42.34)	111	11.58^{***}
	No	5 (20.00)	20 (80.00)	25	
Urban	Yes	70 (56.00)	55 (44.00)	125	8.94^{**}
	No	4 (20.00)	16 (80.00)	20	
VIII	Yes	45 (59.21)	31 (40.79)	76	10.62^{**}
	No	4 (19.05)	17 (80.95)	21	
IX	Yes	42 (55.26)	34 (44.74)	76	4.60^{*}
	No	3 (23.08)	10 (76.92)	13	
X	Yes	49 (55.68)	39 (44.32)	68	5.51^{*}
	No	2 (18.18)	9 (81.82)	11	

characterised by a closer affinity between the members of their families compared to low creatives.

VIII. Are creativity and type of family to which the child belongs associated? It may be seen from Table—6.80 that in the case of the whole group 155 belonged to joint families while the remaining 123 were from nuclear families.[6] Among those who belonged to joint families 44.52 per cent were high creatives while 55.48 per cent were low creatives. With regard to children from nuclear families 60.16 per cent fell in the high creativity group while 39.84 per cent were from the low creativity group. The X^2 test yielded a X^2 value of 6.72, significant at 0.01 level for 1 df. Similar trend of results could be seen in the case of all the subgroups.

This shows that there was a significant difference between the two groups and it may be concluded from the figures in the table that nuclear family seems to contribute to creativity.

It is possible that in the case of nuclear families the children get more personal attention and guidance from the parents. In the case of joint families there will be frequent bickerings between the members of the family because of jealousy, etc. These bickerings, some times leading to open quarrels between the members, leads to adjustmental problems among the children, which may hamper their creativity as it does their achievement.

IX. How does parent's treatment of children affect their creativity? An examination of the responses of the Ss to the question— "Do your parents ask you to do things only as directed by them?: Frequently/Occasionally/ Rarely", shows that in the case of the whole group, 113 Ss reported that their parents frequently insisted that they should do things only as per their instructions. One of them 57.52 per cent were from the high creative group while 42.48 per cent were from the low creative group. 32 children responded that their parents rarely insisted

Table—6.80 Number and Percentage (given in parentheses) of High Creative and Low Creative Ss Giving Different Responses for the Question: "Is Your Family Joint or Nuclear? Joint Family/Nuclear Family" and the Results of X^2 Test

Group		*High creative*	*Low creative*	*Total*	X^2 *(df = 1)*
1	2	3	4	5	6
Whole	Joint families	69 (44.52)	86 (55.48)	155	6.72**
	Nuclear families	74 (60.16)	49 (39.84)	123	
Boys	Joint families	41 (48.81)	43 (51.19)	84	0.70@
	Nuclear families	33 (55.93)	26 (44.07)	59	
Girls	Joint families	26 (37.14)	44 (62.86)	70	8.60**
	Nuclear families	40 (62.50)	24 (37.50)	64	

(Contd...)

Table—6.80 (Contd...)

1	2	3	4	5	6
Rural	Joint families	37 (43.53)	48 (56.47)	85	4.71*
	Nuclear families	32 (62.75)	19 (37.25)	51	
Urban	Joint families	30 (42.25)	41 (57.75)	71	4.29*
	Nuclear families	44 (59.46)	30 (40.54)	74	
VIII	Joint families	27 (47.37)	30 (52.63)	57	0.55@
	Nuclear families	22 (55.00)	18 (45.00)	40	
IX	Joint families	15 (32.61)	31 (67.39)	46	12.28***
	Nuclear families	30 (69.77)	13 (30.23)	43	
X	Joint families	25 (46.30)	29 (53.70)	54	1.30@
	Nuclear families	26 (57.78)	19 (42.22)	45	

that they should act only as per their directions. Out of the 32 who marked rarely for the above question, 53.13 per cent were high creatives, while 46.88 per cent were low creatives (Table—6.81).

X^2 test was applied as in the earlier cases to see whether there was any significant difference between the two groups on this aspect. The X^2 value obtained was 3.36, which was not significant at 0.05 level. Similar results were obtained for all the subgroups.

Thus it may be concluded that, whether the parents insisted that the children should do things only as per their instructions or not, had no effect on the creativity of the children. This was true irrespective of the sex or locality of the children or the class to which they belonged.

X. How does parents' treatment of children's mistakes affect their creativity? An examination of the figures shows in Table—6.82 gives an idea about this. It may be seen from the table that for the question "Do your parents keep quite without making much fuss when you commit mistakes?: Frequently/Occasionally/rarely", 57 Ss marked frequently for the above question, while 65 Ss marked rarely for it. 156 children marked occasionally for the above question.

Among the 57 children whose parents did not punish them for their mistakes 54.39 per cent fell in the high creative group while 45.61 per cent fell in the low creative group. In the case of the 65 children whose parents punished/did not tolerate the mistakes of the children, 64.62 per cent were high creatives while 35.38 per cent were low creatives. The X^2 value was evidently not significant indicating no association between the two attributes. Similar results were obtained in the case of all subgroups except urban children.

Authoritarianism is considered by Anderson and Anderson (1965) to be a crucial factor in limiting the creativity of the children. Watson (1957), Nicholas (1964), Straus and

Table—6.81 Number and Percentage (given in parentheses) of High Creative and Low Creative Ss giving Different Responses for the Question: "Do Your Parents Ask You to Do Things Only As Directed by Them? Frequently/Occasionally/Rarely" and the Results of X^2 Test

Group		*High creative*	*Low creative*	*Total*	X^2 *(df = 1)*
1	2	*3*	*4*	*5*	*6*
	Frequently	65 (57.52)	48 (42.48)	113	
Whole	Occasionally	61 (45.86)	72 (54.14)	133	3.36[@]
	Rarely	17 (53.13)	15 (46.88)	32	
	Frequently	32 (55.17)	26 (44.83)	58	
Boys	Occasionally	32 (47.06)	36 (52.94)	68	1.21[@]
	Rarely	10 (58.82)	7 (41.18)	17	
	Frequently	29 (55.77)	23 (44.23)	52	
Girls	Occasionally	28 (43.08)	37 (56.92)	65	1.97[@]
	Rarely	9 (52.94)	8 (47.06)	17	

(Contd...)

Table—6.81 (Contd...)

1	2	*3*	*4*	*5*	*6*
	Frequently	34 (59.65)	23 (40.35)	57	
Rural	Occasionally	26 (42.62)	35 (57.38)	61	3.42@
	Rarely	9 (50.00)	9 (50.00)	18	
	Frequently	31 (54.39)	26 (41.61)	57	
Urban	Occasionally	34 (47.22)	38 (52.78)	72	0.85@
	Rarely	9 (56.25)	7 (43.75)	16	
	Frequently	18 (47.37)	20 (52.63)	38	
VIII	Occasionally	27 (50.94)	26 (49.06)	53	0.78@
	Rarely	4 (66.67)	2 (33.33)	6	
	Frequently	23 (56.10)	18 (43.90)	41	
IX	Occasionally	19 (48.72)	20 (51.28)	39	1.62@
	Rarely	3 (33.33)	6 (66.67)	9	
	Frequently	20 (62.50)	12 (37.50)	32	
X	Occasionally	24 (52.17)	22 (47.83)	46	4.33@
	Rarely	7 (33.33)	14 (66.87)	21	

Table—6.82 Number and Percentage (given in parentheses) of High Creative and Low Creative Ss Giving Different Responses for the Question: "Do Your Parents Keep Quite Without Making Much Fuss When You Commit Mistakes? Frequently/Occasionally/Rarely" and the Results of X^2 Test

Group		*High creative*	*Low creative*	*Total*	X^2 *(df = 2)*
1	*2*	*3*	*4*	*5*	*6*
Whole	Frequently	31 (54.39)	26 (45.61)	57	
	Occasionally	70 (44.87)	86 (55.13)	156	5.41[@]
	Rarely	42 (64.62)	23 (35.38)	65	
Boys	Frequently	17 (44.74)	2 (55.26)	38	
	Occasionally	40 (50.00)	40 (50.00)	80	3.49[@]
	Rarely	17 (68.00)	8 (32.00)	25	
Girls	Frequently	12 (60.00)	8 (40.00)	20	
	Occasionally	30 (40.00)	45 (60.00)	75	5.85[@]
	Rarely	24 (61.54)	15 (38.46)	39	

(Contd...)

Table—6.82 (Contd...)

1	*2*	*3*	*4*	*5*	*6*
	Frequently	14 (45.16)	17 (54.84)	31	
Rural	Occasionally	36 (50.70)	35 (49.30)	71	0.75$^{@}$
	Rarely	19 (55.88)	15 (44.12)	34	
	Frequently	15 (57.69)	11 (42.31)	26	
Urban	Occasionally	36 (40.91)	52 (59.09)	88	4.73**
	Rarely	23 (74.19)	8 (25.81)	31	
	Frequently	9 (47.37)	10 (52.63)	19	
VIII	Occasionally	32 (48.48)	34 (51.52)	66	1.44$^{@}$
	Rarely	8 (66.67)	4 (33.33)	12	
	Frequently	8 (40.00)	12 (60.00)	20	
IX	Occasionally	20 (45.45)	24 (54.55)	44	4.39$^{@}$
	Rarely	17 (68.00)	8 (32.00)	25	
	Frequently	12 (41.38)	17 (58.62)	29	
X	Occasionally	28 (52.83)	25 (47.17)	53	2.41$^{@}$
	Rarely	11 (64.71)	6 (35.29)	17	

Straus (1964), Torrance (1971), Louise and Fiebert (1977), Venkata Rami Reddy and Salina support the above view. However, Gallahar (1964) observed that fathers who exerted strong control over their sons' activities had sons who performed better on divergent thinking tasks. Garbar, *et al.*, (1979) got similar results.

The results of the present study, however, seem to indicate that there is no association between authoritarianism of the parents and the creativity of the children.

XI. Does order of birth differentiate between high creatives and low creatives? An examination of Table—6.83 shows that in the whole group of high and low creatives, there were 64 who were first born, 129 were middle born while 85 were last born. Among the 64 first borns 33 (51.56 per cent) were high creatives, while 31 (48.44 per cent) were low creatives. This shows that there was not much difference between the incidence of high creatives/low creatives among the first borns. Among the 129 middle borns, 69 (53.49 per cent) were high creatives while 60 (46.51 per cent) were low creatives. Similarly while 48.24 per cent of last borns were high creatives, 51.76 per cent were low creatives. These figures indicate that there is not much difference between the percentage of high creatives and low creatives either in first borns, middle borns or last borns indicating not much difference between the two groups. When X^2 test was applied to test the significance of the difference between the two groups, the X^2 value obtained (0.57) was also not significant at 0.05 level for 2 df.

Similar results were obtained in the case of all subgroups. Thus it may be concluded that order of birth does not seem to have any bearing on the creativity of the children.

Summary

It may be concluded from the above analysis that on the whole high creatives and low creatives were differentiated

Table—6.83 Number and Percentage (given in parentheses) of High Creative and Low Creative Ss Classified According to Their Birth Order and the Results of X^2 Test

Group		*High creative*	*Low creative*	*Total*	X^2 *(df = 2)*
1	2	*3*	*4*	*5*	*6*
	First born	33 (51.56)	31 (48.44)	64	
Whole	Middle born	69 (53.49)	60 (46.51)	129	0.57@
	Last born	41 (48.24)	44 (51.76)	85	
	First born	18 (47.37)	20 (52.63)	38	
Boys	Middle born	36 (54.55)	30 (45.45)	66	0.50@
	Last born	20 (51.28)	19 (48.72)	39	
	First born	16 (59.26)	11 (40.74)	27	
Girls	Middle born	31 (50.00)	31 (50.00)	62	1.99@
	Last born	19 (42.22)	26 (57.78)	45	

(Contd...)

Table—6.83 (Contd...)

1	*2*	*3*	*4*	*5*	*6*
	First born	16 (53.33)	14 (46.67)	30	
Rural	Middle born	29 (50.88)	28 (49.12)	57	0.14@
	Last born	24 (48.98)	25 (51.02)	49	
	First born	18 (50.00)	18 (50.00)	36	
Urban	Middle born	38 (52.78)	34 (47.22)	72	0.19@
	Last born	18 (48.65)	19 (51.35)	37	
	First born	13 (44.83)	16 (55.17)	29	
VIII	Middle born	19 (57.58)	14 (42.42)	33	1.09@
	Last born	17 (48.57)	18 (51.43)	35	
	First born	15 (62.50)	9 (37.50)	24	
IX	Middle born	21 (50.00)	21 (50.00)	42	2.58@
	Last born	9 (39.13)	14 (60.87)	23	
	First born	12 (60.00)	8 (40.00)	20	
X	Middle born	24 (45.28)	29 (54.72)	53	1.80@
	Last born	15 (57.69)	11 (42.31)	26	

by personality factors A, B, C, D, E, F, G, H, I, J, O, Q_2, and Q_3. On factors A, D, E and O (Reserved Vs Out going, Phlegmatic Vs Excitable, Obedient Vs Assertive, and Placid Vs Apprehensive respectively) high creatives obtained a lower mean score compared to low creatives indicating that a lower mean score on the above factors was characteristic of high creatives.

On all the remaining factors—B, C, F, G, H, I, J, Q_2, and Q_3 (Less intelligent Vs More intelligent, Affected by feelings Vs Emotionally stable, Sober Vs Happy-go-lucky, Expedient Vs Conscientious, Shy Vs Venturesome, Tough-minded Vs Tender-minded, Vigorous Vs Doubting, Group—dependent Vs Self—sufficient and undisciplined self—conflict Vs Controlled respectively) high creatives got a higher mean score than the low creatives.

Though there were some differences in the level of significance of the difference between means from subgroup to subgroup, the trend of the results was as cited above, irrespective of the sex, locality or class of the Ss.

With regard to intelligence, there was a significant difference between the level of intelligence of high creatives and low creatives. High creatives were more intelligent than low creatives. This was true for all subgroups without any exception.

Similarly, high creatives and low creatives differed significantly in their socio-economic status also. High creatives came from higher socio-economic strata.

Generally speaking high creatives and low creatives seem to be differentiated by some of the familial and personal characteristics and habits of life.

High creatives were characterised by the habit of frequent reading of magazines, story books etc., they liked to do things in a new way avoiding the beaten track, they were healthier, there was a close affinity between the members of their families, they felt that others did not find it difficult to adjust with them and they came from nuclear families. These were the conclusions that could be drawn from the high and low creatives selected from the whole group of Ss.

As in the case of the personality factors there were some fluctuations in the results obtained from subgroup to subgroup.

SECTION—III

Multiple Regression Analysis of Creativity Vs All Independent Variables

This section deals with the analysis of the relative contribution of each of the different independent variables to the creativity of the children.

Meaning and Nature of Regression Analysis

Before going into the details of regression analysis a word about the meaning and purpose of regression analysis may not be out of place.

If two variables are closely related we may be interested in estimating (predicting) the value of the one variable given the value of the other. For example, if we know that advertising and sales are correlated we may be interested to find out the expected amount of sales for a given advertising expenditure or the required amount of expenditure for attaining a given amount of sales.

Similarly, we may like to predict academic success (in terms of grades received), from a knowledge of intelligence study habits, etc.

The statistical tool using which we can estimate (predict) the unknown values of one variable from the known values of another variable is called regression.

The dictionary meaning of the term 'regression' connotes the act or returning of going back. The term 'regression' was first used by Francis Galton towards the end of the 19th century, while studying the relationship between the height of fathers and sons. His study of the height of about one thousand fathers and sons revealed a very interesting phenomenon: tall fathers tend to have tall sons and short fathers short sons, but the average height of the sons of tall fathers was less than that of the fathers and the average height of the sons of short fathers was greater than that of the fathers. The line describing this tendency to 'regress' or going back was called by Galton as 'Regression Line' (Gupta, 1975).

This term is still used to describe the line drawn for a group of points to represent the trend present, but it no longer necessarily carries the original implication Galton intended. Now a days there is a growing tendency of the modern writers to call the line as estimating line or predicting line instead of regression line.

Regression analysis is most widely used in almost all scientific disciplines now a days. In economics it is the basic technique for measuring or estimating the relationship among economic variables that constitute the essence of economic theory and economic life. For example, if we know the two variables, price (X) and demand (Y) which are closely related, we can find out the most probable value of X for a given value of Y or the most probable value of Y for a given value of X. Similarly, if we know that the amount of tax and the rise in the price of a commodity are closely related, we can find out the expected price for a certain amount of tax levy.

The use of regression analysis is not confined to economics and business fields only. Its applications are extended to almost all the natural, physical and social sciences. The tool of regression analysis can be extended to three or more variables also.

According to Guilford, although we generally emphasise continuous measurement (the highest type of measurement), in terms of interval or ratio scales, very often such measurements are not possible in educational and psychological research. The data are some times merely in terms of classifications only.

With classification or nominal measurement, it is a matter of assigning attributes to cases rather than making quantitative evaluations on linear—scale positions. We can still make predictions from them as we do from linear measurements. We thus have four general cases of prediction:

1. Attributes from other attributes—as when we predict incidence of divorce from race, political party affiliation, or religious creed.
2. Attributes from measurements—as when we predict divorce from scores on tests of personality or ability or other behaviour traits.
3. Measurements from attributes—as when we predict probable test scores from sex, social class, or marital status.
4. Measurements from other measurements—as when we predict academic success or achievement from aptitude scores (Guilford, 1978).

Though correlation and regression are related to each other, their uses are quite varied. Correlation is merely a tool of ascertaining the degree of relationship between two variables and, therefore, we can not say that one variable is the cause and the other the effect (Gupta, 1975).

Whereas correlation coefficient is simply a measure of the degree of relationship between X and Y, the objective of regression analysis is to study the 'nature of relationship' between the variables. The cause and effect relation is clearly indicated through regression analysis, than by correlation.

In the present investigation there were 30 independent variables like sex, locality, personality factors, etc. To assess the relative effect of each of these independent variables on the dependent variable, *viz.,* creativity step-wise multiple regression analysis was used.

As mentioned earlier, for measuring the dependent variable a battery of creativity tests consisting of verbal and nonverbal tests was used. Thus the effect of each of the different independent variables on the dependent variable was analysed separately for verbal tests, nonverbal tests and all the tests put together. This was done separately for fluency, flexibility, originality and composite creativity.

A. Verbal Tests

1. Fluency

In this part the results of the step-wise multiple regression analysis carried out to determine the relative contribution of each of the 30 independent variables to the variance in the fluency component, as measured by the verbal tests are presented. The summary of results at each step of the step-wise multiple regression analysis is presented in Table—6.84.[7]

Step 1: It could be seen from the table that the first variable that entered into the step-wise multiple regression was independent variable 4, viz., intelligence (the variable numbers are shown in column 3 on the table).

The multiple correlation (R) obtained was 0.471 indicating that the strength of the relationship between the two variables, intelligence and creativity as measured by the fluency component was about 47 per cent. It could also be seen that the multiple R was significant at 0.001 level (F = 256.506) for 1 and 898 df.

The coefficient of multiple R^2 was 0.222. This shows that 22.2 per cent of the variance in the creativity of the Ss was accounted for by their intelligence.

The standard error of multiple R (SE of R) was 0.065. From this it may be inferred that nearly 68 per cent of the 'actual' creativity scores would lie within ± 0.065 points of the 'predicted' creativity scores with the help of this factor.

Table—6.84 Results of Step-wise Multiple Regression Analysis Between Fluency and Other Independent Variables (Verbal Tests).

Step No.	IV	VN	R	R^2	SER	F value for R	b	VN	F value for b	Constant	β	γ	Per cent of variance
1	2	3	4	5	6	7	8	9	10	11	12	13	14
1.	Intelligence	4	0.471	0.222	0.065	256.506	1.044	4	256.512	61.214	0.471	0.471	22.184
						(1,898)							
2.	Class/grade	3	0.551	0.304	0.900	196.345	0.842	4	166.745	48.774	0.378	0.419	17.803
						(2,897)	9.273	3	106.151		0.301		12.612
3.	SES	5	0.574	0.329	0.076	146.591	0.765	4	136.539	42.189	0.344	0.267	16.202
						(3,896)	9.122	3	106.275		0.296		12.402
							0.439	5	25.754		0.161		4.298
4.	PF–H	13	0.584	0.341	0.221	116.216	0.733	4	126.090	32.807	0.329	0.165	15.496
						(4,895)	9.237	3	110.817		0.300		12.570
							0.428	5	32.013		0.157		4.192
							0.918	13	17.156		0.113		1.864

(Contd...)

Table—6.84 (Contd...)

1	2	3	4	5	6	7	8	9	10	11	12	13	14
5.	General state of health	24	0.593	0.352	1.283	97.006	0.723	4	124.300	43.082	0.325	–0.195	15.307
						(5,894)	8.959	3	104.960		0.291		12.193
							0.406	5	28.708		0.149		3.978
							0.837	13	14.333		0.103		1.699
							–4.735	24	13.608		–0.099		1.930
6.	PF–B	7	0.599	0.359	0.340	83.503	0.679	4	106.090	39.508	0.305	0.272	14.365
						(6,893)	8.745	3	100.590		0.284		11.899
							0.370	5	23.853		0.136		3.631
							0.786	13	12.716		0.097		1.600
							–4.524	24	12.524		–0.095		1.852
							1.114	7	10.712		0.093		2.530
7	Affinity between the members of the family	23	0.604	0.365	2.007	73.168	0.662	4	100.661	30.704	0.297	0.189	13.988
						(7,892)	8.599	3	97.535		0.279		11.690
							0.353	5	21.687		0.130		3.471
							0.764	13	12.082		0.094		1.551
							–4.456	24	12.236		–0.094		1.833
							1.080	7	10.138		0.090		2.448
							5.501	23	7.507		0.074		1.398

(Contd...)

Table—6.84 (Contd...)

1	*2*	*3*	*4*	*5*	*6*	*7*	*8*	*9*	*10*	*11*	*12*	*13*	*14*
8.	Sex	1	0.607	0.368	1.367	64.934	0.645	4	94.614	35.230	0.290	–0.048	13.659
						(8,891)	8.617	3	98.565		0.280		11.732
							0.382	5	24.760		0.140		3.738
							0.756	13	11.875		0.093		1.534
							–4.539	24	12.737		–0.095		1.852
							1.136	7	11.202		0.095		2.584
							5.422	23	7.328		0.073		1.379
							–3.056	1	4.995		–0.061		0.293
9.	PF–E	10	0.610	0.372	0.228	58.729	0.627	4	88.962	42.603	0.282	–0.156	13.282
						(9,890)	8.563	3	97.634		0.278		11.648
							0.385	5	25.361		0.141		3.764
							0.752	13	11.812		0.092		1.518
							–4.634	24	13.344		–0.097		1.891
							1.038	7	9.284		0.086		2.339
							5.137	23	6.589		0.069		1.304
							–3.594	1	6.775		–0.072		0.346
							–0.565	10	6.110		–0.068		1.061

(Contd...)

Table—6.84 (Contd...)

1	2	3	4	5	6	7	8	9	10	11	12	13	14
10.	PF–I	14	0.612	0.375	0.230	53.492	0.625	4	88.567	38.616	0.281	0.121	13.235
						(10,889)	8.447	3	94.984		0.274		11.480
							0.383	5	25.180		0.141		3.765
							0.744	13	11.634		0.091		1.501
							–4.736	24	13.965		–0.099		1.930
							0.989	7	8.427		0.083		2.257
							4.962	23	6.160		0.067		1.266
							–3.977	1	8.185		–0.079		0.379
							–0.532	10	4.405		–0.064		0.998
							0.481	14	4.355		0.057		0.689
11.	Type of family	22	0.615	0.378	1.352	49.061	0.620	4	87.516	42.298	0.278	–0.098	13.094
						(11,888)	8.531	3	96.864		0.277		11.606
							0.377	5	24.344		0.139		3.711
							0.758	13	12.062		0.093		1.534
							–4.529	24	6.270		–0.095		1.852
							0.942	7	7.606		0.079		2.149
							4.998	23	6.270		0.067		1.266
							–3.988	1	8.248		–0.079		0.379
							–0.515	10	5.076		–0.062		0.967
							0.467	14	4.117		0.055		0.665
							–2.472	22	3.341		–0.049		0.480

Note: 1. IV = Independent Variable
VN = Variable Number
PF = Personality Factor

2. Same pattern is followed in all the foregoing tables of Step-wise Multiple Regression Analysis.

3. All F values are significant at or above 0.05 level.

The partial regression coefficient (b) presented in column 8 was 1.044. This value indicates that the creativity scores would change by 1.044 units for every unit of change in intelligence. The *F* value for b was 256.512 highly significant at 0.001 level (Col. 10).

The value of the constant that would go into the multiple regression equation that could be written to predict creativity at this stage was 61.214.

The general form in which the multiple regression equation may be written is:

$Y = A + b_1 (X_1) + b_2 (X_2) + b_3 (X_3) + \ldots + b_n (X_n)$ where

Y is the predicted score on the dependent, variable,

A is a constant,

$b_1, b_2, b_3 \ldots, b_n$ are partial regression coefficients and

$X_1, X_2, X_3 \ldots, X_n$ are the scores on different independent variables.

Thus the multiple regression equation at the end of the first step could be written as:

$V_F = 61.214 + 1.044$ (IV4)

where

IV4 refers to independent variable number 4,

V_F refers to fluency as measured by the verbal tests, 61.214 is the constant at this stage and

1.044 is the partial regression coefficient.

Step 2: Independent variable 3 (class/grade) entered into the step-wise regression as the second most significant variables. The multiple correlation (R) between creativity on one side and independent variables intelligence and class on the other side was 0.551. Thus the strength of the relationship between the dependent variable and the two in dependent variables put together was about 55 per cent. The multiple R was significant at 0.001 level (*F* = 196.345 for 2,897 df).

The value of R^2 was 0.304. This shows that the two variables put together could explain 30.4 per cent of the variance in the dependent variable. Out of this 17.803 per cent of variance was explained by variable 4, *viz.*, intelligence and the remaining 12.612 per cent of variance was accounted for by variable 3, *viz.*, class/grade (Column 14).[8]

It is evident that by including independent variable 3, the contribution of independent variable 4 was brought down from 22.137 per cent to 17.803 per cent because of the intercorrelation between the two predictor variables.

The partial regression coefficients presented in column 8 show that when both variables 4 and 3 were included as predictor variables, the score on the dependent variable changes by 0.842 and 9.273 units for every unit of change in variables 4 and 3 respectively.

The regression equation to predict creativity with these two variables intelligence and class/grade as predictor variables was:

$V_F = 48.774 + 0.842\ (IV4) + 9.273\ (IV3)$ where,

48.774 is the constant to be considered at this step, 0.842 and 9.273 are partial regression coefficients, and IV4 and IV3 are scores on Independent Variables 4 and 3 respectively.

Step 3: In the third step the predictor variable entered in the multiple regression analysis was independent variable 5, *viz.*, SES.

The values of R and R^2 at this stage were 0.574 and 0.329 respectively. In other words 32.9 per cent of variance in the fluency score of the sample was explained by these three variables. One of this 16.202 per cent, 12.402 per cent and 4.298 per cent of variance was explained by intelligence, class/grade and SES respectively as indicated by the percentages given in column 14 of Table—6.84.

The partial regression coefficients for the three predictor variables indicate that the change in the fluency score was by 0.765, 9.122 and 0.439 units for every unit of change in the above variables, respectively. The regression equation at this stage was:

$$V_F = 42.189 + 0.765\ (IV4) + 9.122\ (IV3) + 0.439\ (IV5).$$

Step 4: The next variable entered into the regression analysis was independent variable 13 (*i.e.,* personality factor H).

The multiple correlation at this stage was 0.584 and R^2 was 0.341. Thus the 4 variables in combination could explain 34.1 per cent of the variance in the dependent variable. Out of this the contribution of intelligence, class, SES and personality factor–H were 15.496 per cent, 12.570 per cent, 4.192 per cent and 1.864 per cent, respectively.

From the partial regression coefficients presented in column 8 it may be said that when the above four independent variables were included in the regression analysis, the creativity scores as measured by the fluency component would change by 0.733, 9.237, 0.428 and 0.918 units respectively for every unit of change in the four variables.

The regression equation which would predict the creativity of the children with the help of the four variables was:

$$V_F = 32.807 + 0.733\ (IV4) + 9.237\ (IV3) + 0.428\ (IV5) + \\ + 0.918\ (IV13).$$

It may be seen from Table—6.84 that there were altogether 11 steps in this analysis. Thus the variable entered in each step, the amount of variance in the dependent variable that was explained upto that stage and the multiple regression equation at that step are presented briefly in the following paragraphs to conserve space, without loss of any essential information.

Step 5: The predictor variable that entered at this step was variable 24 *(i.e.)* general state of health of the children.

The amount of variance explained by the 5 variables as a set was 35.2%. The multiple regression equation at this stage was:

$$V_F = 43.082 + 0.723\ (IV4) + 8.959\ (IV3) + 0.406\ (IV5) + 0.837\ (IV13) - 4.735\ (IV24).$$

Step 6: Variable 7 (*i.e.,*) personality factor—B was the next independent variable that entered into the regression analysis. The pre cent of variance in creativity contributed by these 6 variables was 35.9. The prediction equation with these 6 variables could be written as:

$$V_F = 39.508 + 0.679\ (IV4) + 8.745\ (IV3) + 0.370\ (IV5) + 0.786\ (IV13) - 4.524\ (IV24) + 1.114\ (IV7).$$

Step 7: Variable 23 (*i.e.,*) affinity between the members of the family was the next variable that entered into the regression analysis. The amount of variance explained by the 7 variables that were considered upto this stage was 36.5 per cent, and the multiple regression equation could be written as:

$$V_F = 30.704 + 0.662\ (IV4) + 8.599\ (IV3) + 0.353\ (IV5) + 0.764\ (IV13) - 4.456\ (IV24) + 1.080\ (IV7) + 5.501\ (IV23).$$

Step 8: The next predictor variable that entered into the multiple regression analysis was variable 1, *viz.,* sex and the amount of variance in the creativity explained by the 8 independent or predictor variable increased to 36.8 per cent with the addition of this variable. The multiple regression equation at this stage was:

$$VF = 35.230 + 0.645\ (IV4) + 8.617\ (IV3) + 0.382\ (IV5) + 0.756\ (IV13) - 4.539\ (IV24) + 1.136\ (IV7) + 5.422\ (IV23) - 3.056\ (IV1).$$

Step 9: Variable 10 (*i.e.,*) personality factor—E entered the analysis at this stage. The amount of variance contributed to creativity by these 9 independent variables was 37.2 per cent and the regression equation at this stage could be written as follows:

$$V_F = 42.603 + 0.627\ (IV4) + 8.563\ (IV3) + 0.385\ (IV5) + 0.752\ (IV13) - 4.634\ (IV24) + 1.038\ (IV7) + 5.137\ (IV23) - 3.594\ (IV1) - 0.565\ (IV10).$$

Step 10: The next predictor variable considered in the analysis was independent variable 14 (*i.e.,*) personality factor—I The per cent of contribution to creativity by the 10 independent variables was 37.5. The regression equation at this stage was:

$$\begin{aligned} V_F = 38.616 &+ 0.625\ (IV4) + 8.447\ (IV3) + 0.383\ (IV5) \\ &+ 0.744\ (IV13) - 4.736\ (IV24) + 0.989\ (IV7) \\ &+ 4.962\ (IV23) - 3.977\ (IV1) - 0.532\ (IV10) \\ &+ 0.481\ (IV14). \end{aligned}$$

Step 11: Variable 22 (*i.e.,*) type of family entered into the multiple regression analysis at this stage. The amount of variance explained by these 11 variables was 37.8 per cent and the regression equation was:

$$\begin{aligned} V_F = 42.298 &+ 0.620\ (IV4) + 8.531\ (IV3) + 0.377\ (IV5) \\ &+ 0.758\ (IV13) - 4.529\ (IV24) + 0.942\ (IV7) \\ &+ 4.998\ (IV23) - 3.988\ (IV1) - 0.515\ (IV10) \\ &+ 0.467\ (IV14) - 2.472\ (IV22). \end{aligned}$$

An examination of the contributions of each of the different independent variables at this stage, presented in column 14, shows that the contribution of the last variable entered, *viz.,* type of family was 0.480 per cent. The step-wise regression analysis was continued at this stage since addition of any of the remaining independent variables would not produce considerable increase in the total amount of variance in the dependent variable.

Thus 37.8 per cent of variance in creativity as measured by the fluency component was predicted by the 11 predictor variables. Since all the F values for 'b' were significant at or above 0.05 level, the same percentage of variance in the independent variable explained in the detailed analysis will be seen in the summary table also (Table—6.85).

It may be concluded from the above analysis that the most significant independent variables that contributed to creativity as measured by fluency component on the verbal tests were intelligence, class/grade, SES, personality factor—H, general state of health, personality factor—B, affinity between the members of the family, sex, personality factor—E, personality factor—I and type of family in that order.

The essence of the results at each step could be summarised as shown in the following table.

Table—6.85 Variable Entered at Each Step and the Percentage of Variance Explained Upto that Stage in the Step-wise Multiple Regression Analysis with Fluency as Measured by Verbal Tests as Dependent Variable

Step	*Variable entered*	*Variable number*	*Per cent of variance explained by all the variables put together that entered upto that stage*
1.	Intelligence	4	22.2
2.	Class/grade	3	30.4
3.	SES	5	32.9
4.	Personality factor—H	13	34.1
5.	General state of health	24	35.2
6.	Personality factor—B	7	35.9
7.	Affinity between members of the family	23	36.5
8.	Sex	1	36.8
9.	Personality factor—E	10	37.2
10.	Personality factor—I	14	37.5
11.	Type of family	22	37.8

2. Flexibility

As in the earlier case step-wise multiple regression analysis was carried out to assess the contribution of each of the independent variables to the flexibility score of the subjects. The results obtained are presented in Table—6.86.

Table—6.86 Results of Step-wise Multiple Regression Analysis Between Flexibility and Other Independent Variables (Verbal Tests)

Step No.	IV	VN	R	R^2	SER	F value for R	b	VN	F value for b	Constant	β	γ	Per cent of variance
1	2	3	4	5	6	7	8	9	10	11	12	13	14
1.	Intelligence	4	0.492	0.242	0.035	286.461	0.596	4	286.455	42.312	0.492	0.492	24.206
						(1,898)							
2.	Class/grade	3	0.562	0.317	0.485	208.113	0.488	4	192.598	35.846	0.403	0.413	19.827
						(2,897)	4.819	3	98.605		0.288		11.894
3.	SES	5	0.582	0.339	0.412	153.424	0.448	4	160.655	32.437	0.370	0.264	18.204
						(3,896)	4.741	3	98.465		0.283		11.687
							0.227	5	30.393		0.153		4.039
4.	PF—H	13	0.593	0.352	C.119	121.568	0.431	4	149.279	27.319	0.356	0.168	17.515
						(4,895)	4.804	3	102.839		0.287		11.853
							0.221	5	29.387		0.149		3.934
							0.500	13	17.514		0.113		1.898

(Contd...)

Table—6.86 (Contd...)

1	2	3	4	5	6	7	8	9	10	11	12	13	14
5.	General state of health	24	0.601	0.361	0.693	100.941	0.426	4	147.476	32.595	0.351	–0.190	17.269
						(5,894)	4.661	3	97.337		0.279		11.523
							0.209	5	26.337		0.141		3.722
							0.459	13	14.768		0.104		1.747
							–2.431	24	12.292		–0.095		1.805
6.	Affinity between the members of the family	23	0.606	0.367	1.089	86.268	0.415	4	139.783	27.419	0.342	0.193	16.826
						(6,893)	4.573	3	94.090		0.273		11.275
							0.198	5	23.736		0.134		3.538
							0.445	13	13.995		0.101		1.697
							–2.388	24	11.957		–0.094		1.786
							3.195	23	8.608		0.079		1.525
7.	PF—B	7	0.610	0.372	0.183	75.573	0.395	4	122.633	25.973	0.326	0.264	16.039
						(7,892)	4.478	3	90.459		0.268		11.068
							0.183	5	20.025		0.124		3.274
							0.423	13	12.645		0.096		1.613
							–2.294	24	11.082		–0.090		1.710
							3.086	23	8.082		0.077		1.486
							0.505	7	7.584		0.077		2.033

(Contd...)

Table—6.86 (Contd...)

1	2	3	4	5	6	7	8	9	10	11	12	13	14
8.	Sex	1	0.614	0.377	0.738	67.402	0.384	4	115.176	28.821	0.317	–0.061	15.596
						(8,891)	4.489	3	91.470		0.268		11.068
							0.201	5	23.658		0.136		3.590
							0.417	13	12.411		0.095		1.596
							–2.346	24	11.655		–0.092		1.748
							3.037	23	7.873		0.076		1.467
							0.540	7	8.678		0.083		2.191
							–1.923	1	6.775		–0.070		0.427
9.	Type of family	22	0.616	0.380	0.732	60.821	0.381	4	113.571	31.452	0.314	–0.106	15.445
						(9,890)	4.544	3	93.934		0.272		11.234
							0.197	5	22.686		0.133		3.511
							0.426	13	12.988		0.097		1.629
							–2.206	24	10.284		–0.086		1.634
							3.053	23	7.991		0.076		1.467
							0.504	7	7.540		0.077		2.033
							–1.949	1	6.996		–0.071		0.433
							–1.712	22	5.471		–0.062		0.657
10.	PF—E	10	0.619	0.383	0.123	55.301	0.374	4	108.160	34.521	0.309	–0.144	15.203
						(10,889)	4.519	3	93.122		0.270		11.151
							0.199	5	23.136		0.134		3.538
							0.424	13	12.902		0.096		1.613
							–2.252	24	10.738		–0.088		1.387
							2.930	23	7.360		0.073		1.409
							0.463	7	6.315		0.071		1.874
							–2.179	1	8.549		–0.080		0.488
							–1.652	22	5.094		–0.060		0.636
							–0.242	10	3.853		–0.053		0.763

Note: See note under Table—6.84.

Step 1: The independent variable that entered into the analysis at first was intelligence (IV4) as in the earlier case. The multiple R obtained was 0.492. It was significant (F = 286.461) at 0.001 level for 1 and 898 df. The R^2 was 0.242. Therefore it could be inferred that 24.2 per cent of the variance in flexibility was contributed by this variable, *viz.*, intelligence of the Ss.

The partial regression coefficient (b) was 0.596, significant at 0.001 level. This shows that there was a change of 0.596 units in the flexibility score of the Ss for every unit of change in intelligence. Thus the regression equation at this stage could be written as:

$V_X{}^9 = 42.312 + 0.596$ (IV4).

Step 2: The second most important predictor variable that entered into the step-wise regression analysis was class/ grade (IV3). The values of R and R^2 at this stage were 0.562 and 0.317 respectively. Thus the amount of variance in flexibility explained by these two variables in combination was 31.7 per cent. Out of this, the contribution of variable— 4 (intelligence) was 19.827 per cent. The remaining 11.894 per cent of variance was contributed by variable—3 (Class/ grade).

The multiple regression equation with these two predictor variables—intelligence and class/grade could be written as:

$V_X = 35.846 + 0.488$ (IV4) + 4.819 (IV3)

Step 3: The next predictor variable that entered in the analysis was variable 5 (*i.e.,*) SES. The values of multiple R and R^2 at this stage were 0.582 and 0.339 respectively. Thus the percentage of variance that was explained by these three predictor variables, *viz.*, intelligence, class/grade and SES was 33.9. The regression equation at this stage could be written as:

$V_X = 32.437 + 0.448$ (IV4) + 4.741 (IV3) + 0.227 (IV5).

Step 4: Variable 13 (personality factor—H) was the next variable entered into the analysis. The values of R^2 at this stage was 0.352, indicating that the four predictor variables put together have contributed to 35.2 per cent of the variance in the flexibility score of the Ss. The regression equation obtained was:

$$V_X = 27.319 + 0.431\ (IV4) + 4.804\ (IV3) + 0.221\ (IV5) + 0.500\ (IV13).$$

Step 5: The next variable entered was general state of health (IV24), with the addition which the amount of variance in the dependent variable explained changed from 35.2 per cent to 36.1 per cent; and the regression equation could be written as:

$$V_X = 32.595 + 0.426\ (IV4) + 4.661\ (IV3) + 0.209\ (IV5) + 0.459\ (IV13) - 2.431\ (IV24).$$

Step 6: The next variable entered was affinity between the members of the family (IV23). The per cent of variance explained by six variables put together increased to 36.7 per cent and the multiple regression equation at this step was as follows:

$$V_X = 27.419 + 0.145\ (IV4) + 4.573\ (IV3) + 0.198\ (IV5) + 0.445\ (IV13) - 2.388\ (IV24) + 3.195\ (IV23).$$

Step 7: The next predictor variable entered into the analysis was personality factor—B (variable 7) and the amount of variance in the flexibility score explained by the seven variables was 37.2 per cent while the multiple regression equation obtained at this stage could be written as:

$$V_X = 25.973 + 0.395\ (IV4) + 4.478\ (IV3) + 0.183\ (IV5) + 0.423\ (IV13) - 2.294\ (IV24) + 3.086\ (IV23) + 0.505\ (IV7).$$

Step 8: The next most significant variable entered into the multiple regression analysis was sex (variable 1). The 8 variables that entered up to this stage explained 37.7 per cent of the variance in the flexibility score of the Ss. The regression equation at this stage could be written as:

$$V_X = 28.821 + 0.384\ (IV4) + 4.489\ (IV3) + 0.201\ (IV5) + 0.417\ (IV13) - 2.346\ (IV24) + 3.037\ (IV23) + 0.540\ (IV7) - 1.923\ (IV1).$$

Step 9: Variable 22 (type of family) was entered in the next step and the total amount of variance explained changed to 38 per cent. The regression equation at this stage was:

$$V_X = 31.452 + 0.381\ (IV4) + 4.544\ (IV3) + 0.197\ (IV5) + 0.426\ (IV13) - 2.206\ (IV24) + 3.053\ (IV23) + 0.504\ (IV7) - 1.949\ (IV1) - 1.712\ (IV22).$$

Step 10: Personality factor—E (variable 10) entered next and the amount of variance contributed by all the 10 variables was 38.3 per cent. The regression equation at this stage was:

$$V_X = 34.521 + 0.374\ (IV4) + 4.519\ (IV3) + 0.199\ (IV5) + 0.424\ (IV13) - 2.252\ (IV24) + 2.930\ (IV23) + 0.463\ (IV7) - 2.179\ (IV1) - 1.652\ (IV22) - 0.242\ (IV10).$$

Thus 38.3 per cent of variance in flexibility score of the Ss was explained by all the 10 predictor variables. Since all the *F* values for 'b' were significant at or above 0.05 level, the same percentage of variance in the dependent variable explained in the detailed analysis will be seen in the summary table also (Table—6.87).

Thus it may be concluded from the above analysis that the most significant variables that contributed to the flexibility of the Ss as measured by the verbal tests were, intelligence, class/grade, SES, personality, factor—H, general state of health, affinity between the members of the family, personality factor—B, sex, type of family, and personality factor—E, in that order.

The essence of the results at each step could be summarised as shown in the following Table—6.87.

3. Originality

The results of a similar analysis taking originality as the dependent variable are presented in Table—6.88

Table—6.87 Variable Entered At Each Step and the Percentage of Variance Explained Upto that Stage in the Step-wise Multiple Regression Analysis with Flexibility as Measured by Verbal Tests as Dependent Variable

Step	*Variable entered*	*Variable number*	*Per cent of variance explained by all the variables put together that entered upto that stage*
1.	Intelligence	4	24.2
2.	Class/grade	3	31.7
3.	SES	5	33.9
4.	Personality factor—H	13	35.2
5.	General state of health	24	36.1
6.	Affinity between members of the family	23	36.7
7.	Personality factor—B	7	37.2
8.	Sex	1	37.7
9.	Type of family	22	38.0
10.	Personality factor—E	10	38.3

Step 1: It could be seen from the table that intelligence was the most important predictor variable that entered first into the step-wise multiple regression analysis. The value of multiple R was 0.435 which was significant (F = 210.083) at 0.001 level for 1 and 898 df. The R^2 was 0.189, indicating that this factor alone contributed to 18.9 per cent of the variance in the originality scores of the Ss.

That the partial regression coefficient was 4.073, significant at 0.001 level, shows that for every unit of change in this factor there would be a change of 4.073 units in the

Table—6.88 Results of Step-wise Multiple Regression Analysis Between Originality and Other Independent Variables (Verbal Tests)

Step No.	IV	VN	R	R^2	SER	F value for R	b	VN	F value for b	Constant	β	γ	Per cent of variance
1	2	3	4	5	6	7	8	9	10	11	12	13	14
1.	Intelligence	4	0.435	0.189	0.281	210.083	4.073	4	210.076	199.037	0.435	0.435	18.922
						(1,898)							
2.	SES	5	0.468	0.219	0.346	125.733	3.704	4	171.112	167.978	0.396	0.264	17.226
						(2,897)	2.009	5	33.721		0.171		4.514
3.	Class/grade	3	0.491	0.241	3.954	94.823	3.263	4	10.647	141.736	0.349	0.281	15.181
						(3,896)	1.957	5	3.829		0.171		4.514
							20.162	3	406.506		0.161		4.524
4.	General state of health	24	0.505	0.255	5.750	76.501	3.201	4	121.551	188.469	0.342	–0.188	14.877
						(4,895)	1.834	5	29.117		0.160		4.224
							18.843	3	22.944		0.151		4.243
							–23.420	24	16.589		–0.119		2.237

(Contd...)

Table—6.88 (Contd...)

1	2	3	4	5	6	7	8	9	10	11	12	13	14
5.	PF—B	7	0.516	0.266	1.525	64.818	2.968	4	101.203	167.401	0.317	0.264	13.789
						(5,894)	1.658	5	23.619		0.145		3.828
							17.792	3	20.611		0.142		3.990
							–22.197	24	15.054		–0.111		2.087
							5.653	7	13.764		0.112		2.957
6.	PF—H	13	0.520	0.271	0.988	55.277	2.901	4	96.236	141.254	0.310	0.141	13.485
						(6,893)	1.646	5	23.425		0.144		3.802
							18.216	3	21.715		0.146		4.103
							–20.883	24	13.250		–0.104		1.955
							5.393	7	12.532		0.107		2.825
							2.384	13	5.808		0.070		0.987

(Contd...)

Table—6.88 (Contd...)

1	2	3	4	5	6	7	8	9	10	11	12	13	14
7.	PF—E	10	0.524	0.275	0.017	48.323	2.837	4	91.776	166.173	0.303	–0.151	13.180
						(7,892)	1.636	5	23.232		0.143		3.775
							17.956	3	21.160		0.144		4.046
							–21.195	24	13.764		–0.106		1.993
							4.951	7	10.433		0.098		2.587
							2.370	13	5.760		0.069		0.972
							–2.293	10	5.062		–0.066		0.996
8.	Affinity between members of the family	23	0.528	0.279	5.075	43.073	2.803	4	89.681	154.026	0.300	0.202	13.050
						(8,891)	1.408	5	15.840		0.123		3.247
							16.954	3	18.662		0.135		3.793
							–21.620	24	14.334		–0.108		2.030
							4.789	7	9.734		0.095		2.508
							2.250	13	5.198		0.065		0.917
							–2.359	10	5.382		–0.066		0.996
							11.188	23	4.840		0.067		1.353

Note: See note under Table—6.84.

originality of the Ss. Therefore the regression equation at this stage could be written as:

$$V_O^{10} = 199.037 + 4.073\ (IV4).$$

Step 2: The second variable that entered into the analysis was SES (variable 5). The value of multiple R^2 at this stage was 0.219. Thus the two factors as a set could explain 21.9 per cent of the variance in the originality of the Ss. The multiple regression equation at this stage was:

$$V_O = 167.978 + 3.704\ (IV4) + 2.009\ (IV5).$$

Step 3: In the third step variable 3 (*i.e.,*) class/grade entered the analysis; with this the amount of variance explained increased from 21.9 per cent to 24.1 per cent. The regression equation at this stage was as follows:

$$V_O = 141.736 + 3.263\ (IV4) + 1.957\ (IV5) + 20.162\ (IV3).$$

Step 4: The next variable entered was general state of health of the children (variable 24). With the addition of this variable the amount of variance in the originality scores of the Ss explained increased to 25.5 per cent. The regression equation obtained was:

$$V_O = 188.469 + 3.201\ (IV4) + 1.834\ (IV5) + 18.843\ (IV3) - 23.420\ (IV24).$$

Step 5: Personality factor—B was the next variable entered and the percentage of variance explained by these five variables put together changed to 26.6 from 25.5. The multiple regression equation at this step was as follows:

$$V_O = 167.401 + 2.968\ (IV4) + 1.658\ (IV5) + 17.792\ (IV3) - 22.197\ (IV24) + 5.653\ (IV7).$$

Step 6: The next predictor variable entered in the analysis was personality factor—H. The amount of variance contributed by the six variables that entered so far was 27.1 per cent and the multiple regression equation at this stage was:

$$V_O = 141.254 + 2.901\ (IV4) + 1.646\ (IV5) + 18.216\ (IV3) - 20.883\ (IV24) + 5.393\ (IV7) + 2.384\ (IV13).$$

Step 7: Personality factor—E (IV10) was the next most significant variable entered into the step-wise multiple regression analysis. The amount of variance explained by the 7 variables put together was 27.5 per cent. The multiple regression equation at this stage could be written as:

$$V_O = 166.173 + 2.837\ (IV4) + 1.636\ (IV5) + 17.956\ (IV3) - 21.195\ (IV24) + 4.951\ (IV7) + 2.370\ (IV13) - 2.293\ (IV10).$$

Step 8: In the eighth step the variable entered into the analysis was affinity between the members of the family. The amount of variance in the originality scores of the Ss that could be explained by the 8 variables was 27.9 per cent. The regression equation obtained at this stage was:

$$V_O = 154.026 + 2.803\ (IV4) + 1.408\ (IV5) + 16.954\ (IV3) - 21.620\ (IV24) + 4.789\ (IV7) + 2.250\ (IV13) - 2.359\ (IV10) + 11.188\ (IV23).$$

It may be seen from the above analysis that, the most significant contributors to the originality of the Ss were intelligence, SES, class/grade, general state of health, personality factor—B, personality factor—H, personality factor—E, and affinity between the members of the family, in that order.

Table—6.89 shows in a nut shell the variable entered at each step and the variance explained by all the variable put together upto that step.

4. Composite Creativity

As in the pervious cases the step-wise multiple regression analysis was carried out to predict the amount of variance in the composite creativity score of the Ss that was contributed by the different independent variables. The results are presented in Table—6.90.

Step 1: The most important independent variable that entered into the step-wise regression analysis was variable 4 (*i.e.,*) intelligence as in the case of fluency, flexibility and originality. The multiple R (0.456) was significant at 0.001

level for 1 and 898 df (F = 236.016). The R^2 was 0.208 showing that the amount of contribution of intelligence to the creativity of the Ss was 20.8 per cent.

Table—6.89 Variable Entered At Each Stage and the Amount of Variance Explained Upto that Stage in the Step-wise Multiple Regression Analysis with Originality as measured by Verbal Tests as Dependent Variable

Step No.	*Variable entered*	*Variable number*	*Per cent of variance explained upto that step*
1.	Intelligence	4	18.9
2.	SES	5	21.9
3.	Class/grade	3	24.1
4.	General state of health	24	25.5
5.	Personality factor—B	7	26.6
6.	Personality factor—H	13	27.1
7.	Personality factor—E	10	27.5
8.	Affinity between the members of the family	23	27.9

The partial regression coefficient of 5.721 shows that the creativity of the Ss changed by 5.721 units for every unit of change in the intelligence of the Ss. Thus the regression equation could be written as:

$$V_C^{11} = 302.633 + 5.721\ (IV4).$$

Step 2: The next most important variable that was entered into the multiple regression analysis was class/grade. The two variables—intelligence and class/grade—contributed to 24.4 per cent of the variance in the composite creativity of the Ss as indicated by the multiple R^2 of 0.244. The multiple regression equation at this stage could be written as:

$$V_C = 256.515 + 4.951\ (IV4) + 34.381\ (IV3).$$

Table—6.90 Results of Step-wise Multiple Regression Analysis Between Composite Creativity and Other Independent Variables (Verbal Tests)

Step No.	IV	VN	R	R^2	SER	F value for R	b	VN	F value for b	Constant	β	γ	Per cent of variance
1	2	3	4	5	6	7	8	9	10	11	12	13	14
1.	Intelligence	4	0.456	0.208	0.372	236.016	5.721	4	235.929	302.633	0.456	0.456	20.793
						(1,898)							
2.	Class/grade	3	0.494	0.244	5.286	144.580	4.951	4	167.184	256.515	0.394	0.321	17.966
						(2,897)	34.381	3	42.250		0.199		6.387
3.	SES	5	0.521	0.272	0.448	111.752	4.485	4	136.422	216.700	0.357	0.272	16.279
						(3,896)	33.463	3	41.473		0.193		6.195
							2.655	5	35.046		0.173		4.706
4.	General state of health	24	0.535	0.286	7.544	89.817	4.402	4	133.402	280.117	0.351	–0.195	16.005
						(4.895)	31.672	3	37.577		0.184		5.906
							2.488	5	31.136		0.162		4.406
							–31.781	24	17.741		–0.120		2.340

(Contd...)

Table—6.90 (Contd...)

1	*2*	*3*	*4*	*5*	*6*	*7*	*8*	*9*	*10*	*11*	*12*	*13*	*14*
5.	PF—B	7	0.546	0.298	2.000	75.898	4.086	4	111.513	251.519	0.326	0.274	14.866
						(5,894)	30.245	3	34.680		0.175		5.617
							2.248	5	25.301		0.147		3.998
							–30.122	24	36.192		–0.114		2.223
							7.673	7	14.669		0.114		3.123
6.	PF—H	13	0.550	0.303	1.295	64.895	3.987	4	105.884	231.343	0.318	0.149	14.501
						(6,893)	30.865	3	36.240		0.179		5.745
							2.231	5	25.100		0.146		3.971
							–28.202	24	14.062		–0.107		2.086
							7.295	7	13.322		0.107		2.932
							3.481	13	7.236		0.076		1.132
7.	Affinity between the members of the family	23	0.555	0.308	11.803	56.646	3.903	4	101.002	169.623	0.311	0.173	14.182
						(7,892)	30.150	3	34.692		0.175		5.617
							2.146	5	23.136		0.140		3.808
							–27.868	24	13.838		–0.106		2.067
							7.129	7	12.745		0.105		2.877
							3.373	13	6.812		0.074		1.103
							27.129	23	5.281		0.065		1.124

(Contd...)

Table—6.90 (Contd...)

1	2	3	4	5	6	7	8	9	10	11	12	13	14
8.	Type of family	22	0.557	0.311	6.653	50.367	3.857	4	98.804	151.315	0.307	–0.208	13.299
						(8,891)	28.829	3	31.360		0.167		5.361
							1.848	5	15.761		0.121		3.291
							–28.391	24	14.364		–0.108		2.106
							6.928	7	12.041		0.102		2.795
							3.212	13	6.185		0.071		1.056
							28.335	23	5.760		0.068		1.176
							–14.499	22	4.752		–0.065		1.352
9.	PF—E	10	0.561	0.315	1.329	45.431	3.783	4	94.673	183.295	0.301	–0.152	13.726
						(9,890)	28.514	3	30.802		0.165		5.296
							1.832	5	15.523		0.120		3.264
							–28.802	24	14.876		–0.109		2.125
							6.392	7	10.176		0.095		2.603
							3.196	13	6.145		0.070		1.043
							27.028	23	5.258		0.065		1.124
							–14.879	22	5.013		–0.067		1.394
							–2.790	10	4.406		–0.059		0.897

Note: See note under Table—6.84.

Step 3: The next predictor variable entered into the analysis was SES, and the amount of variance predicted by the 3 variables—intelligence, class/grade and SES was 27.2 per cent. The multiple regression equation at this stage was:

$$V_C = 216.700 + 4.485\ (IV4) + 33.463\ (IV3) + 2.655\ (IV5).$$

Step 4: The independent variable entered next was general state of health of the children (IV24), and the per cent of variance contributed by all the four variables increased to 28.6. The multiple regression equation obtained at this stage was as follows:

$$V_C = 280.117 + 4.402\ (IV4) + 31.672\ (IV3) + 2.488\ (IV5) - 31.781\ (IV24).$$

Step 5: Variable 7 (*i.e.,*) personality factor—B entered the analysis at this stage and the amount of variance in the creativity of the Ss explained by the 5 variables was 29.8, per cent. The regression equation at this stage could be written as:

$$V_C = 251.519 + 4.086\ (IV4) + 30.245\ (IV3) + 2.248\ (IV5) - 30.122\ (IV24) + 7.673\ (IV7).$$

Step 6: The next variable entered into the multiple regression analysis was personality factor—H (variable 13) and the per cent of variance explained increased to 30.3 from 29.8. The multiple regression equation at this stage was:

$$V_C = 231.343 + 3.987\ (IV4) + 30.865\ (IV3) + 2.231\ (IV5) - 28.202\ (IV24) + 7.295\ (IV7) + 3.481\ (IV13).$$

Step 7: Variable 23 (*i.e.,*) affinity between the members of the family was the next to enter the analysis and the amount of variance explained changed from 30.0 per cent to 30.8 per cent. The regression equation at this stage was as given below:

$$V_C = 169.923 + 3.903 + (IV4) + 30.150\ (IV3) + 2.146\ (IV5) - 27.868\ (IV24) + 7.129\ (IV7) + 3.373\ (IV13) + 27.129\ (IV23).$$

Step 8: The predictor variable that entered into the regression analysis at this step was type of family (IV22) and the amount of variance explained by all the 8 variables was 31.1 per cent. The multiple regression equation at this step was:

$$V_C = 151.315 + 3.857\,(IV4) + 28.829\,(IV3) + 1.848\,(IV5) - 28.391\,(IV24) + 6.928\,(IV7) + 3.212\,(IV13) + 28.335\,(IV23) - 14.499\,(IV22).$$

Step 9: The next variable entered was personality factor—E (IV10). The per cent of variance explained by all the variables that entered upto the stage was 31.5. The prediction equation with these 9 variables could be written as:

$$V_C = 183.295 + 3.783\,(IV4) + 28.514\,(IV3) + 1.832\,(IV5) - 28.802\,(IV24) + 6.392\,(IV7) + 3.196\,(IV13) + 27.028\,(IV23) - 14.879\,(IV22) - 2.790\,(IV10).$$

It may be inferred from the above analysis that the most significant independent variables that contributed to the composite creativity of the Ss were intelligence, class/grade, SES, general state of health, personality factor—B, personality factor—H, affinity between the members of the family, type of family and personality factor—E in that order.

The variables that entered at the difference stages and the amount of variance explained at the respective stages is shown in a summary form the Table—6.91.

B. Nonverbal Tests

1. Fluency

In the previous section, results of step-wise multiple regression analysis taking creativity scores, as measured by the verbal tests as the dependent variable were discussed.

This section dealts with the multiple regression analysis taking the creativity scores as measured by the nonverbal tests as the dependent variable. In other words this section deals with the analysis of the relative contribution of each of the independent variables to creativity of the Ss as measured by the nonverbal tests.

Table—6.91 Variable Entered At Each Stage and the Amount of Variance Explained Upto that Stage in the Step-wise Multiple Regression Analysis with Composite Creativity as Measured by Verbal Tests as Dependent Variable

Step No.	*Variable entered*	*Variable number*	*Per cent of variance explained upto that step*
1.	Intelligence	4	20.8
2.	Class/grade	3	24.4
3.	SES	5	27.2
4.	General state of health of children	24	28.6
5.	Personality factor—B	7	29.8
6.	Personality factor—H	13	30.3
7.	Affinity between members of the family	23	30.8
8.	Type of family	22	31.1
9.	Personality factor—E	10	31.5

Step 1: From Table—6.92 it could be seen that the first variable entered in the multiple regression analysis was intelligence (IV4). The values of multiple R and R^2 were 0.305 and 0.093 respectively, indicating that this variable contributed to 9.3 per cent of the variance in the creativity as measured by the fluency component on the nonverbal tests.

The partial regression coefficient 0.172, shows that for every unit of change in this variable there would be a change of 0.172 units in the fluency score of the Ss. The regression equation at this stage was:

$$NV_F{}^{12} = 19.823 + 0.172\ (IV4).$$

Step 2: The second variable that entered into the analysis was variable 23 (*i.e.,*) affinity between the members of the family. The values of multiple R and R^2 were 0.332 and 0.110 respectively. Thus the two variables in combination could explain 11 per cent of variance in the dependent variable. The multiple regression equation at this stage could be written as:

$$NV_F = 15.651 + 0.160\ (IV4) + 2.415\ (IV23).$$

Step 3: In the third step the predictor variable that entered was variable 22 (*i.e.,*) type of family. The multiple R^2 was 0.123. Thus 12.3 per cent of the variance in the nonverbal fluency was explained by these three predictor variables put together and the regression equation at this stage was as given below:

$$NV_F = 18.111 + 0.156\ (IV4) + 2.410\ (IV23) - 1.489\ (IV22).$$

Step 4: The independent variable entered at this stage was sex (IV1). Amount of variance in the dependent variable explained by all the 4 variables put together was 13.4 per cent and the regression equation at this stage could be written as:

$$NV_F = 20.259 + 0.152\ (IV4) + 2.418\ (IV23) - 1.536\ (IV22) - 1.314\ (IV1).$$

Step 5: The next independent variable entered into the analysis was: locality (IV2). The amount of variance predicted by all the 5 variables that entered upto this stage was 14.3 per cent. The multiple regression equation obtained was:

$$NV_F = 18.516 + 0.155\ (IV4) + 2.488\ (IV23) - 1.723\ (IV22) - 1.314\ (IV1) + 1.201\ (IV2).$$

Step 6: SES was the next variable entered into the analysis and the amount of variance explained by these 6 variables put together was 15.4 per cent. The multiple regression equation was:

$$NV_F = 17.337 + 0.143\ (IV4) + 2.317\ (IV23) - 1.699\ (IV22) - 1.565\ (IV1) + 1.593\ (IV2) + 0.078\ (IV5).$$

Table—6.92 Results of Step-wise Multiple Regression Analysis Between Fluency and Other Independent Variables (Non-verbal Tests)

Step No.	IV	VN	R	R^2	SER	F value for R	b	VN	F value for b	Constant	β	γ	Per cent of variance
1	2	3	4	5	6	7	8	9	10	11	12	13	14
1.	Intelligence	4	0.305	0.093	0.018	92.514	0.172	4	92.506	19.823	0.306	0.306	9.363
						(1,898)							
2.	Affinity between members of the family	23	0.332	0.110	0.593	55.351	0.160	4	79.745	15.651	0.285	0.175	8.721
						(2,897)	2.415	23	16.581		0.130		2.275
3.	Type of family	22	0.351	0.123	0.398	42.095	0.156	4	76.213	18.111	0.278	–0.137	8.507
						(3,896)	2.410	23	16.761		0.130		2.275
							–1.489	22	13.987		–0.117		1.603
4.	Sex	1	0.366	0.134	0.395	34.690	0.152	4	72.846	20.259	0.270	–0.119	8.262
						(4,895)	2.418	23	17.048		0.131		2.292
							–1.536	22	15.023		–0.121		1.657
							–1.314	1	11.055		–0.104		1.237

(Contd...)

Table—6.92 (Contd...)

1	*2*	*3*	*4*	*5*	*6*	*7*	*8*	*9*	*10*	*11*	*12*	*13*	*14*
5.	Locality	2	0.378	0.143	0.399	29.815	0.155	4	76.832	18.516	0.276	0.043	8.446
						(5,894)	2.488	23	18.190		0.134		2.345
							–1.723	22	18.619		–0.136		1.863
							–1.314	1	11.162		–0.104		1.237
							1.201	2	9.060		0.095		0.408
6.	SES	5	0.392	0.154	0.023	27.013	0.143	4	62.568	17.337	0.254	0.139	7.772
						(6,893)	2.317	23	15.824		0.125		2.187
							–1.699	22	18.301		–0.134		1.836
							–1.565	1	15.445		–0.124		1.476
							1.593	2	14.853		0.126		0.542
							0.078	5	11.309		0.114		1.585
7.	Order of birth	20	0.402	0.162	0.263	24.704	0.145	4	64.481	18.707	0.258	–0.079	7.895
						(7,892)	2.269	23	15.311		0.123		2.152
							–1.668	22	17.791		–0.132		1.808
							–1.553	1	15.343		–0.123		1.464
							1.648	2	16.008		0.130		0.559
							0.083	5	13.075		0.121		1.682
							–0.803	20	9.302		–0.094		0.742

(Contd...)

1	2	3	4	5	6	7	8	9	10	11	12	13	14
8.	PF—B	7	0.410	0.169	0.098	22.695	0.132	4	51.179	17.759	0.235	0.182	7.191
						(8,891)	2.198	23	14.440		0.119		2.082
							–1.583	22	16.040		–0.125		1.712
							–1.633	1	17.707		–0.129		1.535
							1.668	2	16.516		0.132		0.567
							0.076	5	10.850		0.111		1.543
							–0.773	20	8.685		–0.090		0.711
							0.266	7	7.387		0.088		1.600
9.	Liberty given by the parents to the children	30	0.147	0.174	0.287	20.822	0.130	4	50.367	19.532	0.231	–0.086	7.068
						(9,890)	2.116	23	13.395		0.114		1.995
							–1.597	22	16.394		–0.126		1.726
							–1.746	1	19.210		–0.138		1.642
							1.611	2	15.413		0.127		0.546
							0.074	5	10.240		0.108		1.501
							–0.755	20	8.323		–0.088		0.695
							0.263	7	7.214		0.087		1.583
							–0.643	30	5.022		–0.069		0.593
10.	PF—E	10	0.422	0.178	0.066	19.238	0.126	4	46.512	21.208	0.224	–0.115	6.855
						(10,889)	2.046	23	12.517		0.110		1.925
							–1.565	22	15.769		–0.124		1.699
							–1.875	1	21.697		–0.148		1.761
							1.598	2	15.210		0.126		0.542
							0.075	5	10.530		0.109		1.515
							–0.753	20	8.294		–0.088		0.695
							0.239	7	5.953		0.079		1.438
							–0.643	30	5.035		–0.069		0.593
							–0.137	10	4.293		–0.065		0.747

Note: See note under Table—6.84.

Step 7: At this stage variable 20 (order of birth) entered into the analysis. The amount of variance contributed by these seven independent variables considered so far was 16.2 per cent. The prediction equation at this stage could be written as:

$$NV_F = 18.707 + 0.145\ (IV4) + 2.269\ (IV23) - 1.668\ (IV22) - 1.553\ (IV1) + 1.648\ (IV2) + 0.083\ (IV5) - 0.803\ (IV20).$$

Step 8: Personality factor—B (IV7) entered next into the analysis. The amount of variance predicted by all the 8 variables was 16.9 per cent and the prediction equation at this stage was as follows:

$$NV_F = 17.759 + 0.132\ (IV4) + 2.198\ (IV23) - 1.583\ (IV22) - 1.633\ (IV1) + 1.668\ (IV2) + 0.076\ (IV5) - 0.773\ (IV20) + 0.266\ (IV7).$$

Step 9: Liberty given by parents to the children in doing things (IV30) was the next variable that entered into the analysis and the amount variance explained changed to 17.4 per cent. The regression equation at this stage was:

$$NV_F = 19.532 + 0.130\ (IV4) + 2.116\ (IV23) - 1.597\ (IV22) - 1.746\ (IV1) + 1.611\ (IV2) + 0.074\ (IV5) - 0.755\ (IV20) + 0.263\ (IV7) - 0.643\ (IV30).$$

Step 10: The next predictor variable entered into the regression analysis was variable 10 (*i.e.,*) personality factor—E. The amount of variance contributed by all the 10 variables to the fluency score as measured by the nonverbal tests was 17.8 per cent. The regression equation at this stage could be written as:

$$NV_F = 21.208 + 0.126\ (IV4) + 2.046\ (IV23) - 1.565\ (IV22) - 1.875\ (IV1) + 1.598\ (IV2) + 0.075\ (IV5) - 0.753\ (IV20) + 0.239\ (IV7) - 0.643\ (IV30) - 0.137\ (IV10).$$

From the above analysis it may be seen that the most significant contributors to the variance in the fluency score of the Ss as measured by the nonverbal tests were intelligence, affinity between the members of the family, type of family, sex, locality, SES, order of birth, personality factor—B, liberty given by parents to the children in doing things and personality factor E, in that order.

The variable that entered at each stage and the amount of variance explained upto that stage is given in a summary form in Table—6.93.

Table—6.93 Variable Entered At Each Stage and the Amount of Variance Explained Upto that Stage in the Step-wise Multiple Regression Analysis with Fluency as Measured by Nonverbal Tests as Dependent Variable

Step No.	*Variable entered*	*Variable number*	*Per cent of variance explained upto the step*
1.	Intelligence	4	9.3
2.	Affinity between the members of the family	23	11.0
3.	Type of family	22	12.3
4.	Sex	1	13.4
5.	Locality	2	14.3
6.	SES	5	15.4
7.	Order of birth	20	16.2
8.	Personality factor—B	7	16.9
9.	Liberty given by parents to the children in doing things	30	17.4
10.	Personality factor—E	10	17.8

2. Flexibility

As in the earlier cases step-wise multiple regression analysis was carried out with flexibility scores as the dependent variable. The results obtained are presented in Table—6.94.

Table—6.94 Results of Step-wise Multiple Regression Analysis Between Flexibility and Other Independent Variables (Nonverbal Tests)

Step No.	*IV*	*VN*	*R*	R^2	*SER*	*F value for R*	*b*	*VN*	*F value for b*	*Constant*	β	γ	*Per cent of variance*
1	2	*3*	*4*	*5*	*6*	*7*	*8*	*9*	*10*	*11*	*12*	*13*	*14*
1.	Intelligence	4	0.313	0.098	0.012	98.156	0.123	4	98.148	17.014	0.313	0.314	9.818
						(1,898)							
2.	Sex	1	0.335	0.112	0.280	56.434	0.120	4	94.342	18.637	0.305	–0.135	9.577
						(2,897)	–1.023	1	13.359		–0.115		1.552
3.	SES	5	0.355	0.126	0.015	42.951	0.109	4	73.960	18.028	0.276	0.163	8.666
						(3,896)	–1.217	1	18.490		–0.137		1.849
							0.059	5	14.288		0.123		2.005
4.	Locality	2	0.381	0.145	0.288	37.858	0.110	4	76.492	15.739	0.279	0.072	8.761
						(4,895)	–1.279	1	20.867		–0.144		1.944
							0.080	5	24.512		0.166		2.706
							1.282	2	19.865		0.144		1.037
5.	PF—B	7	0.394	0.155	0.069	32.804	0.099	4	58.828	14.976	0.251	0.184	7.881
						(5,894)	–1.349	1	23.329		–0.152		2.052
							0.074	5	20.784		0.154		2.510
							1.312	2	21.022		0.148		1.066
							0.227	7	10.909		0.107		1.969

(Contd...)

1	2	3	4	5	6	7	8	9	10	11	12	13	14
6.	Affinity	23	0.405	0.164	0.406	29.134	0.094	4	53.261	12.904	0.239	0.155	7.505
	between					(6,893)	–1.335	1	23.069		–0.150		2.025
	members of						0.069	5	18.628		0.144		2.347
	the family						1.322	2	21.529		0.149		1.073
							0.218	7	10.081		0.103		1.895
							1.235	23	9.266		0.095		1.472
7.	Order of	20	0.412	0.170	0.183	26.059	0.096	4	54.923	13.754	0.244	–0.060	7.662
	birth					(7,892)	–1.326	1	22.886		–0.149		2.011
							0.073	5	20.539		0.152		2.477
							1.356	2	22.734		0.153		1.102
							0.210	7	9.437		0.099		1.822
							1.210	23	8.934		0.093		1.441
							–0.469	20	6.523		–0.078		0.468
8.	PF—E	10	0.417	0.174	0.046	23.465	0.092	4	50.723	15.002	0.234	–0.110	7.348
						(8,891)	–1.420	1	25.695		–0.160		2.160
							0.074	5	20.939		0.154		2.510
							1.350	2	22.619		0.152		1.094
							0.193	7	7.879		0.091		1.674
							1.159	23	8.208		0.089		1.379
							–0.467	20	6.487		–0.078		0.468
							–0.099	10	4.575		–0.067		0.737

(Contd...)

Table—6.94 (Contd...)

1	2	3	4	5	6	7	8	9	10	11	12	13	14
9.	General state of health	24	0.422	0.178	0.255	21.416	0.091	4	48.832	16.198	0.231	–0.111	7.253
						(9,890)	–1.437	1	26.409		–0.162		2.187
							0.071	5	19.360		0.148		2.412
							1.326	2	21.855		0.149		1.073
							0.184	7	7.139		0.087		1.601
							1.134	23	7.868		0.087		1.348
							–0.469	20	6.579		–0.078		0.468
							–0.102	10	4.844		–0.069		0.759
							–0.530	24	9.322		–0.064		0.710
10.	Type of family	22	0.425	0.181	0.276	19.678	0.090	4	48.414	16.828	0.228	–0.077	7.159
						(10,889)	–1.446	1	26.729		–0.163		2.200
							0.071	5	19.360		0.148		2.412
							1.404	2	24.049		0.158		1.137
							0.175	7	6.451		0.083		1.527
							1.145	23	8.048		0.088		1.364
							–0.461	20	6.375		–0.077		0.462
							–0.098	10	4.503		–0.067		0.737
							–0.488	24	3.636		–0.059		0.655
							–0.517	22	3.497		–0.058		0.447

Note: See note under Table—6.84.

Step 1: It could be seen from the table that the most important independent variable that entered first into the regression analysis was intelligence (IV4) as in the earlier cases. The multiple R^2 was 0.098, showing that the amount of variance contributed by the intelligence of the Ss to the flexibility score 9.8 per cent.

The partial regression coefficient 0.123 shows that for every unit of change in this variable, there would be a change of 0.123 units in the flexibility of the students as measured by the nonverbal tests. The regression equation could be written as:

$$NV_X^{13} = 17.014 + 0.123\ (IV4).$$

Step 2: The next most important variable that was entered into the multiple regression analysis was sex (IV1). The multiple R^2 at this stage was 0.112. Thus intelligence and sex jointly contributed to 11.2 per cent of the variance in the total nonverbal flexibility of the students. The multiple regression equation at this stage could be written as:

$$NV_X = 18.637 + 0.120\ (IV4) - 1.023\ (IV1)$$

Step 3: The predictor variable entered into the analysis at this stage was SES (IV5) and the amount of variance predicted by 3 variables entered upto this stage was 12.6 per cent. The multiple regression equation at this step could be written as follows:

$$NV_X = 18.028 + 0.109\ (IV4) - 1.217\ (IV1) + 0.059\ (IV5).$$

Step 4: Locality was the next independent variable entered into the analysis and 14.5 per cent of variance was contributed by the 4 variables. The multiple regression equation at this stage was:

$$NV_X = 15.739 + 0.110\ (IV4) - 1.279\ (IV1) + 0.080\ (IV5) + 1.282\ (IV2).$$

Step 5: Variable 7 (*i.e.,*) personality factor—B entered the analysis at this stage and the amount of variance in flexibility explained increased to 15.5 per cent. The regression equation obtained at this stage was:

$$NV_X = 14.976 + 0.099\ (IV4) - 1.349\ (IV1) + 0.074\ (IV5) + 1.312\ (IV2) + 0.227\ (IV7).$$

Step 6: Affinity between the members of the family (IV23) entered next into the analysis and the per cent of variance contributed by these 6 variables increased to 16.4 per cent. The multiple regression equation at this stage was as given below:

$$NV_X = 12.904 + 0.094\ (IV4) - 1.335\ (IV1) + 0.069\ (IV5) + 1.322\ (IV2) + 0.218\ (IV7) + 1.235\ (IV23).$$

Step 7: Variable 20 (order of birth) entered next into the analysis and 17 per cent of variance in the flexibility was explained by the 7 variables. The regression equation at this stage could be written as:

$$NV_X = 13.754 + 0.096\ (IV4) - 1.326\ (IV1) + 0.073\ (IV5) + 1.356\ (IV2) + 0.210\ (IV7) + 1.210\ (IV23) - 0.469\ (IV20).$$

Step 8: In step 8 personality factor—E was the predictor variable that entered into the analysis and the total amount of variance explained increased from 17 per cent to 17.4 per cent. The following regression equation was obtained at this stage:

$$NV_X = 15.002 + 0.092\ (IV4) - 1.420\ (IV1) + 0.074\ (IV5) + 1.350\ (IV2) + 0.193\ (IV7) + 1.159\ (IV23) - 0.467\ (IV20) - 0.099\ (IV10).$$

Step 9: General state of health of the children was the next variable entered and the per cent of variance contributed by the 9 variables considered upto this stage was 17.8 per cent. The prediction equation with these 9 variables could be written as:

$$NV_X = 16.198 + 0.091\ (IV4) - 1.437\ (IV1) + 0.071\ (IV5) + 1.326\ (IV2) + 0.184\ (IV7) + 1.134\ (IV23) - 0.469\ (IV20) - 0.102\ (IV10) - 0.530\ (IV24).$$

Step 10: Variable 22 (*i.e.,*) type of family was the next independent variable that entered into the multiple regression analysis. The amount of variance explained by the 10 variables put together was 18.1 per cent and the prediction equation at this stage was as follows:

$$NV_X = 16.828 + 0.090\ (IV4) - 1.446\ (IV1) + 0.071\ (IV5) + 1.404\ (IV2) + 0.175\ (IV7) + 1.145\ (IV23) - 0.461\ (IV20) - 0.098\ (IV10) - 0.488\ (IV24) - 0.517\ (IV22).$$

Table—6.95 Variable Entered At Each Stage and the Amount of Variance Explained Upto that Stage in the Step-wise Multiple Regression Analysis with Flexibility As Measured by Nonverbal Tests As Dependent Variable

Step No.	*Variables entered*	*Variable number*	*Per cent of variance explained upto the step*
1.	Intelligence	4	9.8
2.	Sex	1	11.2
3.	SES	5	12.6
4.	Locality	2	14.5
5.	Personality factor—B	7	15.5
6.	Affinity between the members of the family	23	16.4
7.	Order of birth	20	17.0
8.	Personality factor—E	10	17.4
9.	General state of health of the children	24	17.8
10.	Type of family	22	18.1

Thus it may be concluded from the above analysis that the most significant variables that contributed to the flexibility of the Ss as measured by the nonverbal tests were intelligence, sex, SES, locality, personality factor—B, affinity between the members of the family, order of birth, personality factor—E, general state of health of the children and type of family, in that order.

The variable that entered at each stage and the amount of variance explained upto each stage are given in a summary form in Table—6.95.

3. Originality

Step 1: In the step-wise multiple regression analysis taking originality as measured by the nonverbal tests as the dependent variable, the first independent variable that entered the analysis was intelligence (IV4), as in all the other analyses discussed so far. The multiple R^2 of 0.083 obtained at this stage indicates that 8.3 per cent of the variance in the originality scores of the Ss was contributed by the variable intelligence (Table—6.96).

The partial regression coefficient (b) shows that the originality score increased by 0.689 units for every unit of increase in the intelligence. Thus the regression equation between originality and intelligence could be written as:

$$NV_O^{14} = 74.439 + 0.689\ (IV4).$$

Step 2: The second most important predictor variable that entered into the analysis was variable 2, *viz.*, locality. The value of R^2 at this stage was 0.097. Thus the amount of variance in the originality score explained by the two variables, intelligence and locality was 9.7 per cent. Out of this, the contribution of intelligence was 8.524 per cent while that of locality was 1.119 per cent. The multiple regression equation with these two predictor variables—intelligence and locality could be written as:

$$NV_O = 64.099 + 0.713\ (IV4) + 6.430\ (IV2).$$

Step 3: The next predictor variable that entered in the analysis was type of family (IV22). From the multiple R^2 of 0.110, it may be inferred that the percentage of variance explained by the three predictor variables, *viz.*, intelligence, locality and type of family was 11 per cent. The regression equation at this stage was:

$$NV_O = 73.168 + 0.697\ (IV4) + 7.441\ (IV2) - 6.494\ (IV22).$$

Table—6.96 Results of Step-wise Multiple Regression Analysis Between Originality and Other Independent Variables (Nonverbal Tests)

Step No.	IV	VN	R	R^2	SER	F value for R	b	VN	F value for b	Constant	β	γ	Per cent of variance
1	2	3	4	5	6	7	8	9	10	11	12	13	14
1.	Intelligence	4	0.288	0.083	0.076	80.881 (1,898)	0.689	4	80.820	74.439	0.287	0.287	8.237
2.	Locality	2	0.314	0.097	1.721	48.001 (2,897)	0.713	4	87.161	64.099	0.297	0.094	8.524
							6.430	2	13.950		0.119		1.119
3.	Type of family	22	0.332	0.110	1.733	37.148 (3,896)	0.697	4	84.272	73.168	0.291	–0.117	8.352
							7.441	2	18.490		0.138		1.297
							–6.494	22	14.040		–0.120		1.404
4.	Affinity between members of the family	23	0.352	0.124	2.514	31.719 (4,895)	0.653	4	73.274	56.640	0.272	0.155	7.806
							7.695	2	20.034		0.143		1.344
							–6.521	22	14.364		–0.121		1.416
							9.354	23	13.831		0.118		1.829

(Contd...)

Table—6.96 (Contd...)

1	2	3	4	5	6	7	8	9	10	11	12	13	14
5.	SES	5	0.367	0.135	0.098	27.854	0.604	4	60.934	50.005	0.252	0.139	7.232
						(5,894)	9.333	2	27.499		0.173		1.626
							–6.381	22	13.898		–0.118		1.380
							8.633	23	11.826		0.109		1.689
							0.324	5	10.975		0.111		1.543
6.	Sex	1	0.378	0.143	1.709	24.926	0.579	4	56.025	57.259	0.241	–0.087	6.917
						(6,893)	9.617	2	28.376		0.178		1.673
							–6.542	22	14.722		–0.121		1.416
							8.538	23	11.669		0.108		1.674
							0.381	5	14.692		0.130		1.807
							–5.138	1	9.036		–0.095		0.827
7.	PF—B	7	0.387	0.150	0.422	22.495	0.529	4	44.209	53.516	0.221	0.171	6.343
						(7,892)	9.709	2	30.129		0.180		1.692
							–6.183	22	13.155		–0.114		1.334
							8.234	23	10.897		0.104		1.612
							0.351	5	12.453		0.120		1.668
							–5.472	1	10.259		–0.101		0.879
							1.111	7	6.912		0.086		1.471

(Contd...)

Table—6.96 (Contd...)

1	2	3	4	5	6	7	8	9	10	11	12	13	14
8.	Order of birth	20	0.395	0.156	1.128	20.587	0.536	4	45.697	58.497	0.226	–0.063	6.486
						(8,891)	9.898	2	31.438		0.183		1.702
							–6.087	22	12.816		–0.113		1.322
							8.078	23	10.549		0.102		1.581
							0.373	5	13.995		0.127		1.765
							–5.414	1	10.099		–0.100		0.870
							1.067	7	6.411		0.083		1.419
							–2.832	20	6.290		–0.078		0.491
9.	PF—H	13	0.400	0.160	0.272	18.884	0.522	4	43.165	53.845	0.218	0.125	6.257
						(9,890)	9.572	2	29.300		0.177		1.664
							–6.119	22	13.010		–0.113		1.322
							7.878	23	10.055		0.099		1.534
							0.364	5	13.322		0.124		1.724
							–5.343	1	9.872		–0.099		0.861
							0.998	7	5.593		0.077		1.317
							–2.876	20	6.502		–0.079		0.498
							0.583	13	4.596		0.067		0.837

Note: See note under Table—6.84.

Step 4: Variable 23 (*i.e.,*) affinity between the members of the family was the next most significant variable that entered into the analysis. 12.4 per cent of the variance in the originality scores was contributed by these four predictor variables put together. The regression equation obtained at this stage was:

$$NV_O = 56.640 + 0.653\ (IV4) + 7.695\ (IV2) - 6.531\ (IV22) + 9.354\ (IV23).$$

Step 5: SES entered the analysis at this stage and the amount of variance explained by all the 5 variables increased from 12.4 per cent to 13.5 per cent. The regression equation obtained could be written as:

$$NV_O = 50.005 + 0.604\ (IV4) + 9.333\ (IV2) - 6.381\ (IV22) + 8.633\ (IV23) + 0.324\ (IV5).$$

Step 6: Sex was the next variable entered into the analysis and the total amount of variance contributed by the 6 variables was 14.3 per cent. The multiple regression equation at this stage was:

$$NV_O = 57.259 + 0.579\ (IV4) + 9.617\ (IV2) - 6.542\ (IV22) + 8.538\ (IV23) + 0.381\ (IV5) - 5.138\ (IV1).$$

Step 7: Personality factor—B entered the analysis next and the amount of variance explained increased to 15 per cent. The regression equation at this stage was:

$$NV_O = 53.516 + 0.529\ (IV4) + 9.709\ (IV2) - 6.183\ (IV22) + 8.234\ (IV23) + 0.351\ (IV5) - 5.472\ (IV1) + 1.111\ (IV7).$$

Step 8: Independent variable 20 (*i.e.,*) order of birth was the next predictor variable that entered into the regression analysis and the amount of variance explained was 15.6 per cent. The multiple regression equation at this step was as given below:

$$NV_O = 58.497 + 0.536\ (IV4) + 9.898\ (IV2) - 6.087\ (IV22) + 8.078\ (IV23) + 0.373\ (IV5) - 5.414\ (IV1) + 1.067\ (IV7) - 2.832\ (IV20).$$

Step 9: Personality factor—H entered as the next most significant predictor variable. 16 per cent of the variance was contributed by the 9 variables put together. The prediction equation with these 9 variables could be written as:

$$NV_O = 53.845 + 0.522\ (IV4) + 9.572\ (IV2) - 6.119\ (IV22) + 7.878\ (IV23) + 0.364\ (IV5) - 5.343\ (IV1) + 0.998\ (IV7) - 2.876\ (IV20) + 0.583\ (IV13).$$

It may be seen from the above analysis that, the most significant contributors to the originality of the Ss were intelligence, locality, type of family, affinity between the members of the family, SES, sex, personality, factor—B, order of birth and personality factor—H, in that order.

The variable that entered at each stage and the amount of variance explained upto that stage are shown in a summary form in Table—6.97.

Table—6.97 Variable Entered At Each Stage and the Amount of Variance Explained Upto that Stage in the Step-wise Multiple Regression Analysis, with originality as measured by nonverbal tests as dependent variable

Step No.	*Variables entered*	*Variable number*	*Per cent of variance explained upto the step*
1.	Intelligence	4	8.3
2.	Locality	2	9.7
3.	Type of family	22	11.0
4.	Affinity between the members of the family	23	12.4
5.	SES	5	13.5
6.	Sex	1	14.3
7.	Personality factor—B	7	15.0
8.	Order of birth	20	15.6
9.	Personality factor—H	13	16.0

4. Composite Creativity

This part deals with the prediction of composite creativity score with the help of the different independent variables. The results obtained are shown in Table—6.98.

Step 1: As in the earlier cases the first independent variable that entered into the regression analysis was intelligence (IV4). The multiple R^2 of 0.089 shows that 8.9 per cent of the variance in the composite creativity score was contributed by the variable intelligence.

The partial regression coefficient, 0.981 shows that for every unit of change in this variable, there would be a change of 0.981 units in the composite creativity score of the Ss. Thus the regression equation could be written as:

$$NV_C{}^{15} = 111.108 + 0.981 \text{ (IV4)}.$$

Step 2: The next variable that entered into the analysis was variable 23 (*i.e.,*) affinity between the members of the family. The multiple R^2 at this stage was 0.102. This shows that intelligence and affinity between the members of the family, jointly contributed to 10.2 per cent of the variance in the creativity scores of the subjects. The multiple regression equation at this stage could be written as:

$$NV_C = 89.585 + 0.921 \text{ (IV4)} + 12.457 \text{ (IV23)}.$$

Step 3: The predictor variable that entered into the analysis in step 3 was locality (IV2). The amount of variance explained by the 3 variables that entered upto this stage was 11.5 per cent. The multiple regression equation at this stage was:

$$NV_C = 74.801 + 0.950 \text{ (IV4)} + 12.964 \text{ (IV23)} + 8.648 \text{ (IV2)}.$$

Step 4: The next independent variable entered was type of family (IV22). The per cent of variance explained at this stage was 13. The multiple regression equation at this step was:

$$NV_C = 87.285 + 0.928 \text{ (IV4)} + 13.020 \text{ (IV23)} + 10.051 \text{ (IV2)} - 9.009 \text{ (IV22)}.$$

Table—6.98 Results of Step-wise Multiple Regression Analysis Between Composite Creativity and Other Independent Variables (Nonverbal Tests)

Step No.	*IV*	*VN*	*R*	R^2	*SER*	*F value for R*	*b*	*VN*	*F value for b*	*Constant*	β	γ	*Per cent of variance*
1	*2*	*3*	*4*	*5*	*6*	*7*	*8*	*9*	*10*	*11*	*12*	*13*	*14*
1.	Intelligence	4	0.298	0.089	0.104	87.911 (1,898)	0.981	4	7.891	111.108	0.299	0.299	8.940
2.	Affinity between members of the family	23	0.319	0.102	3.482	50.926 (2,897)	0.921	4	14.062	89.585	0.280	0.159	8.372
							12.457	23	12.794		0.115		1.828
3.	Locality	2	0.339	0.115	2.337	38.997 (3,896)	0.950	4	82.174	74.801	0.289	0.087	8.641
							12.964	23	14.025		0.119		1.892
							8.648	2	13.690		0.117		1.018
4.	Type of family	22	0.360	0.130	2.349	33.371 (4,895)	0.928	4	79.445	87.285	0.283	–0.120	8.462
							13.020	23	14.372		0.120		1.908
							10.051	2	18.318		0.136		1.183
							–9.009	22	14.699		–0.122		1.464

(Contd...)

Table—6.98 (Contd...)

1	2	3	4	5	6	7	8	9	10	11	12	13	14
5.	SES	5	0.374	0.140	2.337	29.208	0.861	4	66.422	78.193	0.262	0.144	7.834
						(5,894)	12.032	23	12.313		0.111		1.765
							12.295	2	25.593		0.166		1.444
							–8.819	22	14.235		–0.119		1.428
							0.445	5	11.055		0.111		1.598
6.	Sex	1	0.391	0.153	2.329	26.807	0.821	4	60.606	89.987	0.250	–0.105	7.475
						(7,893)	11.878	23	12.159		0.109		1.733
							12.757	2	27.836		0.172		1.496
							–9.079	22	15.272		–0.122		1.464
							0.536	5	15.682		0.133		1.915
							–8.355	1	12.888		–0.113		1.186
7.	PF—B	7	0.400	0.160	0.575	24.367	0.745	4	47.375	84.372	0.227	0.181	6.787
						(7,892)	11.422	23	11.309		0.105		1.669
							12.895	2	28.665		0.174		1.514
							–8.541	22	13.542		–0.115		1.380
							0.492	5	13.177		0.122		1.757
							–8.855	1	14.516		–0.119		1.249
							1.666	7	8.387		0.094		1.701

(Contd...)

1	2	3	4	5	6	7	8	9	10	11	12	13	14
8.	Order of birth	20	0.409	0.167	1.523	22.330	0.756	4	49.014	91.491	0.230	–0.066	6.877
						(8,891)	11.199	23	10.943		0.103		1.637
							13.165	2	30.019		0.178		1.548
							–8.405	22	13.177		–0.113		1.356
							0.523	5	14.822		0.130		1.872
							–8.772	1	14.311		–0.118		1.239
							1.603	7	7.784		0.091		1.647
							–4.047	20	6.938		–0.081		0.535
9.	PF—H	13	0.413	0.171	0.370	20.407	0.737	4	46.444	85.351	0.224	0.124	6.697
						(9,890)	10.934	23	10.452		0.100		1.590
							12.734	2	27.984		0.172		1.496
							–8.447	22	13.373		–0.114		1.368
							0.510	5	14.190		0.127		1.828
							–8.678	1	14.062		–0.117		1.228
							1.512	7	6.927		0.086		1.556
							–4.106	20	7.166		–0.082		0.541
							0.773	13	4.347		0.065		0.806
10.	PF—E	10	0.417	0.174	0.387	18.746	0.714	4	43.112	93.991	0.217	–0.108	6.488
						(10,889)	10.571	23	9.759		0.097		1.542
							12.669	2	27.773		0.171		1.487
							–8.279	22	12.866		–0.112		1.344
							0.514	5	14.440		0.128		1.843
							–9.341	1	15.920		–0.126		1.323
							1.393	7	5.822		0.079		1.429
							–4.091	20	7.129		–0.082		0.541
							0.770	13	4.326		0.064		0.793
							–0.706	10	3.323		–0.057		0.615

Note: See note under Table—6.84.

(Contd...)

Step 5: Variable 5 (*i.e.,*) SES entered the analysis as the next most significant predictor of creativity. The amount of variance in the composite creativity of the Ss explained by all the 5 variables was 14 per cent. The regression equation obtained at this stage was as given below:

$$NV_C = 78.193 + 0.861\ (IV4) + 12.032\ (IV23) + 12.295\ (IV2) - 8.819\ (IV22) + 0.445\ (IV5).$$

Step 6: Sex (variable 1) entered next. The per cent of variance contributed by the 6 variables was 15.3 per cent. The multiple regression equation could be written as:

$$NV_C = 89.987 + 0.821\ (IV4) + 11.878\ (IV23) + 12.757\ (IV2) - 9.079\ (IV22) + 0.536\ (IV5) - 8.355\ (IV1).$$

Step 7: Variable 7 (*i.e.,*) personality factor—B was the next to enter the analysis. The amount of variance explained by these 7 variables was 16 per cent. The regression equation at this stage could be written as:

$$NV_C = 84.372 + 0.745\ (IV4) + 11.422\ (IV23) + 12.895\ (IV2) - 8.541\ (IV22) + 0.492\ (IV5) - 8.855\ (IV1) + 1.666\ (IV7).$$

Step 8: Order of birth (IV20) entered next, and the amount of variance explained was increased to 16.7 per cent. The multiple regression equation at this step was:

$$NV_C = 91.491 + 0.756\ (IV4) + 11.199\ (IV23) + 13.165\ (IV2) - 8.405\ (IV22) + 0.523\ (IV5) - 8.772\ (IV1) + 1.603\ (IV7) - 4.047\ (IV20).$$

Step 9: The next variable entered was personality factor—H (IV13) and the per cent of variance contributed changed from 16.7 per cent to 17.1 per cent. The prediction equation with these 9 variables could be written as given below:

$$NV_C = 85.351 + 0.737\ (IV4) + 10.934\ (IV23) + 12.734\ (IV2) - 8.447\ (IV22) + 0.510\ (IV5) - 8.678\ (IV1) + 1.512\ (IV7) - 4.106\ (IV20) + 0.773\ (IV13).$$

Step 10: Personality factor—E was the next independent variable that entered the regression analysis. The amount of variance explained by the 10 variables put together was 17.4 per cent. The prediction equation at this stage was:

$$NV_C = 93.991 + 0.714\,(IV4) + 10.571\,(IV23) + 12.669\,(IV2) - 8.279\,(IV22) + 0.514\,(IV5) - 9.341\,(IV1) + 1.393\,(IV7) - 4.091\,(IV20) + 0.770\,(IV13) - 706\,(IV10).$$

It may be inferred from the above analysis that the most significant independent variables that contributed to creativity as measured by composite creativity on the nonverbal tests were: intelligence, affinity between the members of the family, locality, type of family, SES, sex, personality factor—B, order of birth, personality factor—H and personality factor—E, in that order.

The variable that entered at each stage and the amount of variance explained upto that stage are presented in a summary form in Table—6.99.

Table—6.99 Variable Entered At Each Stage and the Amount of Variance Explained Upto that Stage in the Step-wise Multiple Regression Analysis with Composite Creativity As Measured by Nonverbal Tests As Dependent Variable

Step No.	*Variable entered*	*Variable number*	*Per cent of variance explained upto the step*
1.	Intelligence	4	8.9
2.	Affinity between the members of the family	23	10.2
3.	Locality	2	11.5
4.	Type of family	22	13.0
5.	SES	5	14.0
6.	Sex	1	15.3
7.	Personality factor—B	7	16.0
8.	Order of birth	20	16.7
9.	Personality factor—H	13	17.1
10.	Personality factor—E	10	17.4

C. Verbal and Nonverbal Tests Put Together

1. Fluency

The total score obtained on all the ten sub-tests was taken as the dependent variable and a similar analysis was carried out. The results are presented in the following pages.

Step 1: It could be seen from Table—6.100 that as in the previous analyses already discussed, intelligence was the first variable entered into the regression analysis.

The multiple correlation (R) obtained was 0.460. This indicated that the strength of the relationship between the two variables—intelligence and fluency component of creativity as measured by the whole test (verbal and nonverbal put together), was 46 per cent. The coefficient of multiple R^2 of 0.212 shows that 21.2 per cent of the variance in fluency as measured by the verbal and nonverbal tests put together was accounted for by intelligence.

The partial regression coefficient (b) obtained was 1.197 (column 8), which indicates that the fluency score would change by 1.197 units for every unit of change in intelligence.

Thus the multiple regression equation at the end of this step could be written as:

$W_F{}^{16} = 81.884 + 1.197$ (IV4).

Step 2: Class/grade (IV3) entered into the step-wise regression analysis as the second most significant variable. The strength of the relationship between fluency and the two independent variables put together was about 52 per cent.

The R^2 of 0.275 shows that the two variables put together could explain 27.5 per cent of variance in the independent variable. Out of this 17.471 per cent of variance was explained by intelligence and the remaining 10.058 per cent of variance was accounted for by class/grade of the Ss.

The regression equation with these two variables—intelligence and class/grade as predictor variable was:

$W_F = 69.221 + 0.986$ (IV4) + 9.442 (IV3).

Table—6.100 Results of Step-wise Multiple Regression Analysis Between Fluency and Other Independent Variables (Verbal + Nonverbal Tests)

Step No.	IV	VN	R	R^2	SER	F value for R	b	VN	F value for b	Constant	β	γ	Per cent of variance
1	2	3	4	5	6	7	8	9	10	11	12	13	14
1.	Intelligence	4	0.460	0.212	0.077	242.506 (1,898)	1.197	4	247.310	81.884	0.461	0.461	21.252
2.	Class/grade	3	0.524	0.275	1.072	170.419 (2,897)	0.986	4	77.633	69.221	0.379	0.381	17.471
							9.442	3	161.427		0.264		10.058
3.	SES	5	0.545	0.297	0.091	125.981 (3,896)	0.903	4	133.356	62.091	0.348	0.253	16.043
							9.277	3	77.071		0.260		9.906
							0.475	5	27.163		0.150		3.795
4.	PF—H	13	0.556	0.309	0.265	100.008 (4,895)	0.866	4	123.253	51.320	0.333	0.163	15.351
							9.409	3	80.515		0.263		10.020
							0.463	5	26.201		0.146		3.694
							1.054	13	15.832		0.112		1.825

(Contd...)

Table—6.100 (Contd...)

1	2	3	4	5	6	7	8	9	10	11	12	13	14
5.	Type of the family	22	0.565	0.319	1.630	83.547	0.850	4	119.719	60.824	0.327	–0.128	15.078
						(5,894)	9.542	3	83.755		0.267		10.173
							0.441	5	23.958		0.139		3.517
							1.070	13	16.522		0.113		1.842
							–5.772	22	12.545		–0.097		1.242
6.	Affinity between members of the family	23	0.573	0.328	2.405	72.590	0.821	4	111.934	47.338	0.316	0.202	14.567
						(6,893)	9.301	3	80.263		0.260		9.906
							0.413	5	21.015		0.130		3.289
							1.031	13	15.528		0.109		1.777
							–5.780	22	12.740		–0.098		1.254
							8.486	23	12.453		0.102		2.060
7.	PF—B	7	0.579	0.335	0.406	64.043	0.775	4	96.590	43.662	0.298	0.265	13.738
						(7,892)	9.052	3	76.178		0.253		9.639
							0.377	5	17.361		0.119		3.011
							0.972	13	13.878		0.103		1.679
							–5.346	22	10.909		–0.091		1.165
							8.218	23	11.765		0.099		1.999
							1.212	7	8.904		0.087		2.301

(Contd...)

1	2	3	4	5	6	7	8	9	10	11	12	13	14
8.	Sex	1	0.584	0.341	1.628	57.631	0.748	4	89.490	50.668	0.288	–0.072	13.276
						(8,891)	9.088	3	77.458		0.255		9.715
							0.423	5	21.409		0.133		3.365
							0.961	13	13.649		0.102		1.662
							–5.431	22	11.353		–0.092		1.177
							8.098	23	11.522		0.097		1.959
							1.300	7	10.279		0.094		2.491
							–4.834	1	8.815		–0.082		0.590
9.	General state of health	24	0.589	0.347	1.514	52.652	0.741	4	88.707	60.279	0.285	–0.182	13.139
						(9,890)	8.831	3	30.905		0.247		9.410
							0.405	5	19.729		0.128		3.238
							0.886	13	11.596		0.094		1.532
							–5.017	22	9.699		–0.085		1.088
							7.955	23	11.210		0.096		1.934
							1.252	7	9.604		0.090		2.385
							–4.967	1	9.219		–0.084		0.605
							–4.489	24	8.792		–0.089		1.620

(Contd...)

Table—6.100 (Contd...)

1	2	3	4	5	6	7	8	9	10	11	12	13	14
10.	PF—E	10	0.594	0.353	0.271	48.578	0.717	4	82.818	70.058	0.276	–0.164	12.724
						(10,889)	8.751	3	72.426		0.245		9.335
							0.410	5	20.402		0.129		3.264
							0.880	13	11.518		0.093		1.516
							–4.823	22	9.020		–0.082		1.049
							7.563	23	10.181		0.091		1.838
							1.123	7	7.423		0.081		2.146
							–5.699	1	12.160		–0.097		0.698
							–4.635	24	9.435		–0.085		1.547
							–0.772	10	8.121		–0.080		1.312
11.	PF—I	14	0.597	0.356	0.273	65.298	0.715	4	82.464	65.298	0.275	0.118	12.677
						(11,888)	8.615	3	70.167		0.241		9.182
							0.408	5	20.266		0.129		3.263
							0.871	13	11.093		0.092		1.499
							–4.717	22	8.647		–0.015		0.192
							7.359	23	9.656		0.088		1.777
							1.069	7	6.961		0.077		2.040
							–6.141	1	13.904		–0.104		0.749
							–4.762	24	9.978		–0.087		1.583
							–0.735	10	7.337		–0.076		1.279
							0.715	14	4.138		0.072		0.849

Note: See note under Table—6.84.

Step 3: In the third step the predictor variable entered into the analysis was SES (IV5).

The value of R^2 at this stage was 0.297. In other words 29.7 per cent of the variance was explained by these three variables, *viz.*, intelligence, class/grade, and SES. The contribution of each of the above variables was 16.043 per cent, 9.906 per cent and 3.795 per cent respectively as indicated in column 14 of Table—6.100. The regression equation at this stage was as follows:

$$W_F = 62.091 + 0.903\,(IV4) + 9.277\,(IV3) + 0.475\,(IV5).$$

Step 4: Personality factor-H entered into the regression analysis next and the amount of variance explained was 30.9%. The regression equation at this stage was:

$$W_F = 51.320 + 0.866\,(IV4) + 9.409\,(IV3) + 0.463\,(IV5) + 1.054\,(IV13).$$

Step 5: Type of family was the next predictor variable entered into the analysis. The amount of variance explained by these 5 variables increased to 31.9 per cent and the multiple regression equation at this stage was:

$$W_F = 60.824 + 0.850\,(IV4) + 9.542\,(IV3) + 0.441\,(IV5) + 1.070\,(IV13) - 5.772\,(IV22).$$

Step 6: Variable 23 (*i.e.,*) affinity between the members of the family was the next independent variable that entered into the regression analysis and the per cent of variance contributed by these 6 variables entered upto this stage was 32.8 per cent. The prediction equation with these 6 variables could be written as:

$$W_F = 47.338 + 0.821\,(IV4) + 9.301\,(IV3) + 0.413\,(IV5) + 1.031\,(IV13) - 5.780\,(IV22) + 8.486\,(IV23).$$

Step 7: Personality factor—B entered next into the analysis and the amount of variance explained increased to 33.5 per cent. The multiple regression equation obtained at this stage was:

$$W_F = 43.662 + 0.775\,(IV4) + 9.052\,(IV3) + 0.377\,(IV5) + 0.972\,(IV13) - 5.346\,(IV22) + 8.218\,(IV23) + 1.212\,(IV7).$$

Step 8: With the addition of sex (variable 1) as the next predictor variable to the regression analysis, the amount of variance explained increased from 33.5 per cent to 34.1 per cent. The multiple regression equation at this stage could be written as:

$$W_F = 50.668 + 0.748\,(IV4) + 9.088\,(IV3) + 0.423\,(IV5) + 0.961\,(IV13) - 5.431\,(IV22) + 8.098\,(IV23) + 1.300\,(IV7) - 4.834\,(IV1).$$

Step 9: Variable 24 (*i.e.,*) general state of health of the Ss entered into the analysis next. The amount of variance contributed to the fluency score of the Ss as measured by the 9 variables was 34.7 per cent and the regression equation was:

$$W_F = 60.279 + 0.741\,(IV4) + 8.831\,(IV3) + 0.405\,(IV5) + 0.886\,(IV13) - 5.017\,(IV22) + 7.955\,(IV23) + 1.252\,(IV7) - 4.967\,(IV1) - 4.489\,(IV24).$$

Step 10: With the addition of personality factor—E as the next most important predictor variable. The per cent of variance explained changed from 34.7 to 35.3. The regression equation at this stage was:

$$W_F = 70.058 + 0.717\,(IV4) + 8.751\,(IV3) + 0.410\,(IV5) + 0.880\,(IV13) - 4.823\,(IV22) + 7.563\,(IV23) + 1.123\,(IV7) - 5.699\,(IV1) - 4.635\,(IV24) - 0.772\,(IV10).$$

Step 11: Personality factor—I (variable 14) entered into the multiple regression analysis at this stage. The amount of variance explained by these 11 variables was 35.6 per cent. The regression equation obtained at this stage could be written as:

$$W_F = 65.298 + 0.715\,(IV4) + 8.615\,(IV3) + 0.408\,(IV5) + 0.871\,(IV13) - 4.717\,(IV22) + 7.359\,(IV23) + 1.069\,(IV7) - 6.141\,(IV1) - 4.762\,(IV24) - 0.735\,(IV10) + 0.715\,(IV14).$$

It may be concluded from the above analysis that the most significant variables that contributed to the fluency score of the Ss as measured by the whole test battery were intelligence, class/grade, SES, personality factor—H, type of family, affinity between the members of the family, personality factor—B, sex, general state of health of the children, personality factor—E, and personality factor—I in that order.

The variable that entered at each stage and the amount of variance explained upto that stage is given in a summary form in Table—6.101.

Table—6.101 Variable Entered At Each Stage and the Amount of Variance Explained Upto that Stage in the Step-wise Multiple Regression Analysis with Fluency As Measured By Verbal and Nonverbal Tests put Together As Dependent Variable

Step No.	*Variable entered*	*Variable number*	*Per cent of variance explained upto the step*
1.	Intelligence	4	21.2
2.	Class/grade	3	27.5
3.	SES	5	29.7
4.	Personality factor—H	13	30.9
5.	Type of family	22	31.9
6.	Affinity between the members of the family	23	32.8
7.	Personality factor—B	7	33.5
8.	Sex	1	34.1
9.	General state of health	24	34.7
10.	Personality factor—E	10	35.3
11.	Personality factor—I	14	35.6

2. Flexibility

Step 1: In step 1 of the analysis, with flexibility as measured by the whole test as dependent variable, the independent variable entered was intelligence (Table—6.102).

Table—6.102 Results of Step-wise Multiple Regression Analysis Between Flexibility and Other Independent Variables (Verbal + Nonverbal Tests)

Step No.	IV	VN	R	R^2	SER	F value for R	b	VN	F value for b	Constant	β	γ	Per cent of variance
1	2	3	4	5	6	7	8	9	10	11	12	13	14
1.	Intelligence	4	0.400	0.159	0.057	169.585 (1,898)	0.738	4	169.583	59.622	0.399	0.399	15.921
2.	Class/grade	3	0.441	0.194	0.806	107.608 (2,897)	0.626	4	114.960	52.909	0.338	0.300	13.486
							5.005	3	38.541		0.195		5.856
3.	PF—H	13	0.456	0.208	0.202	78.467 (3,896)	0.596	4	104.432	44.391	0.322	0.163	12.847
							5.104	3	40.743		0.199		5.972
							0.819	13	16.472		0.121		1.972
4.	PF—B	7	0.465	0.220	0.308	63.039 (4,385)	0.545	4	83.464	40.723	0.294	0.239	11.731
							4.860	3	37.194		0.189		5.670
							0.761	13	14.299		0.113		1.842
							1.132	7	13.477		0.113		3.178
5.	Affinity between members of the family	23	0.478	0.228	1.832	52.768 (5,894)	0.525	4	77.188	31.707	0.284	0.174	11.331
							4.705	3	35.038		0.183		5.490
							0.736	13	13.485		0.109		1.776
							1.005	7	12.474		0.101		2.413
							5.596	23	9.334		0.090		1.566

(Contd...)

Table—6.102 (Contd...)

1	*2*	*3*	*4*	*5*	*6*	*7*	*8*	*9*	*10*	*11*	*12*	*13*	*14*
6.	SES	5	0.484	0.234	0.069	45.494	0.500	4	68.804	30.169	0.270	0.197	10.773
						(6,893)	4.676	3	34.839		0.182		5.460
							0.726	13	13.203		0.107		1.744
							0.970	7	9.831		0.097		2.318
							5.176	23	7.982		0.083		1.444
							0.186	5	7.274		0.082		1.615
7.	Type of family	22	0.489	0.239	1.827	40.024	0.494	4	67.452	35.197	0.267	–0.103	10.654
						(7,892)	4.757	3	36.180		0.186		5.580
							0.737	13	13.685		0.109		1.778
							0.903	7	8.502		0.090		2.151
							5.196	23	8.089		0.083		1.444
							0.177	5	6.583		0.078		1.536
							–2.961	22	5.752		–0.071		0.732
8.	Sex	1	0.493	0.243	1.245	35.686	0.479	4	62.918	38.931	0.259	–0.057	10.334
						(8,891)	4.776	3	36.603		0.186		5.588
							0.731	13	13.519		0.108		1.760
							0.950	7	9.391		0.095		2.271
							5.133	23	7.919		0.082		1.427
							0.201	5	62.917		0.089		1.753
							–3.008	22	5.950		–0.072		0.742
							–2.576	1	4.283		–0.062		0.353

(Contd...)

Table—6.102 (Contd...)

1	*2*	*3*	*4*	*5*	*6*	*7*	*8*	*9*	*10*	*11*	*12*	*13*	*14*
9.	PF—E	10	0.497	0.247	0.208	32.371	0.465	4	58.937	44.453	0.251	–0.142	10.015
						(9,890)	4.734	3	36.094		0.185		5.555
							0.729	13	13.488		0.108		1.760
							0.875	7	7.909		0.088		2.103
							4.907	23	7.246		0.079		1.375
							0.205	5	8.635		0.091		1.793
							–2.901	22	5.555		–0.070		0.721
							–3.000	1	5.692		–0.072		0.410
							–0.451	10	4.674		–0.065		0.923
10.	Locality	2	0.500	0.250	1.257	29.613	0.467	4	59.614	40.708	0.252	–0.011	10.055
						(10,889)	4.676	3	35.279		0.182		5.460
							0.695	13	12.188		0.103		1.679
							0.893	7	8.268		0.089		2.127
							4.974	23	7.464		0.080		1.392
							0.245	5	11.403		0.108		2.127
							–3.241	22	6.822		–0.078		0.803
							–3.131	1	6.200		–0.075		0.428
							–0.445	10	4.573		–0.065		0.923
							–2.537	2	3.857		–0.061		0.067

Note: See note under Table—6.84.

It contributed to 15.9 per cent of the variance to the flexibility score of the Ss.

The partial regression coefficient (0.738) shows that for every unit of change in intelligence of the Ss there would be a change of 0.738 units in their flexibility score. The regression equation at this stage could be written as:

$$W_X{}^{17} = 59.622 + 0.738\ (IV4).$$

Step 2: The second variable that entered into the analysis was class/grade (IV3). The value of multiple R^2 was 0.194 which shows that the two variables intelligence and class/grade put together could explain 19.4 per cent of the variance in the flexibility score. The multiple regression equation at this stage was:

$$W_X = 52.909 + 0.626\ (IV4) + 5.005\ (IV3).$$

Step 3: In the third step the predictor variable entered was personality factor—H (IV13). The multiple R^2 was 0.208. The 20.8 per cent of the variance in the flexibility score was explained by the three predictor variables as a set. The regression equation at this stage could be written as:

$$W_X = 44.391 + 0.596\ (IV4) + 5.104\ (IV3) + 0.819\ (IV13).$$

Step 4: Personality factor—B entered the analysis at this stage and the amount of variance explained upto this stage was 22 per cent. The regression equation at this stage was as follows:

$$W_X = 40.723 + 0.545\ (IV4) + 4.860\ (IV3) + 0.761\ (IV13) + 1.132\ (IV7).$$

Step 5: The next variable entered was affinity between the members of the family and the per cent of variance explained by these five variables put together increased to 22.8 per cent. The multiple regression equation at this step was:

$$W_X = 31.707 + 0.525\ (IV4) + 4.705\ (IV3) + 0.736\ (IV13) + 1.005\ (IV7) + 5.596\ (IV23).$$

Step 6: The independent variable that entered at step 6 was SES. With the addition of this variable, the per cent of variance contributed increased from 22.8 to 23.4. The prediction equation could be written as:

$$W_X = 30.169 + 0.500\ (IV4) + 4.676\ (IV3) + 0.726\ (IV13) + 0.970\ (IV7) + 5.176\ (IV23) + 0.186\ (IV5)$$

Step 7: Type of family (IV22) was the predictor variable that entered into the regression analysis next and the amount of variance in the dependent variable explained at this stage was 23.9 per cent. The multiple regression equation at this stage was as follows:

$$W_X = 35.197 + 0.494\ (IV4) + 4.757\ (IV3) + 0.737\ (IV13) + 0.903\ (IV7) + 5.196\ (IV23) + 0.177\ (IV5) - 2.961\ (IV22)$$

Step 8: The independent variable that entered at this stage was sex (IV1). The amount of variance contributed by the 8 variables considered upto this step was 24.3 per cent. The prediction equation with the eight variables was:

$$W_X = 38.931 + 0.479\ (IV4) + 4.776\ (IV3) + 0.731\ (IV13)\ 0.950\ (IV7) + 5.133\ (IV23) + 0.201\ (IV5) - 3.008\ (IV22) - 2.576\ (IV1).$$

Step 9: Personality factor—E entered next into the analysis and the per cent of variance contributed increased to 24.7. The multiple regression equation at this stage could be written as:

$$W_X = 44.453 + 0.465\ (IV4) + 4.734\ (IV3) + 0.729\ (IV13) + 0.875\ (IV7) + 4.907\ (IV23) + 0.205\ (IV5) - 2.901\ (IV22) - 3.000\ (IV1) + 0.451\ (IV10)$$

Step 10: Locality (variable 2) was the next variable considered in the analysis. The amount of variance explained by all the 10 variables was 25%. The regression equation with the ten variables was:

$$W_X = 40.708 + 0.467\ (IV4) + 4.676\ (IV3) +0.695\ (YV13) + 0.893\ (IV7) + 4.974\ (IV23) + 0.245\ (IV5) - 3.241\ (IV22) - 3.131\ (IV1) - 0.445\ (IV10) - 2.537\ (IV2).$$

Thus it may be inferred from the above analysis that the most significant variables that contributed to the flexibility score of the Ss as measured by the whole test battery were intelligence, class/grade, personality factor—H, personality factor—B, affinity between the members of the family, SES, type of family, sex, personality factor—E and locality, in that order.

Table—6.103 shows in a summary form the variables that entered into the analysis at each step and the variance explained by all the variables put together upto that stage.

Table—6.103 Variable Entered At Each Stage and the Amount of Variance Explained Upto that Stage in the Step-wise Multiple Regression Analysis with Flexibility As Measured by Verbal and Nonverbal Tests Put together As Dependent Variable

Step No.	*Variable entered*	*Variable number*	*Per cent of variance explained upto the step*
1.	Intelligence	4	15.9
2.	Class/grade	3	19.4
3.	Personality factor—H	13	20.8
4.	Personality factor—B	7	22.0
5.	Affinity between the members of the family	23	22.8
6.	SES	5	23.4
7.	Type of family	22	23.9
8.	Sex	1	24.3
9.	Personality factor—E	10	24.7
10.	Locality	2	25.0

3. Originality

The results of multiple regression analysis carried out with originality as measured by the whole test as the dependent variable are presented in Table—6.104.

Table—6.104 Results of Step-wise Multiple Regression Analysis Between Originality and Other Independent Variables (Verbal + Nonverbal)

Step No.	*IV*	*VN*	*R*	R^2	*SER*	*F value for R*	*b*	*VN*	*F value for b*	*Constant*	*β*	*γ*	*Per cent of variance*
1	2	*3*	*4*	*5*	*6*	*7*	*8*	*9*	*10*	*11*	*12*	*13*	*14*
1.	Intelligence	4	0.435	0.189	0.327	209.058	4.735	4	209.058	274.493	0.435	0.435	18.922
						(1,898)							
2.	SES	5	0.464	0.215	0.404	122.628	4.331	4	171.531	240.544	0.398	0.254	17.313
						(2,897)	2.196	5	29.552		0.165		4.191
3.	Class/grade	3	0.484	0.234	4.626	91.284	3.848	4	126.526	211.876	0.353	0.271	15.355
						(3,896)	2.139	5	28.695		0.160		4.065
							22.026	3	22.670		0.154		4.173
4.	General state of health	24	0.498	0.248	6.727	73.795	3.776	4	123.623	266.519	0.347	–0.187	15.095
						(4,895)	1.995	5	25.186		0.150		3.810
							20.483	3	19.810		0.143		3.875
							–27.384	24	16.571		–0.110		2.057

(Contd...)

Table—6.104 (Contd...)

1	2	3	4	5	6	7	8	9	10	11	12	13	14
5.	PF—B	7	0.510	0.260	1.784	62.776	3.498	4	102.617	241.367	0.321	0.264	13.964
						(5,894)	1.785	5	19.981		0.134		3.403
							19.229	3	17.556		0.135		3.658
							–25.925	24	14.977		–0.104		1.945
							6.749	7	14.288		0.115		3.306
6.	PF—H	13	0.515	0.266	1.155	53.797	3.413	4	97.589	208.231	0.313	0.147	13.615
						(6,893)	1.770	5	19.846		0.133		3.378
							19.767	3	18.706		0.138		3.739
							–24.259	24	13.120		–0.097		1.814
							6.420	7	12.972		0.109		2.887
							3.022	13	6.847		0.076		1.117
7.	Type of family	22	0.521	0.271	6.702	47.311	3.380	4	96.153	235.903	0.310	–0.123	13.485
						(7,892)	1.720	5	18.823		–0.129		3.277
							20.347	3	19.894		0.142		3.848
							–22.779	24	11.550		–0.091		1.702
							6.033	7	11.441		0.103		2.719
							3.116	13	7.317		0.078		1.146
							–18.100	22	6.435		–.072		0.886

(Contd...)

Table—6.104 (Contd...)

1	2	3	4	5	6	7	8	9	10	11	12	13	14
8.	Affinity between members of the family	23	0.525	0.276	10.492	42.426	3.298	4	91.249	194.029	0.303	0.172	13.180
						(8,891)	1.637	5	17.032		0.123		3.124
							19.658	3	18.610		0.138		3.739
							−22.445	24	11.276		−0.090		1.683
							5.870	7	10.880		0.010		0.264
							3.011	13	6.864		0.075		1.102
							−18.215	22	6.555		−0.073		0.898
							26.274	23	6.271		0.079		1.358
9.	Order of birth	20	0.529	0.280	5.919	38.397	3.258	4	89.191	176.533	0.299	−0.199	13.065
						(9,890)	1.374	5	11.019		0.103		2.617
							18.464	3	16.252		0.129		3.496
							−22.962	24	11.834		−0.092		1.720
							5.706	7	10.303		0.097		2.561
							2.866	13	6.222		0.072		1.058
							−17.581	22	6.122		−0.070		0.861
							27.339	23	6.802		0.082		1.410
							−12.885	20	4.739		−0.064		1.274

(Contd...)

Table—6.104 (Contd...)

1	2	3	4	5	6	7	8	9	10	11	12	13	14
10.	PF—E	10	0.533	0.284	1.788	35.176	3.191	4	85.257	35.176	0.293	−0.154	12.746
						(10,889)	1.361	5	10.856		0.102		2.591
							18.149	3	15.751		0.127		3.442
							−23.399	24	12.332		−0.094		1.758
							5.226	7	8.548		0.089		2.349
							2.847	13	6.164		0.071		1.044
							−16.880	22	5.656		−0.068		0.836
							26.128	23	6.222		0.078		1.342
							−13.259	20	5.035		−0.066		1.313
							−2.575	10	4.741		−0.064		0.986
11.	Sex	1	0.536	0.287	4.722	32.470	3.220	4	86.938	223.029	0.296	−0.038	12.876
						(11,888)	1.420	5	11.796		0.107		2.718
							17.819	3	15.219		0.125		3.387
							−23.577	24	12.562		−0.094		1.758
							5.077	7	8.082		0.086		2.270
							2.574	13	6.367		0.064		0.941
							−16.430	22	5.372		−0.066		0.812
							25.625	23	6.003		0.077		1.324
							−13.542	20	6.268		−0.068		1.353
							−2.575	10	4.755		−0.064		0.986
							−9.630	1	4.159		−0.058		0.220

Note: See note under Table—6.84.

Step 1: Intelligence was the most important independent variable that entered into the regression analysis. The multiple R^2 obtained was 0.189. Thus the contribution of intelligence to the variance in originality of the Ss was 18.9 per cent. The partial regression coefficient (4.735) shows that for every unit of change in intelligence, there would be a corresponding change of 4.735 units in the originality scores of the Ss. Thus the regression equation could be written as:

$$W_O{}^{18} = 274.493 + 4.735\ (IV4).$$

Step 2: SES was the next most important variable that entered into the regression analysis. The multiple R^2 at this stage was 0.215. Thus intelligence and SES jointly contributed to 21.5 per cent of the variance in originality. The multiple regression equation at this stage was:

$$W_O = 240.544 + 4.331\ (IV4) + 2.196\ (IV5).$$

Step 3: Class/grade (IV3) was the next to enter into the multiple regression analysis. The amount of variance explained by the three variables put together at this stage was 23.4 per cent and the prediction equation was:

$$W_O = 211.876 + 3.848\ (IV4) + 2.139\ (IV5) + 22.026\ (IV3).$$

Step 4: The predictor variable that entered into the analysis in step 4 was general state of health of the Ss (IV24). With the addition of this variable, the amount of variance explained increased to 24.8 per cent. The multiple regression equation with these 4 variables could be written as:

$$W_O = 266.519 + 3.776\ (IV4) + 1.995\ (IV5) + 20.483\ (IV3) - 27.384\ (IV24).$$

Step 5: Personality factor—B entered the regression analysis in this step and the per cent of variance contributed jointly by these 5 variables increased from 24.8 per cent to 26 per cent. The multiple regression equation at this stage was:

$$W_O = 241.367 + 3.498\ (IV4) + 1.785\ (IV5) + 19.229\ (IV3) - 25.925\ (IV24) + 6.749\ (IV7).$$

Step 6: The next predictor variable that entered into the regression analysis was personality factor—H, and the amount of variance explained at this stage was 26.6 per cent. The prediction equation with the 6 variables was:

$$W_O = 208.231 + 3.413\ (IV4) + 1.770\ (IV5) + 19.767\ (IV3) - 24.259\ (IV24) + 6.420\ (IV7) + 3.022\ (IV13).$$

Step 7: Type of family was the next independent variable that entered the regression analysis and 27.1 per cent of the variance in originality was explained at this stage. The multiple regression equation at this stage could be written as:

$$W_O = 235.903 + 3.380\ (IV4) + 1.720\ (IV5) + 20.347\ (IV3) - 22.779\ (IV24) + 6.033\ (IV7) + 3.116\ (IV13) - 18.100\ (IV22).$$

Step 8: Affinity between the members of the family (IV23) was the next variable considered in the analysis, with which the per cent of variance explained changed to 27.6 from 27.1.

The multiple regression equation at this stage could be written as follows:

$$W_O = 194.029 + 3.298\ (IV4) + 1.637\ (IV5) + 19.658\ (IV3) - 22.445\ (IV24) + 5.870\ (IV7) + 3.011\ (IV13) - 18.215\ (IV22) + 26.274\ (IV23).$$

Step 9: With the addition of variable 20 (*i.e.*) order of birth into the analysis in this step, the amount of variance explained increased to 28 per cent and the multiple regression equation obtained was:

$$W_O = 176.533 + 3.258\ (IV4) + 1.374\ (IV5) + 18.464\ (IV3) - 22.962\ (IV24) + 5.706\ (IV7) + 2.866\ (IV13) - 17.581\ (IV22) + 27.339\ (IV23) - 12.885\ (IV20).$$

Step 10: The next most significant predictor variable was personality factor—E and amount of variance contributed to the originality of the Ss at this stage was 28.4 per cent. The prediction equation at this stage could be written as:

$$W_O = 35.176 + 3.191\ (IV4) + 1.361\ (IV5) + 18.149\ (IV3) - 23.399\ (IV24) + 5.226\ (IV7) + 2.847\ (IV13) - 16.880\ (IV22) + 26.128\ (IV23) - 13.259\ (IV20) - 2.575\ (IV10).$$

Step 11: Sex (independent variable 1) entered the analysis in this step and 28.7 per cent of variance was explained by all the 11 variables put together. The regression equation at this state was:

$$W_O = 223.029 + 3.220\,(IV4)\ 1.420\,(IV5) + 17.819\,(IV3) - 23.577\,(IV24) + 5.077\,(IV7) + 2.574\,(IV13) - 16.430\,(IV22) + 25.625\,(IV23) - 13.542\,(IV20) - 2.575\,(IV10) - 9.630\,(IV1).$$

It may be seen from the above analysis that, the most significant contributors to the originality of the Ss were intelligence, SES, class/grade, general state of health, personality factor-B, personality factor-H, type of family, affinity between the members of the family, order of birth, personality factor—E, and sex, in that order.

Table—6.105 shows in a summary form the variable that was entered at each step into the analysis and the variance explained by all the variables put together upto that stage.

Table—6.105 Variable Entered At Each Stage and the Amount of Variance Explained Upto that Stage in the Step-wise Multiple Regression Analysis with Originality as Measured by Verbal and Nonverbal Tests Put together as Dependent Variable

Step No.	*Variable entered*	*Variable number*	*Per cent of variance explained upto the step*
1.	Intelligence	4	18.9
2.	SES	5	21.5
3.	Class/grade	3	23.4
4.	General state of health of the children	24	24.8
5.	Personality factor—B	7	26.0
6.	Personality factor—H	13	26.6
7.	Type of family	22.	27.1
8.	Affinity between the members of the family	23	27.6
9.	Order of birth	20	28.0
10.	Personality factor—E	10	28.4
11.	Sex	1	28.7

Composite Creativity

What is the amount of variance contributed by the different independent variables to the composite creativity as measured by the whole test? To probe into this multiple regression analysis was carried out taking composite creativity score as the dependent variable. The results are shown in Table—6.106.

Step 1: Intelligence was the most important variable that entered into the step-wise multiple regression analysis and its contribution to the creativity of the Ss was 20.5 per cent.

The partial regression coefficient (6.677) indicates that for every unit of change in intelligence of the ss, there would be a change of 6.677 units in their composite creativity as measured by the whole test battery. Thus the regression equation could be written as follows:

$$W_C{}^{19} = 414.285 + 6.677 \text{ (IV4)}$$

Step 2: The next most important variable that entered into the multiple regression analysis was class/grade (IV3). The multiple R^2 at this stage was 0.235. Thus intelligence and class/grade jointly contributed to 23.5 per cent of the variance in the composite creativity. The multiple regression equation at this stage could be written as:

$$W_C = 364.145 + 5.840 \text{ (IV4)} + 37.379 \text{ (IV3)}.$$

Step 3: The next most important predictor variable entered into the analysis was SES (IV5), with the addition of which the amount of variance predicted increased to 26.2 per cent. The multiple regression equation at this stage was:

$$W_C = 318.906 + 5.310 \text{ (IV4)} + 36.336 \text{ (IV3)} + 3.017 \text{ (IV5)}.$$

Step 4: Personality factor—B entered next and the per cent of variance contributed by the 4 variables increased to 27.4. The multiple regression equation obtained at this stage was:

$$W_C = 288.830 + 4.929 \text{ (IV4)} + 34.528 \text{ (IV3)} + 2.722 \text{ (IV5)} + 9.126 \text{ (IV7)}.$$

Table—6.106 Results of Step-wise Multiple Regression Analysis Between Composite Creativity and Other Independent Variables (Verbal + Nonverbal)

Step No.	IV	VN	R	R^2	SER	F value for R	b	VN	F value for b	Constant	β	γ	Per cent of variance
1	2	3	4	5	6	7	8	9	10	11	12	13	14
1.	Intelligence	4	0.453	0.205	0.439	231.201	6.677	4	231.201	414.285	0.454	0.452	20.520
						(1,898)							
2.	Class/grade	3	0.485	0.235	6.256	137.920	5.840	4	166.163	364.145	0.397	0.306	17.944
						(2,897)	37.379	3	35.704		0.187		5.722
3.	SES	5	0.512	0.262	0.531	105.908	5.310	4	136.216	318.906	0.361	0.265	16.317
						(3,896)	36.336	3	34.883		0.182		5.569
							3.017	5	32.269		0.169		4.478
4.	PF—B	7	0.524	0.274	2.389	84.286	4.929	4	113.604	288.830	0.335	0.266	15.142
						(4,895)	34.528	3	31.785		0.173		5.293
							2.722	5	26.114		0.152		4.028
							9.126	7	14.598		0.119		3.166

(Contd...)

Table—6.106 (Contd...)

1	2	3	4	5	6	7	8	9	10	11	12	13	14
5.	General state of health	24	0.533	0.284	8.911	70.931	4.865	4	112.008	354.555	0.331	–0.182	14.961
						(5,894)	32.816	3	28.920		0.164		5.018
							2.569	5	23.416		0.144		3.816
							8.632	7	13.191		0.112		2.980
							–32.121	24	12.993		–0.096		1.747
6.	Affinity between members of the family	23	0.539	0.290	14.047	60.803	4.741	4	106.070	291.041	0.322	0.181	14.554
						(6,893)	31,825	3	27.304		0.159		4.865
							2.447	5	21.245		0.137		3.631
							8.379	7	12.501		0.109		2.899
							–31.560	24	12.628		–0.095		1.729
							38.621	23	7.559		0.077		1.394
7.	PF—H	13	0.544	0.295	7.902	53.427	4.669	4	103.195	262.231	0.317	0.211	14.328
						(7,892)	29.991	3	24.081		0.150		4.587
							2.022	5	13.342		0.113		2.995
							8.070	7	11.641		0.105		2.793
							–32.179	24	13.204		–0.097		1.765
							40.258	23	8.251		0.081		1.466
							20.605	13	6.800		0.082		1.733

(Contd...)

Table—6.106 (Contd...)

1	*2*	*3*	*4*	*5*	*6*	*7*	*8*	*9*	*10*	*11*	*12*	*13*	*14*
8.	Type of family	22	0.548	0.299	1.533	47.674	4.575	4	98.823	226.226	0.311	–0.145	14.057
						(8,891)	30.756	3	25.381		0.134		4.100
							2.030	5	13.342		0.114		3.021
							7.702	7	10.612		0.100		2.660
							–30.181	24	11.567		–0.091		1.656
							38.969	23	6.134		0.078		1.412
							19.552	13	7.758		0.078		1.646
							–3.599	22	5.513		–0.068		0.986
9.	PF—E	10	0.550	0.303	9.465	43.079	4.539	4	97.551	258.261	0.309	–0.114	13.967
						(9,890)	31.475	3	26.614		0.157		4.804
							1.987	5	12.989		0.111		2.942
							7.271	7	9.431		0.095		2.527
							–28.471	24	10.256		–0.085		1.547
							39.107	23	7.846		0.078		1.412
							18.845	13	5.716		0.075		1.592
							–3.713	22	5.885		–0.071		1.030
							–20.509	10	4.723		–0.062		0.706

(Contd...)

1	2	3	4	5	6	7	8	9	10	11	12	13	14
10.	Sex	1	0.554	0.307	1.576	39.322	4.456	4	93.599	293.666	0.303	–0.152	13.696
						(10,889)	31.081	3	26.020		0.155		4.743
							1.971	5	12.822		0.110		2.915
							6.674	7	7.851		0.087		2.314
							–29.016	24	10.679		–0.087		1.584
							37.597	23	7.256		0.075		1.353
							19.316	13	6.018		0.077		1.625
							–3.689	22	5.830		–0.070		1.015
							–19.696	10	4.336		–0.059		0.673
							–3.208	1	4.144		–0.058		0.882
11.	Order of birth	20	0.557	0.310	9.718	33.618	4.375	4	87.682	332.632	0.298	–0.044	13.467
						(11,888)	30.976	3	26.608		0.155		4.743
							2.277	5	15.466		0.128		3.392
							6.781	7	8.560		0.088		2.341
							–29.716	24	11.076		–0.089		1.620
							36.039	23	6.906		0.072		1.303
							17.129	13	4.418		0.069		1.456
							–3.714	22	5.767		–0.071		1.029
							–19.435	10	4.482		–0.058		0.661
							–3.699	1	5.427		–0.067		1.018
							–19.461	20	4.010		–0.058		0.255

Note: See note under Table—6.84.

Step 5: Variable 24 (*i.e.*) general state of health of the Ss entered the analysis at this stage, with the addition of which the amount of variance in the composite creativity explained, changed to 28.4 per cent from 27.4 per cent. The regression equation obtained was as given below:

$$W_C = 354.555 + 4.865\ (IV4) + 32.816\ (IV3) + 2.569\ (IV5) + 8.632\ (IV7) - 32.121\ (IV24).$$

Step 6: In this step the variable affinity between the members of the family entered and the total amount of variance explained increased to 29 per cent. The multiple regression equation at this stage is shown below:

$$W_C = 291.041 + 4.741\ (IV4) + 31.825\ (IV3) + 2.447\ (IV5) + 8.379\ (IV7) - 31.560\ (IV24) + 38.621\ (IV23).$$

Step 7: Personality factor—H entered next into the analysis with the addition of which the amount of variance explained changed to 29.5 per cent. The regression equation at this stage was:

$$W_C = 262.231 + 4.669\ (IV4) + 29.991\ (IV3) + 2.022\ (IV5) + 8.070\ (IV7) - 32.179\ (IV24) + 40.258\ (IV23) + 20.605\ (IV13).$$

Step 8: The predictor variable that entered into the analysis at this step was type of family and the amount of variance explained was 29.9 per cent. The multiple regression equation at this stage could be written as:

$$W_C = 226.226 + 4.575\ (IV4) + 30.756\ (IV3) + 2.030\ (IV5) + 7.702\ (IV7) - 30.181\ (IV24) + 38.969\ (IV23) + 19.552\ (IV13) - 3.599\ (IV22).$$

Step 9: Personality factor—E was the independent variable that entered into the analysis in this step. The amount of variance explained by the 9 variables put together at this stage was 30.3 per cent and the prediction equation was as follows:

$$W_C = 258.261 + 4.539\ (IV4) + 31.475\ (IV3) + 1.987\ (IV5) + 7.271\ (IV7) - 28.471\ (IV24) + 39.107\ (IV23) + 18.845\ (IV13) - 3.713\ (IV22) - 20.569\ (IV10).$$

Step 10: Variable 1 (*i.e.*) sex was the next most significant predictor variable, with whose addition to the analysis the amount of variance experienced increased to 30.7 per cent. The prediction equation with the 10 variables could be written as:

$$W_C = 293.666 + 4.456\ (IV4) + 31.081\ (IV3) + 1.971\ (IV5) + 6.674\ (IV7) - 29.016\ (IV24) + 37.597\ (IV23) + 19.316\ (IV13) - 3.689\ (IV22) - 19.696\ (IV10) - 3.208\ (IV1).$$

Table—6.107 Variable Entered At Each Stage and the Amount of Variance Explained Upto that Stage in the Step-wise Multiple Regression Analysis with Composite Creativity as Measured by Verbal and Nonverbal Tests Put together as Dependent Variable

Step No.	*Variable entered*	*Variable number*	*Per cent of variance explained upto the step*
1.	Intelligence	4	20.5
2.	Class/grade	3	23.5
3.	SES	5	26.2
4.	Personality factor—B	7	27.4
5.	General state of health of the children	24	28.4
6.	Affinity between the members of the family	23	29.0
7.	Personality factor—H	13	29.5
8.	Type of family	22	29.9
9.	Personality factor—E	10	30.3
10.	Sex	1	30.7
11.	Order of birth	20	31.0

Step 11: The next predictor variable to enter the regression analysis was variable 20 (*i.e.*) order of birth. The amount of variance in the composite creativity explained at this stage was 31 per cent and the multiple regression equation was as given below:

$$W_C = 332.632 + 4.375\ (IV4) + 30.976\ (IV3) + 2.277\ (IV5) + 6.781\ (IV7) - 29.716\ (IV24) + 36.039\ (IV23) + 17.129\ (IV13) - 3.714\ (IV22) - 19.435\ (IV10) - 3.699\ (IV1) - 19.461\ (IV20).$$

It may be concluded from the above analysis that the most significant independent variables that contributed to the composite score of the Ss as measured by the whole test battery, were intelligence, class/grade, SES, personality factor—B, general state of health of the children, affinity between members of the family, personality factor—H, type of family, personality factor—E, sex and order of birth, in that order.

The variable entered at each stage and the amount of variance explained upto that stage are presented in a summary form in Table—6.107.

Summary

It may be seen from the above analysis that intelligence was the most significant of all the factors in its contribution to creativity. This was the first independent variable that entered into the step-wise multiple regression analysis. This was true for all dependent variables—fluency, flexibility, originality, composite creativity, as measured by verbal tests, or nonverbal tests or by all the tests put together. The second most important independent variable varied from one dependent variable to another. However, irrespective of the level of their importance, SES, personality factors B, E, H, sex, class/school grade, type of family, affinity between the members of the family, state of general health of the children seems to be the important contributors to the creativity of the children.

References

1 In the present investigation the composite creativity score of the Ss was obtained by adding the scores on the different components of creativity in the line with Gakhar (1974), Badarinath and Satyanarayana (1979), Venkata Rami Reddy and Balakrishna Reddy (1983, 1984), Chadha and Ghose (1985), Misra (1986), Syama Trimurthy (1987), Venkata Rami Reddy and Salina (1988) etc.

2 Cattell (1969) has pointed out that "when one is not dealing with individuals as such, but researching on general relations, in correlations or by examining the significance of difference between means, etc., the calculations can just as readily be done with raw scores". Since in the present investigation the aim was to see the difference between the mean scores of the high creatives and low creatives the calculations were carried out with raw scores instead of converting them to stens.

3. While identifying high creatives and low creatives in any subgroup, those who scored above M+ 1 SD for that subgroup were treated as high creatives while those who scored below M– SD were treated as low creatives, so far as that subgroup was concerned.

Because of slight variations in the means and SDs of different subgroups, the total number of high creatives/low creatives among different subgroups (boys and girls, urban and rural, etc.) do not tally exactly with the number of high creatives/low creatives in the whole group.

4. With regard to the application of X^2 test in different situations, McNemar (1957) states that a contingency type of situation where X^2 test is used 'involves classification into unordered groups for the other, or categories for one variable Vs classificatioon into unordered grouping Vs another. The fundamental problem is apt to be that of comparing 2 or more groups with regard to multiple responses; i.e.. we want a test of the difference between groups...'. In the same vein Lindguist (1968) and Edwards (1971) lists out one of the uses of X^2 test as a test of homogeneity among groups.

5. In some of the chi-square tables for different subgroups presented in Table—6.78 the expected frequencies were small in some cells. But the expected frequency in any cell should not be 'low' in a chi-square table. If it is 'low' 'Yates' correction has to be applied or the category should be meaningfully merged with the adjoining one. But upon what is 'low' there seems to be no agreement. Ostle (1966) says, "Some authors say that 'too small' means less than 3; others say less than 5. Since not every one is agreed on the interpretation of what is too small, you should feel free to use any reasonable definition. Personally I favour the value '3'". In line with Ostle whenever the expected frequency for a particular cell was 'small', that category was meaningfully merged with the adjoining category before calculating the X^2. In such cases, naturally the degrees of freedom was reduced.

6. Joint families are those in which families of two or more brothers live together.

   Nuclear families are those in which husband and wife and their children live in a separate home (away from their brothers and sometimes even their parents).

7. The scoring weights given to the different alternatives in the case of unmeasured variables for the purpose of carrying out multiple regression analysis is given in Appendix—I.

8. The percentage given in column 14 can be obtained by multiplying the B coefficients or standard partial regression coefficients given in column 12, with the corresponding simple correlations between the dependent variable and the respective independent variables given in column 13.

9. V_X = refers to the flexibility as measured by the Verbal tests.

10. V_O refers to originality as measured by the verbal tests.

11. V_C refers to composite creativity score as measured by the verbal tests.

12. NV_F refers to the score on the Fluency component as measured by the NonVerbal tests.

13. NV_X refers to the score on the flexibility component as measured by the NonVerbal tests.

14. NV_O refers to originality as measured by the NonVerbal tests.

15. NV_C refers to composite creativity score as measured by the Non Verbal tests.

16. W_F refers to fluency as measured by the whole test (*i.e.,*) Verbal and Nonverbal tests put together.

17. W_X refers to the flexibility score as measured by the whole test (*i.e.*) Verbal and Nonverbal tests put together.

18. W_O refers to Originality as measured by the whole test.

19. W_C refers to Composite creativity score as measured by the whole test (verbal and nonverbal tests put together).

7

Summary and Conclusions

I. THE PROBLEM

There is no gainsaying creativity is the very life and blood of human civilization. None can deny that our future depends upon creative talents. Hence, creativity has become a chief psycho-social motif of the 20th century. Creativity is more than a word today. It is an incantation. It is a kind of psychic wonder. Creative talent makes history through reshaping man's world. The progress of any civilization depends upon new insights, fresh ideas and original productions. The future of a nation that does not recognise this fact, to say the least, will be at peril.

Creativity of the citizens is a national asset. Those who have creative abilities can manage, control and organise new materials and experiences. Creativity is a distinguishing characteristic of outstanding individuals in almost every field. It has been generally conceded that the possession of high intelligence, special talent, and technical skills are not enough for outstanding success. A tinge of creativeness is as important as, if not more important than, the above abilities in scientific discovery and invention.

Progress in varied dimensions like economic growth, technological development and psychological well being of a nation rests basically upon the creative talents of individuals.

Interests in the concept of creativity is not new. Mankind down the ages, has always been curious to explore, examine and understand nature. Man's curiosity in himself and in his environment has cut new grounds in understanding the very nature of man. His abilities to search, discover, and invent have contributed to unimaginable progress of man.

Butcher (1972) observed "Any society, to avoid stagnation, needs a constant supply of original ideas at all levels; but profoundly original men who are the most fertile source of these ideas are often the very people who most disturb the society by threatening its established ways of thought and familiar structure". Yet they are needed nay, they are most needed, to assure betterment of mankind.

Today, the focus of the entire world is on this specialised area 'creativity'. The modern educators are concerned with the identification of the creative abilities so as to nourish them and explore all the possibilities to make use of the unusual productive talents for the development of science, technology, literature, art, music and so on. Research in the field of creativity has been an outcome of this realisation. But this realisation is a rather late realisation and is itself due to the creative genius of one great psychologist—Guilford.

He kindled to spark of creativity and it has resulted in an explosion of research activity on creativity. Yet, the amount of research that has been carried out on creativity is negligible in comparison to the hundred years of experimental psychological research on the mechanistic dimensions of man, which has utilised untold amounts of time, personnel, equipment, and laboratory animals; and still has not moved any closer to the core of what is human and, more important than that, what is humane (Venkata Rami Reddy and Vijayakumari).

Great efforts are made today to study more scientifically the nature of creativity, its measurement and its possible development. As a result of these studies many important aspects of creativity seem to have been unravelled. The main contributors to this field are Guilford and his associates at the University of California, Getzels and Jackson at Chicago, Torrance at Minnesota and Taylor at Utah.

Nevertheless, creativity is a vast area and research is creativity is still in its embryonic stage, filled to the brim with unknowns. Among the unsolved questions are its very nature, typical psychological and behavioural pattern of creatives, teachability, etc. Controversial views are also expressed whether creativity is possessed by a blessed few or it is more or less normally distributed over the whole range of the population. Whatever may be the answers to these controveries, it is essential for any country to discover the creative child, understand him, and utilise him to the fullest extent. This is especially so for a developing country like India. According to Curle (1962) underdeveloped countries have remained such because they have not cultivated human resources.

Though creativity is no less important than any other human characteristic for the progress of mankind, research on creativity has been of recent origin due to various reasons, even in advanced countries like USA, UK, not to speak of a developing country like India. Though many studies have been carried out on creativity in recent years, they yielded contradictory results, showing that much is yet to be known about the relationship between creativity and various other factors.

Further, according to Arasteh and Arasteh (1976) research studies on creativity and the development of talent have proceeded from both childhood and adulthood with an obvious gap in between (*i.e.*) the adolescent period. Torrance (1964) also observed that of the different educational levels, the high school years have been the most neglected in creativity research.

While research on creativity is of recent origin even in the advanced countries, it is needless to point out that not many studies have been carried out in this area in the Indian context. There are several aspects of creativity on which clear cut answers are yet to be foundout by sustained empirical research. For example, what is the effect of differences in rural and urban environment on creativity of the individual? Do boys and girls differ on the various components of creativity—like fluency, flexibility and originality? What are the personality characteristics of high creative and low creative children? How does creativity develop during the adolescent period, etc. The present investigation is designed to find answers to questions such as the above.

II. STATEMENT OF THE PROBLEM

Hence, the present investigation was aimed at analysing the creativity of adolescent boys and girls in relation to certain variables like sex, locality, length of schooling (school grade/class), personality traits, mental ability, socio-economic status, etc.

III. OBJECTIVES OF THE STUDY

1. To find out whether boys and girls differ in their creativity.
2. To find out whether children belonging to urban and rural localities differ in their creativity.
3. To examine whether differences in length of schooling (school grade/class) are significantly related to the creativity of the children.
4. To examine whether high and low creatives differ with regard to their personality characteristics.
5. To find out whether high creatives and low creatives differ in their mental ability.
6. To find out whether SES differentiates between high and low creative children.

In addition to the above the relation between creativity and certain familial variables (like type of family, affinity between members of the family, liberty given by parents in doing things, punishment given by parents for mistakes etc.) and certain habits of life like (reading other general books, attitude towards stereotypy in work etc., was also sought to be analysed.

IV HYPOTHESES

Based upon the above objectives the following hypotheses were formulated for the investigation:

1. There would not be any significant difference between the creativity of boys and girls.
2. There would not be any significant difference between the creativity of the children belonging to rural and urban localities.
3. There would be a significant difference between the creativity of children belonging to different classes.

The above hypotheses were tested separately for each of the four aspects, *viz.*, fluency, flexibility, originality and composite creativity.

Further, to find out whether the relationship between creativity and different variables differed from verbal tests to nonverbal tests, this analysis was carried out separately for the verbal tests, nonverbal tests and both types of tests put together.

4. There would not be any significant difference between the personality characteristics of high creative and low creative children.
5. High creative children would have a higher level of mental ability compared to low creative children.
6. There would not be any significant difference between the socio-economic status of high creative and low creative children.

7. There would not be any significant difference between high creative and low creative children with regard to the frequency with which they study story books, magazines, etc.
8. High creatives would be more unconventional in doing things compared to low creatives.
9. High and low creative children would not differ significantly with regard to the frequency with which they get silly ideas.
10. High creatives and low creatives would not differ with regard to the number of friends they have.
11. Others would find it difficult to adjust with creative children.
12. There would not be any significant difference between high creatives and low creatives with regard to the frequency with which they fall ill.
13. There would be greater affinity between the members of the families of high creative children than that in the case of low creative children.
14. High and low creatives would not differ with regard to the type of family to which they belong.
15. High creatives and low creatives would differ significantly with regard to the liberty given to them by their parents in doing various things.
16. High creatives and low creatives would differ significantly with regard to the frequency with which they are punished for their mistakes.
17. There would not be any significant difference between high creatives and low creatives with regard to their order of birth.

V. VARIABLES STUDIED

The variables chosen for the investigation were: *(i)* Sex, *(ii)* Locality, *(iii)* Length of schooling (school grade/class), *(iv)* Personality traits, *(v)* Mental ability, *(vi)* Socio-economic status.

In addition information about a few familial and personal characteristics and habits of life of the children was also obtained, to see the relation between each of the above and the creativity of the children.

VI. DESIGN AND SAMPLE

The study was of a 2×2×3 factorial design with 2 sexes × 2 localities × 3 classes.

The sample for the investigation consisted of 900 students equally distributed between the two sexes (boys and girls), the two localities (rural and urban) and the three classes (VIII, IX and X). The sample was selected by a multi-stage stratified random sampling procedure from 30 high schools located in rural and urban areas of Chittoor, Cuddapah and Nellore districts of Rayalaseema in Andhra Pradesh State.

VII. TOOLS USED

The following tools were used in the study to measure the creativity, personality, mental ability, etc., of the subjects.

1. Creativity test battery.
2. Cattel's High School Personality Questionnaire (HSPQ) — Form A.
3. Raven's Standard Progressive Matrices—Sets A, B, C, D and E.
4. Socio-economic Status Scale.
5. Personal Data Sheet.

1. ***Creativity:*** The creativity of the Ss was measured with the help of a battery of creativity tests containing ten subtests developed by Venkata Rami Reddy. The tests were developed in line with those of Torrance (1962), Getzels and Jackson (1962) and Wallach and Kogan (1965), giving due consideration to the familiarity of the items/objects to the average Indian children of the age

group under consideration. The reliability and validity of the tests were established.

2. ***Personality:*** Cattell's High School Personality Questionnaire—Form A was used to measure the personality characteristics of the Ss. The HSPQ assesses the personality of the respondents on 14 factors.

3. ***Mental Ability:*** Mental ability of the Ss was assessed by Raven's Standard Progressive Matrices, sets A, B, C, D and E.

4. ***Socio-economic Status:*** The socio-economic status of the Ss was measured by a socio-economic status scale developed by Venkata Rami Reddy.

5. ***Personal Data Sheet:*** The information regarding the familial and personal characteristics and habits of life included in the study was obtained through a carefully designed personal data sheet.

VIII. ADMINISTRATION

The sample of Ss were administered the tools under normal classroom conditions in groups of not exceeding 20 at a time. After establishing proper rapport, they were told about the nature and importance of the work so as to motivate them. Before administering each sub-test, the children were explained what they had to do, with the help of the example given in the instructions for each sub-test.

Each of the ten sub-tests of the creativity test battery were administered separately, in a game like manner in line with Wallach and Kogan (1965) without any time limit.

Four of the ten sub-tests were administered in the morning sessions of the school giving a gap of 15 minutes after the first two sub-tests. The next four sub-tests were administered in the afternoon session with a small gap of fifteen minutes after two sub-tests. The remaining two sub-tests and Raven's Progressive Matrices were administered in the morning session of the next day with a pause of 15 minutes after the two sub-tests of creativity. Cattell's High School Personality Questionnaire, Socio-economic Status Scale and Personal Data sheet were administered in the afternoon session. All these instruments were administered as per the instructions given in the respective manuals which were explained to the children in Telugu, the regional language of the Ss.

The total time taken to administer all the instruments put together was about 8½ hours including the time taken to give instructions.

IX. SCORING

As there are no right or wrong responses for the creativity test items much care has to be exercised in scoring them. The responses of the subjects were scored based upon the following procedure suggested by Guilford (1951), Torrance (1962), Child (1973) and followed by various investigators like Gakhar (1974), Badrinath and Satyanarayana (1979), Venkata Rami Reddy and Balakrishna Reddy (1983, 1984), Chadha and Ghose (1985), Mishra (1986), Syama Thrimurthi (1987), Venkata Rami Reddy and Salina (1988) etc.

1. A fluency score was obtained by counting the number of relevant responses given by the subject. Responses that were nonsensical or which did not answer the question as posed, were eliminated before counting them.

2. A flexibility score was obtained by categorizing the responses into as many discrete classifications as suggest themselves. Evidently, the subjectivity of the scorer comes into any measure of flexibility so derived; but consensus agreement among different scorers was employed by way of making the final flexibility score more objective.

3. Originality was assessed by the relative infrequency of the responses by giving appropriate scoring weights to the different responses.

Cattell's High School Personality Questionnaire, Raven's Progressive Matrices, and the Socio-economic Status scale were scored as per the procedure given in the respective manuals.

X. ANALYSIS OF THE DATA

The data thus collected was analysed employing appropriate statistical techniques like analysis of variance, *t* test, chi-square test, multiple regression analysis, etc., to find out the relation between the different independent variables and creativity. The numerical results were also graphically represented wherever necessary.

Conclusions

From the results obtained in the investigation, the following conclusions appear warranted:

1. There was no significant difference between the creativity of boys and girls as measured by the verbal tests. But in the case of nonverbal tests boys scored significantly better than girls. This was true for all the components of creativity-fluency, flexibility and originality, and also for the composite creativity. Considering verbal and nonverbal tests put together, there was no significant difference between the two sexes in the case of flexibility, originality and composite creativity score. On the fluency component, however, boys scored significantly better than girls.

Hence, the first hypothesis, viz., "There would not be any significant difference between the creativity of boys and girls", was accepted in the case of verbal tests and also in the case of flexibility, originality and composite creativity score as measured by verbal and nonverbal tests put together.

The hypothesis was rejected in the case of creativity as measured by nonverbal tests and also in the case of the fluency component as measured by verbal and nonverbal tests put together.

2. Considering the locality variable, rural and urban children differed significantly with regard to their creativity as measured by verbal tests, urban children scoring better than rural children. This was true for all the components of creativity. In the case of nonverbal tests, rural children scored significantly better than their urban counterparts on flexibility, originality and composite creativity. In the case of fluency component, however, there was no significant difference between the two localities.

When creativity as measured by both verbal and nonverbal tests put together was considered, it was found that there was no significant difference between rural and urban children on flexibility, originality and composite creativity.

On the basis of the above results, the second hypothesis, *viz.*, "There would not be any significant difference between the creativity of the children belonging to rural and urban localities", was rejected in the case of verbal tests and the flexibility, originality and composite creativity score as measured by nonverbal tests, and also in the case of the fluency component as measured by verbal and nonverbal tests put together.

It was accepted in the case of flexibility, originality and composite creativity as measured by verbal and nonverbal tests put together and also in the case of the fluency component of nonverbal tests.

3. With regard to the variable, school grade/class, there was a significant difference between the creativity of children belonging to different classes in the case of the fluency and flexibility components of verbal tests and verbal and nonverbal tests put together, and also in the case of fluency originality and composite creativity as measured by nonverbal tests.

There was no significant difference between IX and X class children on originality and composite creativity as measured by verbal tests and verbal and nonverbal tests put together and in the case of the flexibility component as measured by nonverbal tests.

In view of the above results, the third hypothesis that, "There would be a significant difference between the creativity of children belonging to different classes", was accepted with regard to fluency and flexibility components of verbal tests and verbal and nonverbal tests put together, and also in the case of fluency, originality and composite creativity as measured by nonverbal tests. It was rejected in all other cases, *viz.,* originality and composite creativity as measured by verbal tests, and verbal and nonverbal tests put together and flexibility component of nonverbal tests.

The above conclusions are, however, somewhat limited in scope in view of the significant interaction effects between sex, locality and class.

4. It was found that on the whole high creatives and low creatives differed significantly on the Personality factors A, B, C, D, E, F, G, H, I, J, O, Q_2 and Q_3. High creatives obtained a lower mean score compared to low creatives on factors A, D, E and O. On the remaining factors high creatives obtained higher personality scores than the low creatives.

Thus, the fourth hypothesis, "There would not be any significant difference between the personality characteristics of high creative and low creative children", was rejected in the case of the above personality factors. The hypothesis was accepted in the case of the only remaining factor, *viz.,* Q_4.

Though the results varied slightly from subgroup to subgroup, with regard to the level of the significance of the difference between means, the above trend seen in the case of the whole group was true for all the subgroups in general.

5. High creatives were found to be more intelligent than low creatives. This was true for all the subgroups without any exception.

As such the hypothesis, "High creative children would have a higher level of mental ability compared to low creative children", was accepted.

6. The next hypothesis, *viz.*, "There would not be any significant difference between the socio-economic status of high creatives and low creative children", was rejected because high creatives belonged to higher socio-economic strata compared to low creatives. This was also true for all the subgroups of Ss.

7. On the basis of the analysis of the difference between high creatives and low creatives drawn from the whole group of Ss, it was found that high creatives were characterised by the habit of frequent reading of story books, magazines, etc.

Similar results were obtained in the case of all subgroups except VIII and IX class children. In these two subgroups also the trend of results was similar to that found in the whole group and other subgroups, but the differences were not significant.

In view of the above results, the hypothesis, "There would not be any significant difference between high creative and low creative children with regard to the frequency with which they study story books, magazines, etc.", was rejected in the case of the whole group as well as all the subgroups, except VIII and IX class children.

8. When high and low creatives drawn from the whole sample were considered, it was found that high creatives liked to do things in a new way rather than in a conventional way. This was true in the case of boys and VIII class children.

As such, the hypothesis, "High creatives would be more unconventional in doing things compared to low creatives" was accepted in the above cases and rejected in the case of all other subgroups.

It may be said in passing, however, that as in the earlier case, similar results were obtained in all the subgroups as those obtained in the case of the whole group. But the differences between the two groups were not significant in the case of the some subgroups.

9. Do high creatives get silly ideas more often than low creatives? It was found in the present investigation that there was no significant difference between high and low creatives in this regard.

Thus, the hypothesis that "High and low creative children would not differ significantly with regard to the frequency with which they get silly ideas", was accepted. This was true for all the subgroups of Ss except the urban children.

10. The 10th hypothesis, "High creatives and low creatives would not differ with regard to the number of friends they have", was accepted, because it was found in the investigation that high and low creatives did not differ significantly on this aspect. This was true for the whole group as well as all the subgroups without any exception.

11. It was observed from the results of the investigation that larger percentage of low creatives than high creatives felt that others find it difficult to adjust with them. Hence, the hypothesis, "Others would find it difficult to adjust with creative children", was rejected. This was true for all the subgroups of Ss except X class children.

12. High creatives were found to be healthier than low creatives. As such the next hypothesis, "There would not be any significant difference between high creatives and low creatives with regard to the frequency with which they fall ill", was also rejected. This was true for all the subgroups of Ss except VIII and X class children.

13. Larger percentage of high creatives rather than low creatives expressed that there was a close affinity

between the members of their families. Hence the hypothesis, "There would be greater affinity between the members of the families of high creative children than that in the case of low creative children", was accepted. This was true for the whole group as well as all the subgroups except in the case of boys.

14. More number of high creatives than low creatives hailed from nuclear families. Hence, the hypothesis, "High and low creatives would not differ with regard to the type of family to which they belong", was rejected. This was true for all the subgroups except boys, VIII and X class children.

15. It was found that whether parents insisted that the children should do things only as per their instructions or not, had no effect on the creativity of the children, leading to the rejection on 15th hypothesis, "High creatives and low creatives would differ significantly with regard to the liberty given to them by their parents in doing various things". This was true for the whole group, as well as all subgroups.

16. Similarly, the high creative and low creative groups did not differ with regard to the frequency with which their parents punished them for their mistakes. Hence, the hypothesis, "High creatives and low creatives would differ significantly with regard to the frequency with which they are punished for their mistakes" was also rejected. This was true for the whole group as well as all the subgroups except VIII class children.

17. There was no significant difference between high and low creatives with regard to the order of their birth. Hence, the last hypothesis, *viz.*, "There would not be any significant difference between high creatives and low creatives with regard to their

order of birth", was accepted. This was true for the whole group as well as all the subgroups without any exception.

It was found from the multiple regression analysis that the most significant contributor to the creativity of the Ss was intelligence. This was true in all cases, irrespective of the fact whether creativity was measured by verbal tests or nonverbal tests, or what component—fluency, flexibility, originality or composite creativity—was considered. The next most significant variable in a majority of the cases was school grade/class of the children with variations depending on the type of tests (verbal or nonverbal or both) used, and the component of creativity under consideration. On the whole the significant contributors to creativity were: the SES of the children, personality factors B, E and H, sex, type of family, affinity between the members of the family and general state of health of the children.

16 to 38.3 per cent of variance in the creativity of the Ss was explained by different independent variables, with variations depending upon the type of test and the component under consideration.

Educational Implications, Limitations and Suggestions for Further Research

1. Educational Implications

The recent interest in creativity as a field of research, not only in United States and other developed countries but also in India, is due to a changed outlook on the part of educators with regard to the desired outcomes or education and a feeling based on observation and empirical research that people who make creative contributions to the society are not necessarily those who possess high intelligence, but those who possess high levels of creative talent. Educators have further felt that, if the fullest use of the nation's potential has to be made, people with creative abilities should be identified early, and their talents nourished and cultivated.

There is no gainsaying creative children are assets to the society. Development and progress in various fields of national life depend on creative individuals. Hence, it is our duty to prepare the children to cope up with the fast changing environment.

It may be asserted at the same time that creativity is not the monopoly of a few. Creativity is an unique ability possessed by almost all individuals but its dimensions vary from individual to individual. The differences may be attributed to factors such as intelligence, personality traits sex, socio-economic status, age, teaching-learning process, etc. Torrance (1975) remarked that almost no individual difference in creative thinking ability can be attributed to heredity. This implies that individuals are not born creative. They become creative.

However, the seeds of creative thinking which are present in all children, are more often than not, blocked on account of unfavourable climate in the school, the family and the society. Studies of Osborn (1963), Khatena (1973, 1975), Treffinger (1975), Torrance (1965, 1972), *etc.*, emphasised on the acceleration of development of creative mental functioning through planned environmental enrichment. This should give a new meaning to our system of education. There should be a shift of emphasis from routine type of teaching to creative teaching. Further, the home environment is an equally important factor which affects the development of creativity in the child.

According to the Report of the Education Commission (1966), even the little talent that enters schools and succeeds in climbing the educational ladder, does not blossom fully because it is not discovered sufficiently early and is often engulfed in 'poor schools', poor with respect to the environment they provide to the children. Creative ability which is a true barometer of our present and future progress, needs to be identified early and nurtured properly. But can it blossom in a vacuum? The necessity of favourable environment for its promotion can not be exaggerated. Therefore, conditions congenial to creativity at home and in the school should be studied thoroughly and identified correctly.

It has been found in this investigation that though sex differences were not significant in all cases, boys tended to score better than girls. Therefore, girls should be given special attention and they should be encouraged to take up various types of creative activities. Stereotyped traditional sex role fixation should be avoided by the parents and the teachers. The curriculum should also depict ideal creative female personalities. Equal emphasis should be given to male and female characters depicted in the books and in curricular and cocurricular activities, thereby instilling confidence among girls. Parents should also think in terms of equality of sexes and should give equal importance to both the boy and the girl, avoiding preferential treatment to the male child in any activity. There is no gainsaying giving preferencial treatment to the boy in the family, kills the self confidence of the girl, who is forced to watch helplessly the partial treatment matted out to her in the traditional Indian culture.

Further, it was also found that children from rural areas excelled their urban counterparts in nonverbal creativity. It was also suggested that, factors that contribute to better development of nonverbal creativity among the rural children may have to be isolated through further researches. If certain factors of this type can be identified, it would be worthwhile to see that these factors are taken care of in the case of urban children so that they do not lag behind with regard to their performance on nonverbal tests.

It has also been observed in the study that there was a progressive improvement in the creativity of the Ss from class to class as measured by verbal tests, though the improvement from IX to X class was not as much as that from VIII to IX class. But with regard to creativity as measured by nonverbal tests there was a slight decline at the X class level.

Sullivan (1953), Torrance (1962) opined that creativity gets hampered whenever there is pressure of some sort or the other on the child. Results of the study of Venkata Rami Reddy and Salina (1988) on creativity and age have confirmed the above observation. It is an accepted fact that over emphasis on academic achievement (convergent thinking) affects the creativity of the child.

In Andhra Pradesh there is a great stress on the child, that too imposed on him all of a sudden, at the X class level because of the non-detention system as mentioned earlier. This would have affected the creativity of the X class children. Accepting that the non-detention system will be continued because of its merits in some aspects, teachers and parents must seen that the student is regular in his work in all the classes, instead of waking up all of a sudden at the X class level, so that the growth of the creativity of the children is not hampered at this level. For this, the teachers must be regular in conducting the unit tests, and in sending progress reports to the parents. The parents should be guided to see that children are not negligent in their work because of the non-detention system. This may be done through parent-teacher association meetings, parent conferences, by sending phamplets, etc.

It has been found in this investigation that rural children were poor with regard to their creativity as measured by the verbal and nonverbal tests put together and also on the verbal tests. Hence, it is necessary for the teachers working in rural schools to be more alert to provide situations for the children that can foster their creativity. Their verbal powers are to be exercised by giving more practice by conducting competitions, quiz programmes, debates, etc. The teacher should give necessary guidance to the parents through parent-teacher associations and parent conferences about the various ways and means of developing creative talent among the children.

Whatever may be the locality to which the children may belong, it is essential that the schools should nourish creativity among the children. The major responsibility in this task is vested with the teachers since the children spend quiet a good amount of a time with them. This aspect assumes greater importance in the Indian context in view of the fact that most of the parents especially in rural areas, are illiterate.

Further, teachers should find ways in which they can help to promote the creativity of the children through various activities right from their entry into the first class or even the kindergarten. The formal school programmes should always be accompanied by opportunities for creative efforts. This aspect should be taken care of even while planning and preparing the curriculum.

Teachers should provide opportunities for free expression of thought by adopting modern scientific methods of teaching. They should avoid authoritarian teaching to liberate and widen the intellectual horizons of the students. There is no gainsaying that it is the responsibility of the teachers to provide safe and permissive atmosphere to the children wherein they feel accepted and their ideas are encouraged without the threat of evaluation.

Teacher's appreciation of imaginative ideas, encouragement to implement and try new modes of doing things, are some of the well known ways of enhancing the creativity of the children. But these are more said than done. Probably they are never practised. That encouragement to do new things and to articulate about their whims and fancies instills confidence in the children can not be denied. Teachers should therefore provide exciting and new experiences in the day today classroom teaching and allow freedom to the children to think, act and express their ideas freely without the threat of either evaluation or punishment. It was found in an investigation by Venkata Rami Reddy and Vijayakumari (b) that practice in free thinking and story telling and discussion on the various aspects of the episodes in the fictitious stories improved the creativity and also scientific attitude among the children. As suggested by the authors teachers can easily try such simple techniques in their classes without much difficulty. Educational administrators should inculcate creative attitude among the teachers through inservice programmes and motivate them to try simple techniques for the development of creativity among the children.

It has been found in the present investigation that high creative children were characterised by wider reading of magazines, story books, etc. Schools should take a clue from this and encourage their wards to read as many story books, magazines and other general books to help them enhance their creativity.

Towards this end, sufficient library facilities must be provided to the children. Providing facilities is not the be all and end all of the matter. The children should be motivated to use the library. They should be guided properly in the selection of the books suited to their interests by an efficient and affectionate librarian, who should have a knowledge of the psychology of the children which stands him in good stead to understand and cater to their needs.

Even the mass media can do much in the betterment of creativity by communicating the various sources that can help in this regard. Teachers and parents should make the fullest use of these avenues to explore the creativity of their children.

Outside the classroom parents can also do much to foster creative thinking in the child. Most of the suggestions for stimulating creativity in the school apply equally well to the child's home environment.

It has been found in the investigation that the high creatives come from higher socio-economic strata. As such, to help improve the creativity of the children belonging to low socio-economic strata, special programmes should be taken up by the schools. Parents should also provide them better facilities within their means. Every father and mother should be alert to notice the child's creative work and give him proper encouragement, guidance and assistance. The feeling of confidence in one's own original ideas should have its foundations in childhood and the parents can do as much as, if not more than the teachers, to encourage that attitude. Since the child spends more time at home, parents have many opportunities for encouraging creative ability by carefully looking after their interests and accepting their ideas.

Parents should also encourage the habit of reading among their wards. They should be encouraged to record what they think about the different episodes in what they read.

This is advantageous in that it makes them appreciate the value of their imagination.

It has been found in the study that high creatives come from nuclear families, and also that there was greater affinity between the members of the families of creative children. Teachers must disseminate this ideas and provide necessary guidance to the parents to have mutual understanding and affinity between the members of their families, and also to provide a permissive atmosphere in the home to help promote creativity of the children.

As mentioned earlier affinity between the members of the family will be lacking in the joint families. On the other hand there will be frequent bickerings and even open quarrels among the members of the family. Hence, teachers must be much more watchful in the case of children hailing from joint families, and help them overcome the negative effect of joint families on the development of their creativity by bestowing personal attention and by providing them extra facilities and also by giving guidance to the parents through personal contact.

It may not be out of place to mention that all these are more easily said than done. However, it may be asserted in the same vein that for any teacher or parent willing to do something there will always be a way out, and every teacher and parent *can* do something within their own limitations for the betterment of the creativity of the children.

It may be reiterated that, in the age of explosion of constructive as well as destructive knowledge, it is the creative individual who can adopt himself to the changed environment in which he will find himself sooner or later. Hence, creativity is the urgent need of the coming generations and the schools must raise to the occasion and train the children in creative work.

2. Limitations and Suggestions for Further Research

In this investigation an attempt was made to assess the creativity of boys and girls belonging to VIII, IX and X classes, hailing from rural and urban localities. The study was limited to only two localities and three classes. More elaborate and extensive investigations including other localities like semiurban and metropolitan cities may be undertaken.

The study was limited to children from VIII, IX and X classes comprising terminal stage of secondary education. More elaborate studies taking all age groups starting from pre-primary to collegiate level may be conducted to trace out the developmental trends of creativity with age. Such studies may throw light on the controversial issue of slumps in creativity observed by Torrance (1962), Sullivan (1953), Venkata Rami Reddy and Salina (1988) and contradicted by others like Olshin (1965), Raina (1970), Ogletree (1971, 1972), and Dexie (1985). It is needless to mention that longitudinal rather than cross-sectional studies would be more suitable in the above context, to unravel the age trends in creativity.

An interesting phenomena found in this investigation was with regard to the locality effect on the creativity of the children as measured by different types of tests. Urban children scored better in the case of verbal tests whereas rural children performed better on nonverbal tests.

As mentioned earlier according to Anderson (1968) certain psychological characteristics like 'slight dominance of hippocampal or cortical inhibitory activity over reticular or cortical arousal activity' are necessary for nonverbal creativity. This leads to the questions like—Is there any urban rural difference in this characteristic?

It has been found in the study that X class children scored less than IX class children. One of the important reasons for this was thought of as the non-detention system which is being practiced in Andhra Pradesh. It was suggested that this system has its negative effect on creativity at the X class level because of over emphasis on success and achievement in the public examination conducted at the end of that class. Is this negative effect on creativity more in the case of nonverbal tests than in the case of verbal tests? Further investigations into this aspect may be worthwhile.

Do the characteristics mentioned above which are necessary for nonverbal creativity, fluctuate with age? Or with stress and anxiety? If so, is it possible that these fluctuations have resulted in the decline of creativity at the X class level? Further studies on these aspects may be really fascinating and unravel many mysteries about creative thinking ability.

An aspect very much related to the hypothesised negative effect of over emphasis on achievement on the development of creativity of the children, is with regard to the creativity of children in residential schools and residential junior colleges, where the children's motivation and along with its tension is whipped up to score well at the X class public examination and at the Intermediate (+2) level. A comparative study of the creativity of the children in residential schools and residential junior colleges and those from non-residential schools and colleges may shed more valuable light on this issue.

In this study the relation between intelligence and creativity was studied. The relation of creativity to other variables like academic achievement, reading abilities, etc., would be worthwhile.

In the affective domain, this study was limited to the analysis of the relationship between personality and creativity. The relation between creativity and other affective variables like values, level of adjustment, aspirations, etc., may be studied.

In this study the relation between socio-economic status and creativity was analysed. No attempt was made, however, to analyse the effect of economic status, or the level of parental education or occupation as such, on creativity. Studies on the effect of each of these ingredients, which constitute the SES may throw more light on factors affecting creativity.

A study in the same arena that may be worth trying would be on the much talked of creativity of children of working Vs nonworking mothers. Studies on comparable groups of children of working and nonworking mothers controlling all other variables would reveal the effect of employment of the mother *perse* on the creativity of the children.

Similarly, an investigation to study the effect of school environment on creativity can throw valuable light on the role of the school in the development of creativity of the children.

In this study no attempt was made to compare the creativity of the students belonging to schools coming under different managements (like private schools, government schools, municipal schools, zilla praja parishad schools, *etc.,*). Will there be any difference in the creativity of children coming from schools belonging to different managements? An attempt to answer this may be worthwhile to guide the educational administrators to improve the school environment to help foster the creativity of the children.

India is a multilingual, multicultural, multiracial country. What is the impact of the differences in cultures and races on the creativity of the children? Are certain cultures more conducive for development of creativity among the children? A comparative study of the creativity of the students belonging to different cultures and different races would be very fascinating to unravel cultural and racial effects on creativity. Further, are students belonging to bilingual localities more creative than those hailing from unilingual localities? A study on this also may be worthwhile.

Similarly, the effect of medium of instruction on creativity may be of much relevance because of the great controversy that is raging in the country about introducing regional media even at the college and university level, much against the wishes of a majority of students, parents and even educationists (Venkata Rami Reddy and Chandra Reddy, 1980).

In the present investigation it was found that high creatives obtained lower personality scores than the low creatives on factors A, D, E and O while on all other factors high creatives scored higher than low creatives. Cattell and Butcher (1968), however, found that high creatives scored higher than the average on factors, B, C, D, E, H, I, J, Q_2 and Q_3 while they scored lower than the average on factors A, F, G and O. There was a disagreement between the results of the present investigation with regard to factors, D, E, F and G.

As mentioned earlier, this contradiction may be due to the differences in the type of sample on which the two investigations were conducted. It may also be mentioned in this context that Pearce (1968) in his study on the creativity of high school students picked up for science talent, found that his sample of students differed significantly from other high school students on factors, B, C, D, H, I, J, O, Q_2, Q_3 and Q_4. They scored lower than the average high school students on factors D, O and Q_4. These results warrant the need for further investigations on this aspect.

In the present investigation it was found that it is the low creatives who feel that many find it difficult to adjust with them rather than the high creatives, contradicting the observation of Torrance (1962). Similarly, Torrance (1962) suggested that high creatives get silly ideas and would have fewer friends than others, whereas in the present investigation it was found that there was no significant difference between the high creatives and low creatives on these aspects.

These results seem to suggest an urgent need for an indepth study of the familial and personality characteristics of high creative children in contrast to low creative children, controlling other variables to isolate the characteristics of high creative children. According to Lugo and Hershey (1976) a 'major thrust in the development of creative thinking has been directed to specifiable personality characteristics'. Isolating characteristics of high creative children assumes greater importance in this context because, if certain characteristics that distinguish high creatives are identified, attempts at developing these characteristics among the children and their parents (where applicable) may be made. Thus a well designed comprehensive investigation in this regard may be highly valuable and worth the time, money and energy spent on that.

That creativity of teachers is no less important than that of students can not be denied. But how creative are the teachers working in the schools? The present study was limited to students only. No attempt was made to study the creativity of the teachers and its effect on the creativity of the children. A study on this aspect may be very useful to the educational administrators in devising ways of enhancing the creativity of the children since it is only the creative teacher that can fruitfully implement creative programmes in the schools.

Bibliography

Aaron, P.G., Marihal, V.G., and Malatesha, A.N., 1969. The Rural and Urban Schools—A Comparative Study of the Socio-Psychological Conditions of the Pupils and the Teachers. Dept. of Education, Karnataka University, 98-99.

Agarwal, S.C. and Gupta, S.P., 1982. A Study of Biographical Attributes of High and Low Creative Student-teachers. *Indian Education*, 12, 8.

Ahmed, N. 1969. A Study of the Personality Correlates of Creative Girls at the Middle School Age. *Unpublished M.A. (Psy) Dissertation*, Aligarh Muslim University.

Ahmed, S. 1980. Effect of Socio-Cultural Disadvantage on Creative Thinking. *Journal of Psychological Researches,* 24, 2, 96-106.

Alka Bajpai, and Asta Ahmed. 1986. A Study of Creativity in Relation to Anxiety and Level of Aspiration in Male and Female Teacher Trainees. *M.Ed Dissertation Abstract* Devi Ahilya Visva Vidyalaya, Indore.

Alschuler, R.H. and Hattwick, L.B.W. 1947. *A Study of Painting and Personality in Young Children*, University of Chicago Press, Chicago, 111.

Anastasi, A. 1958. *Differential Psychology*, Macmillan, New York, 17, 30, 221, 223, 228, 422, 426-27.

Anderson, C.C. 1968. A Theory of Nonverbal Creativity in Microfiche No. ED 025 814, U.S. Department of Health, Education and Welfare, June.

Anderson H. and Anderson, G. 1965. A Cross National Study of Children: A Study of Creativity and Mental Health, *Paper Presented at Sixth International Congress on Mental Health.* Technical Session, Paris 1961 (In) I.J. Corden (Ed.) Human development, Chicago, 111, Scatt, Foresman, 307–314.

Anderson, H.H. 1965. *Creativity in Childhood and Adolescence: A Diversity of Approach*, Science and Behaviour Books Inc., Polo, Alto, California.

Anderson, J.E. 1960. The Nature of Abilities. (In) Torrance, E.P. (Ed.) *Talent and Education: Present Status and Future Directions*, The University of Minnesota Press, Minneapolis, 9–31.

Andrews, E.G. 1930. The Development of Imagination in the Preschool Child. *University of Iowa Studies of Character*, 3, 1–64.

Anisworth, M.A. 1962. The Effects of Maternal Deprivation: A Review of Findings and Controversy in the Context of Research Strategy. *WHO Reassessment*, 97–165 (In) Asha, C.B. 1983. Creativity of Children of Working Mothers *Psychological Studies*, 28, 2.

Arasteh, A.R. and Arasteh, J.D. 1976. *Creativity in Human Development*, Schenkman Publishing Company: John Wiley and Sons, New York.

Arnold, J.E., 1962. Useful creative techniques, (In) Parnes, S.J. and Harding, H.F. (Eds.) *A Source Book for Creative Thinking*, Charles Serifner's Sons, New York, 251–268.

Arnold, J.E., 1963. Creative imagination: A Course in mechanical engineering. *Paper Presented at Regional Meeting of ASEE University of Vermount fall*, Mimeographed.

Arora, G.L. 1976. A Study of Relationship Between Anxiety and Creative Thinking Ability. *Indian Educational Review,* 11, 3, 91–96.

—— 1978. Relationship of Sex with Creativity, General Anxiety, Vocational Anxiety and Teaching Success. *Journal of Education and Psychology*, 36, 3, 133–139.

Asha, C.B. 1983. Creativity of Children of Working Mothers. *Psychological Studies*, 28, 2, 104–106.

Ashok, K. Kalia, 1985. Creativity Correlates of Intelligence, Academic Achievement and Extroversion Neuroticism. *Journal of Educational Research and Extension*, 21, 4, 214–222.

Awasthy, M. 1979. A Study of Creativity, Intelligence, Scholastic Achievement and the Factors of Socio-economic Status, *Unpublished M.Ed. Dissertation*, Indore University, Indore.

Babu, N. 1977. A Comparative Study of the Personality Factors of High Intelligence—High Creative Thinkers and High Intelligence—Low Creative Thinkers in Secondary Schools *Doctoral Thesis*, Kerala University, Trivandrum.

Badrinath, S. and Satyanarayana, S.B. 1979. Correlates of Creative Thinking of High School Students. *Creativity News Letter*, 7–8, 2 and 1, 16–23.

Bajpai, A. and Ahmed, A. 1986. A Study of Creativity in Relation to Anxiety and Level of Aspiration in Male and Female Teacher Trainees, M.Ed. Dissertation Abstract, Devi Ahalya Visvavidyalayam, Indore.

Barron, F. 1958. The Psychology of Imagination, *Scientific American*, 199, 151–666.

—— 1961. Creativity: What Research Says About It. NEAJ, 50, 17–19.

Barron, F., 1965. The Psychology of the Creative Writer. *Paper Presented at the Annual Meeting of the American Psychological Association*, Chicago.

—— 1969. *Creative Person and Creative Process*. New York, Holt, Rinehart and Winston, Inc., New York.

Baquer, Mehdi, B. 1977. Creativity, Intelligence and Achievement—A Correlational Study. *Psychological Studies*, 22, 1, 55–62.

Bedi, R.K. 1974. Experimental Attitude and Creativity. *Unpublished M.Ed. Dissertation*, Indore University, Indore.

Bee, H.L. 1962. Divergent and Convergent Abilities Compared (In) Maccoby and L. Rau (Eds.), *Differential Cognitive Abilities*, Cooperative Research Project No. 1040, Office of Education, U.S. Department of Health, Education and Welfare, Washington, D.C., 146–149.

Bennet, S.N. 1973. Divergent Thinking Abilities, a Validation Study. *British Journal of Educational Psychology,* 43, 1–7.

Berdyaev, 1969. The Meaning of the Creative Act. (In) Frank Barron, *Creative Person and the Creative Process*, Rinehart and Winston, Inc., New York, 154.

Bhan, R. 1972. Social Factors in Creative Potentiality. *Journal of Education and Psychology,* 29, 4, 263–267.

—— 1973. Relationship Between Creative Potential and the Level of Aspiration. *Journal of Education and Psychology,* 31, 1, 52–54.

Bharadwaj, R. 1985. Intelligence, Sex and Age as Correlates of the Components of Creativity. *Asian Journal of Psychology and Education*, 16, 3, 41–44.

—— and Sharma, A.D., 1986. Intelligence, Fixation, Frustration and Economic Status as Correlates of the Originality. *Journal of Educational Psychology*, 44, 2, and 3, 158–161.

Bhargava, M. 1979. Personal Variables and second Order Personality Correlates of Creativity. *Indian Psychological Review*, 17, 3–4, 63–67.

Bhattacharya, P.S. 1956. A Psychological Study of the Artists. *Proceeding of the 47th Indian Science Congress*, Part III, 544 (Abstr).

—— 1960. (In) Passi, B.K. 1982. *Creativity in Education*, National Psychological Corporation, Agra.

Bhoodev Singh 1986. Role of Personality Vs. biographical factors in creativity. *Psychological Studies*, 31, 2, 90–92.

Bill, K. 1977. Differences in Creativity Among Homogeneous Groups of Pupils Using Torrance Tests of Creative Thinking. *Psychological Reports*, 38 3, 1283–1284.

Blood, R.O. 1965. Long-range Causes and Consequences of the Employment of Married Women. *Journal of Marriage and Family*, 27, 43–47 (In) Asha, C.B. 1993. Creativity of Children of Working Mothers, *Psychological Studies*, 26, 2.

Bloom, B.S. (Ed.) (1958). Some Effects of Cultural, Social and Educational Conditions on Creativity. (In) Calvin, W. Taylor (Ed.) *The Second (1957) University of Utah Research*

Conference on the Identification of Creative Scientific Talent, University of Utah Press, 55–65.

Bowers, J. 1960. *Explorations of Creative Thinking in the Early School Years: XIV a Preliminary Factor Analytic Study of the Creative Thinking Abilities of Children*. Bureau of Educational Research, Minneapolis, Minnesota.

Brodley, F.K. 1976. The Effect of Frustration on the Figural Creativity Thinking of 5th Grade Students. *Journal of Experimental Education*, 44, 3, 20–23.

Bruner, J.S. 1962. *On Knowing: Essays for the Left Hand*. Cambridge University Press, Cambridge.

Buhl, H.R. 1960. *Creative Engineering Design*, Iowa State University Press, Iowa.

Buhl, H.R. 1961. *Understanding the Creative Engineer*, American Society of Mechanical Engineers, New York.

Burgess, W.V. 1971. The Analysis of Teacher Creativity, Pupil Age and Pupil Sex as Sources of Variation Among Elementary Pupil's Performance on Pre and Post-tests of Creative thinking. *Dissertation Abstracts International*, 32, 2, 747.

Burns, M.J. 1969. Selected Characteristics of Children's Individual Tests of Creativity. *Dissertation Abstracts International*, 30, 5, 1859A.

Burt, C. 1962. Introduction: the Gifted Child, (In): Beredy, G.Z.F. and Laurways, J.A. (Eds.) *The Gifted Child*, Brace and World, New York.

—— 1964. Forward. (In) Koestler, A. *The Act of Creation*, Hutchinson, London.

Cacha, F.B. 1971. A Study of Creative Thinking Abilities of Personality Factors and Peer Nominations of Fifth Grade Children. *Dissertation Abstracts International*, 32, 3, 1329 A.

Campbell, D.T. and Fiske, D.W. 1959. Convergent and Discriminant Validation by the Multi Trait—Multimethod Matrix. *Psychology Bulletin*, 56, 81–105.

Cattell, R.B. 1956. Second Order Personality Factors in the Questionnaire Realm. *Journal of Consulting Psychology*, 20, 411–418.

—— 1963. The Personality and Motivation of the Researcher from Measurements of Contemporaries and from Biography. Ch. 9 (In) Taylor and Barron (Eds.) *Scientific Creativity: Its Recognition and Development*, John Wiley and Sons, New York, 119–131.

—— 1969. *Handbook for the Junior-Senior High School Personality Questionnaire "HSPQ"*, Published by the Institute for Personality and Ability Testing, Illinois, USA.

Cattell, R.B. and Butcher, J. 1968. *The Prediction of Achievement and Creativity*, Indianapolis, Ind. Bobbs-—Merrill.

—— and Drevdahl, J.C. 1955. A Comparison of the Personality Profile (16 PF) of Eminent Researchers with that of Eminent Teachers and Administrators, and of the General Population. *British Journal of Psychology*, 46, 248–261.

——, Eber, H.W. and Delhees, K.H. 1968. A Large Sample Cross Validation of the Personality Trait Structure of the 16 PF with Some Clinical Implications. (In) Cattell, R.B. (Ed.) *Progress in Clinical Psychology Through Multivariate Experimental Design*: Society of Multivariate Experimental Psychology, Fort, Texas, 107–132.

—— and Sealy, A.P. 1965. The General Relations of Changes in Personality and Interest to Changes in School Performance: An Exploratory Study. Coop. Res. Proj. No. 1411, Urbana, III, Laboratory of Personality Assessment and Group Behaviour; Univer. III.

Chadha, N.K. and Sen, A.K. 1981. Creativity as a Function of Intelligence, Socio-Economic Status and Sex Among 12th Grade School Students. *Journal of Education and Psychology,* 39, 1, 52–56.

—— and Ghose, P. 1985. Sex Differences in Creativity, Risk taking, Intelligence and Frustration: An Inferential Study, *Journal of Educational Research and Extension*, 21, 4.

Champney, H. 1941. The Measurement of Parent Behaviour. *Child Development*, 12, 131–166.

Chandrakant, Bhogayata. 1987. The Effect of Birth Order, Sex and Urban—Rural Dimensions of Culture on Creativity of Secondary School Students. *Journal of Education and Psychology*, 44, 4, 212–216.

Chaplin, J.P. 1982. *Dictionary of Psychology*, Dell, New York.

Chatterjee, B.B. 1970. *Exploration of Some Structural Components of Creativity Through Projective Tests*, Gandhian Institute of Studies, Varanasi.

Chauhan, N.S. 1977. Second Stratum Personality Factors, Sex and age Adolescence as Correlates of Originality. *Indian Psychological Review*, 14, 1, 15–21.

Chawla, V. 1976. (In) Passi, B.K. 1982. *Creativity in Education,* National Psychological Corporation, Agra, 12.

Cheek, J.F. 1979. An Analysis of Differences in Creative Ability Between White and Negro Students, Public and Parochial, Three Different Grade Levels and Males and Females. *APA Experimental Publication System*, 9, Ms No. 349–54.

Child, D. 1973. *Psychology and the Teacher*. London: Rinehart and Winston Holf.

—— and Croucher, A. 1977. A Divergent Thinking and Ability: Is there a Threshold? *Educational Studies,* 3, 101–110.

Cicirelli, V.G. 1965. The relationship Between Creativity, IQ and Academic Achievement. *Journal of Educational Psychology*, 56, 303–308.

Clark *et al.*, 1965. Quoted in Chauhan, N.S and Tiwari, G. *Manual of Creativity Test*, Agra Psychological Research Cell, Agra.

Coan, R.W. and Cattell, R.B. 1958. Reproducible Personality Factors in Middle Childhood. *Journal of Clinical Psychology*, 14, 339–345.

Colvin, S.S. and Meyer, I.F. 1906. Imaginative Elements in the Written Work of School Children. *Pedagogical Seminary,* 13, 17–28.

Conrad, H.S. 1933. The Personal Equation in Ratings: II. A Systematic Evaluation, Journal of Educational Psychology, 24, 39–46.

Couch, A. and Keniston, K. 1960. Yea-sayers and Nay-sayers, Agreeing Response Set as a Personality Variable. *Journal of Abnormal Social Psychology*, 60, 151–174.

Cropley, A.J. 1966. Creativity and Intelligence. *British Journal of Educational Psychology*, 36, 259–266.

—— 1967. Originality, Intelligence and Personality. *Unpublished Doctoral Thesis*, University of Alberta, Reported in the *Australian Journal of Education*, 2, 2, 120–135.

—— 1968. A note on Wallach—Kogan tests of Creativity (Research Note). *British Journal of Educational Psychology*, 38, 2, 1–4.

Cross, P. Cattell, R.B. and Butcher, H.J. 1967. The Personality Pattern of Creative Artists. *British Journal of Educational Psychology*, 37, 292–299.

Crutchfield, R.S. 1967. Instructing the Individual in Creative Thinking. (In) Ross, L. Mooney and Taher, A. Razik (EDs.) *Explorations in Creativity*, Harper and Row, New York, 196–205.

Curle, 1962. Measurement of Creative Ability: An Investigation—Smt. P. Dey, *Indian Educational Review*, 1, 1, 68.

Curry, R.L. 1962. The Effect of the Socio-Economic Status on the School Achievement of VI Grade Children. *British Journal of Educational Psychology*, 46–49.

Das, 1957. (In) Passi, B.K. 1982. *Creativity in Education*, National Psychological Corporation, Agra.

Das Gupta, S. 1977. (In) Passi, B.K. 1982. *Creativity in Education*, National Psychological Corporation, Agra.

Datta, L. 1968. Birth Order and Potential Scientific Creativity. *Sociometry*, 31, 76–87.

Dauw, D.C. 1966. Life Experiences, Vocational Needs and Choices of Original Thinkers and Good Elaborators. *Dissertation Abstracts*, 26, 9, 5223.

Dave, Janakaray, G. 1980. Evolving and Trying Out of Creativity in Writing in Gujarati for Std. X Pupils of Sourashtra Area, *Doctoral Thesis*, Sourashtra University.

Dearborn, G.V. 1898. A Study of Imaginations. *American Journal of Psychology*, 9, 183–190.

Degan, J.W. 1952. *Dimensions of Functional Psychosis*, Richmond: Wm. Byrd Press.

De Haan, R.F. and Havighurst, R.J. 1961. *Educating Gifted Children*, University of Chicago Press, Chicago, III.

Dehlavi, Nahid, S. 1980. Relationship Between Creativity and Personality Characteristics in an Indian Sample. *Psychological Abstracts*, 50, 3, 823–828.

Dellas, M. and Gaier, E.L. 1970. Identification of Creativity. *Psychological Bulletin*, 73, 55–73.

Deshmukh, M.N. 1984. *Creativity in Classroom*, Chand and Company Ltd., New Delhi.

Dewing, K. 1970. Some Correlates of Creativity and Test Performance in Seventh Grade Children. *Australian Journal of Psychology*, 22, 269–276.

—— and Taft, R. 1973. Some Characteristics of the Parents of Creative Twelve-year Olds. *Journal of Personality*, 41, 71–85.

Dexie, F. 1985. Test of Creative Thinking Potentials, Academic Achievement, 7th—12th Graders. *Information of Psychological Sciences*, 2, 20–25.

Dharmangadan, B.C. 1976. Creativity in School Children: An Analytical Study. *Unpublished Ph.D Thesis*, University of Kerala, Trivandrum.

—— 1981. Creativity in Relation to Sex, Age and Locality. *Psychological Studies*, 26, 1, 28–33.

Doppelt, J.E. 1964. *What is Creativity?* III. Definitions of creativity. Transactions, Academy of Sciences, New York, 26, 788–793.

Drevdahl, J.E. 1954. An Exploratory Study of Creativity in Terms of its Relation to Various Personality and Intellectual Factors. *Unpublished Ph.D. Thesis*, University of Nebr.

—— 1956. Factors of Importance for Creativity. *Journal of Clinical Psychology*, 12, 21—26.

—— 1964. Some Developmental and Environmental Factors in creativity (In) Taylor, C.W. (Ed.) *Widening Horizons in Creativity*, John Wiley and Sons, Inc., New York, 170–185.

Dreyer, A.S. and Wells, M.B. 1966. Parental Values, Parental Control and Creativity in Young Children. *Journal of Marriage and the Family*, 28, 83–88.

Dutt, N.K. Prem Bountra, and Sabharawal, V.K. 1977. A Study of Creativity in Relation to Intelligence, Extraversion and Neuroticism. *Indian Educational Review*, 8, 2, 81–87.

Editorial, 1971. Automatic Promotions. *The Educational Review*, 77, 7, 168.

—— 1977. Need to Evaluate the A.Ps New Evaluation Scheme. *Educational India*, 43, 7, 159–164.

Edwards, A.L. 1971. *Experimental Design in Psychological Research*, 3rd ed. Amerind Publishing Co., New York.

Eisenman, Russel, 1988. Creativity Birth Order and Risk Taking. *Bulletin of Psychonomic Society*.

Essenman, R. and Robinson, 1967. (In) Chauhan, N.S. and Tiwari G. 1974. *Manual of Creativity Test,* Agra Psychological Research Cell, Agra.

Ezekeil, N. 1966. Teacher Participation in School Administration in Greater Bombay. *Doctoral Thesis*, Bombay University, Bombay.

Fenske, R.H. 1969. Who Selects Vocational Technical Post High School Education? (In) Torsten Husen and T. Neville Postlethwaite (Eds,) 1986. *The International Encyclopaedia of Education*, Pergamon Press, Oxford, 9, 5532.

Fine, Reuben, 1980. Work, Depression and Creativity. *Psychological Reports*, 46, 3, 1195–1221.

Flanagan, J.C. 1958. Definition and Measurement of Ingenuity. (In) Taylor, C.W. (Ed.) *The Second University of Utah Research Conference on the Identification of Creative Scientific Talent*, University of Utah Press, Salt Lake city, 109–118.

Flang, Dexie. 1985. Test of Creative Thinking Potentials, Academic Achievement, 7th—12th Graders. *Information of Psychological Sciences*, 2, 20–25.

Fleming, E.S. and Weintraub, S. 1962. Additional Rigidity as a Measure of Creativity in Gifted Children. *Journal of Educational Psychology*, 53, 81–85.

Fletcher, I. 1963. Anxiety and Achievement of Intellectually Gifted and Creative Children. *Journal of Psychology*, 56.

Foster, J. 1971. *Creativity and the Teacher*, Macmillan Education Ltd., London.

Freud, S. 1949. The Unconscious (In) Jones, Earnest (Ed.), *Collected Papers*, 4, 98–139.

Fromm, E. 1959. The Creative Attitude. (In) Anderson, H.H. (Ed.) *Creativity and its Cultivation*, Harper and Row, New York, 44–54.

Gage, N.L and Berliner, D.C. 1975. *Educational Psychology,* Rand McNally College Publishing Company, Chicago.

Gagneja, S.L. 1972. A Study of Creativity in Ninth Class Students in Relation to Sex, Residential Background, Academic Achievement and Parental Occupation. *Master's Dissertation*, Punjab University.

Gakhar, S. 1974. Creativity in Relation to Age and Sex. *Journal of Education and Psychology*, 32, 3.

—— 1975. Intellectual and Personality Correlates of Creativity. *Doctoral Thesis*, Punjab University.

Gakhar, S. and Kaura, N. 1977. Creativity—Intelligence: A Study of Structural Relationship and Threshold Hypothesis. *Creativity News Letter*, 5 and 6 Combined, 27–37.

—— and Joshi, J.N. 1980. Creativity with in the Framework of personological Context. *Psychological Studies*, 26, 1, 48–57.

Gallagher, J.J. 1963. *A Conference on Research on the Education of Gifted Children*, Cooperative Research Project, No. F. 006, U.S. Dept. of Health, Education and Welfare, Washington, D.C.

—— and Haffman, W. 1964. Productive thinking. (In) M.L. Lois and W. Hoffman (Eds.) *Review of Child Development Research*, Russel Sage Foundation, New York, 349–381.

Ganapathy, M. and Singh, M.R. 1981. The Impact of Socio-Economic Conditions on Achievement. *Experiments in Education*, 9, 8, 144–147.

Garber, J.A., Resnick, T., Kepees, M. and Vedhan, V. 1979. Levels of Creative Thinking in Pre-School Age Children from Orthodox and Nonorthodox Homes. *Journal of Psychology and Judaism*, 3, 217–226 (In) *Psychological Abstracts*, 65, 1981, Abstract No. 2987.

Getzels, J.W. 1964. Creative Thinking, Problem Solving and Instruction. (In) Hilgard, E.R. (Ed.) *Theories of Learning and Instruction*, 63rd year book, NSSE, U. Chicago Press, 240–267.

—— and Csikszentmihalyi, M. 1964. Creative Thinking in Art Students: an Exploratory Study. Cooperative Research Project No. E. 008, U. Chicago, 202.

—— and Dillon, J.M. 1973. Giftedness and the Education of the Gifted (In) Travers R.M.W. (Ed.) 1973. *Second Handbook of Research in Teaching*. A Project of the American Educational Research Association, Rand McNally, Chicago, 689–731.

Getzels, J.W. and Jackson, P.W. 1961. Family Environment and Cognitive Styles: A Study of the Sources of Highly Intelligent and Highly Creative Adolescents. *American Psychological Review*, 26, 351–359.

—— 1962. *Creativity and Intelligence: Explorations with Gifted Students*, John Wiley and Sons Inc., New York.

—— and Madaus, G.F. 1969. *Encyclopedia of Educational Research: A Project of the American Educational Research Association*. The Macmillan Company, Collier-Macmillan Limited, London, 267–273.

Ghiselin, B. 1952. *The Creative Process*. New American Library, 293.

Ginsberg, G.P. and Whittmore, R.G. 1968. Creativity and Verbal Ability. A Direct Examination of their Relationship. *British Journal of Educational Psychology*, 38, 133–139.

Girijesh Kumar, 1978. Creative functioning in Relation to Personality, Value Orientation and Achievement Motivation. *Indian Educational Review*, 13, 2.

Goertzel, M.G. and Goertzel, V.H. 1960. Intellectual and Emotional Climate in Families Producing Eminence. *Gifted Child Quarterly*, 4, 59–60.

Golann, S.E. 1961. Psychological Study of Creativity. *Psychological Bulletin*, 60, 548–565.

Goldenson, R.M. 1984. Longman Dictionary of Psychology and Psychiatry. A Walter, D. Glanze Book, New York.

Gopal, A.K. 1975. Certain Differentiating Personality Variables of Creative and Noncreative Science and Engineering Students. *Doctoral Thesis*, Kurukshetra University, Kurukshetra.

Goralski, P.S. 1964. Creativity: Student Teacher's Perceptions of Approaches to Classroom Teaching. *Dissertation Abstracts*, 25, 5, 2851.

Goyal, R.P. 1972. A Study of Some Personality Traits of High Creative Children at School Stage. *Indian Educational Review*, 7, 2, 92.

—— 1974. A Study of Some Personality Correlates of Creativity in Secondary School Teachers under Training. *Doctoral Thesis*, Punjab University.

Gray, 1954. (In) Skinner, C.E. 1962. *Essentials of Education* (In) Venkateswaran, S. 1987. Academic Achievement and Creativity. *Journal of Educational Research and Extension*, 24, 52–58.

Greenacre, P. 1959. Play in Relation to Creative Imagination. *Psychoanalytic Study of the Child*, 14, 61–80.

Griffths, R.A. 1945. *A Study of Imagination in Early Childhood.* Routledge, London.

Grippen, V.B. 1933. A Study of Creative Artistic Imagination in Children by the Constant Procedure. *Psychological Monographs*, 35, 63–81.

Guilford, J.P. 1950. Creativity. *American Psychologist,* 5, 9, 444–454.

—— 1952. Some Recent Findings on Thinking Abilities and their Implications. *T.A. and D Information Bulletin,* U.S. Air Force, III, 3, 61.

—— 1954. *Psychometric Methods*, McGraw Hill, New York, 529–530.

—— 1956. The Structure of Intellect. *Psychological Bulletin*, 53, 267–293.

—— 1957. *A Revised Structure of Intellect*, (Rep. Psychol. Lab., No. 19), University of Southern California, Los Angles, 69–95.

—— 1959. Factors and Psychological Theory, *American Psychologist*, 434.

—— 1962. Creativity: Its Measurement and Development (In) Parnes, S.J. and Harding, H.P. (Eds.) *A Source Book for Creative Thinking*, New York: Scribner, 151–168.

Guilford, J.P. 1964. Some Theoretical Views of Creativity. Chapter XI (In) Helson, H. and Bevan, W. (Eds.) *Contemporary Approaches to Psychology*, Von Nostrand Reinhold Co., New York, 419–459.

—— 1967a. *Nature of Human Intelligence*, McGraw Hill, New York.

—— 1967b. Creativity: Yesterday, Today and Tomorrow *Journal of Creative Behaviour*, 1, 3–14.

—— 1971. *The Analysis of Intelligence*, McGraw-Hill New York.

—— and Fruchtor, B. 1978. *Fundamentals of Statistics in Educational Psychology*, Mc-Graw Hill, New York.

—— and Hoepfner, R. 1966. Creative Potential as Related to Measures of IQ and Verbal Comprehension. *Indian Journal of Psychology*, 41, 7–16.

——, Merrifield, P.R. and Cox, A.B. 1961. *Creative Thinking in Children at the Junior High School Level*, Psychological Laboratories, University of Southern California, Los Angels.

——, Wilson, R.C., Chirstenson, P.R., and Lewis, D.J. 1951. *A Factor-analytic Study of Creative Thinking Hypothesis and Description of Tests*. University of Southern California, Los Angels.

Gulati, G.S. 1979. A Comparative Psychological Study of Creativity of Indian Adolescent Students at Various Educational Levels. *Indian Psychological Review*, 18, 1 and 4, 42–44.

Gulati, S. 1979. Creativity as a Function of Intelligence, Artistic Aptitude and Neuroticism. *Educational Trends*, 14, 1, 35–44.

Gupta, A.K. 1977. A Study of the Personality of Creativity with Self Concept Among the School Going Children of 12+ in Jammu city, *Doctoral Thesis*, Punjab University.

Gupta, A.K. 1978. Study of Pupil Creativity in two Institutional Settings. *Creativity News Letter*, 7, 1, 14–21.

—— 1979. Adolescents with High and Low Creativity. *Indian Educational Review*, 14, 2, 31–41.

—— 1980. A Factorial Study of Verbal and Nonverbal Creativity Intelligence and Socio-Economic Status. (In) Buch, M.B. (Ed.) 1986. *Third Survey of Research in Education 1978—83*, NCERT, New Delhi, 355.

Gupta, G.S. 1977. Developing Creative Thinking Amongst X Grade Students Through Brain Storming. *M.Ed. Dissertation*, M.S. University, Baroda.

Gupta, K.K. 1979. Creativity, Intelligence and Achievement. *The Educational Review*, 85, 11, 208–212.

Gupta, S. 1982. Relationship Between Reading Ability and Father's Profession and Birth Order. (In) Buch, M.B. (Ed.) 1986. *Third Survey of Research in Education (1978–83)* NCERT, New Delhi, 652.

Gupta, S.P. 1975. *Statistical Methods*, Sultan Chand, New Delhi.

Gupta, V.A. 1976 (In). Passi, B.K. 1982. *Creativity in Education,* National Psychological Corporation, Agra.

Hadden, F.A. and Lytton, H. 1968. Teaching Approach and the Development of Divergent Thinking Abilities in Primary Schools. *Journal of Educational Psychology*, 38, 171–180.

Hallman, R.J. 1963. The Necessary and Sufficient Conditions of Creativity. *Journal of Humanistic Psychology*, 3: 1, Spring.

Hammer, E.F. 1961. *Creativity*. Random House, New York.

Harlow, S.D. 1967. The Development of the Originality Indicator of Creativity. *Dissertation Abstracts*, 28 6, 2094A.

Harnek, S. Kaile, 1989. Relationship of Intelligence, Creativity and Language Usage with Achievement in Languages at three Levels of Socio-economic Status. *Experiments in Education*, 17, 9, 225–232.

Harnek, S. Kaile Gurusagar, Sadhu and Manjit, K. Sekhon, 1988. Creativity in Relation to Sex and Birth Order. *The Educational Review*, XCIV, 11, 195–197.

Harriman, P.L. 1947. *Dictionary of Psychology,* The Wisdom Library, New York.

Hasan, P. and Butcher, H.J. 1966. Creativity and Intelligence: A Partial Replication with Scottish Children of Getzels and Jacksons Study, *British Journal of Psychology,* 57 129–133.

Heer, D.M. 1958. Dominance and the Working Wife. *Social Forces*, 36, 341–347. (In) Asha, C.B. 1983. Creativity of Children of Working Mothers.

Herrenstein, R.J. 1971. IQ. *Atlantic Monthly*, 228 (September), 43, 58, 206–223.

Hoepfner, 1967. (In) Passi, B.K. 1982. *Passi's Tests of Creativity (Verbal and Nonverbal)*, National Psychological Corporation, Agra.

Holland, J.L. 1961. Creative and Academic Performance Among Talented Adolescents. *Journal of Educational Psychology*, 52, 136–147.

Hollender, J.W. 1967. Development of a Realistic Vocational Choice. *Journal of Counselling Psychology*, 18, 244–248.

Houtz, J.C and Sylvia, R. and Tetenbaum, T.J. 1978. Creative Thinking in Gifted Elementary School Children. *Gifted Child Quarterly*, 22, 513–519.

Hudson, L. 1966. Contrary Imaginations, A Psychological Study of the English School Boy, London, Methuen.

—— 1966a. Contrary Imaginations: A Psychological Study of a Young Student, New York.

Hussain, M.G. 1974. Creativity and Sex Differences. *Psychological Studies*, 19, 2, 127–129.

—— 1976. Creativity and Sex Differences. *Psychological Abstracts*, 56, 1186.

Hutchinson, E.D. 1949. *How to Think Creativity*. Nashville: Abingdon Press, 97.

Hutchinson, W.L. 1967. Creative and Productive Thinking in the Classroom. *Journal of Creative Behaviour*, 1, 4, 419–427.

Iscoe, I. and Pierce Jones, J. 1963. Divergent Thinking, Age and Intelligence in White and Negro Children. *Child Development,* 34, 785–797.

Jackson, R.L. 1968. An Investigation of the Creative Growth Curves of University Students. *Dissertation Abstracts*, 28, 9, 3508A.

Jackson, P.W. and Messick, S. 1965. The Person, the Product and the Responses—Conceptual Problems in the Assessment of Creativity. *Personality*, 33 309–329.

Jain, J. 1975. (In) Passi, B.K. 1982. *Creativity in Education,* National Psychological Corporation, Agra.

Jalota, S. Pandey, R.N. Kapoor, S.D. and Singh, R.N. 1970. Manual of Directions for Socio-economic Status Scale Questionnaire, *The Psychocentre,* New Delhi.

Jansevek, Norbert, 1981. The Influence of Family Environment on Child Creativity. *Psychological Abstracts,* 1983, January—June, 69, 6–2.

Janson, 1968. Creativity and Socio-economic States in Status of Indian Researches in Creativity (In Zargar, A.H., and Neelam Dhar 1988. Creativity and Socio-economic Status: A Study. *The Educational Review*, 64, 2, 29–32.

Jarial, Gurpal Singh. 1979. Verbal Creative Thinking Among the Students with Different Socio-economic Status Backgrounds and Birth Orders. *Psycho Lingua*, 9, 2, 85–90.

—— 1981. Effect of Birth Order Upon Creative Thinking Abilities Among Adolescents. *Psychological Studies*, 1981 (In Press).

—— 1981a. Creativity and Family Size. *Journal of Education and Psychology*. (in Press).

Jarial Gurpal Singh, 1981b. Creativity, Intelligence, Academic Achievement—Their Relationships and Differences to Sex and Academic Subjects. *Journal of Education and Psychology*, 39, 2.

—— 1983. Creativity and Family Size, *Journal of Education*, 1, 1, 13–17.

—— and Sarma, A.K. 1980. Creativity and its Components as Affected by Intelligence, Personality and Their Interaction. *Asian Journal of Psychology and Education*, 6, 21, 26–32.

—— 1981. Effect of Personality Types, Grade Levels and their Interaction Upon Creativity and its Components. *The Educational Review,* (In Press).

—— 1981a. The Effect of Birth Order Upon Intelligence: A Review of Studies. *Journal of the Institute of Educational Research*, 5, 30–33.

Jayaswal, V.K. 1977. A Study of Creativity in Relation to Anxiety in Male and Female Teacher Trainees. *Doctoral Thesis*, Gorakhpur University.

Jha, S.K. 1975 (In) Passi, B.K. 1982. *Creativity in Education,* National Psychological Corporation, Agra.

—— 1978. An Analysis of Certain Dimensions of Creativity. *Himalaya Publishing House*, Bombay.

Jones, F.E. 1964. Predictor Variables for Creativity in Industrial Science, *Journal of Applied Psychology,* 48, 134–136.

Joshi, R.J. 1974. A Study of Creativity and Some Personality Traits of the Intellectually Gifted High School Students. *Doctoral Thesis*, M.S. University, Baroda.

—— 1973. (In) Passi, B.K. 1982. *Creativity in Education*, National Psychological Corporation, Agra.

Joshi, S.P. 1982. A Study of Verbal Creativity in Marathi Language in Relation to Achievement in Marathi and Environmental Factors of the Students as well as Teaching in High Schools. *Doctoral Thesis*, Bombay University, Bombay.

Joshi, D. and Joshi, K.K. 1986. Creativity as a Function of Intelligence and Self Disclosure among Teacher Trainees. *Indian Journal of Applied Psychology*, 23, 1, 30–34.

Jyotsna, 1980. A Study of Personality Correlates of High and Low Creative Students—A Cross Cultural Study of Western U.P. Doctoral Thesis, Rohilkhand University, Bareilly.

Kaltsounis, B. 1971. Differences in Creative Thinking of Black and White Deaf Children. *Perceptual and Motor Skills*, 32 243–248.

Kaur, B. 1980. A Factor Study of Self Concept, Creativity and Problem Solving among Higher Secondary students of Indore city. *Unpublished M.Ed. Dissertation*, Indore University, Indore.

Kaur, Maninder, 1986. Relationship of Creativity with Demographic Factors Such as Occupation of Father, Birth Order and Family Type. *Indian Psychological Review*, Special Issue, 31, 41–46.

Kaur, R. 1978. Personality Characteristics of High School Creative Children. *Unpublished M.A. (Edn.) Dissertation*, Punjab University.

—— 1980. A Study of Creative Thinking of IX Grade Boys in Relation to their Problems and Adjustment. *Unpublished M.Phil Dissertation*, Punjab University.

Kelly, G.R. 1965. Creativity, School Attitude and Intelligence Relationships in Grades Four, Six and Eight. *Dissertation Abstracts*, 25, 11, 6300.

Ketcham, W.A. and Kheiralla, S. 1963. Creativity in Relation to Intelligence and School Achievement (In) Inter Institute Seminar on Child Development, *Collected Papers,* 1962, Edision Institute, Greenfield Village, Dearborn, 79–85.

Khatena, J. 1973. Creativity, Concept and Challenge, *Educational Trends*, 8 (1–4), 7–18.

Khatena, J. 1975. (In) Bhoodev Singh. *Teaching Learning Strategies and Mathematical Creativity*, Mittal Publications, New Delhi.

Khire, U.S. 1971. Creativity in Relation to Intelligence and Personality Factors. *Doctoral Thesis*, Poona University, Poona.

Kilpatrick, E.A. 1900. Individual Tests of School Children. *Psychological Review*, 7, 274–275.

Kloss, M.G. 1972. The Relation Between Adolescent Creativity and Selected Variables, Sex, Adjustment, Art—Science Preference, Complexity—Simplicity, and Type of School. *Dissertation Abstracts International*, 33, 5, 2324 B.

Kogan, N.A. 1971. Clarification of Cropley and Maslany's Analysis of the Wallach—Kogan Creativity Tests. *British Journal of Psychology*, 62, 113–117.

Kovac, Tomas. 1985. Relationship Between Creativity and Intelligence at Pre-school Age, *Psychological Abstracts,* 72, 4.

Kumar, A. 1981. Personality Identification of High and Low Creatives at Age 13 or Older. *Journal of Creative Behaviour*, 15, 1, 73.

Kumar, G. 1978. Creative Functioning in Relation to Personality, Value Orientation and Achievement Motivation. *Indian Educational Review*, 13, 2, 110–114.

—— 1981. Creative Functioning in Relation to Cognitive Style. *Trends in Education,* 8, 1 and 2, 12–17.

Kumari, K. 1975. (In) Passi, B.K. 1982. *Creativity in Education*, National Psychological Corporation, Agra.

Kundu, Dibakar, 1987. Creative Development in school children. *The Education Quarterly*, 37, 3, 6.

Kuppuswamy, B. 1962. *Manual of Socio-economic Status Scale*. Manasayan, New Delhi.

Lal, G. 1977. Relationship of Sex with Creativity, General Anxiety, Vocational Anxiety and Teaching Success. *Journal of Educational Research and Extension*, 14, 2.

Lal, B.N. and Chilana, M.R. 1977. Relationship of Creativity with Achievement, Motivation in Science Students. *The Educational Trends*, 12, 1 and 2, 99–103.

Lalitha, M.S. 1957. (In) Passi, B.K. 1982. *Creativity in Education*, National Psychological Corporation, Agra.

—— 1973. Self-concept and Creativity of Over, Normal and Under Achievers Amongst Grade X Students of Baroda city. *Unpublished M.Ed. Dissertation*, M.S. University, Baroda.

Lehman, H.C. 1953. *Age and Achievement*, Princeton, New Jersey.

—— and Heidler, J.B. 1949. Chronological age Vs. Quality of Literary Output. *American Journal of Psychology*, 62, 75–89.

Lewis, R.A., Jr. 1973. Ability and Creativity in Maths. *Review of Educational Research*, 43 4, 405–432.

Lewis, Carol, D. and Houtz, John C. 1986. Sex Role Stereotyping and Young Children's Divergent Thinking. *Psychological Reports*, 59, 3, 1027–1033.

Liberman, J.N. 1965. Playfulness and Divergent Thinking: An Investigation of their Relationship at the Kidergarten Level. *Journal of Genetic Psychology,* 107, 219–224.

—— 1966. Playfulness: An Attempt to Conceptualize a Quality of Play and of the Player. *Paper Read at the Eastern Psychological Association*, New York.

Ligon, E.M. 1957. *The Growth and Development of Christian Personality*. The Union College Character Research Project, New York.

Lindquist, E.F. 1968. *Statistical Analysis in Educational Research*, Oxford and IBH Publishing House, Calcutta.

Long, B.H. and Handerson, E.H. 1965. Opinion formation and Creativity in Elementary School Children. *Psychological Reports*, 17, 219–223.

Lorr, M., Schaefer, E., Rubenstein, E.S. and Jenkins, R.L. 1953. An Analysis of an out Patient Rating Scale. *Journal of Clinical Psychology*, 9, 296–299.

Louise and Fiebert, M. 1977. Creativity in the Pre-school Child and its Relationship to Parental Authoritarianism. *Perceptual and Motor Skills*, 45 170 (In) *Psychological Abstracts*, 60, 1978, Abstract No. 5021.

Lovell, K. and Shields, J.B. 1967.. Some Aspects of a Study of the Gifted Children. *British Journal of Educational Psychology*, 37, 201–208.

Lowenfeld, V. 1957. *Creativity and Mental Growth*, MacMillan, New York.

—— and Brittain, W.L. 1966. *Creative and Mental Growth*, Collier—MacMillan, London.

Lugo, James O and Hershey, 1976. *Living Psychology, Research in Action*, Mac Millan, New York, 135–139.

Lytton, H. and Cotton A.C. 1969. Divergent thinking Abilities in Secondary Schools. *British Journal of Educational Psychology*, 39 188–190.

Maccoby, E.E. 1958. Children and Working Mothers. *Children* 5, 82–89 (In) Asha, C.B. 1983. Creativity of Children of Working Mothers.

—— and Jacklin, C.N. 1974. *The Psychology of Sex Differences,* Stanford University Press, Stanford.

Mac Gregor, M. and Smith, J.L. 1965. Originality and Role Perception in Elementary and Junior High School Children. *Dissertation Abstracts,* 25, 11, 6762.

Mackinnon, D.W. 1962. The Nature and Nurture of Creative Talent. *American Psychologist*, 17 484–495.

—— 1964. The Creativity of Architects (In) Taylor, C.W. (Ed.) *Widening Horizons in Creativity*, John Wiley and Sons Inc., New York, 359–378.

Mackler and Shontz 1965. (In) Khatena, J. 1973. Creativity: Concept and Challenge, *Educational Trends*, 8, (1–4), 7–18.

Madaus, 1967. Quoted in Chauhan, N.S. and Tiwaṛi: *Manual of Creativity Test*, Agra Psychological Research Cell, Agra.

Maish, S. 1979. Creativity and Teacher Effectiveness. *Quest in Education*, 16, 2.

Mallappa, K.R. and Upadhyaya, R.C. 1977. Creativity and Personality. *Indian Psychological Review*, 14, 2, 31–35.

Manikya Rastogi, and Nathawat, S.S. 1982. Effect of Creativity on Mental Health. *Psychological Studies,* 27, 2, 74–76.

Mar'I, S.K. 1971. Creativity of American and Arab Rural Youth: A Cross Cultural Study. *Dissertation Abstracts International*, 31, 12, 6407 A.

Marjoribanks, K. 1977. Sibsize, Family Environment, Cognitive Performance and Affective Characteristics. *The Journal of Psychology*, 94, 195–204.

Markey, F.V. 1935. *Imaginative Behaviour in Preschool Children*, Bureau Publishers, New York.

Marsh, R.W. 1964. A Statistical Analysis of Getzels and Jacksons Data. *British Journal of Educational Psychological*, 34, 91–93.

Maslow, A.H. 1963. The Creative Attitude. *The Structurist,* 3, 4–10.

—— 1972. A Holistic Approach to Creativity. In C.W. Taylor (Ed.), Climate for Creativity. *Report of the Seventh National Research Conference on Creativity*. Pergamon Press Inc., New York, 287–293.

Mason, J.G. 1960. *How to be a More Creative Executive*. McGraw Hill, New York.

May, R. 1953. The Nature of Creativity. (In) Harold, H.A. 1959 (Ed.) *Creativity and its Cultivation,* Harper and Row, New York.

Mc Clelland, D.C and Others (Eds.) 1958. *Talent and Society*. Princeton: Van Nostrand, 1–28.

Mc Cloy, W. 1939. Creative Imagination in Children and Adults. *Psychological Monographs,* 51, 88–102.

—— and Meier, N.C. 1939. Re-creative imagination. *Psychological Monographs*, 51, 5, 108–116.

Mc Crae Robert R. 1987. Correlation of Creativity and Divergent Thinking with Openness to Experience, Male Participants in Baltimore Longitudinal Study of Aging. *Journal of Personality and Social Psychology*, 52 6, 1258–1265.

Mc Dowell, M.S. and Howe. S.R. 1941. Creative Use of Play Materials by Preschool Children. *Childhood Education,* 17, 321–326.

Mc Elvain, J.L. Fretwell, L.N and Lewis, R.B. 1963. Relationship Between Creativity and Teacher Variability. *Psychological Reports*, 13, 186.

Mc Guire, C. 1960. *Talented Behaviour in Junior High Schools,* University of Texas, Texas.

Mc Kinnon, D.W. 1962. The Personality Correlates of Creativity: A Study of American Architects (In) Cooper Smith, S. (Ed.) Personality Research, *International Association of Applied Psychology Proceedings Volume II*: Copenhagen, Munksgaard.

Mc Nemar, Q. 1957. *Psychological Statistics,* (II Ed.), John Wiley and Sons, New York.

—— 1964. Lost: Our Intelligence. Why? *American Psychologist*, 19, 871–882.

Mearns, H. 1941. *The Creative Adult*, Double Day and Company, Inc., Garden City, New York.

Mednick, S. 1962. The Associative Basis of the Creative Process. *Psychological Review*, 69 3, 220–232.

Mednick, S.H. and Mednick, M.T. 1964. An Associative Interpretation of the Creative Process. (In) Taylor, C.W. (Ed.) *Widening Horizons and in Creativity*, John Wiley and Sons, Inc., New York, 54–68.

Meer, B. and Stein, H.I. 1955. Measures of Intelligence and Creativity. *Journal of Psychology*, 39, 117–126.

Mehdi, B. 1973. *Manual: Verbal Test of Creative Thinking*. Mrs. Qumar Fatima, Aligarh.

—— 1977. Creativity, Intelligence, Academic Achievement: A Relational Study, *Psychological Studies, 22*, 1.

Mendel, G. 1965. Children's Performance for Differing Degrees of Novelty. *Child Development*, 36, 453–465.

Merrifield, P. 1976. How an Educational Psychologist use the Creative process. *Educator*, 18, 2, 16 TEEN, 22 WO.

Merrifield, P.R., Guilford, J.P. and Gershon, A. 1963. *The Differentiation of Divergent Production Abilities at the Sixth Grade Level*, Psychological Laboratories, University of Southern California, Los Angles.

Middents, G.J. 1968. The Relationship of Creativity and Anxiety. *Dissertation Abstracts,* 28, 7, 2562 A.

Milgram, R.M. and Milgram, N.A. 1976. Creative Thinking and Creative Performance in Israeli Students. *Journal of Educational Psychology*, 68, 3, 253–259.

Mishra, K.S. 1977. (In) Passi, B.K. 1982. *Creativity in Education*, National Psychological Corporation, Agra.

—— 1986. *Effect of Home and School Environment on Scientific Creativity*. National Psychological Corporation, Agra.

Moorhead, G.E. and Pond, D. 1942. *Music for Young Children: II General Observations*, Pittsbury Foundation Studies, Santa Barbara, California.

Morgan, E.S. 1960. What Every Yale Fresh Man Should Know, *Saturday Review*, 43, 4, 13–14.

Morrow, W.R. and Wilson, R.C. 1961. Family Relations of Bright High-achieving and Underachieving High School Boys. *Child Development*, 32, 502–510.

Moss, J. (Jr.) 1966. Measuring Creative Abilities in Junior High School Industrial Arts. *Monograph—2*, American Council of Industrial Arts Teacher Education, Washington, D.C.

—— and Duenk, L.G. 1967. Estimating the Concurrent Validity of the Minnesota Tests of Creative Thinking. *American Educational Research Journal*, 4, 386–396.

Mulk Raj, Tuli, 1982. Sex and Regional Differences in Mathematical Creativity. *Journal of Educational and Psychology*, 39, 4, 211–217.

Nagia, S. 1977. (In) Passi, B.K. 1982. *Creativity in Education*, National Psychological Corporation, Agra.

Nair, M. 1976. Personality Characteristics of Creative High School Pupils. *Masters' Thesis*, Kerala University, Trivandrum.

Nair, S. and Babu, N. 1977. A Factor Analytical Comparison of Personality Variables Related to High and Low Creative Thinkers. *Quest in Education*, 14 1, 54–63.

Narayanan, S. 1984. Creativity and Intelligence, Band Width Categorisation Style, 15 year Old Males. *Psychological Research Journal*, 8 (1–2), 12–17.

Narayana Rao, S. 1967. Student Performance and Adjustment. S.V. University, Tirupati.

NCERT, 1975. The Curriculum for the Ten-year School: A Framework. New Delhi.

Neufeld, J.J. 1964. The Relationship of Creative Thinking Abilities to the Academic Achievement of Adolescents. *Dissertation Abstracts*, 25, 3404.

Newell, A. and Others 1962. The Process of Creative Thinking (In) Graber, H.E. *et al*., (Eds.) *Contemporary Approaches to Creative Thinking*, Altherton Press, 63–119.

Nichols, R.C. Quoted from Morrow and Wilson, 1961.

Nichols, R.C. 1964. Parental Attitudes of Mothers of Intelligent Adolescents and Creativity of their Children. *Child Development*, 35, 1041–1050.

Nisha, B., Singh, R.P. and Gupta, K. 1976. Creative Thinking Abilities and Creative Personality. A Study of Relationship Verbal Creative Thinking Abilities and Creative Personality. *Psycho-Lingua*, 6, 1 and 2, 15–18.

Northway, M.L. and Rooks, M.M. 1955. Creativity and Sociometric Status in Children. *Sociometry,* 18. 194–201.

Nunnally, J.O. 1959. *Tests and Measurements: Assessment and Prediction*. McGraw Hill Book Company, New York.

Nye, F. and Hoffman, L.W. 1963. *The Employed Mother in America*. Rand Mac Nally, Chicago (In) Asha, C.B. 1983.

O'Brien, M.S. Sibley, L.A. and Ligon. 1953. Developing Creativity in Children's use of Imagination: Theoretical Statement. *Union College Studies in Character Research*, 1, 17–26.

Ogletree, E.J.A. 1968. Cross Cultural Exploratory Study of the Creativeness of Steiner and State School Pupils in England, Scotland and Germany, *Dissertation Abstracts* 29, 2, 516 A.

—— 1971. A Cross-cultural Examination of the Creative Thinking Ability of Public and Private School Pupils in England, Scotland and Germany. *Journal of Social Psychology*, 83, 301–302.

—— 1972. Creative Discontinuties of European School Children. *The Journal of Social Psychology*. 88, 147–148.

Olive, M. 1972. The Relationship of Divergent Thinking to Intelligence, Social Class and Achievement in High School Student. *Journal of Genetic Psychology,* 12, 179–186.

Olshin, G.M. 1965. The Relationship Among Selected Subject Variables and Level of Creativity. *Exceptional Children*, 31, 588–589.

Olton, R.M., Wardrop, J.C., Covington, M.V., Crutchfield, R.S., Goodwin, W.L. Klausmeier, H.J. and Ronda, T. 1969. *The Development of Productive Thinking Skills in Fifth Grade Children*. Wisconsin Research and Development, Centre for Cognitive Learning, University of Wisconsin, Madison.

Orcutt, L. 1968. Conformity Tendencies Among Three and Five Year Olds in an Impersonal Situational Task. *Psychological Reports*, 23, 387–390.

Osborn, A.F. 1948. *Your Creative Power: Now to Use Imagination,* Charles Scribner's Sons, New York.

—— 1957, *Creative Imagination,* 3rd Ed., Charles Scribner's Sons, New York.

—— 1963. (In) Bhoodev Singh. *Teaching Learning Strategies and Mathematical Creativity*, Mittal Publications, New Delhi.

Ostle, B. 1966. *Statistics in Research,* Oxford and IBH Publications, Bombay.

Pandey, K. 1980. A Comparative Study of Personality Characteristics and Values of Creative and Non-creative Pupil-teachers. *Unpublished M.Ed. Dissertation*, Allahabad University, Allahabad.

Pandey, R.C. and Pandey, R.N. 1984. A Study of Creativity in Relation to Sex of High School Students. *Indian Psychological Review*, 26, 2, 53–57.

Pandit, R. 1976. A Study of Creativity in Relation to Adjustment, Socio-economic Status and Scholastic Achievement of the students. *Unpublished M.Ed. Dissertation*, Indore University, Indore.

Panucci, M.R. 1978. The Relationship of Sex and Ethnicity to Anxiety, Self Concept and Creativity Among Continuation High School Students. *Dissertation Abstracts*, 38, 7, 4056.

Papanek, V.J. 1964. Solving Problems Creatively. *Management Views*, IX (Pt. 3), Selected Speeches, Academic Year 1963–64, U.S. Army Management School, Fort Belvoir, 169–196.

Paramesh, C.R. 1970. Value Orientation of Creative Persons. *Psychological Studies*, 15, 2, 108–112.

—— and Narayanan, S. 1974. Creativity, Intelligence and Vocational Interests. *Indian Journal of Psychology*, 51, 221–224.

—— 1977. Effect of Creativity and Intelligence on Temperament. *Journal of Education and Psychology*, 34, 3 and 4, 159–161.

Pareek, U. and Trivedi, G. 1964. *Manual of the Socio-Economic Status Scale*. Manasayan, Delhi.

Parnes, S.J. 1966. *Work Book for Creative Problem Solving Institutes and Courses*, Creative Education Foundation, Buffalo.

Passi, B.K. 1972. An Exploratory Study of Creativity and its Relationship with Intelligence and Achievement in School Subjects at Higher Secondary Stages. *Doctoral Thesis*, Punjab University.

—— 1979. *Passi Test of Creativity* (Verbal and nonverbal), National Psychological Corporation, Agra.

—— 1982. *Creativity in Education*, 1st Edition. National Psychological Corporation, Agra, 1–19.

—— and Lalithamma, M.S. 1973. Self Concept and Creativity of Over, Normal and Under Achievers Amongst Grade X Students of Baroda. *Indian Journal of Psychometry and Education*, 4, 1, 1–11.

Patel, A.S. 1978. An Enquiry into the Relation of Creativity to Intellectual Giftedness. *Indian Journal of Psychology*, 53, 3, 140–144.

—— and Joshi, R.J. 1976. An Inquiry into the Relation of Creativity to Intellectual Giftedness. *A Paper Submitted to the Indian Science Congress,* Waltair.

Pearce, C. 1968. Creativity in Young Science Students. *Journal of Exceptional Children*, 35, 121–126.

Pegnato, C.V. and Birch, J.W. 1959. Locating Gifted Children in Junior High Schools. *Exceptional Children*, 25, 300–304.

Pestonjee, D. and Usmani, S.M. 1982. Creativity in Relation to Alienation, Ego Strength and Intelligence. *Journal of Education and Psychology*, 40, 1–2, 39–44.

Phatak, P. 1961. Exploratory Study of Creativity and Intelligence and Creativity and School Achievement. *Proceedings of the 48th Indian Science Congress*, Part IV, 570–571.

—— 1962. Experimental Study of Creativity and Intelligence and School Achievements. *Psychological Studies*, 7, 1–9.

Philips, V.K. and Torrance, E.P. 1971. Divergent Thinking Remote Associations and Concept Attainment Strategies. *Journal of Psychology*, 77, 223–228.

Piers, F.V. Daniels, and Quackenbush, 1960. The Identification of Creativity in Adolescents. *Journal of Educational Psychology*, 51, 346–351.

Pogue, B.C. 1964. A Study to Determine Whether or Not There is a Relationship Between Creativity and Self Image. *Doctoral Dissertation,* Bale State University.

Prakash, A.O. 1966. Understanding the Fourth Grade Slump: A Study of the Creative Thinking Abilities of Indian children. *Master's Dissertation*, University of Minnesota.

Praugh, D.G. and Halow, R.G. 1962. Marked Deprivation in Infants and Young Children. *WHO Reassessment*, 97–165 (In) Asha, C.B. 1983.

Qureshi, Anjum Naseer, 1982. A Study of Creativity in Relation to Intelligence, Manifest Anxiety and Level of Aspiration of High School Girls. *Doctoral Thesis*, Agra University.

Raina, M.K. 1968. A Study of Some Correlates of Creativity in Indian Students. *Doctoral Thesis*. University of Rajasthan.

—— 1969. A Study of Sex Differences in Creativity in India. *Journal of Creative Behaviour*, 3, 111–114.

—— 1970. A Study of Creativity in Teachers. *Psychological Studies*, 15, 1 and 2, 28–33.

—— 1971. Verbal and Non-verbal Creative Thinking Ability: A Study in Sex Differences. *Journal of Education and Psychology*, 29, 3, 175–179.

Rainer, K. 1979. Relationships Between Sex, Mental Health, Socialization and Creativity. *Zeitschrift fur Klinische Psychologie and Psychotherapie*, 27, 49–74 (In). *Psychological Abstracts*, 65, January 1981. Abstract No. 3073.

Ramachandra, Mohanty and Katiyar, P.C. 1986. A Study of Creativity in Relation to Intelligence, Academic Achievement and Problem Solving Ability of Students. *M.Phil Abstract*, Devi Ahalya Visvavidyalayam, Indore.

Rao, B.P. 1976. Some Cognitive Correlates of Creativity. *Doctoral Thesis*, Jabalpur University.

Rasool, G. 1977. A Study of Divergent Thinking of School Going Children. *Creativity News Letter*, 6, 2, 23–26.

Rastogi, P. 1967. Intelligence and Intellectual Situations Received by VIII Grade Students Under Different Styles of Junior High Dchool Education in Uttar Pradesh. *Doctoral Thesis*, University of Agra.

Rastogi, Manikya. 1987. A Study of Cognitive Style in Relation to Intelligence and Creativity. *Journal of Personality and Clinical Studies*, 3, 2, 161–164.

Raven, J.C. 1951. The Instinctive Disposition to Act Intelligently. *British Journal of Psychology*, XLII, 4.

Rawat, M.S and Agarwal, S. 1977. A Study of Creative Thinking with Reference to Intelligence, Age, Sex, Communities and Income Group. *Indian Psychological Review,* 14, 2, 36–40.

Rawat, M.S. and Garg, M.K. 1977. A Study of Creativity and Level of Aspiration of High School Students. *Indian Psychological Review*, 14, 2, 51–53.

Ray Choudhary, Manas 1962. An Investigation into the Personality Structure of Musicians. *Doctoral Thesis*, University of Calcutta.

—— 1965. Personality Correlates of Creativity. *Samiksha*, 19, 3, 107–134.

—— 1966. Studies in Artistic Creativity. *Rabindra Bharti*, Calcutta.

Razik, T.M.A. An Investigation of Creative Thinking Among College Students. *Dissertation Abstracts*, 24, 7, 2775.

Rehman, A. and Hussain, M.G. 1973. Creativity and Social Desirability. *The Educational Trends*, 8, 1–4, 163–165.

Reid, J.B. King, E.J. and Wickwire, P. 1959. Cognitive and Other Personality Characteristics of Gifted Children. *Psychological Reports,* 5, 729–739.

Report of the Education Commission. 1966. Government of India, Ministry of Education, New Delhi.

Richards, J.M. *et al.*, 1964. Creativity Tests and Teacher and Self-Judgement of Originality. *Journal of Experimental Education*, 32, 281–285.

Rimoldi, H.J.A. 1948. Study of Some Factors Related to Intelligence: *Psychometrika*, 13, 27–46.

Riqz, Mohnazir, 1979. A Study of Intelligence, Creativity Distinction and their Relationship with Academic Achievement. *Psychological Studies*, 3, 58–70.

Rittmyer, J.F. 1968. Relationship Among High Verbal, High Nonverbal and High Total Creativity Scores and Intelligence, Academic Achievement, SES, and Teacher Judgement. *Dissertation Abstracts International*, 28, 12A, 4913–4914.

Roe, A. 1951. A Psychological Study of Eminent Biologists. *Psychological Monographs*, 65.

Roe, A. 1953. A Psychological Study of Eminent Psychologists and Anthropologists, and a Comparison with Biological and psychological scientists. *Psychological Monographs*, 67, 352.

—— 1960. Crucial life Experiences in the Development of Scientists (In) Torrance, E.P. (Ed.), *Talent and Education*, University of Minnesota Press, Minneapolis, Minn. 66–67.

Rogers, C.R. 1962. Toward a Theory of Creativity. (In) Parnes, S.J. and Harding, H.F. (Eds.), *A Source Book for Creative Thinking*, 63–72. Scribner, New York.

—— 1969. Toward a Theory of Creativity (In) Anderson H.H. (Ed.), *Creativity and its Cultivation*, Harper and Row, New York, 70.

Rossman, J. 1931. *The Psychology of the Inventor*, Inventors Publishing Co., Washington, D.C.

Rossman, J.E. and Campbell, D.P. 1965. Why College Trained Mothers Work? *Journal of Personnel Guidance*, 43, 986–92. (In) Asha, C.B. 1983.

Runco, Mark, A. and Bahleda, Michael, D. 1987. Implicit Theories of Artistic, Scientific and Everyday Creativity. *Journal of Creative Behaviour*, 20 (2), 93–98.

Ruth, Jen-Erik and Birren James, E. 1985. Creativity in Adulthood and Old Age, Relations to Intelligence, Sex and Mode of Testing. *International Journal of Behavioural Development*, 8, 1, 99–109.

Safaya, R. 1981. Academic Achievement of B.Ed. Trainees as Related to Intelligence, Creativity and Adjustment. *Trends in Education*, 8, 1 and 2, 18–25.

Sandhu, T.S. 1979. Relationship of Creativity with Academic Achievement in Science Subjects. *Creativity News Letter,* 7 and 8, 1–2.

Sansanwal, N. 1987. Creativity and its Components in Relation to Different Levels of Intelligence and Academic Subjects Among High School Students. *Journal of Educational Research and Extension*, 23, 3, 122–128.

Sansanwal, D.N. and Jarial, Gurpal Singh. 1979. Personality Differences Among High and Low Creative Teacher Trainees. *Journal of the Institute of Educational Research*, 3, 3, 24–26.

—— 1979a. Creativity and its Components in Relation to Different Levels of Intelligence and Academic Subjects Among High School Dtudents. *Asian Journal of Psychology and Education*, 4, 3.

—— 1980. Creativity and Age. *Creativity News Letter.*

—— 1981. (In) Passi, B.K. 1982. *Creativity in Education*, National Psychological Corporation, Agra.

Saran, V. 1970. A Study of Personality Traits of Nursery School Children Against the Background of their Home Environment. *Doctoral Thesis*, University of Agra.

Saxena, Saroj. 1981. A Study of Need Achievement in Relation to Creativity, Values, Level of Aspiration and Anxiety. *Doctoral Thesis,* Agra University.

Schaefer, C.E. 1968. The Barron-welsh Art Scale as a Predictor of Adolescent Creativity. *Perceptual and Motor Skills* 27, 1099–1102.

—— 1969. The Self Concept of Creative Adolescents. *Journal of Psychology*, 72, 2, 232–242.

—— 1972. Predictive Validity of the Biographical Inventory of Creativity: Five Year Follow-up Study. *Psychological Reports*, 30, 471–76.

Schaie, K.W. 1965. A General Model for the Study of Developmental Problems, *Psychological Bulletin*, 64, 92–107.

Scheier, I.H. 1965. Creative Personality and the Nature of the Creative Process. *High School Journal*, April, 1965.

Seetharam, R. and Vedanayagam, E.G. 1979. Creativity and Socio-economic Status. *Journal of the Institute of Educational Research*, 3, 4, 35–37.

Sehgal, K. 1978. School Systems as Related to Creativity of Students. *The Progress of Education*, 52, 10 and 11, 207–211.

Sen Gupta, M. 1982. Purdue Creativity Test: Psychometric Properties on an Indian sample. *Psychological Studies*, 27, 1, 23–28.

Shapiro, R.J. 1972. The Criterion Problem. (In) Vernon, P.E. (Ed.) *Creativity*, Harmonds Worth, Penguin Books.

Sharma, A.K. 1979. A Study of Creativity in Relation to Intelligence, Personality, Socio-economic Status and Sex of the High School Students of Indore city. *Unpublished M.Ed. Dissertation*, Indore University, Indore.

—— 1980. Creativity and its components as Affected by Socio-economic Status and Personality. *Experiments in Education*, 8, 7, 129–133.

—— 1981. Divergent Thinking in Relation to Academic Achievement and Sex. *Trends in Education*, 8, 1 and 2, 9–11.

—— and Jarial, Gurpal Singh. 1980. Factorial Study of the Effect of SES, Grade Levels and their Interaction Upon Creativity and its Components. *Trends in Education*, 7, 1 and 2, 37–42.

Sharma, K.N. 1971. Creativity as Function of Intelligence, Interest and Culture. *Doctoral Thesis*, Agra University.

—— 1972. Rural Urban Differences in Creativity. *Journal of Psychological Researches*, 16, 3, 121–122.

—— 1974. Creativity as a Function of Intelligence, Fine Arts Interests and Culture. *Indian Journal of Psychology*, 49, 4, 313–319.

—— 1979. Multi-trait, Multidimensional Approach to Creativity. *Creativity News Letter*, 7 and 8, 2 and 1.

Shukla, Prakash Chandra. 1982. A Study of Creativity in Relation to Sex, Locality and School Subjects. *Indian Educational Review*, 17, 2, 128–132.

Simpkins, R. and Eisenman, R. 1968. Sex Differences in creativity. *Psychological Reports*, 22, 3, 996.

Simpson, R.M. 1922. Creative Imagination. *American Journal of Psychology*, 33, 234–243.

Singh, J.L. 1961. Imagination and Waiting Ability in Young Children. *Journal of Personality*, 29, 396–413.

Singh, A. 1977. A Study of Creativity of Populars, Isolates and Rejects in Relation to their Socio-economic Status and Scholastic Achievement. *Unpublished M.Ed Dissertation*, Indore University.

—— 1978. A Study of Creativity in School Teachers and Measured by Mehdi's Test in Relation to their Self-concept, Attitude Towards Teaching and Classroom Verbal Interaction. *Doctoral Thesis*, Meerut University.

Singh, B. 1981. An Exploratory Study of Mathematical Creativity test and its Relationship to Personality among class X Science Students. *Indian Educational Review,* 16, 108–114.

Singh, D. 1978. A Study of the Personality Correlates of Creativity Children (15+) Studying Science Subjects. *Doctoral Thesis*, Bhopal University.

—— 1979. Personality Correlates of Creative Children Studying in Science Subjects. *Doctoral Thesis*, Bhopal University.

Singh, R.J. 1975. A Study of Creativity Among X Class Students in Relation to their Adjustment and Sex. *Unpublished M. Lit Dissertation*, Punjab University.

—— 1977. An Investigation into the Psychological Make up and Sociological Background of Creative and Non-creative Student Teachers. *Doctoral Thesis*, Lucknow University.

Singh, R.J. 1978. The Psychological make up and Sociological Background of Creative and Non-creative Student Teachers. *Indian Educational Review*, 13, 4, 119–123.

—— 1979. Creativity and the Age of Student Teachers. *Journal of the Institute of Educational Research*, 3, 3, 27–31.

—— 1980. Teacher Creativity and Family Background: A Study of Relationship. *Asian Journal of Psychology and Education*, 6, 3, 42–48.

—— 1980a. Value Orientations of Creative and Non-creative Student Teacher in India. *Quest in Education*, 17, 4, 318–326.

—— 1980b. Personality Adjustment of Creative and Non-creative Student Teachers in India. *Indian Educational Review*, 15, 4, 49–56.

Singh, R.P. 1978. Divergent Thinking Abilities and Creative Personality Dimensions of Bright Adolescent Boys and Girls: A Comparative Study. *Indian Educational Review*, 13, 4.

—— 1980. A Study of Creativity in Relation to Adjustment, Level of Aspiration. *Indian Educational Review*, 15, 3, 85–87.

Singh, Bhoodev and Singh, Prameela. 1984. A Comparative Study of Mathematical Creativity and its Relationship to Personality Factors Among Different Types of School Children. *Journal of Psychological Researches*, 28, 3, 162–166.

Singh, R.B. Mathur, S.R. and Saxena, S. 1977. Creativity as Related to Intelligence, Achievement and Security—insecurity. *Indian Psychological Review*, 14, 3, 84–88.

Sinha, N.C.P. and Sharma, M. 1978. Creativity and adjustment. *Indian Psychological Review*, 16, 2, 4–7.

Smith, R.M. 1965. The Relationship of Creativity to Social Class, *Cooperative Research Project* No. 2250, U.S. Department of Health Education and Welfare, Washington.

Smolucha, Larry, W. and Smolucha, Francine, C. 1984. Creativity as a Maturation of Symbolic Play. *Journal of Aesthetic Education*, 18, 4, 113–118.

Solomon, A.O.1968: A Comparative Analysis of Creative and Intelligent Behaviour of Elementary School Children with Different Socio-economic Backgrounds. *Dissertation Abstracts*, 29, 5, 1457A.

Srinivasan, T. 1984. Originality in Relation to Extraversion, Introversion, Neuroticism and Psychoticism. *Journal of Psychological Researches,* 28, 2, 65–70.

Srivastava, J.O. 1967. A Study of the Effect of Academic and Personality Characteristics on the Academic Achievement of Boys Reading in Class X. Ph.D. Education. Rajasthan University (In) Buch, M.B (Ed.) 1979. *Second Survey of Research in Education* (1972—1978). Society for Educational Research and Development, Baroda, 360.

Srivastava, R. 1978. Creativity as a Function of Birth Order, Socio-economic Status and Personality Types. *Journal of Education and Psychology*, 41, 3, 113–117.

Srivastava, S.S. 1977. Creativity as Related to Birth Order and Number of Siblings. *Indian Psychological Review*, 14, 2, 1–4.

Starkweather, E.K. 1964. Conformity and Non-conformity as Indicators of Creativity in Pre-school Children. Cooperative Research Project No. 1967, U.S. Department of Health Education and Welfare, Washington, D.C.

—— and Cowling, F.G. 1964. The Measurement of Conforming and Non-conforming Behaviour in Pre-school Children. *Proceedings of Oklahama Academy of Science*, 1963, 44, 168–80.

—— and Azbill, P.L. 1965. An Exploratory Study of Preschool Children's Freedom of Expression. *Proceedings of Oklsahama Academy of Science*, 45, 176–180.

Starr, J.W. and Nicholl, C. 1975. Creativity and Achievement in Nuffield Physics. *British Journal of Educational Psychology*, 45, 3, 322–326.

Stein, M.I. 1960. Transactional Approach to Creativity. (In) Taylor, C.W. and Frank Barron (Eds.) *Scientific Creativity:*

Its Recognition and Development, John Wiley and Sons, Inc., New York.

—— 1962. Survey of the Psychological Literature in the Area of Creativity with a View Toward Needed Research. *Cooperative Research Project* No. E—3, U.S. Dept. of Health Education and Welfare, Washington, D.C.

—— and Heinze, S.J. 1960. *Creativity and the Individual.* Free Press of Gencoe, Inc., Glencoe.

Stolz., L.M. 1960. Effects of Maternal Employment on Children: Evidence from Research. *Child Development*, 31, 749–782. (In) Asha, C.B. 1983.

Straus, J.H. and Straus, M.A. 1968. Family Roles and Sex Differences in Creativity in Children in Bombay and Minneapolis. *Journal of Marriage and Family*, 30, 1, 46–53.

Sullivan, H.S. 1953. *The Interpersonal Theory of Psychiatry,* W.W. Norton and Company, Inc., New York.

Sultan Ahmed and Joshi, R.K. 1980. Effect of Socio-cultural Disadvantages on Verbal Creative Thinking Ability Among School Going Children. *Journal of Education and Psychology,* 37, 4, 231–238.

Sunil Dutt, 1988. Relationship of Creativity with Achievement in Science and Socio-economic Status of X Grade Students, *Journal of Educational Research and Extension*, 25, 2, 106–110.

Syama Thrimurthy, 1987. Creative Thinking Ability as a Function of Sex, Intelligence and Study Habits. *Journal of Education and Psychology,* 45, 1, 51–56.

Tagiuri. 1960. Movement as a Cue in Person Perception. (In) David, HP. and Brengelnann (Eds.) *Perspectives in Personality Research.*

Taylor, C.W. 1956. (Ed.) *The 1955 University of Utah Research Conference on the Identification of Creative Scientific Talent*, University of Utah Press, Salt Lake City.

—— 1957. *The Second University of Utah Research Conference on the Identification of Creative Scientific Talent*, University of Utah Press, Salt Lake City.

—— 1959. *The Third University of Utah Research Conference of the Identification of Creative Scientific Talent*. University of Utah Press, Salt Lake City.

—— 1960. The Creative Individual: A New Protrait in Giftedness. *Educational Leadership*, 18, 1, 7–12.

—— 1964. *Creativity: Progress and Potential*, McGraw-Hill, New York.

—— and Barron, F. 1963. *Scientific Creativity: Its Recognition and Development,* Wiley, New York, 119–131.

—— 1964. Cited by Passi, B.K. 1979. *Passi Test of Creativity (Verbal and Nonverbal)*, National Psychological Corporation, Agra.

—— and Holland, J.K. 1962. Development and Application of Tests of Creativity. *Journal of Educational Research*, 32, 91–102.

—— 1964. Predictors of Creative Performance. (In) Taylor, C.W. (Ed.) *Creativity: Progress and Potential,* McGraw-Hill, New York, 15–48.

Terman, L.M. 1921. Intelligence and its Measurement: A Symposium. *Journal of Educational Psychology*, 12, 127–133.

—— 1925. *Genetic Studies of Genius; Vol. 1, Mental and Physical Traits of a Thousand Gifted Children*, Stanford University Press, Stanford, California.

—— 1937. *Measuring Intelligence*, Houghton Mifflin, Boston.

Thamma Prateep, V. 1976. A Comparative Study of Creativity of Indian Students (Baroda) and Thai students (Nakornsawan) of Grade IX. *Unpublished M.Ed. Dissertation*, M.S. University, Baroda.

Thorat Nirbala, P.C. Katiyar, 1977. A Study of Creativity of Student Players in Relation to their Scholastic Achievement and Socio-economic Status. *M.Ed. Dissertation Abstract.* Indore University.

Thorndike, R.L. 1963. Some Methodological Issues in Study of Creativity (In) Gardner, E.F. (Ed.) *Proceedings of 1962 Invitational Conference on Testing Problems*. Princeton: Educational Testing Service.

Through different States. 1972. Abolition of Detentions to Create Proper Climate, *Educational India*, 39, 1, 23.

Torrance, E.P. 1961. Status of Knowledge Concerning Educational and Creative Scientific Talent. *Working Paper for a Project on the Status of Knowledge about Creative Scientific Talent,* Directed by Taylor, C.W. University of Utah, with support by the National Science Foundations.

—— 1962. *Guiding Creative Talent*, Prentice Hall (Indian Reprint, 1969).

—— 1962a. Cultural Discontinuities and the Development of Originality of Thinking. *Exceptional Children,* 29, 2–13.

—— 1963. *Education and the Creative Potential.* Minneapolis, University of Minnesota Press, Minnesota.

—— 1963a. Changing Reactions of Pre-adolescent Girls to take Requiring Creative Scientific Thinking. *Journal of Genetic Psychology*, 102, 217–223.

—— 1964. Education and Creativity (In) Taylor, C.W. (Ed.) *Creativity: Progress and Potential,* McGraw-Hill, New York, 50–128.

—— 1964a. The Minnesota Studies of Creative Thinking (In) Taylor, C.W. (Ed.) *Widening Horizons in Creativity*, New York, John Wiley and Sons, Inc.

Torrance, E.P. 1965. *Rewarding Creative Behaviour*. Englewood Cliffs, Prentice Hall, New Jersey.

—— 1967a. The Minnesota Studies of Creative Behaviour: National and International Extensions. *Journal of Creative Behaviour*, 1, 2, 137–154.

—— 1967b. Nurture of Creative Talents. (In) Mooney, R.L. and Razik, T.A. (Eds.) *Explorations in Creativity,* Harper and Row Publishers, New York, 185–195.

—— 1968. Examples and Rationales of Tests for Assessing Creative Abilities. *Journal of Creative Behaviour,* 2, 165–178.

—— 1971. Freedom Control Orientation and Need for Structure in Group Creativity. Sciences del' Art, 8, 61–64. (In) *Psychological Abstracts,* 54, March, 1974, Abstract No. 5072.

—— 1972. Can We Teach Children to Think Creatively? *Journal of Creative Behaviour*, 16, 2.

—— 1975. (In) Bhoodev Singh. *Teaching Learning Strategies and Mathematical Creativity*, Mittal Publications, New Delhi.

—— 1977. Creativity and the Older Adult. *Child and Adult Quarterly*,. 2, 136–144.

—— *et al.*, 1960. Minnesota Studies of Creative Thinking in the Yarly School Years. *Research Memorandum* BER—60—1, University of Minnesota, Minneapolis, Minnesota, 30–31.

—— 1960a. An Experimental Attempt to Increase Quantity and Quality of Ideas. (In) Torrance, E.P. *et al.*, The Minnesota Studies of Creative Thinking in the Early School Years, *Research Memorandum*. BER—60—1, University of Minnesota, Minneapolis, Minnesota, 30—31.

—— 1960b. Explorations in Creative Thinking. *Education*, 81, 216–220.

Torrance, E.P. and His Associates 1960c. Exploration in Creative Thinking in the Early School Years: XI Changing Reactions of Girls in Grades Four Through Six to Tasks Requiring Creative Scientific Thinking. *Research Memorandum* No. 60–12, University of Minnesota, Bureau of Educational Research, Minneapolis, Minnesota.

—— 1961. Factors Affecting Creative Thinking in Children. An Interim Research Report, *Merril Palmer Quarterly*, 7, 171–180.

—— 1962a. Cultural Discontinuities and the Development of Originality of Thinking. *Exceptional Children*, 29, 2–13.

—— 1963a. Changing Reactions of Preadolescent Girls to Take Requiring Creative Scientific Thinking. *Journal of Genetic Psychology*, 102, 217–223.

—— 1964. Education and Creativity (In) Taylor, C.W. (Ed.) *Creativity, Progress and Potential*, McGraw-Hill, New York, 50–128.

—— and Gowan, 1963 (In) Passi, B.K. *Passi Tests of Creativity (Verbal and Nonverbal)*, National Psychological Corporation, Agra.

—— and Myers, R.E. (1970). *Creative Learning and Teaching.* Dodd, Mead and Company Inc., New York.

Townsend, J.C. 1953. *Introduction to Experimental Method,* McGraw-Hill, New York.

Treffinger, D.J. 1975 (In) Bhoodev Singh. *Teaching Learning Strategies and Mathematical Creativity*, Mittal Publications, New Delhi.

——, Renzulli, J.S. and Feldhusen, J.F. 1971. Problems in the Assessment of Creative Thinking. *Journal of Creative Behaviour*, 5, 2, 104–112.

Trivedi, R.C. 1969. To Establish the Reliability and Validity of the Tests of Creativity. *Unpublished M.Ed. Dissertation*, Punjab University.

Trowbridge, N. 1966. Research on Creativity (In) Patel, A.S. and Shah, G.B. (Eds.) *Education of Backward and the Gifted Children.* Centre for Advanced Study in Education, Baroda.

Tuddenham, R.D. 1969. Intelligence. (In) Ebel, R. 1969. (Ed.) *Encyclopedia of Educational Research*, Macmillan, London, 662.

Tuli, Mulkh Raj, 1982. Sex and Regional Differences in Mathematical Creativity. *Indian Educational Review*, 17, 3, 128–134.

Tyler, L.E. 1965. *The Psychology of Human Differences*, Applelton Century Crafts, New York.

Tylor, R.W. 1965. Some Persistent Questions on the Defining of Objectives (In) Lindvall, C.M. (Ed.) *Defining Educational Objectives*, University of Pittsburgh Press, Pittsburg, 77–83.

Upadhyacys, R. 1982. An Experimental Study of the Effect of Stimulating Environment on Change in Creative Ability of Young Children. *Doctoral Thesis*, Bombay University.

Van Mering, F.H. 1955. Professional and Non-professional Women as Mothers. *Journal of Social Psychology*, 42, 21–34.

Venkata Rami Reddy, A. and Balakrishna Reddy, P. 1983. Creativity and Intelligence. *Psychological Studies*, 28, 1, 20–24.

—— 1984. Creativity of Adolescent Boys and Girls in Relation to Some Variables, *Indian Educational Review*, 19, 1.

—— and Bhaskara Naidu, G. 1962. Effect of the Non-detention System on High and Low Achievers. *Journal of Psychological Researches*, 26, 49–57.

—— 1988. Achievement of Students Under Detention and Non-detention Systems. *Indian Educational Review*, 41–45.

Venkata Rami Reddy, A. and Chandra Reddy, T. 1980. Attitude of Students Towards Introduction of Regional Medium at the Post-graduate level. *The Education Quarterly*, 32, 16–18.

—— and Saleena, K. 1988. Creativity Vs. Age. *Perspectives in Education*, 4, 245–250.

—— and Tulasi Devi, S. Creativity in Relation to SES and Birth Order (Communicated).

—— and Vijaya Kumari, G. (a) Can creativity and scientific attitude be developed? *Psychological Studies* (communicated).

—— (b). Tryout of a Technique for the Development of Creativity and Scientific Attitude Among Children and the Results of a Follow-up Study. National Award Winning Article for Innovations in Education, Presented and Discussed at the Educational Conference Held from 29–3–1989 to 2–4–1989 at the National Council for Educational Research and Training Campus, Azmir.

Venkata Rao, 1971. The New Remedy. *Educational India*, 38, 3, 89.

Verma, L.K. 1980. A Study of Locus of Control of High and Low Creative School Students at Different Levels of Socio-economic Status. *Journal of Educational and Psychology*, 38, 2, 99–104.

Verma, O.P. 1979. Personality Traits of Creative Students in Biology. *Education*, 2, 6.

Verma, R.S. 1973. A Factor Analytic Study of Divergent Thinking in Relation to Certain Personality Dimensions of Higher Secondary School Adolescents. *Doctoral Thesis*, Aligarh Muslim University.

Vernon, M.D. 1948. The Development of Imaginative Construction in Children. *British Journal of Psychology*, 39, 102–111.

Vernon, P.E. 1950. The Structure of Human Abilities, Methuen, London.

Vernon, P.E. 1964. Creativity and Intelligence. *Educational Research*, 6, 163–196.

Vijayalakshmi, J. 1980. Academic Achievement and Socio-economic Status as Predictors of Creative Talent. *Journal of Psychology Resources*, 24, 1, 43–47.

Vinake, E. 1952. *The Psychology of Thinking*, McGraw-Hill, New York.

Vohra, I.N. 1975. A Study of Nonverbal Creativity in Relation to Socio-economic Status, Age, Sex, Medium of Instruction and Personality Characteristics Amongst the Pupils of English and Gujarati Medium of 'Bazm-E-Hidayat' Primary School from Baroda city. *Unpublished M.Ed. Dissertation*, M.S. University.

Walker, P.C. 1969. A Study of Creativity Among Mexican School Children. *Doctoral Dissertation*, University of Georgia.

Wall, W.B. 1960. Highly Intelligent Children, Part 2. The Education of the Gifted, *Educational Research*, 2, 3.

Wallach, M. and Kogan, N. 1965. *Modes of Thinking in Young Children*, Holt, Rinehart and Winston Inc., New York.

—— and Wing, 1963. (In) Khatena, J. 1973. Creativity: Concept and Challenge. *Educational Trends*, 8 (1–4), 7–18.

Wallas, G. 1926. *The Art of Thought*, Harcourt Brace and World, Inc., New York.

Watson, G. 1957. Some Personality Differences in Children Related Strict or Permissive Parental Discipline. *Journal of Psychology*, 4A, 227–49.

Weisberg, P.S. and Springer, K.J. 1961. *Environmental Factors Influencing Creative Function in Gifted Children*. Cincinnati: Dept. of Psychiatry. Cincinnati General Hospital (Mimeographed).

Welch, L. 1946. Combination of Ideas in Creative Thinking. *Journal of Applied Psychology*, 30, 638–643.

Westerland, C. 1980. Age and Creativity, Nordisk Psykologi, 32, 284–292. (In) Psychological Abstracts, 67, April, 1982, Abstract No. 9654.

Wilson, R.C., Guilford, J.P. and Christinsen, P.R., 1974. (In) Dutt, N.K. *Psychological Foundation of Education,* Deoba House, Delhi, 208.

—— and Lewis, D.J. 1954. A Factor Analytical Study of Creative Thinking Abilities. *Psychometrics*, 19, 297–311.

Wittenborn, J.R. 1951. Symptom Patterns, in a Group of Mental Hospital Patients. Journal of Consult Psychology, 15, 245–257.

Witty, P.A. 1962. A Decade of Progress in the Study of the Gifted and Creative Pupil (In) Barbe, W.B. (Ed.) *Attention to the Gifted—A Decade Later*, Columbus, Department of Education, Ohio, 3–7.

Wodtke, K.H. 1964. Some Data on the Reliability and Validity of Creativity Tests at the Elementary School Level. *Educational and Psychological Measurement*, 24 2, 339–408.

Yamamoto, K. 1960. The Role of Creative Thinking and Intelligence in high school achievement. Research Memorandum, BER—60–10. Bureau of Educational Research, College of Education, University of Minnesota, 1–245.

—— 1961. Creativity and Intellect: Review of Current Research and Protection. *Paper Presented at Minnesota Psychological Association*, Minneapolis.

—— 1964a. *Experimental Scoring Manuals for Minnesota Tests of Creative Thinking and Writing*. Kent, Bureau of Educational Research, Kent State University, Kent, Ohio.

—— 1964b. Creative thinking: Some Thoughts on Research. *Exceptional Children*, 403–410.

Yamamoto, K. 1965. Effects of Restriction of Range and Test Unreliability on Correlation Between Measures of Intelligence and Creative Thinking. *British Journal of Educational Psychology*, 35, 300–305.

Zargar, A.H. and Neelam Dhar. 1988. Creativity and Socio-economic Status: A Study. *The Educational Review,* XCIV, 29–31.

Additional Reading

Bhaskara Rao, Digumarti (1994). *Scientific Aptitude*. New Delhi: Ashish Publishing House. pp: 100. Rs. 100. ISBN 81-7024-658-X.

Bhaskara Rao, Digumarti (1995). *Animal Kingdom*. New Delhi: Discovery Publishing House. pp: 135. Rs. 200. ISBN 81-7141-274-2.

Bhaskara Rao, Digumarti (1995). *Batracology*. New Delhi: Discovery Publishing House. pp: 174. Rs. 250 ISBN 81-7141-279-3.

Bhaskara Rao, Digumarti (1996). *Scientific Attitude vis-a-vis Scientific Aptitude*. New Delhi: Discovery Publishing House. pp: 143 Rs. 275. ISBN 81-7141-308-0.

Bhaskara Rao, Digumarti, ed. (1996). *Encyclopaedia of Education For All*, 5 vols. New Delhi: APH Publishing Corporation. pp: 1460. Rs. 3000. ISBN 81-7024-759-4. (set).

Vol. I Education For All: The World Conference pp: 440. ISBN 81-7024-760-8.

Vol. II Education For All: The EPA—9 Summit. pp: 340. ISBN 81-7024-761-6.

Vol. III Education For All: Quality Education For All. pp: 250. ISBN 81-7024-762-4.

Vol. IV Education For All: Planning and Monitoring. pp: 170. ISBN 81-7024-763-2.

Vol. V Education For All: The Indian Scenario. pp: 260. ISBN 81-7024-764-0.

Bhaskara Rao, Digumarti, ed. (1996). *Global Perceptions on Peace Education*, 3 vols. New Delhi: Discovery Publishing House. pp: 980 Rs. 1800. ISBN 81-7141-319-6.

Bhaskara Rao, Digumarti, ed. (1996). *National Policy on Education,* 2 Vols. New Delhi: Anmol Publications Pvt. Ltd. pp: 710. Rs. 1000. ISBN 81-7488-323-1.

Bhaskara Rao, Digumarti, ed. (1997). *Care the Child*, 2 Vols. New Delhi: Discovery Publishing House. pp: 616. Rs. 1000. ISBN 81-7141-394-3.

Bhaskara Rao, Digumarti, ed. (1997). *Education for the 21st Century*. New Delhi: Discovery Publishing House. pp: 288. Rs. 500. ISBN 81-7141-389-7.

Bhaskara Rao, Digumarti, ed. (1997). *Reflections on Scientific Attitude*. New Delhi: Discovery Publishing House. pp: 310. Rs. 500. ISBN 81-7141-328-5.

Bhaskara Rao, Digumarti (1997). *Scientific Attitude*. New Delhi: Discovery Publishing House. pp: 120. Rs. 225. ISBN 81-7141-381-1.

Bhaskara Rao, Digumarti, ed. (1997). *Success Story of a Primary Education Project*. New Delhi: APH Publishing Corporation. pp: 260. Rs. 400. ISBN 81-7024-850-7.

Bhaskara Rao, Digumarti, ed. (1997) *World Food Summit*. New Delhi: Discovery Publishing House. pp: 153. Rs. 300. ISBN 81-7141-386-2.

Bhaskara Rao, Digumarti, ed. (1998). *Adolescence Education*. New Delhi: Discovery Publishing House. pp: 238. Rs. 350. ISBN 81-7141-432-X.

Bhaskara Rao, Digumarti, ed. (1998). *Community and School Nutrition Education*. New Delhi: Discovery Publishing House. pp: 425. Rs. 650. ISBN 81-7141-435-4.

Bhaskara Rao, Digumarti, ed. (1998). *District Primary Education Programme*. New Delhi: Discovery Publishing House. pp: 506. Rs. 650. ISBN 81-7141-396-X.

Bhaskara Rao, Digumarti, ed. (1998). *Earth Summit*, 2 vols. New Delhi: Discovery Publishing House. pp: 930. Rs. 1500. ISBN 81-7141-435-4.

Bhaskara Rao, Digumarti, ed. (1998). *National Policy on Education: Towards an Enlightened and Humane Society*. New Delhi: Discovery Publishing House. pp: 542. Rs. 860. ISBN 81-7141-426-5.

Bhaskara Rao, Digumarti, ed. (1998). *Reforming School Education*. New Delhi: Discovery Publishing House. pp: 575. Rs. 750. ISBN 81-7141-403-6.

Bhaskara Rao, Digumarti, ed. (1998). *Teaching Education in India*. New Delhi: Discovery Publishing House. pp: 424. Rs. 600. ISBN 81-7141-406-0.

Bhaskara Rao, Digumarti, ed. (1998). *World Summit for Social Development*. New Delhi: Discovery Publishing House. pp: 278. Rs. 450. ISBN 81-7141-420-6.

Bhaskara Rao, Digumarti, ed. (2000). *Education For All: Achieving the Goal*. 3 vols. New Delhi: APH Publishing Corporation. pp: 830. Rs. 2000. ISBN 81-7648-152-1.

Vol. I The Global Consensus. pp: 285. ISBN 81-7648-153-X.

Vol. II Mid-Decade Review Reports of Regional Seminars. pp: 198. ISBN 81-7648-154-8.

Vol. III Issues and Trends. pp: 346. ISBN 81-7648-155-6.

Bhaskara Rao, Digumarti, ed. (2000). *International Encyclopedia of AIDS*, 11 Vols. in 13 parts. New Delhi: Discovery Publishing House. pp: 3676. Rs. 7500. ISBN 81-7141-465-6 (set).

Vol. 1 Introduction to HIV/AIDS. pp: 246. Rs. 500. ISBN 81-7141-523-7.

Vol. 2 HIV/AIDS—Issues and Challenges, 2 parts. pp: 805. Rs. 1700. ISBN 81-7141-524-5.

Vol. 3 HIV/AIDS—Socio Economic Realities. pp: 436. Rs. 900. ISBN 81-7141-525-3.

Vol. 4 HIV/AIDS Law Ethics and Human Rights, 2 parts. pp: 859. Rs. 1800. ISBN 81-7141-526-1.

Vol. 5 AIDS and NGOs. pp: 215. Rs. 450 ISBN 81-7141-527-X.

Vol. 6 Aids and Home Care pp: 183. Rs. 400 ISBN 81-7141-528-8.

Vol. 7 STD Case Management pp: 223. Rs. 475 ISBN 81-7141-529-6.

Vol. 8 HIV Prevention and Care—Teaching Modules for Nurses and Midwives. pp: 125. Rs. 275. ISBN 81-7141-530-X.

Vol. 9 HIV/AIDS Prevention Education for Educational Institutions. pp: 75. Rs. 150. ISBN 81-7141-531-8.

Vol. 10 Instructional Modules for AIDS Education. pp: 111. Rs. 250. ISBN 81-7141-532-6.

Vol. 11 School Health Education to Prevent AIDS and STD—A package for curriculum planners. pp: 298. Rs. 600. ISBN 81-7141-533-4.

Bhaskara Rao, Digumarti, ed. (2000). *International Encyclopaedia of Science and Technology Education.* 11 Volumes. New Delhi: Discovery Publishing House. pp: 4892. Rs. 8500. ISBN 81-7141-548-2 (set).

Vol. 1 Science and Technology Education. pp: 557. Rs. 975 ISBN 81-7141-568-7.

Vol. 2 Science Education in Developing Countries. pp: 334. Rs. 600 ISBN 81-7141-570-9.

Vol. 3 Organisational Structure of Science. pp: 334. Rs. 600. ISBN 81-7141-570-9.

Vol. 4 Science Education in Asia and the Pacific. pp: 429. Rs. 750 ISBN 81-7141-571-7.

Vol. 5 Science and Technology Education For All. pp: 464. Rs. 800 ISBN 81-7141-572-5.

Vol. 6 Values, Ethics, Talent and Girls in Science and Technology Education. pp: 463. Rs. 800 ISBN 81-7141-573-3.

Vol. 7 Popularization of Science and Technology Education. pp. 334. Rs. 600. ISBN 81-7141-574-1.

Vol. 8 Science, Power and Society. pp: 357. Rs. 625 ISBN 81-7141-575-X.

Vol. 9 Information Technology. pp: 442. Rs. 775. ISBN 81-7141-576-8.

Vol. 10 Teacher Training in Science and Technology Education. pp: 536. Rs. 975. ISBN 81-7141-577-6.

Vol. 11 Science, Technology and Society: A Curriculum Framework. pp: 642. Rs. 1000. ISBN 81-7141-578-4.

Bhaskara Rao, Digumarti, ed. (2001). *Distance Education in Different Countries*. New Delhi: APH Publishing Corporation. pp: 574. Rs. 1500. ISBN 81-7648-229-3.

Bhaskara Rao, Digumarti, ed. (2001). *Decentralised Management of Education (Management of Education in Panchayati Raj and Municipal Bodies)*. New Delhi: Discovery Publishing House. pp: 116. Rs. 250. ISBN 81-7141-617-9.

Bhaskara Rao, Digumarti, ed. (2001). *Electrochemistry for Environmental Protection*. New Delhi: Discovery Publishing House. pp: 208. Rs. 400. ISBN 81-7141-619-5.

Bhaskara Rao, Digumarti, ed. (2001). *Global Educational Studies*. New Delhi: Discovery Publishing House. pp: 145. Rs. 300. ISBN 81-7141-616-0.

Bhaskara Rao, Digumarti, ed. (2001) *Global Synthesis of Educational Assessment*. New Delhi: Discovery Publishing House. pp: 152. Rs. 300. ISBN 81-7141-613-6.

Bhaskara Rao, Digumarti, ed. (2001). *International Encyclopaedia of Human Rights*, 7 volumes in 13 parts. New Delhi. Discovery Publishing House, pp: 6500 (Royal size). Rs. 22000. ISBN 81-7141-567-9 (set).

Vol. 1 International Instruments of Human Rights, 2 parts Rs. 3500. ISBN 81-7141-595-4.

Vol. 2 Regional Instruments of Human Rights. Rs. 1500 ISBN 81-7141-604-7.

Vol. 3 Human Rights and the United Nations, 2 parts. Rs. 2800. ISBN 81-7141-605-5.

Vol. 4 Fact Files of Human Rights, 2 parts. Rs. 3000. ISBN 81-7141-606-3.

Vol. 5 Study Stories of Human Rights, 3 parts. Rs. 5200. ISBN 81-7141-607-1.

Vol. 6 International Meetings on Human Rights, 2 parts. Rs. 3800. ISBN 81-7141-608-X.

Vol. 7 Professional Training in Human Rights. Rs. 2200. ISBN 81-7141-609-8.

Bhaskara Rao, Digumarti, ed. (2001). *Jomtein Decade of Education*. New Delhi: Discovery Publishing House. pp: 106. Rs. 225. ISBN 81-7141-618-7.

Bhaskara Rao, Digumarti, ed. (2001). *Nuclear Materials: Issues and Concerns*, 2 vols. New Delhi: Discovery Publishing House. pp: 1100. Rs. 2200. ISBN 81-7141-611-X.

Bhaskara Rao, Digumarti, ed. (2001). *World Conference on Education for All*. New Delhi: APH Publishing Corporation. pp: 380. Rs. 995. ISBN 81-7648-274-9.

Bhaskara Rao, Digumarti, ed. (2001). *World Conference on Higher Education*. New Delhi: Discovery Publishing House. pp: 306. Rs. 600. ISBN 81-7141-610-1.

Bhaskara Rao, Digumarti, ed. (2001). *World Conference on Science*. New Delhi: Discovery Publishing House. pp: 85. Rs. 200. ISBN 81-7141-612-8.

Bhaskara Rao, Digumarti, C.A.P. Swamy and R.S.V. Dutt (1997). *Self Evaluation in Student Teaching*. New Delhi: Discovery Publishing House. pp: 762. Rs. 150. ISBN 81-7141-374-9.

Bhaskara Rao, Digumarti, C. Sridevi and K. Vijaya (1995). *Achievement in Social Studies*. New Delhi: Discovery Publishing House. pp: 102. Rs. 150. ISBN 81-7141-281-5.

Bhaskara Rao, Digumarti and Digumarti Pushpa Latha (1994). *Achievement in Biology*. New Delhi: Discovery Publishing House. pp: 102. Rs. 125. ISBN 81-7141-264-5.

Bhaskara Rao, Digumarti and Digumarti Pushpa Latha (1995). *Achievement in English*. New Delhi: Discovery Publishing House. pp: 214. Rs. 275. ISBN 81-7141-283-1.

Bhaskara Rao, Digumarti and Digumarti Pushpa Latha (1995). *Achievement in Science*. New Delhi: Discovery Publishing House. pp: 159. Rs. 225. ISBN 81-7141-280-7.

Bhaskara Rao, Digumarti and Digumarti Pushpa Latha (1995). *Achievement in Mathematics*. New Delhi: Discovery Publishing House. pp: 125. Rs. 175. ISBN 81-7141-278-5.

Bhaskara Rao, Digumarti and Digumarti Pushpa Latha, eds. (1998). *International Encyclopaedia of Women*, 5 vols. New Delhi: Discovery Publishing House. pp: 2172. Rs. 4000. ISBN 81-7141-410-9.

Vol. 1 Status of World's Women pp: 427. Rs. 750. ISBN 81-7141-494-X.

Vol. 2 Women, Education and Empowerment. pp: 467. Rs. 875. ISBN 81-7141-498-2.

Vol. 3 Women Challenges and Advancement. pp: 354. Rs. 650. ISBN 81-7141-497-4.

Vol. 4 Women and Family Health. pp: 470. Rs. 875. ISBN 81-7141-497-4.

Vol. 5 Women and International Action. pp: 453. Rs. 850. ISBN 81-7141-498-2.

Bhaskara Rao, Digumarti, Digumarti Pushpa Latha and Digumarti Harshitha, eds. (2001). *Biological Warfare*. New Delhi: Discovery Publishing House. pp: 422. Rs. 800. ISBN 81-7141-597-0.

Bhaskara Rao, Digumarti, Digumarti Pushpa Latha and Digumarti Harshitha, eds. (2001). *Women as Educators*. New Delhi: Discovery Publishing House. pp: 112. Rs. 200. ISBN 81-7141-602-0.

Bhaskara Rao, Digumarti and Digumarti Harshitha (2000). *Education in India*. New Delhi: APH Publishing Corporation. pp: 280. Rs. 700. ISBN 81-7648-207-2.

Bhaskara Rao, Digumarti, and Digumarti Harshitha eds. (2001). *Assessing Learning Achievement*. New Delhi: Discovery Publishing House. pp: 128. Rs. 225. ISBN 81-7141-601-2.

Bhaskara Rao, Digumarti and Digumarti Harshita, eds. (2001). *Energy Security*. New Delhi: Discovery Publishing House. pp: 564. Rs. 1000. ISBN 81-7141-598-9.

Bhaskara Rao, Digumarti, D. Harshitha and K.R.S.S. Rao. eds. (1999). *Advanced Biotechnology*. New Delhi: Discovery Publishing House. pp: 335. Rs. 550. ISBN 81-7141-516-4.

Bhaskara Rao, Digumarti and K.R.S. Sambasiva Rao, eds. (1996). *Current Trends in Indian Education*. New Delhi: Discovery Publishing House. pp: 234. Rs. 400. ISBN 81-7141-311-0.

Bhaskara Rao, Digumarti and K. Vijaya (1995). *A Text Book Evaluation*. Ambala Cantt: The Associated Publishers. pp: 100. Rs. 160.

Bhaskara Rao, Digumarti, V.V. Rao, V.V. Lakshmi and V.V. Krishna, eds. (2000). *Status and Advancement of Women*. New Delhi: APH Publishing Corporation. pp: 570. Rs. 1100. ISBN 81-7648-169-6.

Bhagya Lakshmi, Lingineni and Digumarti Bhaskara Rao, ed. (2000). *Reading and Comprehension*. New Delhi: Discovery Publishing House. pp: 108. Rs. 175. ISBN 81-7141-543-1.

Bhuvaneswara Lakshmi, G. and Digumarti Bhaskara Rao, ed. (2000). *Attitude Towards Science*. New Delhi: Discovery Publishing House. pp: 128. Rs. 250. ISBN 81-7141-541-6.

Devraj, T.A.S. and Digumarti Bhaskara Rao, ed. (1997). *Trace Analysis of Uranium and Thorum*. New Delhi: Discovery Publishing House. pp: 195. Rs. 350. ISBN 81-7141-375-7.

Durgani Rani, K. and Digumarti Bhaskara Rao, ed. (2000). *Educational Aspirations and Scientific Attitudes*. New Delhi: Discovery Publishing House. pp: 130. Rs. 250. ISBN 81-7141-555-55.

Dutt, B.S.V. and Digumarti Bhaskara Rao (2001). *Empowering Primary Teachers*. New Delhi: Discovery Publishing House. pp. 283. Rs. 475. ISBN 81-7141-615-2.

Ediger, Marlow and Digumarti Bhaskara Rao (1996). *Science Curriculum*. New Delhi: Discovery Publishing House. pp: 309. Rs. 450. ISBN 81-7141-321-8.

Ediger, Marlow and Digumarti Bhaskara Rao (2000). *Teaching Mathematics Successfully*. New Delhi: Discovery Publishing House. pp: 279. Rs. 525. ISBN 81-7141-552-0.

Ediger, Marlow and Digumarti Bhaskara Rao (2000). *Teaching Reading Successfully*. New Delhi: Discovery Publishing House. pp: 386. Rs. 750. ISBN 81-7141-556-3.

Ediger Marlow and Digumarti Bhaskara Rao (2001). *Teaching Science Successfully*. New Delhi: Discovery Publishing House. pp: 320. Rs. 600. ISBN 81-7141-600-4.

Ediger, Marlow and Digumarti Bhaskara Rao (2001). *Teaching Social Studies Successfully*. New Delhi: Discovery Publishing House. pp: 296. Rs. 575. ISBN 81-7141-596-2.

Jayasree, Kandi and Digumarti Bhaskara Rao, ed. (1999). *Correlates of Socialisation*. New Delhi: Discovery Publishing House. pp: 160. Rs. 375. ISBN 81-7141-517-2.

John Babu, Ch., T.J.R. Prasad, G.M. Madhukar and Digumarti Bhaskara Rao, eds. (2001). *Problem Solving in Mathematics*. New Delhi: APH Publishing Corporation. pp: 125. Rs. 250. ISBN 81-7648-273-0.

Marja, Talvi and Digumarti Bhaskara Rao, eds. (1996). *Educational Leadership and Social Changes*. New Delhi: Discovery Publishing House. pp: 236. Rs. 400. ISBN 8-7141-320-X.

Prabhakaram, K.S. and Digumarti Bhaskara Rao, ed. (1998). *Concept Attainment Model in Mathematics Teaching*. New Delhi: Discovery Publishing House. pp: 122. Rs. 200. ISBN 81-7141-424-9.

Prasanth Kumar, J. and Digumarti Bhaskara Rao, ed. (1998). *Effectiveness of Distance Education System*. New Delhi: Discovery Publishing House. pp: 152. Rs. 275. ISBN 81-7141-437-0.

Prasanth Kumar, J., and Digumarti Bhaskara Rao and G. Sundara Rao, eds. (2000). *Open University Student Support Services*. New Delhi: Discovery Publishing House. pp: 100. Rs. 200. ISBN 81-7141-550-4.

Rama Krishnaiah, D. and Digumarti Bhaskara Rao, ed. (1998). *Job Satisfaction of College Teachers*. New Delhi: Discovery Publishing House. pp: 251. Rs. 400. ISBN 81-7141-438-9.

Ramesh, Ganta and Digumarti Bhaskara Rao, eds. (1998). *Environmental Education: Problems and Prospects*. New Delhi: Discovery Publishing House. pp: 324. Rs. 525. ISBN 81-7141-423-0.

Rathaiah, L. and Digumarti Bhaskara Rao, eds. (1997). *International Innovations in Education*. New Delhi: Discovery Publishing House. pp: 514. Rs. 750. ISBN 81-7141-359-5.

Rathaiah, Lavu, Digumarti Bhaskara Rao and Paturi Koteswara Rao. (1997). *Achievement Correlates*. New Delhi: Discovery Publishing House. pp: 116. Rs. 225. ISBN 81-7141-385-4.

Sanjeeva Rao, P.C. and Digumarti Bhaskara Rao, ed. (1996). *A Text Book of Geology*. New Delhi: Discovery Publishing House. pp: 320. Rs. 525 ISBN 81-7141-313-7.

Satya Narayana, V. and Digumarti Bhaskara Rao, ed. (2001). *Physical Education, Social Attitudes and Leadership Qualities*. New Delhi: Discovery Publishing House. pp: 296. Rs. 575. ISBN 81-7141-593-8.

Srinivasulu Reddy, M., K.R.S. Sambasiva Rao and Digumarti Bhaskara Rao, ed. (1999). *A Text Book of Aquaculture*. New Delhi: Discovery Publishing House. pp: 296. Rs. 525. ISBN 81-7141-482-6.

Vanaja, M. and Digumarti Bhaskara Rao, ed. (1999). *Inquiry Training Model*. New Delhi: Discovery Publishing House. pp: 189. Rs. 325. ISBN 81-7141-515-6.

Veena Kumari, Balusu and Digumarti Bhaskara Rao (1996). *Operational Black Board*. New Delhi: APH Publishing Corporation. pp: 140. Rs. 200. ISBN 81-7024-711-X.

Veena Kumari, B. and Digumarti Bhaskara Rao, ed. (2000). *Psycho Social Correlates of Achievement*. New Delhi: Discovery Publishing House. pp: 136. Rs. 300. ISBN 81-7141-547-4.

Venkata Rao, P. and Digumarti Bhaskara Rao (1989). *A Text Book of Zoology—Junior Intermediate*. Guntur: Vignan Publishers. pp: 370. Rs. 57.

Venkata Rao, P. and Digumarti Bhaskara Rao (1989). *A Text Book of Zoology—Senior Intermediate*. Guntur: Vignan Publishers. pp: 480. Rs. 68.

Venugopala Rao, K. and Digumarti Bhaskara Rao, ed. (2000). *Teacher Morale in Secondary Schools*. New Delhi: Discovery Publishing House. pp: 300. Rs. 575. ISBN 81-7141-551-2.

Vidya, C. and Digumarti Bhaskara Rao, ed. (1996). *A Text Book of Nutrition*. New Delhi: Discovery Publishing House. pp: 438. Rs. 650. ISBN 81-7141-309-9.

Vijaya Bharathi, D. and Digumarti Bhaskara Rao, ed. (2000). *Educational Philosophies of Swami Vivekanand and John Dewey*. New Delhi: APH Publishing Corporation. pp: 200. Rs. 500. ISBN 81-7648-202-1.

Bhaskara Rao, Digumarti. (1986). *Dhrushya Sravana Bodhanapakaranalu* (Audio Visual Teaching Aids). Guntur: Nagarjuna Publishers.

Bhaskara Rao, Digumarti (1993). *Jeevasashtra Bodhana* (Teaching of Biology). Guntur: Nagarjuna Publishers.

Bhaskara Rao, Digumarti (1995). *Vignanasasthra Bodhana*. (Teaching of Science). Guntur: Nagarjuna Publishers.

Bhaskara Rao, Digumarti (1997). *Vidya Manovignana Sashtram*. (Educational Psychology). Guntur: Creative Press. pp. 434. Rs. 79.

Bhaskara Rao, Digumarti (1998). *DSC Study Material*. Guntur: Nagarjuna Publishers.

Bhaskara Rao, Digumarti (1998). *Upadhyayudu Vidya* (Teacher and Education). Guntur: Nagarjuna Publishers.

Bhaskara Rao, Digumarti (1998). *Vidya Dhrukpadhalu.* (Perspectives of Education). Guntur: Nagarjuna Publishers.

Bhaskara Rao, Digumarti (1999). *EdCET Teaching Aptitude.* Guntur: Nagarjuna Publishers.

Bhaskara Rao, Digumarti (2001). *Bharata Samajamulo Upadhayayudu Vidya.* (Teacher and Education in Emerging Indian Society). Guntur: Nagarjuna Publishers. pp: 256. Rs. 59.

Bhaskara Rao, Digumarti (2001). *Bhoutika Sastra Bodhana Padhatulu* (Methods of Teaching Physical Science). Guntur: Nagarjuna Publishers. pp: 324. Rs. 77.

Bhaskara Rao, Digumarti (2001). *Jeeva Sastra Bodhana Padhatulu* (Methods of Teaching Biological Science). Guntur: Nagarjuna Publishers. pp: 224. Rs. 59.

Bhaskara Rao, Digumarti (2001). *Vidya Manovignana Sastram* (Educational Psychology). Guntur: Nagarjuna Publishers. pp: 344. Rs. 77.